PREJUDICE

THE TARGET'S

PERSPECTIVE

PREJUDICE

THE TARGET'S

PERSPECTIVE

EDITED BY

JANET K. SWIM
Psychology Department
The Pennsylvania State University
University Park, Pennsylvania

CHARLES STANGOR
Department of Psychology
University of Maryland
College Park, Maryland

ACADEMIC PRESS
San Diego   London   Boston   New York   Sydney   Tokyo   Toronto

Academic Press
a division of Harcourt Brace & Company
525 B Street, Suite 1900, San Diego, California 92101-4495, USA
http://www.apnet.com

Academic Press Limited
24-28 Oval Road, London NW1 7DX, UK
http://www.hbuk.co.uk/ap/

Library of Congress Card Catalog Number: 97-80793

International Standard Book Number: 0-12-679130-9

PRINTED IN THE UNITED STATES OF AMERICA
98 99 00 01 02 03 QW 9 8 7 6 5 4 3 2 1

CONTENTS

2

EXPERIENCING EVERYDAY PREJUDICE
AND DISCRIMINATION

JANET K. SWIM, LAURIE L. COHEN, AND LAURI L. HYERS

3

NO LAUGHING MATTER: WOMEN'S VERBAL AND
NONVERBAL REACTIONS TO SEXIST HUMOR

MARIANNE LAFRANCE AND JULIE A. WOODZICKA

PART II

CONSEQUENCES OF PREJUDICE

4

STEREOTYPE THREAT AND THE ACADEMIC UNDERPERFORMANCE OF MINORITIES AND WOMEN

JOSHUA ARONSON, DIANE M. QUINN, AND STEVEN J. SPENCER

5

CONCEPTUALIZING THE DETERMINANTS OF ACADEMIC CHOICE AND TASK PERFORMANCE ACROSS SOCIAL GROUPS

CHARLES STANGOR AND GRETCHEN B. SECHRIST

6

VULNERABILITY TO THE AFFECTIVE CONSEQUENCES OF THE STIGMA OF OVERWEIGHT

DIANNE M. QUINN AND JENNIFER CROCKER

7

STRESS AND OPPRESSED SOCIAL CATEGORY MEMBERSHIP

KEVIN W. ALLISON

8

UNDERMINED? AFFIRMATIVE ACTION FROM THE TARGETS' POINT OF VIEW

KATHRYN TRUAX, DIANA I. CORDOVA, AURORA WOOD, ELISABETH WRIGHT, AND FAYE CROSBY

PART III

COPING WITH PREJUDICE

9

COMPENSATING FOR PREJUDICE: HOW HEAVYWEIGHT PEOPLE (AND OTHERS) CONTROL OUTCOMES DESPITE PREJUDICE

CAROL T. MILLER AND ANNA M. MYERS

10

COPING WITH STIGMA THROUGH PSYCHOLOGICAL DISENGAGEMENT

BRENDA MAJOR AND TONI SCHMADER

11

COPING WITH GROUP-BASED DISCRIMINATION: INDIVIDUALISTIC VERSUS GROUP-LEVEL STRATEGIES

NYLA R. BRANSCOMBE AND NAOMI ELLEMERS

12

THE EVERYDAY FUNCTIONS OF AFRICAN AMERICAN IDENTITY

WILLIAM E. CROSS, JR. AND LINDA STRAUSS

13

IMPLICATIONS OF CULTURAL CONTEXT: AFRICAN AMERICAN IDENTITY AND POSSIBLE SELVES

DAPHNA OYSERMAN AND KATHY HARRISON

14

NEGOTIATING SOCIAL IDENTITY

KAY DEAUX AND KATHLEEN A. ETHIER

Contributors

Numbers in parentheses indicate the pages on which the authors' contributions begin.

Kevin W. Allison (145) Department of Psychology, Virginia Commonwealth University, Richmond, Virginia 23284.

Joshua Aronson (83) Department of Educational Psychology, University of Texas at Austin, Austin, Texas 78712.

Nyla R. Branscombe (243) Department of Psychology, University of Kansas, Lawrence, Kansas 66045.

Laurie L. Cohen (37) Psychology Department, The Pennsylvania State University, University Park, Pennsylvania 16801.

Diana I. Cordova (171) Department of Psychology, Yale University, New Haven, Connecticut 06520.

Jennifer Crocker (125) Department of Psychology, University of Michigan, Ann Arbor, Michigan 48109.

Faye Crosby (171) Smith College, Northampton, Massachusetts 01063.

William E. Cross, Jr. (267) Department of Student Development and Pupil Personnel Services, School of Education, University of Massachusetts, Amherst, Massachusetts 01003.

Kay Deaux (301) Graduate Center, City University of New York, New York, New York 10036.

Naomi Ellemers (243) Department of Social Psychology, Free University, Amsterdam, 1081 BT Amsterdam, The Netherlands.

Kathleen A. Ethier (301) Connecticut Women's Health Project, Yale University, New Haven, Connecticut 06510.

Lisa Feldman Barrett (11) Department of Psychology, Boston College, Chestnut Hill, Massachusetts 02167.

Kathy Harrison (281) Psychology Department, Wayne State University, Detroit, Michigan 48202.

Lauri L. Hyers (37) Psychology Department, The Pennsylvania State University, University Park, Pennsylvania 16801.

Marianne LaFrance (61) Department of Psychology, Boston College, Chestnut Hill, Massachusetts 02167.

Brenda Major (219) Department of Psychology, University of California, Santa Barbara, Santa Barbara, California 93106.

Carol T. Miller (191) Psychology Department, University of Vermont, Burlington, Vermont 05401.

Anna M. Myers (191) Psychology Department, University of Vermont, Burlington, Vermont 05401.

Daphna Oyserman (281) Research Center for Group Dynamics (RCGD), Institute for Social Research, University of Michigan, Ann Arbor, Michigan 48106.

Diane M. Quinn (83, 125) Department of Psychology, University of Michigan, Ann Arbor, Michigan 48109.

Toni Schmader (219) Department of Psychology, University of California, Santa Barbara, Santa Barbara, California 93106.

Gretchen B. Sechrist (105) Department of Psychology, University of Maryland, College Park, Maryland 20742.

Steven J. Spencer (83) Department of Psychology, University of Waterloo, Waterloo, Ontario, Canada N2L 3G1.

Charles Stangor (1, 105) Department of Psychology, University of Maryland, College Park, Maryland 20742.

Linda Strauss (267) The Pennsylvania State University, University Park, Pennsylvania 16801.

Janet K. Swim (1, 11, 37) Psychology Department, The Pennsylvania State University, University Park, Pennsylvania 16801.

Kathryn Truax (171) Department of Psychology, Yale University, New Haven, Connecticut 06520.

Aurora Wood (171) Smith College, Northampton, Massachusetts 01063.

Julie A. Woodzicka (61) Boston College, Chestnut Hill, Massachusetts 02167.

Elisabeth Wright (171) Smith College, Northampton, Massachusetts 01063.

INTRODUCTION

JANET K. SWIM

The Pennsylvania State University

CHARLES STANGOR

University of Maryland

> *"The lion's story will never be told as long as the hunter is telling the story"*
> African Proverb (Stevenson, 1997)

Virtually all existing social-psychological research and theorizing on prejudice has focused on the people who hold prejudiced beliefs. For instance, an examination of books on prejudice (e.g., Brown, 1995; Duckitt, 1992) as well as current social psychology textbooks reveals that most research on prejudice covers such topics as the characteristics of racism and sexism, the cognitive and motivational processes that lead to the formation and maintenance of prejudice, and possible methods of changing prejudice and reducing discrimination. Even one of the classic works on stigma (Jones *et al.,* 1984) has more to do with those who are prejudiced against the stigmatized than the study of the stigmatized themselves or their experiences with and perceptions of prejudice.

This relatively one-sided focus on the perpetrators of prejudice is surprising, given the practical importance of studying the target's perspective, and the potential theoretical advances that could be made by doing so. The target person represents a classic social psychological individual—one who is highly motivated, in interests of self-defense and opportunity maximization, to carefully peruse the behaviors of others with the goal of accurately understanding the attitudes of those others toward him or her, and to attempt to tailor his or her behavior to reduce or avoid negative actions from others (see Eberhardt & Fiske, 1996).

One can find research and theory that has included the target's perspective in every decade of this century starting at least from the 1930s. For instance, one can go back to Horowitz's (1939), Clark and Clark's (1939; 1947), and Lewin's (1948) research on ethnic group identification and internalization of prejudice, as well as Goffman's (1963) discussions about the experiences of the stigmatized. There are also books and edited volumes that include research and theory on prejudice that focuses on both the perpetrator and the target (e.g., Watson, 1973; Simpson & Yinger, 1985). Yet, this research has not been centrally integrated, until recently, into the social psychological literature, or into discussions and reviews of research on prejudice (see Sigelman & Welch, 1991, for a view about why the target's perspective may have been neglected). Further, much of this past research, like research on prejudice in general, has tended to focus on African Americans, but has not examined the experiences of other target groups.

This lack of integration of this research within social psychology has produced continued pleas for more attention to targets' perspectives. This idea was raised during the "crisis in confidence" within social psychology in the late 1960s and early 1970s (Collier, Minton, & Reynolds, 1991). At that time Harrison (1974) argued "that the current social psychology of prejudice has a bias in predominantly studying the prejudiced, or how they compare with those whom they injure, and in far less considering the victims of prejudice" (p. 202). More recently, other researchers (for instance, Graham, 1992) have noted the lack of inclusion of minority groups in psychological research, and have called for more research including the minority groups' perspectives and interpretations. Sue (1983) noted that ". . . many ethnic minority group individuals do not feel that research and practice represents their viewpoints, their interests, and their gestalts of society. Minority group status and the history of racism have made it difficult for them to have a strong voice in influencing directions." (p. 586). Further, Washington and McLoyd (1983) noted that it is important to include minority groups' interpretation of events in order to counteract the myths and distorted images of African American's lives.

CURRENT RESEARCH

Despite a relatively slow start, over the past decade there has been an explosion of research studying the target's perspective, and this literature is now being integrated more fully into the literature (see Crocker, Major, & Steele, 1998 for a review). In line with previous suggestions, this research is aimed at providing a more complete picture of prejudice by more fully studying the impact of prejudice on its targets as well as targets' perceptions and responses to prejudice. The general goal of the present book is to review the current state of this quickly growing field of research. We have recruited many of the most active researchers in the field as contributors, and asked them to write chapters that present contemporary theoretical and empirical approaches. The book is divided into three sections, that relate respectively to encountering prejudice, consequences of prejudice, and coping with prejudice.

ENCOUNTERING PREJUDICE

Questions of relevance in this first section involve how and when stigmatized group members perceive that they have encountered prejudice or discrimination and their immediate reactions to these events. Research related to these topics includes individual differences in perceptions of the prevalence of prejudice against themselves and others (cf. Taylor, Ruggiero, & Louis, 1996; Taylor, Wright, & Porter, 1994) and the extent to which people feel that prejudice and discrimination is a relevant social problem (e.g., Schuman & Hatchet, 1974; Terrell & Terrell, 1981). It also includes perceptions of societal equity and fairness (Major, 1994; Pratto, Sidanius, Stallworth, & Malle, B. F., 1995; Stangor & Jost, 1996) and the role of anxiety in intergroup contact (Devine, Evett, Vasquez-Suson, 1997; Hyers & Swim, 1998; Stephan and Stephan, 1985).

The issues raised in this section naturally include concerns about the accuracy of such perceptions, the energy that it takes to maintain vigilance in the face of potential threats, and the immediate emotional consequences of the encounters. One of the thorny issues that follows in the study of perceptions is that of the criterion used to determine whether targets are accurately perceiving the presence or absence of prejudice directed at them. One approach to this issue might be to compare the target's own interpretations of prejudice with third-party assessments of the impact of prejudice on targets or to some predetermined definitional criteria. Another approach would be to compare definitions and labeling of various events between potential perpetrators and potential targets across a variety of circumstances rather than focus on who is accurate. Both types of research might allow inferences to be made about potential biases that occur in the target's judgments about the behavior of those who judge them. These biases might be expected to be related to the development and differentiation among different types of self and social identity, self-esteem, and beliefs about prejudice and perpetrators. In short, this research could be seen as the mirror image of the more traditional study of prejudice that involves documenting individual and contextual determinants of biases in perpetrators' judgments about targets. This line of research seems to present a relatively fertile field of potential research opportunities, and the chapters by Feldman Barrett and Swim; Swim, Cohen, and Hyers; and LaFrance and Woodzicka begin to tackle these topics. Further, these issues reemerge in other chapters because perceptions and reaction to prejudice have implications for the consequences of prejudice on targets as well as on their selection of coping strategies.

CONSEQUENCES OF PREJUDICE

This second section of the book concerns how the actual or perceived prejudice and discrimination of others can influence the thoughts, feelings, and behaviors of the targets of prejudice and discrimination. Such research includes investigation of potential long- and short-term effects on mental health due to prejudice and discrimination, as well as the impact of ethnic and sexual crimes on members of target groups.

Of the general issues covered in the present book, social psychological research on the debilitating effects of prejudice has perhaps received the most attention over the years (Clark & Clark, 1947; Cohen & Swim, 1995; Crocker & Major,

1989; Cross, 1991; Dion, 1975; Katz, Goldston, & Benjamin, 1958; Katz, Roberts, & Robinson, 1965; Lewin, 1948; Lord & Saenz, 1985; Maruyama & Miller, 1979; Saenz, 1994; Stangor & Carr, 1997). This has included research on the impact of prejudice on target's self-esteem, identity, and academic performance. Following this tradition, one chapter by Aronson, Quinn, and Spencer, and a second by Stangor and Sechrist, provide theoretical models for understanding the negative impact of prejudice and perceptions of prejudice on academic performance and school persistence, and the chapters by Quinn and Crocker and by Allison examine the impact of prejudice on targets' psychological well-being. Assessing the effects of prejudice also allows us to draw conclusions about the importance and effects of social remedies, such as the necessity and consequences of affirmative action programs. This particular social issue is explored in the chapter by Truax, Wood, Wright, Cordova, and Crosby. The consequences of prejudice are important to understand because they are a driving force for the coping mechanism targets employ.

COPING WITH PREJUDICE

This third section of our book addresses how individuals attempt to eliminate or minimize the impact of prejudice in their lives. In contrast to considering prejudice as an attitude held by perpetrators, from the target's perspective prejudice can be conceived of as a stressor (Allison; Feldman Barret & Swim) that leads to cognitive, emotional, and behavioral responses to buffer its impact. Also relevant to this topic is research on targets' attempts to disconfirm others' beliefs about them (Deaux & Major, 1987) or to accept the negative beliefs of others with the goal of verifying their own perceptions of themselves (Swann & Ely, 1984; Swann, 1997). Social identity research has also included efforts to understand how group members cope with and attempt to change the status of their social group (Tajfel & Turner, 1979; Taylor & Moghaddan, 1994), and the recognition of a differentiation between personal and social or collective identity and responses to prejudice (Cross, 1991; LaLonde & Cameron, 1984). Along these same lines, chapters in this section of the present volume address both personal and collective responses to prejudice (Branscombe & Ellemers; Major & Schmader), attempts to prevent or reduce the impact of prejudice on the individual (Miller & Myers), as well as the formation and functions of social identity as a buffer (Cross & Clark; Deaux & Ethier; Oyserman & Harrison).

While we have partitioned the research into the three areas of encountering, consequences of, and coping with prejudice, it is clear that these three sections are interrelated. The consequences of prejudice are likely a function of one's identification of and immediate response to an encounter as well as the success of one's coping responses. Similarly, the coping method one selects will be dependent upon the quality of one's encounters with prejudice and the consequences the encounters have for individuals and their groups. Finally, the quality of one's encounters will likely be influenced by past experiences with prejudice and the coping strategies chosen.

CONSEQUENCES OF STUDYING THE
TARGET'S PERSPECTIVE

We believe that the ideas in this book will contribute to the growing literature studying prejudice from the target's perspective, and we see a number of potentially positive outcomes of such research. For one, our contributors as a group recognize that it is important to study targets in their own right and see the target of prejudice as a legitimate and informative focus of research. Most basically, the chapters highlight the importance of taking into account the experience of being a potential target of prejudice in order to fully understand prejudice and its impact.

The importance of including targets' frame of reference was nicely discussed by Rosenberg (1986) who argued that the reason social scientists were mistaken when they proposed that African Americans would have lower self-esteem than European Americans is because they were not taking into account the phenomenological experience of being an African American (see also Crocker & Major, 1989). That is, they were not taking into account the subjective world in which African Americans lived. As Rosenberg notes, research on targets of prejudice requires "a shift from an external to an internal frame of reference" (p. 178), and from an observer's to an actor's frame of reference. Understanding the target's perspective can help explain the struggles targets face in their attempts to develop the least personally costly way to deal with prejudice. The chapters in this book illustrate the recurring theme that coping with prejudice represents walking a fine line between over and under protecting oneself from prejudice (Aronson, Spencer, & Quinn; Miller; Feldman Barrett & Swim; Stangor & Sechrist). Further, taking into account targets' perspectives highlights the flexibility of their own identity (Deaux & Ethier) as well as the unique aspects of their identity that are not defined by their stigmatized status (Cross & Clark).

Second, just as a feminist perspective has informed research on women and gender (Worell and Etaugh, 1994), a focus on the target individual will likely lead to a fuller appreciation for the experiences of minority group members and women as a legitimate focus in the study of prejudice apart from the standard of the majority group and men, and to a more complete understanding of the strengths and capabilities as well as the particular problems of minority group members and women. Such research can lead not only to an expansion of topic areas studied but also to changes in how prejudice is conceived and a fuller understanding of the targets themselves. Instead of prejudice being an objectively identified phenomenon within perceivers, prejudice becomes a subjective phenomenon with differences in perceptions and interpretations occurring between observers and actors, among target groups, and even within target groups (e.g., variations in perceptions among women from different ethnic groups; differences in group identity and in resilience to prejudice).

Third, we hope this focus will lead to more research studying different target groups as well as variations within target groups, without the necessity of always directly comparing targets and perpetrators. For example, African Americans and

Asian Americans could be compared as could differences among women in terms of their specific psychological demands and responses to prejudice, without including European Americans or men as comparison groups. In addition to having more ethnically and economically diverse samples, greater emphasis on alternative methodologies may also evolve. For instance, we may need to place greater emphasis on descriptive and qualitative data, such as observational approaches, in order to fully understand different group's perspectives.

Finally, in addition to the scientific advantages, there are also valuable social consequences to including a target's perspective on prejudice in our science. A focus on target's experiences gives a voice to target groups, validates their experiences, helps pinpoint their unique strengths and weaknesses, and can potentially increase empathy for the targets of prejudice in today's society. We and our contributors will have succeeded in our endeavor if we have accomplished any of these goals.

REFERENCES

Brown, R. (1995). *Prejudice: Its social psychology.* Oxford, UK: Blackwell.

Clark, K. B., & Clark, M. P. (1939). The development of consciousness of self and the emergence of racial identification in Negro pre-school children. *The Journal of Social Psychology, 10,* 591–599.

Clark, K. B., & Clark, M. P. (1947). Racial identification and preference in Negro children. In T. M. Newcomb & E. Hartley (Eds.), *Readings in social psychology.* New York: Hold & Company, 1969–1978.

Cohen, L. L., & Swim, J. K. (1995). The differential effect of gender ratios on women and men: Tokenism, self-confidence, and expectations. *Personality and Social Psychology Bulletin, 21,* 876–884.

Collier, G., Minton, H. L., & Reynolds, G. (1991). *Currents of thought in American social psychology.* Oxford, UK: Oxford University Press.

Crocker, J., & Major, B. (1989). Social stigma and self-esteem: The self-protective properties of stigma. *Psychological Review, 96,* 608–630.

Crocker, J., & Major, B. & Steele, C. (1998). Social stigma. In D. Gilbert, S. T. Fiske, & G. Lindzey (Eds.), *Handbook of social psychology* (4th ed.). Boston: McGraw Hill.

Cross, W. E. (1991). *Shades of black: Diversity in African-American identity.* Philadelphia, PA: Temple University Press.

Devine, P. G., Evett, S. R., Vasquez-Suson, K. A. (1997). Exploring the interpersonal dynamics of intergroup contact. In Sorrentino & E. T. Higgins (Eds.), *Handbook of motivation and cognition: The interpersonal context* (Vol. 3). New York: Guilford.

Deaux, K., & Major, B. (1987). Putting gender into context: An interactive model of gender-related behavior. *Psychological Review, 94,* 369–389.

Dion, K. L. (1975). Women's reactions to discrimination from members of the same or opposite sex. *Journal of Personality, 9,* 294–306.

Duckitt, J. (1992). *The social psychology of prejudice.* New York: Praeger.

Eberhardt, J. L., & Fiske, S. T. (1996). Motivating individuals to change: What is a target to do? In C. N. Macrae, C. Stangor, & M. Hewstone (eds.), Stereotypes and stereotyping (pp. 369–418). New York: Guilford.

Goffman, E. (1963). *Stigma: Notes on the management of spoiled identity.* Englewood Cliffs, NJ: Prentice-Hall, Inc.

Graham, S. (1992). "Most of the subjects were White and middle class": Trends in published research on African Americans and selected APA journals, 1970–1989. *American Psychologist, 47,* 629–639.

Harrison, G. (1974). A bias in the social psychology of prejudice. In N. G. Armistead (Ed.), *Reconstructing social psychology* (pp. 189–204). Baltimore, MD: Penguin Education.

Horowitz, R. (1939). Racial aspects of self-identification in nursery school children. *Journal of Psychology, 7,* 91–99.

Hyers, L. L., & Swim, J. K. (1998). *A comparison of experiences of stigmatized and non-stigmatized individuals during an intergroup encounter.* Paper submitted for publication.

Jones, E. E., Farina, A., Hatorf, A. H., Markus, H., Miller, D. T., & Scott, R. A. (1984). *Social stigma: The psychology of marked relationships.* New York, NY: Freeman.

Katz, I., Goldston, J., & Benjamin, L. (1958). Behavior and productivity in biracial work groups. *Human Relations, 11,* 123–141.

Katz, I., Roberts, S. O., & Robinson, J. M. (1965). Effects of task difficulty, race of administrator, and instructions on digit-symbol performance of Negroes. *Journal of Personality and Social Psychology, 2,* 53–59.

LaLonde, R. N., & Cameron, J. E. (1994). Behavioral responses to discrimination: A focus on action. In M. P. Zanna & J. M. Olson (Eds.), *The psychology of prejudice: The Ontario symposium, 7,* (pp. 257–288). Hillsdale, NJ: Lawrence Erlbaum Associates, Publishers.

Lewin, K. (1948). Self-hatred in Jews. In G. W. Lewin (Ed.), *Resolving social conflicts—Selected Papers of K. Lewin* (pp. 186–200). New York: Harper & Brothers.

Lord, C. G., & Saenz, D. S. (1985). Memory deficits and memory surfeits: Differential cognitive consequences of tokenism for tokens and observers. *Personality and Social Psychology, 49,* 918–926.

Major, B. (1994). From social inequality to personal entitlement: The role of social comparisons, legitimacy appraisals, and group members. *Advances in Experimental Social Psychology, 26,* 293–355.

Maruyama, G., & Miller, N. (1979). Reexamination of normative influence processes in desegregated classrooms. *American Education Research Journal, 16,* 273–283.

Rosenberg, M. (1986). Self-esteem research: A phenomenological corrective. In J. Prager, D. Longshore, & M. Seeman (Eds.), *School desegregation research: New directions in situational analysis.* New York, NY: Plenum Press.

Saenz, D. S. (1994). Token status and problem-solving deficits: Detrimental effects of distinctiveness and performance monitoring. *Social Cognition, 12,* 61–74.

Schuman, H., & Hatchet, S. (1974). *Black racial attitudes: Trends and complexities.* Ann Arbor, MI: Institute for Social Research.

Simpson, G. E., & Yinger, J. M. (1985). *Racial and cultural minorities: An analysis of prejudice and discrimination* (5th ed.). New York: Plenum Press.

Pratto, F., Sidanius, J., Stallworth, L. M., & Malle, B. F. (1995). Social dominance orientation: A personality variable predicting social and political attitudes. *Journal of Personality and Social Psychology, 67,* 741–763.

Sigelman, L., & Welch, S. (1991). *Black Americans' views of racial inequality.* Cambridge, UK: Cambridge University Press.

Stangor, C., & Carr, C. (1997). *Interactive effects of minority status and perceived group similarity upon choice to engage in group versus individual activities.* Manuscript under editorial review.

Stangor, C., & Jost, J. T. (1996). Individual, group and system levels of analysis and their application to intergroup relations. In R. Spears, P. Oakes, N. Ellemers & S. Haslam (Eds.), *Social psychology of stereotyping and group life* (pp. 336–358). Oxford: Blackwell Press.

Stephan, W. G., & Stephan, C. W. (1985). Intergroup anxiety. *Journal of Social Issues, 41,* 157–175.

Stevenson, H. (1997). Personal communication.

Sue, S. (1983). Ethnic minority issues in psychology. *American Psychologist, X,* 583–592.

Swann, W. B., & Ely, R. J. (1984). A battle of wills: Self-verification versus behavioral confirmation. *Journal of Personality and Social Psychology, 46,* 1287–1302.

Swann, W. B. (1997). *Self-traps. The elusive quest for higher self-esteem.* New York: W. H. Freeman.

Tajfel, H., & Turner, J. C. (1979). An integrative theory of intergroup conflict. In W. G. Austin & S. Worchel (Eds.), *The social psychology of intergroup relations* (pp. 33–47). Monterey, CA: Brooks/Cole.

Taylor, D. M. & Moghaddan, F. M. (1994). *Theories of intergroup relations: International social psychological perspectives* (2nd ed.). Westport, CT: Praeger Publishers/Greenwood Publishing Group.

Taylor, D. M., Wright, S. C., & Porter, L. E. (1994). Dimensions of perceived discrimination: Their personal/group discrimination discrepancy. In M. P. Zanna & J. M. Olson (Eds.), *The psychology of prejudice: The Ontario Symposium* (Vol. 7, pp. 233–256). Hillsdale, NJ: Lawrence Erlbaum Associates.

Taylor, D. M., Ruggiero, K. M., & Louis, W. R. (1996). Personal/group discrimination discrepancy: Towards a two-factor explanation. *Canadian Journal of Behavioral Science, 28,* 193–202.

Terrell, F., & Terrell, S. (1981). An inventory to measure cultural mistrust among Blacks. *The Western Journal of Black Studies, 5,* 180–185.

Washington, E. D., & McLoyd, V. C. (1982). The external validity of research involving American minorities. *Human Development, 25,* 324–339.

Watson, P. (1973). *Psychology and race.* Chicago, IL: Aldine Publishing Company.

Worell, J., & Etaugh, C. (1994). Transforming theory and research with women: Themes and variations. *Psychology of Women Quarterly, 18,* 443–450.

ENCOUNTERING PREJUDICE

1

APPRAISALS OF PREJUDICE
AND DISCRIMINATION

LISA FELDMAN BARRETT

Boston College

JANET K. SWIM

The Pennsylvania State University

Like other daily hassles, encountering prejudice and discrimination can be stressful (Allison, this volume; Feagin & Sikes, 1994). It can cause people to feel mistreated, disrespected, and angry, and it can prevent people from meeting their goals. The frequency with which an individual identifies encounters as prejudicial or discriminatory has important implications for his or her psychological functioning: it bears directly on whether feedback about the self should be discounted or accepted, and it helps identify strategies for protecting oneself from current and future encounters with prejudice and discrimination.

The purpose of this chapter is to examine targets' perceptions of prejudice and discrimination using a modified version of Lazarus and Folkman's (1984) cognitive appraisal perspective. In 1984, Lazarus and Folkman presented a comprehensive theory of stress and coping based on a central tenant: both environmental presses and attempts to cope with those presses must be considered to fully understand the ways in which an individual defines and evaluates the environment. They called the process of defining and evaluating the environment "appraisal," and proposed two types of appraisal processes. During primary appraisal, the individual assesses whether a threat is present in the environment; during secondary appraisal, the individual assesses whether he or she has the resources to cope with the threat, should it materialize. Lazarus and Folkman (1984) focused largely

11

on the ways in which the secondary appraisal process influenced well-being. In the present chapter, we focus on the primary appraisal process.

Recently, Feldman Barrett (1996; Feldman Barrett & and Fong, 1996) proposed an elaboration of the Lazarus and Folkman model, drawing on signal detection theory (SDT) to explain variations in the primary appraisal process. Although it was originally used as a model for understanding perceptual errors (misses and false alarms) in judging psychophysical signals, SDT has been applied to judgments in many psychological domains. Feldman Barrett and Fong (1996) argued that there are different psychological and interpersonal costs associated with misses and false alarms when applied to appraisals of threat. They suggest that people weigh the psychological costs of each type of error when making threat appraisals, thereby providing a motivational explanation for people's judgment strategies.

We suggest that deciding whether or not one has encountered prejudice or discrimination is a type of threat appraisal. A perception of threat is a subjective probability that danger to the self will develop (Milburn & Watman, 1981). In the case of prejudice and discrimination, the harm can be psychological, structural, and even physical. Psychologically, prejudice and discrimination can cause a person to internalize negative beliefs about the self. Negative beliefs may leave a person with lowered self-esteem or a damaged identity and produce a feeling that one is stigmatized (Crocker & Major, 1989). Structurally, prejudice and discrimination can restrict a person's access to opportunities or information, thereby producing a lack of personal or professional growth (e.g., Benokraitis & Feagin, 1995). Physically, prejudice and discrimination can be associated with physical attacks. In addition, prejudice and discrimination serve as a constant source of stress that can affect physical health (see Allison, this volume). Even if an event has occurred in the past, individuals might appraise the event as threatening after the fact because it presented a psychological or physical danger that they were unaware of when the event occurred, or because it presents a psychological danger when they are thinking about it in the present.

In this chapter, we examine perceptions of prejudice and discrimination as primary appraisals that are subject to misses and false alarms. Our goal is to use signal detection theory to provide a framework for understanding how people decide when they are the targets of prejudice and discrimination. More specifically, we believe our framework provides insight into the cognitive and motivational processes that underlie the identification of prejudice and discrimination. We begin by briefly reviewing components of signal detection theory and the application of SDT to perceptions of threat. We then elaborate on the specific application of SDT to perceptions of prejudice and discrimination.

SIGNAL DETECTION THEORY

Signal detection theory (SDT) was originally designed to assess an observer's behavior when attempting to detect weak psychophysical signals (Green & Swets,

1966/1974; McNicol,1972). Considerable evidence suggests that SDT provides a good framework for investigating a wide range of human judgment behavior, including judgments of subtle, covert psychological experiences (e.g., pain, stress, fear, and memory), and judgments of ambiguous social information (Grossberg & Grant, 1978; Harvey, 1992; Swets, 1986).

SDT's most significant theoretical contribution to understanding the judgment process lies in its ability to separate an observer's actual judgment behavior into two subprocesses: sensitivity and response style or bias (Harvey, 1992). Sensitivity has been defined as an observer's ability to accurately detect sensory information when it is present and its absence when it is not present. A target's sensitivity to prejudice would reflect her or his ability to accurately detect the presence or absence of cues indicating prejudice and discrimination. Sensitivity may vary because people differ in their perceptual abilities or because of the properties of the stimulus. A stimulus' probability of occurrence, intensity, and imminence (i.e., proximity to danger) will affect its ambiguity, and therefore a perceiver's sensitivity (McNicol, 1972; Miller, 1979; Paterson & Neufeld, 1987).

In contrast to sensitivity, response style or bias is defined as the observer's tendency to favor one response over another, independent of the base rate for the stimulus. Thus, a response bias for prejudice exists when an individual judges a situation or person as prejudiced or discriminatory more or less frequently than prejudice or discrimination objectively occurs in that environment. Response bias (i.e., the placement of an observer's decision criteria) is influenced by two factors: the observer's beliefs about the base rates of the stimuli; and the goals that she or he has when making a judgment about a stimulus (Egan, 1975; Green & Swets, 1966; 1974; Healy & Kubovy, 1978), in particular, the perceived severity and consequences of a miss or false alarm (Feldman Barrett & Fong, 1996). There is no requirement that individuals are consciously aware of their response biases, and in fact they may function outside the observer's awareness (Harvey, 1992).

According to STD, the observer perceives situationally relevant information that he or she then compares to an internal decision criterion. The location of this decision criteria determines the observer's response bias (Harvey, 1992). If the available evidence is stronger than the decision criterion, then the observer will say "yes" the stimulus is present; if the evidence is not stronger than the decision criterion, then the observer will say "no" (see Harvey, 1992, and Macmillan, 1993, for a discussion of responses using continuous or probability ratings). Cognitive and motivational processes will influence where an individual sets his or her decision criterion. To determine the accuracy of the oberver's perception, his or her judgment can then be compared to a stimulus criterion indicating whether the stimulus actually did occur. For a given decision criterion and stimulus criterion there are four possible judgment outcomes. A *positive hit* occurs when the observer responds "yes" and the target stimulus did appear; a *correct rejection* occurs when the observer responds "no" and the target stimulus did not appear; a *false alarm* occurs when the observer responds "yes" but the target stimulus did not appear, and a *miss* occurs when the observer responds "no" but the target stimulus did appear.

The notion of judgment outcomes can be applied to perceptions of prejudice and discrimination. For example, an African American individual may be in a situation where he or she is barred from entering a store that is about to close, but he or she notices that the manager allows a European American to enter. In this scenario, sensitivity is indicated by whether or not the African American individual notices the incongruence at all; response bias is indicated by how the person interprets the incongruence. A person with a stringent decision criterion may not judge the event to be discriminatory. A person with a more lenient decision criterion, however, will be more likely to perceive the event as discriminatory. The extent to which a person has a stringent or lenient decision criterion (response bias) is likely to be a function of many things, including his or her previous experience with prejudice in that environment (i.e., the perceived base-rates), and his or her need to be self-protective versus accurate (i.e., the goal associated with making the judgment). The goal associated with making the judgment is strongly linked to the perceived cost of making a judgment error (i.e., the cost of a miss versus the cost of a false alarm).

In many cases, the value of the stimulus criterion is difficult to assess because the actual status of the stimulus is ambiguous and no concrete criterion for the judgment exists. For instance, in our scenario above, the accuracy of the target's judgment (hits, correct rejections, misses, and false alarms) should be determined by comparing his or her decision to the presence or absence of the stimulus criterion. We know that the store manager engaged in differential behavior toward both parties involved in the scenario, but we do not know for certain whether the store manager was actually being discriminatory toward the target individual (i.e., engaging in the differential behavior because of the race or ethnicity of the target). When there is no clear objective stimulus criterion, judgment accuracy is difficult to assess. There are strategies for creating a criterion where one does not exist, however. For example, a third party observer who is independent of the target and the store manager can be used to determine the presence or absence of the stimulus criterion. This third party observer is not necessarily "objective," but is independent of the victim–perpetrator system. Although the third party observer may have motivations that influence where he or she sets the stimulus criterion, they are not the same motivations as those of the perceiver (which constitute bias). Thus, the actual absence or presence of the stimulus cue is decided by an external source; it is ambiguous and probabilistic, but the relativity is taken out of the hands of the perceiver/target, and this allows us to distinguish between the decision criterion, which is bias, and the stimulus criterion, which is not. Furthermore, the ability to determine accuracy may not be necessary to understand the factors that affect appraisals. SDT can be used as a heuristic for understanding the stimulus and person characteristics that should affect judgment strategies. Moreover, it should be possible to assess the advantages and disadvantages of different decision-making strategies, as we discuss below, with out knowing precisely whether a specific judgment instance was accurate or not.

PRIMARY APPRAISALS OF THREAT FROM A SIGNAL DETECTION THEORY PERSPECTIVE

Feldman Barrett and Fong (1996) recently employed the logic of SDT to discuss how sensitivity, response style, and base rates are involved with primary appraisal of threat. They argue that the ambiguity typically associated with threat cues limits sensitivity (Fiske & Taylor, 1991; Paterson & Neufeld, 1987). When making judgments under uncertainty, most researchers agree that it is adaptive to use the base rates of the stimulus in question (Nisbett, Krantz, Jepson, & Fong, 1982; Tversky & Kahneman, 1982). Although psychologists have argued that individuals fail to use base rates for a number of cognitive reasons (e.g., they attend to the wrong information or they fail to apply statistical logic), Feldman Barrett and Fong (1996) argue that there is a motivation for not relying on base rates: self-protection. That is, judgment errors differ in their consequences and reinforcement power and this will affect people's judgment strategies. Failing to detect a threat (i.e., a miss) will cause an individual to experience the full force of the threat and incur psychological, structural, or physical damage. In contrast, detecting a threat when none is there (i.e., a false alarm) will cause interpersonal disruption, behavioral restriction, and needless anxiety (e.g., Mathews & MacLeod, 1994), resulting from the erroneous perception of the self as vulnerable and others as intending harm when this is not the case (Leary, 1957, Sullivan, 1953; Horney, 1950).

As illustrated below, the likelihood of obtaining misses and false alarms is a function of both the prior probability of threat and the perceiver's decision-making strategy. Let the stimulus-response matrix in Fig. 1.1a represent an environment with a high base rate for threat where the observer can accurately appraise the presence or absence of threat in every event; he or she has a hit rate of 100% with no misses or false alarms. Considering the ambiguous and inconsistent nature of most threats (Fiske & Taylor, 1991; Paterson & Neufeld, 1987), however, it is unlikely that a person would obtain this perfect hit rate because the ambiguity and unpredictability of stimuli makes accurate detection quite difficult. One decision-making strategy available to the individual would be to rely on base-rates. Consider the stimulus-response matrix of an individual who relies on the base rates to appraise threat (Fig. 1.1b): the individual experiences misses 16% of the time and false alarms 16% of the time. Thus, 16% of the time the individual would face a threat unprepared because she or he failed to detect it, and 16% of the time he or she would prepare for a threat that never materialized.

If the individual is concerned about maximizing self-protection, he or she will use a judgment strategy that minimizes the error in judgment that is perceived to

a

		Reality			
		Threat	No Threat		
Appraisal	Threat	80	0	80	
	No Threat	0	20	20	
		80	20		

FIGURE 1.1A   Correct judgments in a threatening environment.

b

		Reality			
		Threat	No Threat		
Appraisal	Threat	64	16	80	
	No Threat	16	4	20	
		80	20		

FIGURE 1.1B   Use of base-rate information in a threatening environment.

c

		Reality			
		Threat	No Threat		
Appraisal	Threat	80	20	100	
	No Threat	0	0	0	
		80	20		

FIGURE 1.1C   Use of zero-miss strategy in a threatening environment.

be the most costly (Feldman Barrett & Fong, 1996); the base rate for threat in the environment will contribute to the relative costs of misses and false alarms. If we assume that the magnitude of threat is associated with the frequency of threat, then a large prior probability of threat in the environment (i.e., a high base rate for threat) should be associated with a goal to reduce the number of misses more than false alarms. Although random acts of violence do occur, we have assumed for the moment that a threat in a relatively threatening environment will be more harmful than that in an environment where the base rate for threat is lower. The magnitude of the harm, along with the frequency of misses, will produce aversive learning associated with failing to detect a threat when it is present. To reduce the number of misses, the individual can substantially lower her or his decision criterion, thereby causing most cues to exceed threshold and be perceived as a threat; Feldman Barrett and Fong (1996) call this a "zero-miss" strategy. As a result, any cue, however weak, will exceed threshold and the individual will perceive the presence of a threat. By responding to every event as a potential threat, the individual maximizes his or her positive hit rate and minimizes misses (Fig. 1.1c). For some portion of the time, however, an individual will perceive threat where the probability of danger is low or nonexistent (i.e., the number of false alarms will increase from 16% to 20%). In a high-threat environment, however, the costs associated with false alarms may be preferred over the cost of misses.

a

		Reality			
		Threat	No Threat		
Appraisal	Threat	4	16	20	
	No Threat	16	64	80	
		20	80		

FIGURE 1.2A   Use of base-rate information in a nonthreatening environment.

b

		Reality			
		Threat	No Threat		
Appraisal	Threat	0	0	0	
	No Threat	20	80	100	
		20	80		

FIGURE 1.2B   Use of positive-illusions strategy in a nonthreatening environment.

In contrast, a small prior probability of threat will be associated with a goal to reduce the number of false alarms rather than misses. The stimulus-response matrix in Fig. 1.2a represents an environment with a low base rate for threat where the individual relies on the base rates to appraise threat. The individual experiences false alarms 16% of the time and misses 16% of the time. Although misses may still be harmful in a low-threat environment, we assume that they are less problematic because the threat itself may be less intense. Relative to the costs of a miss in a relatively benign environment, false alarms may be more costly; preparing for threats that never appear can have serious emotional, behavioral, and interpersonal consequences. To reduce the number of false alarms, the individual can adopt a more stringent decision criterion. As a result, most cues will fail to exceed threshold and will not be perceived as a threat. Feldman Barrett and Fong (1996) call this a "positive-illusion" strategy (Fig. 1.2b). By responding to the environment in this way, the individual maximizes his or her correct rejection rate and minimizes false alarms.[1] For some portion of the time, the individual will fail to perceive a threat when it is really there (i.e., the number of misses will increase from 16% to 20%). Although an increased miss rate can be associated with psychological costs, the consequences of a false alarm may outweigh those of a miss in a relatively benign environment.

Both misses and false alarms are associated with costs. As a general principle, individuals will try to avoid the error that is most costly to their psychological functioning. By using either strategy, the individual is protecting the self from the harm associated with a particular type of error. Yet each strategy has its own cost, because it is associated with an increase in the other judgment error. Although we might not describe such strategies as accuracy-seeking or rational (i.e., using statistical information and formal logic to make primary appraisals), they are

[1]It should also be noted that this strategy also minimizes positive hits. There are costs associated with positive hits when appraising prejudice (discussed below). The goal of minimizing these costs could might also lead to a positive illusion strategy.

optimal rules learned through interactions with the environment (Einhorn, 1980; Funder, 1987). Similarly, although misses and false alarms are considered "errors" in the strict sense of the word, they are not "mistakes" from this perspective. Thus, individuals are likely to adopt zero-miss or positive illusion strategies when making judgments about prejudice and discrimination, depending on which strategy results in the least costly of errors.

If the detection of threat is under the control of feedback and reinforcement contingencies, then the individual will develop a model of the world that is based on the judgment strategies learned in the formative environment. The result is an individual who is well adapted to the conditions of the current environment. If base rates change and people do not adjust their decision criteria, however, their error rate will change as well. For example, if an environment becomes safer, a person maintaining a zero-miss strategy will make more false alarms (e.g., from 20% to 80%; Fig. 1.3a). In contrast, if an environment becomes more threatening, a person maintaining a positive illusion strategy will experience more misses (e.g., from 20% to 80%; Fig. 1.3b). As the base rates increasingly deviate from an individual's judgment strategy, the individual's error rate will increase, the psychological consequences associated with each type of error will intensify, and a decrease in adaptation and well-being will result.

Failure to change a decision criteria in response to new base rates for threat can occur for three reasons. First, individuals using a zero-miss strategy may fail to calibrate to the base rates of the larger environmental context because of behavioral restriction. Avoiding certain situations or people is one way to avoid a miss. Such avoidance also prevents individuals from encountering disconfirming evidence, however, and that in turn contributes to maintaining the use of a zero-miss strategy.

Second, individuals using either a zero-miss or a positive illusion strategy may fail to detect changes in their environment because of cognitive biases. Previous experience will produce cognitive structures that direct attention to information that is consistent with the formative environment and filter out that which is inconsistent. An individual will develop cognitive structures that facilitate or inhibit threat detection, associated with expectancy that either most, or few, experiences have the potential to be dangerous or harmful. In either case, the individual develops well-entrenched assumptions about how to interpret ambiguous stimuli (Ittlesone & Kilpatrick, 1951) and will be chronically prepared to deal with ambiguous events (Kahneman & Tversky, 1982) in a way that matches their formative environment. Previous research suggests that implicitly held expectancies mediate the large effects of context on recognition, and exert their greatest influence on the interpretation of ambiguous stimuli (Epstein & Roupenian, 1970). Expectancies that have developed over a lifetime of previous experience not only have a profound effect on judgments, but they are usually inaccessible to conscious knowledge or intention, function automatically and effortlessly, and essentially constitute a dispositional preparedness for detecting threat (Ittlesone & Kilpatrick, 1951; Kahneman & Tversky, 1982; Posner, 1978). As a result, the

a

Appraisal		Reality		
		Threat	No Threat	
	Threat	20	80	100
	No Threat	0	0	0
		20	80	

FIGURE 1.3A   Use of zero-miss strategy in a nonthreatening environment

b

Appraisal		Reality		
		Threat	No Threat	
	Threat	0	0	0
	No Threat	80	20	100
		80	20	

FIGURE 1.3B   Use of positive-illusions strategy in a threatening environment.

individual may not be consciously aware that he or she has been trained to detect or avoid threat and may have limited sensitivity to the increase or decrease in threat cues in a new or changed environment. In addition, decision rules are typically learned deductively (Einhorn, 1982) and are used without intention or awareness (Lewicki, Hill, & Sasaki, 1989). These decision rules structure the encoding of ambiguous information such that it will be seen as confirming evidence and thereby strengthen the further use of the rule (Kahneman & Tversky, 1982). As a result, confirmatory biases will lead people to try to verify, rather than falsify, their working hypotheses about the world.

Third, individuals using either strategy may fail to calibrate to a change in environmental conditions for emotional reasons. Threat appraisals may constitute an aversive learning context that has intense emotional consequences for judgment errors. If individuals modify their learned judgment strategy in any way, they will encounter more errors of the type that they have learned to avoid. Not only will the individual suffer the full consequences of the current judgment error, but he or she will have to tolerate the emotional arousal associated with an error; the individual may even recall or even re-experience similar previous situations where he or she suffered in some way by making the error. Thus, the error will likely have a strong emotional currency because in the formative environment, it was psychologically, structurally, or physically costly . Because judgment errors will be emotionally disruptive to the individual, they may retain strong reinforcement power and may subsequently reinforce the readoption of the original appraisal strategy.

This theoretical framework suggests the critical role that previous experiences can play in affecting the judgment strategies that individuals use to determine whether or not they have been a target of prejudice or discrimination. As with other types of primary appraisals, previous experience with prejudice and discrimination will influence the type judgment error that a person is motivated to reduce. At this point, we should clarify that when we talk about "response bias" or "judgment error," we are not using the term pejoratively to mean a given judgment is unjustified or not understandable. Rather, we are using the term as a description of a perceiver's judgments about the presence or absence of a stimulus relative to the actual base rates for the stimuli in the environment. In the remainder of the chapter, we explore what sensitivity and response bias can contribute to an understanding of perceptions of prejudice and discrimination. We also consider whether there is any evidence to suggest that judgments of prejudice are associated with the cost–benefit analysis that we have presented.

SIGNAL DETECTION THEORY AND PERCEPTIONS OF PREJUDICE

According to SDT, sensitivity and response bias are separable processes that together produce one judgment. Previous research on perceptions of prejudice and discrimination has examined variation in individuals' judgments of prejudice or discrimination, but most studies have not examined whether an individual *accurately* detected the presence (or absence) of prejudice or discrimination cues. To our knowledge, there is no direct research evaluating how differential sensitivity to prejudice cues and response biases combine to form the judgments that are made by research participants. Because there is no clear-cut objective stimulus value for most social behaviors, the task of separating sensitivity from response bias becomes especially difficult. Even though we use SDT for its heuristic value in examining the processes associated with appraisals of prejudice, it is fair to say that the boundary between sensitivity and bias is blurred by the lack of objective criteria to indicate when prejudice or discrimination occur.

SENSITIVITY

A target's sensitivity to prejudice would reflect her or his ability to accurately detect the presence or absence of cues indicating prejudice and discrimination. Sensitivity to prejudice and discrimination can vary because of properties of the observer or properties of the stimulus cues.

Properties of the Individual

Theoretically, one could argue that some people are more able to detect prejudice and discrimination than others and that this ability is separate from their response biases. Sensitivity might be a function of people's general knowledge about social interactions or their specific knowledge about prejudice (Essed, 1991). People's knowledge about prejudice can come from either their own personal experience with prejudice, from accounts of friends, or from other sources such as explicit training from parents (Essed, 1991). For example, people who are more socially aware might be more likely to notice when a person has been overlooked than those who are less socially aware. (These individuals might also be more adept at delineating possible attributions for this behavior, but this is a matter of response bias, rather than sensitivity.) In addition, people who are knowledgeable about the history of prejudice might be aware of and notice a larger range of behaviors that can indicate possible prejudice. (Again, if they are also more able to determine whether there is a specific connection between an action and the larger social implications of that action, then this is a matter of response bias, rather than sensitivity.) Practically, individual differences in knowledge about prejudice are likely to be confounded with factors that influence the perceptions of base-rates, which in turn have their influence on response biases.

Properties of the Stimulus

Like the difficulty associated with identifying person-based differences in sensitivity, the stimulus characteristics that affect sensitivity blur the boundaries between sensitivity and response bias. Evidence from social psychology suggests that people tend to consider many alternative explanations for behaviors that might be motivated by prejudice (Essed, 1991; Louw-Potgieter, 1989) and this is especially so when the stimulus is attributionally ambiguous (Crocker & Major, 1989; Crocker, Major, & Steele, 1998). Research on stimulus properties indicates that the probability of occurrence, the intensity, and the imminence of a stimulus all influence the ambiguity of the information, which in turn should affect the sensitivity for when the information is or is not presented, as well as what the information actually means.

Probability of Occurrence

Cues to prejudice and discrimination are probabilistic in nature, and this enhances their ambiguity. The probability of occurrence is reflected in actual base rates. Ruggiero and colleagues (Ruggiero & Major, 1997; Ruggiero & Taylor, 1995, 1997) have conducted several studies testing the impact of base rates on attributing (or not attributing) negative evaluations to prejudice. In these studies, participants first completed a test of their abilities. They were then told that their tests would be graded by one of eight outgroup members (e.g., males for female participants). Participants were also told that of these eight people, either all (100%), 6 (75%), 4 (50%), 2 (25%), or none (0%), were known to discriminate against members of the participant's group. After a delay period, participants received a failing grade on the test, making them ineligible for a lottery. Finally, participants completed dependent measures that included a rating of the extent to which they attributed the grade they received to discrimination. Consistent with the prediction that prejudice is likely to be perceived when the probability of occurrence is high, participants were most likely to judge negative feedback as prejudicial when 100% of the evaluators discriminated against their group. Similarly, a base rate of 90% led individuals to more frequent judgments of discrimination than did lower base rates (Ruggiero & Taylor, 1995). Interestingly, the relationship between probability of occurrence and judgments of prejudice was not linear, because attributions to discrimination did not differ when the base rates were 75%, 50%, 25%, and 0%. The one exception to this finding was for European American men, whose attributions to discrimination decreased in a stepwise fashion from the 100% to the 0% conditions (Ruggiero & Major, 1997).[2] Findings from all four groups suggest that probability of occurrence does affect attributions to discrimination. The absence of complete reliance on base rates, however, suggests that other factors (i.e., response biases) were also influencing attributions.

Intensity of Stimulus

Cues to prejudice and discrimination vary in intensity, and this further determines their ambiguity. Generally, the intensity of a threat cue increases as more harm is incurred (Milburn & Watman, 1981). We would predict that as the intensity of threat increases, ambiguity decreases, and greater sensitivity is possible. As a result, people will be more able to perceive when they have encountered prejudice or discrimination. Evidence for this relationship comes from the literature on perceptions of harassment of women. People are more likely to identify an event that has occurred to someone else as sexual harassment when the event had negative repercussions for the target than when the same event had no repercussions (York, 1989).[3] Additionally, the presence of positive as well as negative outcomes could reduce the perceived intensity of the negative outcomes and thereby reduce the judgments of prejudice. For instance, the positive aspects of benevolent forms of discrimination such as paternalism (Glick & Fiske, 1995; VandenBerghe, 1967) may make it difficult for people to recognize this type of differential treatment as indicative of prejudice (Swim, Cohen, Hyers, Fitzgerald, & Bylsma, 1997).

Imminence of the Stimulus

Finally, the imminence of prejudice is associated with the ambiguity of threat cues. In general, the closer the individual is to danger, the more likely he or she will judge a stimulus as threatening (Milburn & Watman, 1981) and possibly prejudicial. We are unaware of any studies demonstrating that proximity to danger influences judgments of prejudice and discrimination. We would predict, however, that attributions to prejudice will become more likely as the negative consequences and the behavior in question become increasingly contiguous. For, example, perhaps quid pro quo harassment ("sexual cooperation that is coerced by promises of rewards or threats of punishment," Fitzgerald & Hesson-McInnis, 1989, p. 310) is more likely to be perceived as sexual harassment than is a hostile work environment (Frazier, Cochran, & Olson, 1995) because the harm from the former is perceived to be more imminent.

---

[2]Although we have interpreted these studies as evidence that probability of occurrence influences sensitivity to prejudice cues, participants were aware of the base-rate information and therefore the observed effects might also reflect response bias as well as sensitivity differences.

[3]It is also possible to interpret this effect in terms of response bias. Perceived base rates for harmful events that are prejudicial may be higher than those for nonharmful events that are prejudicial and this perception may result in judgment biases.

RESPONSE BIASES

Response biases are influenced by two factors: the individual's beliefs about the base rates of the stimuli and the goals that the individual has when making a judgment about the stimulus (i.e., the perceived costs of a miss or false alarm). We review research evidence suggesting that both of these factors can influence judgments about prejudice and discrimination.

Beliefs about Base Rates

According to SDT, people will set a very low threshold for identifying the presence of a stimulus when they believe that the base rate for the stimulus is high; alternatively, people will set a high threshold when they believe the base rate for the stimulus is low. Low thresholds and high base rates will lead to a greater likelihood, whereas high thresholds and lower base rates will lead to a lower likelihood, of identifying an event as prejudicial or discriminatory. There are several types of base-rate information that might be relevant to assessments of prejudice and we address each of these below.

Base Rates about People

People have beliefs about who is prejudiced against whom. These beliefs (like stereotypes) can be defined as perceived base rates or perceptions of the probability that certain people will be prejudiced (Locksley, Borgida, Brekke, & Hepburn, 1980; McCauley & Stitt, 1978). For example, participants are more likely to label a male (versus a female) instigator as sexist, even when instigators engaged in identical behavior (Baron, Burgess, & Kao, 1991, Inman & Baron, 1996). Similarly, European American instigators are labeled as racist more often than are African American instigators, even when they engaged in identical behavior (Inman & Baron, 1996).

Base Rates about Behaviors

Behaviors are likely to vary in the extent to which they are perceived to represent prejudice against one's group (Swim, Cohen, & Hyers, this volume). Differences in judgments of what constitutes a prototypic prejudicial behavior could explain why Blacks (primarily of West Indian heritage) were more likely than East Asians to indicate that a low grade was a result of discrimination (Ruggiero and Taylor, 1997). Even though both the East Asian and Black participants underutilized base-rate information, the Black participants were more likely to do this than the East Asian participants. Ruggiero and Taylor (1997) suggest that this group difference might be the result of differences in the tendency to make internal attributions for the low grade. An alternative explanation, however, is that negative evaluations in academic contexts are less prototypic for Asian students than for Black students. Hence, the Black participants may have believed that low academic scores are a prototypical cue of prejudicial treatment more so than did the Asian participants.

Base Rates about Encounters with Prejudice

People have beliefs about the extent to which they or members of their social group have experienced prejudice and discrimination. The available evidence suggests that some of these beliefs influence attributions to prejudice. In the previously described study by Ruggiero and Taylor (1996), women were asked to indicate the extent to which they themselves, and women in North America, had experienced discrimination from men. The first question represents participants' perceived base rates for their own personal experiences with discrimination, and the latter represents their perceived base rates for women in general. Ruggiero & Taylor (1996) found that perceptions of personal experience with discrimination were associated with attributing a failing grade to discrimination. Similarly, African American teenagers who believed that they were more likely to be personally discriminated against were also more likely to indicate that scenarios describing prototypical incidents of discrimination were indicative of discrimination (Taylor, Ruggiero, & Louis, 1996). Unlike beliefs about personal encounters with prejudice, however, beliefs about the tendency for one's group to experience discrimination were not predictive of women's or African Americans' judgments (see Taylor et al., 1996, for a possible explanation for the difference in predictive power for the two types of base rates).

A daily diary study of perceived prejudice indicated that perceptions of both personal and group discrimination affected the number of prejudicial events that women reported experiencing during a 2-week period (Swim et al., 1997). Prior to completing the daily diaries, women estimated the number of the prejudicial events that they typically experienced in a week (personal base-rate information) and the number of events they thought a typical woman experienced in a week (group base-rate information). During the diary portion of the study, participants recorded the number of gender-related events that they experienced and they judged the extent to which each event was prejudicial. Both personal and group base rates were positively associated with the number of events judged as prejudicial.[4]

Goals

The social psychological literature is replete with references to the ways that goals can influence judgments about other people (Fiske & Taylor, 1991). Judgments of prejudice and discrimination are no different. When we judge a person to be prejudicial, we are using stereotype information about who is likely to be prejudiced against whom. Therefore, past research on cognitive and motivational factors influencing the use of stereotypes (e.g., Brewer, 1996; Neuberg & Fiske, 1987) is likely to inform us about how goals of accuracy and self-protection influence the types of judgment strategies that people use when making appraisals of prejudice and discrimination.

[4]In contrast to these findings for women and Ruggerio and collegues findings, Swim et al. (1997) found no support for the relationship between African American participants' personal base-rate estimates and the number of events they recorded in their diaries as being prejudicial. African American participants were not asked about their perceived group base rates in this study.

Costs

We have argued above that the major goal associated with strategies for appraising the presence or absence of prejudice is self-protection: individuals try to maximize correct judgments while minimizing the judgment errors that are most costly. The costs associated with errors in judgment (misses and false alarms) will influence an individual's decision criteria and, therefore, his or her response tendencies. We address each of these costs in turn.

Costs of Misses

Evidence suggests that missing a prejudice cue can endanger an individual's self-esteem. For example, early research on reactions to discrimination indicated that after receiving negative feedback from a male evaluator, women who did not identify the evaluators as prejudiced had lower global self-esteem than women who did make this attribution (Dion, 1975, 1986). Results consistent with these conclusions have been found for the impact of negative evaluations on African, Jewish, and Asian Americans (Dion, 1986; Dion, Earn, & Yee, 1978; Miller, Boye, & Gerard, 1968 as cited in Dion et al., 1978). Recent research indicates that state rather than stable or trait self-esteem may be most vulnerable to misses. In addition, performance self-esteem (e.g., "I feel as smart as others," Heatherton & Polivy, 1991, p. 58) is hurt by failing to appraise prejudice, whereas social self-esteem (e.g., "I feel concerned about the impression I am making," Heatherton & Polivy, 1991, p. 58) increases with misses (Ruggiero & Taylor, 1997). Furthermore, a miss can be costly because the individual will incur the negative consequences of encountering prejudice, such as internalization of unfavorable or restrictive stereotypic beliefs about one's group (e.g., Quinn & Crocker, this volume). Misses can also be costly at a societal level as well. If prejudice and discrimination are not identified as a source of political and economic disadvantage, then targets of prejudice bear the burden of responsibility for improving their status. (Taylor, Ruggiero, & Louis, 1996).

Costs of False Alarms

Incorrectly judging the presence of prejudice is associated with several different types of psychological disruption. First, false alarms can be associated with interpersonal disruption. Openly labeling events as prejudiced or discriminatory can cause an individual to be identified as overly sensitive (Crosby, 1984; Feagin & Sikes, 1994; Swim, Cohen, & Hyers, this volume). Furthermore, interpersonal disruption can result from the distrust of outgroup members. In the late 1960s, Grier and Cobbs (1968) proposed that African Americans have a "healthy cultural paranoia." Following this characterization, researchers have examined the tendency for African Americans to distrust and be suspicious of European Americans (Terrell & Terrell, 1981; Thompson, Neville, Weathers, Poston, & Atkinson, 1990). This distrust (or "racism reaction") is thought to stem from feelings of threat from European Americans (Thompson et al., 1990). While the distrust may be justifiable, the disruption that results from mistrust can hinder the formation of specific relationships, even when there is primary importance placed on the relationship between two individuals. For example, African American individuals who have high mistrust levels are more likely to expect their European American counselors to be less accepting, trustworthy, credible, satisfactory, and more likely to expect less help with general anxiety, shyness, inferiority feelings, and dating difficulties (Nickerson, Helms, & Terrell, 1994; Watkins & Terrell, 1988; Watkins, Terrell, Miller, & Terrell, 1989). Cultural mistrust can also affect the counseling process by affecting the amount of disclosure during a counseling session (Thompson, Worthington, & Atkinson, 1994), possibly leading to self-fulfilling prophecy combined with a confirmatory bias. These findings from the counseling literature may also apply to other forms of interactions (e.g., Kleck & Strenta, 1980). For example, research indicates that stigmatized individuals' expectations about how others will treat them can lead them to perceive unfavorable treatment even when none is given (Kleck & Strenta, 1980).

Second, false alarms can be associated with behavioral restriction. One way to manage the perceived presence of prejudice is to structure one's life to decrease the likelihood of encountering it (Swim *et al.,* this volume). While complete avoidance is unattainable for the most part (Simpson & Yinger, 1985), targets can make choices about when (or when not) to enter particular situations or interactions. For instance, women (and not men) are likely to prefer to change groups and gender composition of groups when they anticipate being the solo member of their gender in the group and this preference is related to women's perception that they will be treated stereotypically (Cohen and Swim, 1995). Similarly, distrust of European Americans may lead African Americans to terminate employment (Terrell & Terrell, 1981) and prematurely terminate counseling with European American counselors (Terrell & Terrell, 1984). Also, reduced numbers of African American applicants to jobs has been attributed to a desire to avoid the rejection and interpersonal stress that results from prejudice from European American employers (Pettigrew & Martin, 1987).

The behavioral restriction that results from such avoidance has costs (Stangor & Sechrist, this volume). Descriptive research from counseling psychology illustrates that avoidance has potential costs for African Americans (Pinderhughes, 1982). Past experience with misdiagnoses by clinicians and intrusiveness of social service workers has lead many African American families to avoid seeking mental health services. As Biafora, Warheit, Zimmerman, Apospori, and Taylor (1993) note, ''While racial mistrust may provide an adaptive coping mechanism for some individuals, it could also be hypothesized that mistrust may be maladaptive for others in that it may motivate them to withdraw from activities that are essential if they are to access the opportunity and reward structures of the dominant society—for example, school completion and/or seeking employment'' (p. 894).

Third, false alarms are associated with anxiety (Mathews & MacLeod, 1994). If targets of prejudice believe that they are going to be evaluated in terms of their social group rather than on their own merits, anxiety may result and interfere with their performance (see Steele & Aronson, 1995; Aronson, Quinn, & Spencer, this volume). For example, women can be distracted when they are solo members of their gender in a group, and this interferes with their work even when they are not treated differently from other group members (Lord & Saenz, 1985; Saenz, 1984); this occurs particularly when women are socially worried and believe they are being scrutinized (Lord, Saenz, & Godfrey, 1987). Thus, the anxiety associated with anticipating a threat can interfere with task performance.

SUMMARY

We have tried to demonstrate that SDT provides a useful framework for understanding how sensitivity and response biases can affect people's appraisals of prejudice. In particular, we discussed how response biases (either under- or overestimating prejudice) are associated with minimizing the costs of one judgment outcome at the expense of the other. Next, we elaborate on the use of zeromiss and positive-illusion judgment strategies when perceiving prejudice and discrimination.

APPRAISALS OF PREJUDICE: A COST–BENEFIT ANALYSIS OF JUDGMENTS UNDER UNCERTAINTY

MINIMIZING FALSE ALARMS: A POSITIVE-ILLUSION STRATEGY

There have been two primary lines of research that have addressed how and why individuals minimize perceptions of prejudice and discrimination. First, the act of denying or minimizing prejudice has been used to explain the robust finding that people report lower frequency and severity of discrimination directed at themselves than directed at members of their group (Crosby, 1984; Ruggiero & Taylor, 1994; Taylor et al., 1996; Taylor et al., 1994). It is difficult to rule out alternative explanations for this finding, however (e.g., the overestimation of group-based experiences).

Second, the previously mentioned laboratory studies by Ruggiero and colleagues (Ruggiero & Taylor, 1995, 1997; Ruggiero & Major, 1997) have nicely demonstrated women's, Blacks' (of West Indian heritage), and East Asians' tendency to underutilize base-rate information about the presence of prejudice. These researchers note that minimizing appraisals of prejudice may reflect a general tendency for people to hold "positive illusions" or "illusions of unique invulnerability." Because other groups (e.g., European American men) are willing to make attributions to prejudice, however, it is unlikely that the minimization of prejudice is a result of simply a general tendency for people to hold positive illusions (Ruggiero & Major, 1997). Instead, as Ruggiero and colleagues note, the positive illusions in this context are likely a function of the relatively greater psychological benefits of attributing negative feedback to something about oneself rather than to discrimination. These benefits include higher social self-esteem and greater perceptions of control at the cost of performance self-esteem (Ruggiero & Taylor, 1997).

MINIMIZING MISSES: A ZERO-MISS STRATEGY

Some individuals might engage in judgment strategies that allow them to minimize the number of times that they fail to correctly identify prejudicial situations. Before we begin this section, we would like to offer a clarification: we are by no means "blaming the victim" by suggesting that people who perceive themselves to be the target of prejudice are "oversensitive." Rather, we are suggesting that anyone who has previous, pervasive experiences with threat will be preattentively prepared to see threat in a current situation because they have learned a decision rule through interactions with the environment. If individuals learn decision rules (i.e., response biases) that are adaptive to their life circumstances, then people who have previous experience with prejudice will be more likely to perceive it in the present, all other things being equal. If the current environmental context has a high probability of prejudice, then a zero-miss strategy will be adaptive for that individual. In such an environment, the individual using a zero-miss strategy will not only have a high positive hit rate, but may also have a slightly higher false alarm rate (i.e., perceive more prejudice than is actually there). Despite this small increase in false alarms, however, the zero-miss strategy is likely adaptive when living in conditions where prejudice and discrimination thrive. We do argue, however, that a zero-miss strategy may be less adaptive when the base rate of prejudice in the current environment is reduced. We are not denying that prejudice exists, nor that it is prevalent in many environments or contexts. Rather, we are suggesting that overestimations of prejudice may be more prevalent in some contexts than in others. Thus, the zero-miss strategy may be less adaptive in circumstances where there is a lower base rate for prejudice and discrimination, and may make it more difficult for a person to learn that the danger of being a target of prejudice is not lurking in a new environment.

Grier and Cobbs' (1968) essentially described a zero-miss strategy (i.e., cultural mistrust) as healthy because it can be an optimal coping strategy for those living in a highly prejudicial environment (see also Vorauer & Ross, 1993). Judgment strategies designed to minimize misses may be a result of living in a threatening environment where European Americans have demonstrated prejudice against African Americans in educational, political and legal, work and business, and interpersonal and social contexts (Terrell & Terrell, 1981). Furthermore, preparedness to detect and deal with prejudice can be taught at home (Biafora et al., 1993; Essed, 1991). Hines and Boyd-Franklin (1982) note that "This suspiciousness is frequently a direct, learned, survival response that black children are socialized at an early age to adopt" (p.101). Thus, cultural mistrust can be explained in terms of miss-reducing strategy such that personal or collective past experiences with prejudice and discrimination increase the likelihood that African Americans will be distrustful of European Americans.

Some of the findings from Ruggiero and colleagues suggest that a tendency to use a zero-miss strategy can be heightened when threat is made salient and when the costs of false alarms and positive hits are lessened. In one condition of the previously described studies (Ruggiero & Major, 1997; Ruggiero & Taylor, 1995, 1997), participants were led to believe that the base rate for discrimination was zero (i.e., participants were told that none of the eight people who evaluated participant's work had discriminated against members of the participant's group). In these conditions, any attribution to discrimination could arguably be an over-estimation of prejudice. While participants in this condition were more likely to attribute negative evaluations to their own ability or effort than to discrimination, the mean attribution to discrimination was significantly greater than zero (K. M. Ruggiero, personal communication, February 14, 1997).

An additional study suggests that attributions to discrimination in the zero percent base rate condition is a function of heightened threat. Participants were not told any information about the probability that their evaluators discriminated against women (Ruggiero & Major, 1997). Women's attributions to discrimination in this condition were significantly lower than when they were told that none of their evaluators discriminated against women. In fact, the attributions to discrimination in the no-information condition were not significantly different from zero. An interpretation of the zero percent base rate–no-information contrast is that being reminded of the possibility of discrimination increased partici-pants' perceived threat, thereby increasing their motivation to avoid a miss, which in turn caused them to be more likely to attribute the negative feedback to discrimination.

A second study by Ruggiero suggests that decreasing the cost of labeling an event as discriminatory (i.e., the cost of a positive hit or a false alarm) serves to increase the likelihood that events will be labeled as discriminatory (Ruggiero, Taylor, & Lydon, 1997). In this study, women were told that their test responses would be evaluated by one of eight men and that half of the men discriminated against women. After receiving a failing grade for their test, participants were told that they would be given either one type of social support, two types of social support, or they were not told anything. Women anticipating two types of support were more likely to attribute the negative feedback to discrimination than to their own ability. Women receiving only one type of support were equally likely to attribute the negative evaluation to their ability and discrimination. Women re-ceiving no support were more likely to attribute the negative evaluation to their ability than to discrimination. Armed with the knowledge that they would receive some form of social support, women may have felt that they would not incur the costs of a positive hit or false alarm (e.g., decreased social self-esteem or being told that they were overly sensitive). Thus, the relative costs of saying "yes" versus "no" was altered by providing social support, such that a miss may have been seen as more costly.

FAILURE TO CALIBRATE TO NEW CONDITIONS

The costs associated with engaging in zero-miss strategies are greatest in situations where threat is minimal or nonexistent; in contrast, the costs associated with engaging in a positive illusion strategy are greatest in high threat situations. As noted previously, people may have difficulty shifting their decision criteria when the base rates for threat change. First, for those using a zero-miss strategy, the behaviors people have employed to protect themselves from prejudice may prevent them from detecting when threat is reduced. For instance, behavioral restriction means that people are less likely to enter situations where their beliefs will be disconfirmed. As Pettigrew and Martin (1987) note with regard to avoiding prejudice, "Avoidance learning reduces the possibility of experiencing corrective situations, such as acceptance and positive interaction" (p. 54).

Second, schematic processing, such as interpreting ambiguous information in line with one's beliefs or focusing on confirming rather than disconfirming evidence, may make it difficult to change decision criteria. Confirmatory biases can decrease the likelihood that people will notice changes in the occurrence of prejudice and discrimination. For instance, stigmatized individuals believe that people will treat them unfavorably even when their is no evidence of negative behavior (Kleck & Strenta, 1980). In general, the research indicating that people tend to maintain their stereotypes, despite disconfirming evidence, suggests that people who hold stereotypes about perpetrators of prejudice will do the same (Baron *et al.*, 1991; Inman & Baron, 1996; Rettew, Billman, & Davis, 1993).

Third, the emotional currency of encountering a miss or false alarm can make it difficult for people to stop using a positive illusion or zero-miss strategy, respectively. No research evidence is available to test whether this hypothesis holds for appraisals of prejudice, but previous authors have suggested the possibility that, in particular, misses may be so aversive as to make it very difficult to change judgment strategies. As Pettigrew and Martin (1987) note, ". . . because personal and vicarious experiences as a victim of prejudice and discrimination are highly emotional, this avoidance learning is deeply emotional—and emotional condition has an extremely slow extinction curve (Solomon, 1964). For these reasons, negative black responses to recruitment efforts are often especially resistant to change" (p. 54).

SUMMARY

Applying a cost-benefit analyses provides a motivational explanation for people's perceptions of prejudice and discrimination. This analysis can be used to explain both a tendency to overestimate (i.e., use a zero-miss strategy) or to minimize (i.e., use a positive illusion strategy) one's encounters with prejudice. Situational factors that affect perceptions of costs are likely to influence the strategies that people use. The behavioral restriction, schematic processing, and emotional learning associated with misses may make it difficult for people to avoid using a zero-miss strategy, even though such a strategy is particularly costly. Similarly, the schematic processing and emotional learning associated with false alarms (and positive hits) may make it difficult to avoid using a positive illusion strategy, even though such a strategy would be particularly costly.

DISCUSSION AND FUTURE RESEARCH

A goal of the present chapter is to illustrate how SDT can provide a useful framework for understanding perceptions of prejudice and discrimination. The distinction between sensitivity and response biases helps organize, clarify, and differentiate the psychological processes and stimulus characteristics that might influence judgments of prejudice. SDT suggests specific characteristics, (probability of occurrence, intensity, and imminence) that might affect a target's ability to detect prejudice and also highlights person factors (perceived base rates and goals) that are likely to influence response styles to label (or not label) events as prejudicial or discriminatory. The differentiation between types of costs resulting from misses and false alarms provides clarity as to why people may under- or overestimate prejudice.

A consideration of two response biases, the positive illusion and the zero-miss strategies, highlights the need to expand the understanding of perceptions of prejudice as judgments that are made under uncertainty. Judgments of prejudice, like all human judgments, are subject to error. These errors are best seen as the result of adaptation attempts, rather than as "faults" associated with deficits in the perceiver (Funder, 1987). For example, a zero-miss strategy, although it might produce an overperception of prejudice in certain conditions, should be considered a reasonable response to situations with high base rates for prejudice and discrimination; in such situations, even a single encounter with prejudice may be so harmful that one reverts to this self-protective strategy. Furthermore, applying this framework to perceptions of prejudice suggests that it would be fruitful to examine the role of past experiences with prejudice on perceptions of current experiences particularly in situations where actual base rates have changed. It would also be fruitful to examine situational characteristics that are likely to heighten or reduce perceived threat and alter the relative costs of misses, false alarms, and positive hits. For example, goal orientation (accuracy versus self-protection) may be the result of differences in power between groups (Vorauer & Ross, 1993). It may be the case people are likely to adopt a zero-miss strategy when they are in a situation that highlights their membership in a group that is lower in power than some outgroup. Similarly, it might be beneficial to examine individual differences in perception of threat and relative costs of errors, perhaps related to differences in past experiences or extent to which people are group-identified (Branscombe & Ellemers, this volume; Deaux & Ethier, this volume).

While our analysis emphasized the target's perspective on prejudice, the SDT framework could also be applied to third-party observers' perceptions or to perpetrators' perceptions of their own attitudes and behaviors. Like targets of prejudice, third-party observers and perpetrators will likely vary in sensitivity and response biases. Perpetrators may prefer a positive-illusion strategy over a zero-miss strategy because this would yield a more favorable self-image. The extent to which third-party observers, as well as targets of prejudice, sympathize or identify with perpetrators of prejudice could increase their likelihood of sharing a perpetrators' preference for positive illusions.

While we emphasize the role of sensitivity and response biases in perceptions of prejudice, researchers might also consider how to determine the stimulus criterion. One strategy might be to take a conservative approach of only defining an event as prejudiced when there is "clear and convincing evidence." Alternatively, one can consider taking a more liberal approach of "preponderance of evidence." Another possibility is to use criteria that have been used to define when a threat is present: the extent of harm, social norms, and intent of the perpetrator (Milburn & Watman, 1981). There are issues that should be kept in mind if these criterion are used. For instance, if one is able to protect oneself from the harmful consequences of an event, would it not be considered prejudice? If social norms are different for targets and perpetrators, whose social norms should apply? If prejudice occurs from automatic processes or ignorance, does the lack of intent justify not labeling the behavior as discriminatory? The selection of the stimulus criterion will affect accuracy rates with some criteria being more stringent than others. Thus, discrepancies in stimulus criteria, as well as sensitivity and response biases, are likely an additional source of differences in perceptions of prejudice.

In general, research on perceptions of prejudice can benefit from insights gained through a more general theory of judgmental processes such as signal detection theory. SDT provides a framework for understanding stimulus characteristics and psychological processes that likely influence perceptions of prejudice. It helps differentiate psychological factors (e.g., sensitivity and response bias; costs of positive hits, misses, and false alarms) that likely impact perceptions of prejudice. Finally, it helps us understand the cognitive and motivational reasons why errors or biases in judgments come about.

REFERENCES

Allison, A. (1998; this volume). Stress due to category membership. In J. K. Swim & C. Stangor (Eds.), *Prejudice: The target's perspective.* San Diego: Academic Press.

Aronson, J., Quinn, D., & Spencer, S. (1998; this volume). Stereotype threat. In J. K. Swim & C. Stangor (Eds.), *Prejudice: The target's perspective.* San Diego: Academic Press.

Baron, R. S., Burgess, M. L., & Kao, C. F. (1991). Detecting and labeling prejudice: Do female perpetrators go undetected? *Personality and Social Psychology Bulletin, 17,* 115–123.

Benokraitis, N. V., & Feagin, J. R. (1995). *Modern Sexism* (2nd ed.). Englewood Cliffs, NJ: Prentice Hall.

Biafora, F. A., Warheit, G. J., Zimmerman, R. S., Gil, A. G., Apospori, E., & Taylor, D. (1993). *Journal of Applied Social Psychology, 23,* 891–910.

Branscombe, N., & Ellemers, N. (This volume). Coping with group-based discrimination: Individualistic versus group-level strategies. In J. K. Swim & C. Stangor (Eds.), *Prejudice: The target's perspective.* San Diego: Academic Press.

Brewer, M. B. (1996). When stereotypes lead to stereotyping: The use of stereotypes in person perception. In C. N. Macrae, C. Stangor, & M. Hewstone (Eds.), *Stereotypes and stereotyping,* (pp 254–276). New York, NY: The Guilford Press.

Cohen, L. L., & Swim, J. K. (1995). The differential impact of gender ratios on women and men: Tokenism, self-confidence, and expectations. *Personality and Social Psychology Bulletin, 9,* 876–884.

Crocker, J., & Major, B. (1989). Social stigma and self-esteem: The self-protective properties of stigma. *Psychological Review, 96,* 608–630.

Crocker, J., Major, B., & Steele, C. (1998). Social Stigma. In D. Gilbert, S. T. Fiske, & G. Lindzey (Eds.), *Handbook of social psychology* (4th ed.). Boston: McGraw Hill.

Crosby, F. (1984). The denial of personal discrimination. *American Behavioral Scientist, 27,* 371–386.

Deaux, K., & Ethier, K. (This volume). Negotiating social identity. In J. K. Swim & C. Stangor (Eds.), *Prejudice: The target's perspective.* San Diego: Academic Press.

Dion, K. L. (1975). Women's reactions to discrimination from members of the same or opposite sex. *Journal of Research in Personality, 9,* 294–306.

Dion, K. L. (1986). Responses to perceived discrimination and relative deprivation. In J. M. Olson, & C. P. Herman, & M. P. Zanna (Eds.), *Relative deprivation and social comparison: The Ontario Symposium,* (Vol. 4, pp. 159–179). Hillsdale, NJ: Lawrence Erlbaum Associates.

Dion, K. L., Earn, B. M., & Yee, P. H. N. (1978). The experience of being a victim of prejudice: An experimental approach. *International Journal of Psychology, 13,* 197–214.

Egan, J. P. (1975). *Signal detection theory and ROC analysis.* New York: Academic Press.

Einhorn, H. J. (1982). Learning from experience and suboptimal rules in decision making. In D. Kahneman, P. Slovic, & A. Tversky (Eds.), *Judgment under uncertainty: Heuristics and biases* (pp. 268–283). New York: Cambridge University Press.

Epstein, S., & Roupenian, A. (1970). Heart rate and skin conductance during experimentally induced anxiety: The effect of uncertainty about receiving a noxious stimulus. *Journal of Personality and Social Psychology, 16,* 20–28.

Essed, P. (1991). *Understanding everyday racism.* Newbury Park, CA: Sage.

Feagin, J. R., & Sikes, M. P. (1994). *Living with racism: The black middle-class experience.* Boston, MA: Beacon Press Books.

Feldman Barrett, L. (1996, June). *Primary appraisals of threat: A signal detection model.* Paper presented at the annual meeting of the American Psychological Society, San Francisco.

Feldman Barrett, L., & Fong, G. T. (1996). *Primary appraisals of threat: A signal detection model.* Unpublished manuscript.

Fiske, S. T., & Taylor, S. E. (1991) *Social cognition.* New York, NY: McGraw-Hill, Inc.

Fitzgerald, L. F., & Hesson-Mcinnis, M. (1989). The dimensions of sexual harassment: A structural analysis. *Journal of Vocational Behavior, 35,* 309–326.

Funder, D. C. (1987). Errors and mistakes: Evaluating the accuracy of social jugment. *Psychological Bulletin, 101,* 75–90.

Frazier, P. A., Cochran, C. C., & Olson, A. M. (1995). Social science research on lay definitions of sexual harassment. *Journal of Social Issues, 51,* 39–52.

Green, D. M., & Swets, J. A. (1966/1974). *Signal detection theory and psychophysics.* New York: Wiley.

Glick, P., & Fiske, S. T. (1995). The Ambivalent Sexism Inventory: Differentiating hostile and benevolent sexism. *Journal of Personality and Social Psychology, 70,* 491–512.

Grier, W., & Cobbs, P. (1968). *Black rage.* New York: Bantam Books.

Grossberg, J. M., & Grant, B. F. (1978). Clinical psychophysics: Applications of ratio scaling and signal detection methods to research on pain, fear, drugs, and medical decision making. *Psychological Bulletin, 85,* 1154–1176.

Harvey, L. O. (1992). The critical operating characteristic and the evaluation of expert judgment. *Organizational Behavior and Human Decision Processes, 53,* 229–251.

Healy, A. F., & Kubovy, M. (1978). The effects of payoffs and prior probabilities on indices of performance and cutoff location in recognition memory. *Memory and Cognition, 6,* 544–553.

Heatherton, T. F., & Polivy, J. (1991). Development and validation of a scale for measuring state self-esteem. *Journal of Personality and Social Psychology, 60,* 895–910.

Hines, P. M., & Boyd-Frankline, N. (1982). Black Families. In M. McGoldrick, J. K. Pearce, & J. Giordano (Eds.), *Ethnicity and family therapy,* (pp. 84–107). New York: The Guilford Press.

Horney, K. (1950). *Neurosis and human growth.* New York: Horton.

Inman, M. L., & Baron, R. S. (1996). The influence of prototypes on perceptions of prejudice. *Journal of Personality and Social Psychology, 70,* 727–739.

Ittleson, W. H., & Kilpatrick, F. P. (1951). Experiments in perception. *Scientific American, 185,* 50–55.

Kahneman, D., & Tversky, A. (1982). Variants of uncertainty. In D. Kahneman, P. Slovic, & A. Tversky (Eds.), *Judgment under uncertainty: Heuristics and biases* (pp. 509–520). New York: Cambridge University Press.

Kleck, R. E., & Strenta, A. (1980). Perceptions of the impact of negatively valued physical characteristics on social interaction. *Journal of Personality and Social Psychology, 39,* 861–873.

Lazarus, R. S., & Folkman, S. (1984). *Stress, appraisal, and coping.* New York: Springer.

Leary, T. (1957). Interpersonal diagnosis of personality. New York: Ronald.

Lewicki, P., Hill, T., & Sasaki, I. (1989). Self-perpetuating development of encoding biases. *Journal of Experimental Psychology: General, 118,* 323–37.

Locksley, A., Borgida, E., Brekke, N., & Hepburn, C. (1980). Sex stereotypes and social judgment. *Journal of Personality and Social Psychology, 39,* 821–831.

Lord, C. G., & Saenz, D. S. (1985). Memory deficits and memory surfeits: Differential cognitive consequences of tokenism for tokens and observers. *Journal of Personality and Social Psychology, 49,* 918–926.

Lord, C. G., Saenz, D. S., & Godfrey, D. K. (1987). Effects of perceived scrutiny on participants memory for social interaction. *Journal of Experimental Social Psychology, 23,* 498–517.

Louw-Potgieter, L. (1989). Covert racism: An application of Essed's analysis in a South African context. *Journal of Language and Social Psychology, 8,* 307–313.

Macmillan, N. A. (1993). Signal detection theory as a data analysis method and psychological decision model. In G. Keren & G. Lewis (Eds.), *A handbook for data analysis in the behavioral sciences: Methodological issues* (pp. 21–58). Hillsdale, New Jersey: Erlbaum

Mathews, A., & MacLeod, C. (1994). Cognitive approaches to emotion and emotional disorders. *Annual Review of Psychology, 45,* 25–50.

McCauley, C., & Stitt, C. L. (1978). An individual and quantitative measure of stereotypes. *Journal of Personality and Social Psychology, 36,* 929–940.

McNicol, D. (1972). *A primer of signal detection theory.* London: Allen & Unwin.

Milburn, T. W., & Watman, K. H. (1981). *On the nature of threat: A social psychological analysis.* New York: Praeger.

Miller, S. M. (1979). Controllability and human stress: Method, evidence, and theory. *Behavioral Research and Therapy, 17,* 287–304.

Neuberg, S. L., & Fiske, S. T. (1987). Motivational influences on impression formation: Outcome dependency, accuracy-driven attention, and individuating processes. *Journal of Personality and Social Psychology, 53,* 431–444.

Nickerson, K. J., Helms, J. E., & Terrell, F. (1994). Cultural mistrust, opinions about mental illness, and Black students' attitudes toward seeking psychological help from White counselors. *Journal of Counseling Psychology, 41,* 378–385.

Nesbitt, R. E., Krantz, D. H., Jepson, C., & Fong, G. T. (1982). Improving inductive inference. In D. Kahneman, P. Slovic, & A. Tversky (Eds.), *Judgment under uncertainty: Heuristics and biases* (pp. 445–459). New York: Cambridge University Press.

Paterson, R. J., & Neufeld, W. J. (1987). Clear danger: Situational determinants of the appraisal of threat. *Psychological Bulletin, 101,* 404–416.

Pettigrew, T. F., & Martin, J. (1987). Shaping the context for Black American nclusion. *Journal of Social Issues, 43,* 41–78.

Pinderhughes, E. (1982). Afro-American Families and the victim system. In M. McGoldrick, J. K. Pearce, & J. Giordano (Eds.), *Ethnicity and Family Therapy,* (pp. 108–123). New York: The Guilford Press.

Posner, M. I. (1978). *Chronometric explorations of the mind.* Hillsdale, NJ: Erlbaum.

Quinn, D. & Crocker, J. (This volume). Vulnerability to the affective consequences of the stigma of overweight. In J. K. Swim & C. Stangor (Eds.), *Prejudice: The target's perspective.* San Diego: Academic Press.

Rettew, D. C., Billman, D., & Davis, R. A. (1993). Inaccurate perceptions of the amount others stereotype: Estimates about stereotypes of one's own group and other groups. *Basic and Applied Social Psychology, 14,* 121–142.

Ruggiero, K. M. (1997). Personal communication.

Ruggiero, K. M., & Major, B. (1997). *Gender and coping with attributional ambiguity.* Manuscript submitted for publication.

Ruggiero, K. M., & Taylor, D. M. (1994). The personal/group discrimination discrepancy: Women talk about their experiences. *Journal of Applied Social Psychology, 24,* 1806–1826.

Ruggiero, K. M., & Taylor, D. M. (1995). Coping with discrimination: How disadvantaged group members perceive the discrimination that confronts them. *Journal of Personality and Social Psychology, 68,* 826–838.

Ruggiero, K. M., Taylor, D. M., & Lydon, J. E. (1997). How disadvantaged group members cope with discrimination. When they perceive that social support is available. *Journal of Applied Social Psychology.*

Ruggiero, K. M., & Taylor, D. M. (1997). Why minority group members perceive or do not perceive the discrimination that confronts them: The role of self-esteem and perceived control. *Journal of Personality and Social Psychology, 72,* 373–389.

Saenz, D. S. (1994). Token status and problem-solving deficits: Detrimental effects of distinctiveness and performance monitoring. *Social Cognition, 12,* 61–74.

Simpson, G. E., & Yinger, J. M. (1985). *Racial and cultural minorities: An analysis of prejudice and discrimination* (5th ed.). New York: Plenum Press.

Stangor, C., & Sechrist, G. B. (1998; this volume). Conceptualizing the determinants of academic choice and task performance accross social groups. In J. K. Swim & C. Stangor (Eds.), *Prejudice: The target's perspective.* San Diego: Academic Press.

Steele, C. M., & Aronson, J. (1995). Stereotype threat and the intellectual test performance of African-Americans. *Journal of Personality and Social Psychology, 69,* 797–812.

Sullivan, H. S. (1953). *Conceptions of modern psychiatry.* New York: Norton.

Swets, J. A. (1986). Indices of discrimination or diagnostic accuracy: Their ROCs and implied models. *Psychological Bulletin, 99,* 100–117.

Swim, J. K., Cohen, L. L., Hyers, L. L., & Bylsma, W. H. (1997). *Everyday experiences with prejudice: A daily diary study.* Unpublished manuscript.

Swim, J. K., Cohen, L. L., & Hyers, L. L. (This volume). Experiencing everyday prejudice. In J. K. Swim & C. Stangor (Eds.), *Prejudice: The target's perspective.* San Diego: Academic Press.

Taylor, D. M., Ruggiero, K. M., & Louis, W. R. (1996). Personal/group discrimination discrepancy: Towards a two-factor explanation. *Canadian Journal of Behavioral Science, 28,* 193–202.

Terrell, F., & Terrell, S. (1981). An inventory to measure cultural mistrust among blacks. *The Western Journal of Black Studies, 5,* 180–185.

Terrell, F., & Terrell, S. (1984). Race of counselor, client sex, cultural mistrust level, and premature termination from counseling among Black clients. *Journal of Counseling Psychology, 31,* 371–375.

Thompson, C. E., Neville, H., Weathers, P. L., Poston, W. C., & Atkinson, D. R. (1990). Cultural mistrust and racism reaction among African-American students. *Journal of College Student Development, 31,* 162–168.

Thompson, C. E., Worthington, R., & Atkinson, D. R. (1994). Counselor content orientation, counselor race, and Black women's cultural mistrust and self-disclosures. *Journal of Counseling Psychology, 41,* 155–161.

Tversky, A., & Kahneman, D. (1982). Evidential impact of base rates. In D. Kahneman, P. Slovic, & A. Tversky (Eds.), *Judgment under uncertainty: Heuristics and biases* (pp. 153–160). New York: Cambridge University Press.

VandenBerghe, P. L. (1967). *Race and racism: A comparative perspective.* New York: John Wiley & Sons, Inc.

Vorauer, J. D., & Ross, M. (1993). Making mountains out of molehills: An informational goals analysis of self- and social-perception. *Pesonality and Social Psychology Bulletin, 19,* 620–632.

Watkins, C. E., & Terrell, F. (1988). Mistrust level and its effects on counseling expectations in Black client–White counselor relationships: An analogue study. *Journal of Counseling Psychology, 35,* 194–197.

Watkins, C. E., Terrell, F., Miller, F. S., & Terrell, S.L. (1989). Cultural mistrust and its effects on expectational variables in Black client-White counselor relationships. *Journal of Counseling Psychology, 36,* 447–450.

York, K. M. (1989). Defining sexual harassment in workplaces: A policy-capturing approach. Academy of Management Journal, 32, 830-850.

2

EXPERIENCING EVERYDAY PREJUDICE AND DISCRIMINATION

JANET K. SWIM, LAURIE L. COHEN,
AND LAURI L. HYERS

The Pennsylvania State University

In the 1947 Academy Award-winning movie *Gentlemen's Agreement,* Phil Green, played by Gregory Peck, was a journalist assigned to write about anti-Semitism. At the beginning of this film, Green who was explicitly instructed not to write a story focusing exclusively on cold statistical facts, struggled to come up with a "new angle" on anti-Semitism. His resolution was to present himself as a Jewish person to experience prejudice and discrimination firsthand in his new residency of New York. As a result of this experience, Green gained a great deal of insight into the ways in which both subtle and blatant forms of prejudice infiltrate the lives of targets of prejudice. He learned about the extent to which prejudice can constrain one's actions and the effort required to fight everyday prejudice and discrimination. This story highlights the fact that rich and invaluable information can be gained by examining the target's perspective on prejudice. However, while Green had the advantage of being able to leave the prejudice behind when he returned to his real identity, most people from groups that are often the targets of prejudice have no such luxury. That is, their experience as a target of prejudice is ongoing and is experienced in a multitude of ways within their everyday lives.

An aim of our research has been to provide similarly rich information about the personal experience of being the target of prejudice, by examining everyday encounters with prejudice and discrimination. These encounters are not rare and isolated experiences but are recurrent and familiar events that can be considered commonplace (Essed, 1991; Feagin & Sikes, 1994). These experiences consist of short-term interactions (e.g., street remarks, glares) as well as encounters embedded in long discussions. They include incidents where the individual is directly targeted and those in which the target is an entire social group (e.g., women or African Americans in general). Perpetrators of these events range from people who have intimate relationships with the target to strangers. These concrete and specific events are the building blocks of the experience of being a target of prejudice and contribute toward targets' general knowledge about prejudice. As both Essed (1991) and Feagin and Sikes (1994) point out, everyday racism represents African Americans' "lived experience" with racism. This idea of "lived experiences" with prejudice applies to other target groups as well. In the research reviewed below, we focus on African American's experiences with racism and women's experiences with sexism.

An overarching goal of our research has been to study targets of prejudice not as passive victims who are unable or unwilling to try to deflect the negative consequences of encountering prejudice and discrimination but as active agents who make choices in their lives about when to face potential prejudice and when to challenge or confront prejudice. We take an approach of understanding targets of prejudice as persons who are empowered to make choices about their lives, while still acknowledging the limiting, threatening, and hurtful aspects of being a target of prejudice. Our aim is to examine how targets manage aspects of their social worlds rather than how they are only manipulated by the prejudice of others. This includes an examination of how targets make choices about which situations to enter and which to avoid and when and how to publicly respond to prejudice. By examining the ways in which targets anticipate, describe, and react to specific events, we hope to provide insight on the breadth and depth of targets' personal experiences with prejudice and discrimination.

ANTICIPATING ENCOUNTERS

Since the experience of everyday prejudice and discrimination is ongoing and targets of prejudice are aware even at a young age of the possible influence of prejudice on their lives (Crosby, 1982, Phinney & Tarver, 1988; Rosenberg, 1979; Taylor, Casten, Flinkinger, Roberts, & Fulmore, 1994), it is likely that people from stigmatized groups become able to anticipate prejudicial situations and develop strategies for dealing with them. Research on responses to prejudice and discrimination has suggested that many individuals utilize psychological strategies to protect themselves, such as attributing negative outcomes to prejudice (Crocker & Major, 1989; Rosenberg, 1986). In addition to these strategies, individuals can engage in proactive coping, "efforts undertaken in advance of a potentially stressful event to prevent it or to modify its form before it occurs" (Aspinwall & Taylor, 1998, p. 3). Proactive coping includes the anticipation of stressful events and preparations to prevent or mute the effects of the stressor. In the case of prejudice and discrimination, targets can use their knowledge and awareness of when, where, by whom, and in what manner prejudice is most likely to occur in order to assess the likelihood that they will encounter prejudice in particular situations and to structure their interactions and environment to minimize or avoid the hurtful aspects of encountering prejudice and discrimination. Thus, the anticipation of prejudice and discrimination may affect people's choices about what to say in certain interactions, how to present themselves, and where to socialize, live, go to college, and work (see also, Miller & Myers, this volume).

While some incidents can be anticipated because they occurred previously within the same context or because of information provided by or sought from other people, anticipating prejudice and discrimination in new situations may require an ability to identify and interpret particular environmental cues. Characteristics of potential interaction partners can be used as one potential cue. Baron and his colleagues (Baron, Burgess, & Kao, 1991; Inman & Baron, 1996) have found, in a series of scenario studies, that individuals are more likely to perceive racism when the perpetrator is a European American (rather than African American) and are more likely to perceive sexism when the perpetrator is male (rather than female). The authors argue that this reflects prototypes or expectations about the types of people who are most likely to be perpetrators and victims. These prototypes may be largely based in reality, given the differences in economic, social, and political conditions between these groups. Thus, gender and race can be useful, albeit broad cues for anticipating whether prejudice and discrimination is likely to occur. Other person characteristics that may serve as cues include past knowledge about another individual's or group's attitudes, such as when a potential interaction partner is known to have a history of making sexist comments or when groups have a history of discrimination. A person's age, political orientation, and religiosity may also serve as cues (e.g., people might expect older, more conservative, and more religious individuals to have more traditional gender role beliefs). These stereotypic cues (which may themselves be based on stereotypes) can lead to certain expectations about stereotypic treatment (see Casas, Ponterotto, & Sweeney, 1987, and Rettew, Billman, & Davis, 1993 for further discussion of "stereotypes of stereotypers").

In addition, when anticipating group situations, an important cue is the gender or racial composition of the group that is being considered. In the past 20 years, many researchers have examined the often negative effects of being a numerical minority in groups with skewed gender compositions (Izraeli, 1983; Kanter, 1977; Ott, 1989; Rosenberg, Perlstadt, & Phillips, 1993; Spangler, Gordon, & Pipkin, 1979; Theberge, 1993; Yoder, Adams, & Prince, 1983; Yoder & Sinnett, 1985). While this research has often focused on consequences of these skewed gender ratios for people already in a group or in an occupation, group composition may also serve as a cue for the likelihood of encountering prejudice and discrimination and may affect aspirations of going into those groups. Pettigrew and Martin (1987) proposed that women and racial minorities often decide not to pursue opportunities in organizations with small representations of their group members because they believe that they would be unlikely to be accepted as equals in such contexts. They state that minorities avoid potential rejection and often decide not to pursue such opportunities because "they personally or vicariously know the performance difficulties and interpersonal stresses associated with being a minority in a context dominated by majority members" (p. 51).

Cohen and Swim (1995) examined the role of gender composition in expectations about group encounters, exploring how the anticipated gender composition of a group influences expectations of being stereotyped and preferences to change one's group. They showed that both women and men who anticipated being solos working on a group task were more likely than nonsolos to expect to be treated stereotypically by their group members. However, women were more likely than men to prefer to change groups and to change the gender composition of the current group. This preference was correlated, for women but not men, with their beliefs about being treated stereotypically.

In addition, there are likely to be individual differences in the extent to which cues are recognized and interpreted as prejudicial in the first place. These individual differences may include the person's past experiences, belief in a just world, sex role beliefs, and feminist and/or racial identity. An illustration of the role of sex role beliefs was given by Chatterjee and McCarrey (1989), who compared the extent to which women in both traditional and nontraditional training programs believe that women in male-dominated jobs experience difficulties due to discrimination. They found that regardless of program, egalitarian women predicted more discrimination than traditional women.

AVOIDANCE

Once an assessment is made that prejudicial treatment may occur within a particular context, the individual must make a decision. She or he must choose to enter the situation despite the possibility of experiencing prejudice and discrimination or choose to avoid the situation altogether. Some authors have discussed avoidance as a preventative response to anticipated racial prejudice. Pettigrew (1964), in his discussion of African Americans' responses to oppression, identified avoidance or "moving away from the oppressor" as one type of response to oppression. He discusses several psychological as well as behavioral types of avoidance ranging from passivity and psychological withdrawal to insulating oneself from society. Simpson and Yinger (1985) developed a similar framework, discussing such strategies as developing separatist communities, migrating to less discriminatory locations, and reducing contacts with the majority. However, Simpson and Yinger (1985) also maintain that complete avoidance of the out group is neither possible nor desired by most African Americans. They argue that instead, avoidance often takes less extreme forms (e.g., ordering from catalogues to avoid intergroup contact). Whether subtle or extreme, such strategies may function as an active way of shaping one's environment to avoid potential prejudice and discrimination, but also have the negative consequence of placing limitations on the lives of minorities while leaving majority group members "off the hook."

Women may also avoid situations where they believe that gender prejudice is most likely to be expressed. For example, Junger (1987) found that women often attempted to avoid sexual harassment by avoiding certain situations with known and unknown men. Warr (1985) also found that fear of rape led to high rates of avoidance behaviors among women, including not going out alone, not going out at night, staying away from certain locations in the city, and not answering one's door. Finally, Adams, Kottke, and Padgitt (1983) found that 13% of the female students they surveyed had avoided taking a class with or working with a professor who was reputed to have made sexual advances to students. Avoidance has also been characterized as a response to past discriminatory treatment. Fitzgerald, Swan, and Fischer (1995) argue that one of the most frequent responses to sexual harassment is physically avoiding the harasser. Thus, avoidance may be conceptualized both as a response to deal with previous harassment and a strategy to avoid future incidences of harassment

The decision to avoid situations likely involves an evaluation of the costs and benefits associated with both entering and avoiding, including an examination of the comparison level for alternatives (Thibaut & Kelley, 1959). In this framework, prejudice and discrimination can be seen as a cost of entering certain situations and this cost will be weighed along with other costs and benefits. For example, although African Americans are less positive about housing advertisements that do not include African Americans models than those that do include these models, the advertisements do not discourage their belief that they would pursue the housing perhaps due to other favorable aspects of the living conditions (e.g., price, proximity to schools; Williams, Qualls, & Grier, 1995). The evaluation of costs and benefits may also be affected by the person's anticipation of their ability to cope with prejudice and discrimination that may be encountered. When people believe that they are able to cope with the situation, they may choose to enter, despite the potential of being treated stereotypically. In contrast, people who are not adequately prepared to deal with the situation may opt to avoid it regardless of the availability of desirable alternatives. Such people may thus end up settling for an objectively less desirable alternative (e.g., a lower paying job, a less prestigious military school).

People who are confident about their ability to succeed on a task may feel better equipped to deal with a prejudiced person or situation. Cohen and Swim (1995) found that confidence played an important role in determining whether solo women preferred to change groups and change the group's gender composition. Solo women were only more likely than nonsolos to prefer to avoid or change the group when self-confidence was low (as the result of receiving negative performance feedback). This preference was not exhibited when self-confidence was high, even though expectations of stereotypic treatment remained, regardless of confidence level. They argued that self-confidence may act as a buffer to allow these women to better deal with the possibility of being stereotyped. Being confident in one's abilities on the task at hand may enhance anticipated coping skills such that women may feel that they can perform well on a group task, increasing potential power in the group (Mowday, 1980; Instone, Major, & Bunker, 1983). It is possible that self-confidence leads to expectations that one may be able to disconfirm stereotypes, change the behavior of sexist individuals, and exert influence despite other's prejudice.

Anticipating prejudice and discrimination can help prepare people for situations, including allowing them to decide whether to avoid situations. However, not all potential prejudice can be avoided and it is probably neither practical nor desirable to avoid all situations where it might occur. Thus, people from groups that have traditionally been the targets of prejudice are likely to encounter prejudicial discriminatory incidents at some point in their lives if not on a frequent basis.

ENCOUNTERING PREJUDICE
AND DISCRIMINATION

We consider targets' descriptions of encounters with prejudicial events as a rich and valuable source of information about the experience and nature of prejudice and discrimination. As Essed (1988) notes, we need to give ". . . due credit to the knowledge about racism displayed in the accounts of those who deal with the problem on a daily basis" (p. 7). While others may sometimes disagree with targets' interpretations of particular events, their accounts are important to examine for several reasons. First, these accounts represent target's perceptions, and, as such, they reflect their personal experience and interpretation of events. Second, these accounts can provide insights into the psychological processes of identifying events as prejudicial or discriminatory. For instance, it is informative to examine the decision-making processes that lead to attributions of prejudice. This is particularly important given attributional ambiguity and subtlety associated with modern forms of prejudice (Crocker, Major, & Steele, 1998; Swim & Cohen, 1998).

Third, targets' accounts can provide insights about prejudice and discrimination. Compared to out group members, targets of prejudice may be considered experts on prejudice against their in group given their varied experiences and sources of knowledge about prejudice (Essed, 1992). Targets of prejudice may experience more prejudice or discrimination than others may be aware because a target's presence may activate stereotypes about their own group (Deaux & Major, 1987) and targets who represent numeric minorities are likely to have more intergroup contact experiences than nonminorities (Jackman, 1994). Moreover, because incidents that are directed at one's own group are self-relevant, it is likely that targets are more likely than nontargets to attend to and remember such incidents (Fiske & Taylor, 1991). Finally, targets may be exposed to more information about prejudice than nontargets through discussion with other members of their social group and perhaps family socialization (Essed, 1991; Jackson, McCullough, Gurin, & Broman, 1991). Thus, targets of prejudice may be more able than nontargets to place an experience that could potentially be considered prejudicial within a broader social context, for instance, by making a connection between particular incidents and typical incidents indicative of prejudice or by observing reoccurring themes. Targets may also have more elaborated schemas about characteristics of prejudiced behaviors, situations, and people and these schemas can help them augment or discount an attribution to prejudice. In order to convey what it is like to encounter everyday prejudice, we describe the characteristics of the events that targets often encounter, some attributional processes involved in identifying events as prejudicial, and the prevalence of these events.

DESCRIPTIONS OF INCIDENTS

We conducted a daily diary study examining African American women's and men's experiences with racism and women's (primarily European American) experiences with sexism (Swim, Cohen, Hyers, Fitzgerald, & Bylsma, 1997). The types of experiences typically reported by African Americans consisted primarily of three types of behaviors: (1) being stared at, glared at, or watched (such as while shopping in stores); (2) verbal expressions of prejudice (racial slurs, insensitive comments, and stereotyping); and (3) bad service. Our results support findings reported by Feagin (1991) and Feagin and Sikes (1994) who interviewed middle class African American women and men about their experiences with racism. Consistent with our study, their participants recalled avoidance, poor service, verbal epithets and attacks, threats, and harassment. In addition, their participants recalled several incidents of police threats, rejections such as from jobs, and physical attacks (see also Feagin, 1992, for another classification of types of behaviors experienced by African American college students.).

For the women in our study who reported experiences with sexism, the most frequent experiences were tied to gender roles and stereotypes. These incidents included comments reflecting beliefs that women have less ability than men in particular areas (e.g., driving), that they possess stereotypic traits such as passivity, and that they should restrict themselves to certain domains or tasks (e.g., housework). Objectifying sexual comments (e.g., comments about women's bodies) and behaviors (e.g., unwanted touching) were also common experiences. Finally, many women were also the targets of demeaning labels and street remarks.

The first two dimensions of sexism, (1) traditional gender roles and stereotyping, and (2) unwanted and objectifying sexual behaviors and comments, also emerged in a questionnaire study we conducted with 344 undergraduate women. We gave respondents a list of several different types of sexist behaviors that women in the daily diary study had experienced and asked them to indicate, on a five-point scale ranging from "never" to "about two or more times a week," how often they had experienced the behaviors over the last semester. These behaviors included those directed at themselves personally and those directed at women in general (see the Appendix). Exploratory factor analyses with oblique rotation resulted in a two-factor structure. One factor represented traditional gender stereotypes and roles and the other factor represented objectifying sexual behaviors and comments.[1]

The content of women's experiences with sexism as reported in the daily diary studies is consistent with findings reported 15 years ago by Trenhom and deMancillas (1978) in a study where women and men were asked to list their own experiences with sexism as well as behaviors and comments that they would find to be indicative of sexism. The two-factor structure found with the questionnaire study also parallels a distinction between gender harassment and other forms of sexual harassment (Fitzgerald & Hesson-McInnis, 1989; Gelfand, Fitzgerald, & Drasgow; 1995). Similar to the factor measuring traditional gender stereotypes and roles, gender harassment consists of "generalized sexist remarks and behavior, not necessarily designed to elicit sexual cooperation. Rather they convey insulting, degrading, or sexist attitudes about women" (p. 311, Fitzgerald & Hensson-McInnis, 1989). Like the factor measuring unwanted and objectifying sexual behavior and comments, other forms of sexual harassment deal more exclusively with unwanted sexual attention and coercion.

ASSESSMENT OF EVENTS

Part of the experience of being a frequent target of prejudice is deciding whether particular events are indicative of prejudice or discrimination. The decision process can be thought of as involving the initiation of the attribution process, and the accumulation and evaluation of relevant information. Support for this general process is found in Essed's (1988; 1991; 1992) work with women of African descent in the United States and the Netherlands (see also, Louw-Potguiter, 1989). Essed (1991; 1992) describes the first step in the assessment of events as deciding whether an event is acceptable. If the event is not perceived to be acceptable than the person decides whether there are acceptable excuses for the behavior or a specific event and whether the behavior can be attributed to the target's ethnicity.

Using the acceptability of an event as a starting point is consistent with research demonstrating that people are more likely to seek attributions for unexpected and negative events (Hastie, 1984; Malle & Knobe, 1997). With regard to incidents of everyday racism and sexism, people likely have expectations about normal or ideal interaction patterns and violations of these patterns can facilitate a search for explanations. Descriptions of events in our daily diary studies suggest that the attributional process could also start from two other points related to, but potentially distinct from the acceptability of behaviors.

The attributional process could begin with noticing whether an event is consistent with prototypes of prejudice and discrimination against one's group. For

---

[1]The scale also included four behaviors directed at men in general. A factor analysis of 144 male respondents reported experiences with behaviors directed at themselves and directed at men in general resulted in the same two dimensions with one exception. One item, "sexual behaviors one might do or want to do with respondent" loaded on the traditional gender stereotypes and roles factor rather than the unwanted and objectifying sexual behavior and comments factor.

instance, when women hear someone make sexual comments about their bodies or about women in general, they may start assessing whether the comments are prejudicial. Similarly, when African Americans receive bad service they may start assessing whether the service is a result of their race. In many cases, prototypically prejudiced incidents are also likely to be negative and hence may start the attributional process simply because of this negativity. However, we would predict that an attribution of prejudice is more likely to be considered when the incident is prototypic. Further, not all prototypic prejudicial behavior will be unambiguously negative (Glick & Fiske, 1996).

Another possible starting point may be when the individual notices an event is race- or gender-related. Noticing that an African American and a European American are treated differently may lead people to try to figure out if the differential treatment is unacceptable. In this case the cue would be the unequal treatment, rather than the acceptability of the behavior. Our daily diary data indicate that more women will experience gender-related events that they do not label as indicative of prejudice than African Americans will experience race-related events that they do not label as indicative of prejudice. This may be explained in part because some gender-related events, such as heterosexual dating patterns, are perceived to be acceptable. Thus, there may be a closer connection between differential treatment and unacceptability for racist than sexist events. Yet, in both cases, differential treatment rather than the acceptability may be the observation that starts the attributional process.

After the attributional process has begun, then the search for and evaluation of alternative explanations occurs. Based on Essed's interviews with women of African dissent (1991; 1992), this includes a search for information about whether people of European dissent were treated in the same manner and whether they and others of African dissent are typically treated in the same manner in similar situations or by the same person. Thus, Essed's description of the accumulation and evaluation information is consistent with classic descriptions of attributional processes including the search for consistency, consensus, and distinctiveness information (Kelly, 1967). Essed also notes that an important component of the decision to label events as prejudicial is one's general knowledge about prejudice. For instance, deciding whether an event is a result of a person's ethnicity can require knowledge about whether a specific experience is related to other people's experience within one's social group. Further, defining an event as prejudicial may also involve discussions with others to obtain their perspective and insights about their experiences. It should also be kept in mind that response biases and motivations, such as a desire to maintain perceived control over one's outcomes (Ruggiero & Taylor, 1995), can influence attributions of prejudice and discrimination (see Feldman Barrett & Swim, this volume).

PREVALENCE OF EVERYDAY RACISM AND SEXISM

An assumption behind the concept of everyday prejudice and discrimination is that these incidents occur frequently. The prevalence of prejudice has been documented in studies that examine people's endorsement of prejudiced beliefs and situational characteristics that affect the likelihood that perpetrators act out their prejudices. However, such investigations do not provide information about the frequency of targets' experiences with prejudice. There is relatively little literature on the frequency of targets' experiences compared to the research assessing the extent to which people endorse prejudiced beliefs, make prejudicial judgments, and engage in discriminatory behavior. The research that has examined the frequency of targets' experience with prejudice and discrimination indicates that these experiences are common.

One source of information about the prevalence of experiences with prejudice and discrimination comes from interviews with African Americans. These studies report the number of individuals who have had personal experiences with racism and the number of experiences they recall (e.g., Bullock & Houston, 1987; Essed, 1991; Feagin 1991). Findings from these investigations suggest that these experiences are quite common. However, these studies are more able to convey the content of salient experiences than they are to assess the frequency of events experienced per individual.

Several surveys have addressed African Americans' perceptions of the extent to which prejudice and discrimination is a problem either for themselves or African Americans in general (e.g., Adams & Dressler, 1988; Shuman & Hatchett, 1974; Sigelman and Welch, 1991; Terrell & Terrell, 1981). These studies, however, tend to ask participants about their general perceptions of prejudice and discimination rather than their personal experiences with specific everyday behaviors. As Sigelman and Welch (1991) note, "The questions national surveys use to tap perceptions of discrimination are fairly crude; they deal with broad dimensions of the quality of life (such as housing and education) and ignore possible discrimination in the daily routines of life (shopping, enrolling children in a sports or art program, getting medical care, dealing with coworkers, and so on)" (p. 59). We are aware of only a few studies that specifically looked at African Americans' assessments of the frequency of experiences with specific behaviors. In one study, D'Augelli and Hershberger (1993) surveyed 73 college students about their experiences with prejudice while in college. Only 11% reported they never heard disparaging remarks about African Americans on campus. In contrast, 41% reported occasionally hearing these remarks, 28% reported hearing them often, and 28% reported hearing them frequently. Further, 59% of the respondents indicated that they had been a target of verbal insults with most noting that this occurred once or twice. In a second study, African Americans reported the percent of time they experienced various everyday forms of racism (Landrine & Klonoff, 1996). While most questions on the survey instrument asked about experiences with specific types of people or reactions to events, three questions asked about experiences with specific behaviors (being falsely accused or suspected, called names, and made fun of or harmed). A majority reported experiencing these events during their lives and more than one-third reported these experiences over the previous year.

While there is a fair amount of survey research on women's experiences with sexual harassment (Arvey & Cavanaugh, 1995), survey research on the frequency of women's experiences with a wide range of everyday sexist events is limited. To provide more information about the frequency of women's experiences with this broader range of events, we constructed a survey instrument to assess women's experiences with everyday sexism (see also Haslett & Lipman, 1997; Klonoff & Landrine, 1995; and Fitzgerald *et al.,* 1988, for similar scales). The first item on our scale asks participants how often, on a five-point scale ranging from "never" to "about two or more times per week," in the previous semester they had experienced being treated in a sexist manner in the previous semester. The next 25 items asked how often they had experienced a range of typical everyday behaviors generated from our previously described daily diary study of women's experiences with sexism (Swim *et al.,* 1997).

As noted above, factor analyses indicated that these behaviors can be divided into those that represented unwanted and objectifying sexual behaviors and comments and those representing traditional gender stereotypes and roles. Conceptually, this latter category can also be divided into those that represent behaviors and comments directed at respondents themselves, women in general, and men in general (see the Appendix). We were interested in the total number of sexist events students experienced over the course of the semester as well as comparisons within different subtypes of experiences (i.e., unwanted and objectifying behaviors and comments and the three different targets of the comments about traditional gender stereotypes and roles). Thus, we summed responses from 344 female and 144 male introductory psychology students responses to all the behaviors directed at themselves and their own gender group as well as the behaviors within different subgroups of the items.[2]

Compared to men, women reported experiencing nearly twice as many total number of sexist events directed at themselves and their own gender group (see Table 2.1). The most pronounced differences occurred for experiences with unwanted and objectifying sexual behaviors and comments. Interestingly, men reported hearing more stereotypical comments directed at women in general than women reported experiencing, perhaps because many such comments are not

[2]This is only an approximation of the number of experiences participants had for two reasons. First, any one experience could include more than one type of behavior. Second, the sum of responses across items provides a conservative estimate of the number of experiences participants had. For instance, giving a response of "4" indicated that they had experienced the event "about two or more times a week during the semester" which would be indicative of approximately 15 to 30 experiences. By summing responses to the 0 to 4 scale, we probably understimated the number of experiences. However, the estimate is probably not far off because the means on almost all of the individual items were about equal to one (indicating that the event occured "about once during the last semester"). Items with substantially lower frequencies were reports about being excluded from jobs, college, class, or organizations, and violence from the opposite sex. The only mean greater than two was for male respondents reports about the frequency with which they had heard sexist jokes about women. Further, even though these sums may underestimate the number of experiences people had, the results still indicate that the experiences were common.

TABLE 2.1   Summed Number of Events Women and Men Experienced over a Semester

Event	Mean (SD)		Percent at least once		p-value[a]
	Women	Men	Women	Men	
1. Unwanted and objectifying sexual behaviors and comments	8.39 (5.83)	3.61 (3.91)	94%	72%	<.001
2. Traditional gender stereotypes and roles					
A. Directed at respondent	4.12 (3.54)	3.04 (2.92)	84%	77%	.001
B. Directed at women in general	8.76 (4.47)	9.78 (4.93)	99%	97%	.03
C. Directed at men in general	5.33 (2.99)	5.24 (3.36)	97%	90%	.77
3. Total directed at self and own gender group	21.27 (11.80)	11.89 (7.92)	100%	95%	<.001
4. Treated in a sexist manner	1.13 (1.00)	.38 (.76)	71%	27%	<.001

Note: Means for the item "being treated in a sexist manner" were on 0 (never) to 4 (2 or more times per week over the last semester) scale. The means for the subtypes of experiences represent sums of responses on this same five-point scale for eight behaviors for the sexual behaviors and comments, and seven, six, and four behaviors for the traditional gender stereotypes and roles directed at the respondent, women in general, and men in general, respectively. Means for total number of experiences represent 21 behaviors for women and 19 behaviors for men. When the two unique behaviors directed at women in general are excluded, the mean for women's total experiences is 18.44 ($SD = 10.62$).

[a]The p-value is for the χ^2 for comparing the percent who reported being treated in a sexist manner at least once because of skewed data for the male sample. For the remaining comparisons, the p-value is for t-tests comparing women's and men's means.

made in the presence of women. We did expect and find that there were more stereotypical comments directed at women, in general, than directed at men, in general (difference for female respondents: $M = 5.93$, $SD = 3.09$ versus $M = 5.33$, $SD = 12.99$; $t(327) = 5.18$, $p < .001$ for comments directed at women versus men, in general; difference for male respondents: $M = 6.84$ $SD = 3.52$ versus $M = 5.24$, $SD = 3.26$, $t(145) = 7.23$, $p < .001$ for comments directed at women versus men, in general).[3]

Finally, as noted in Table 1, one interesting result is that the mean number of times that respondents indicated having been treated in a sexist manner is low compared to the total number of times they experienced specific sexist behaviors.

[3]The means for the comments directed at women are different from those provided in Table 2 because the means in the text exclude the two behaviors directed at women that did not have parallel behaviors for men (using words that exclude women, and expressions of negative attitudes about women's equality).

We predicted that this would occur because it is likely that people do not think about the full range of possible types of everyday behaviors when considering how often they experienced sexism. Further, it is possible that some individuals would not define some of the behaviors in the survey as sexist. This is also consistent with research on rape and sexual harassment that shows that women are much less likely to indicate that they have been raped or sexually harassed than they are to indicate that they have experienced behaviors consistent with these acts (Arvey & Cavanaugh, 1995; Fitzgerald *et al.*, 1988; Koss & Oros, 1982).

While the above results illustrate that perceived experiences with sexist and racist behaviors are common, a limitation of both the interview and survey studies is that they rely on participants' recall of events. People's recall may be biased in the direction of highly salient events and they may have difficulty recalling subtle forms of prejudice. Moreover, when events occur frequently and are mundane, it may be difficult to retrospectively assess how often they have occurred (see Swim *et al.*, 1997, for an elaboration on the limitations of this past research). In contrast to the interview and survey studies, our previously described daily diary study was able to minimize the amount of delay between experiencing the event and recalling the event (Swim *et al.*, 1997). Results from this daily diary study indicated that, on average, each African American experienced about one racist event over the 2-week period and each woman experienced about two sexist events over the 2-week period that were labeled probably or definitely prejudicial. A limitation of the daily diary studies is that participants knew that the study was about their experiences with prejudice and this may have increased the likelihood that they noticed and identified prejudicial incidents. Despite such limitations, the converging evidence across methodologies is that these targets frequently encounter everyday racism and sexism.

RESPONDING TO PREJUDICE
AND DISCRIMINATION

Part of the experience of being a target of prejudice is the everyday decision making about whether to respond to the prejudice and discrimination that is encountered. Targets routinely face decisions not only about whether to respond, but also about how to respond. As described by Feagin and Sikes (1994), there is often a "struggle to keep some kind of balance and to contain one's frustrations in searching for the best response" (p.279). Decisions about prompt responses to events are likely to require split-second judgments about the perpetrators and the immediate and long term costs of responding (Haslett & Lipman, 1997). Since there are a number of response options that are available to members of stigmatized groups, individual and situational constraints will affect which responses are chosen. This process of determining how to respond is an important part of the complexity of the target's experience.

TYPES OF RESPONSES

There are a variety of categorizations proposed to describe the possible response strategies available to targets (Feagin, 1991; Feagin & Sikes, 1994; Fitzgerald & Ormerod, 1993; Gruber & Bjorn, 1982; Lalonde & Cameron, 1994; Tajfel & Turner, 1979; Taylor, Casten, Finkinger, Roberts, & Fulmore, 1994; Wright, Taylor, & Moghaddam, 1990). The types of responses can be characterized as assertive, nonassertive, or psychological.

Assertive Responses

Assertive responses communicate one's displeasure in a way that is visible to the perpetrator. Assertive responses have been characterized as physical actions as well as verbal comments engaged in as an immediate response to the event (Feagin, 1991; Gruber & Bjorn, 1986; Simpson & Yinger, 1985). However, in some cases, an assertive response may involve more formal processes, such as reporting the incident to an official or filing a lawsuit. It should also be noted that within the general category of assertive responses are those carried out through collective rather than individual action. As targets' exposures to everyday prejudice accumulate, more organized, contemplated actions may be chosen. Social organizing, political activism, and organized boycotting are examples of these collective responses to everyday prejudice (Simpson & Yinger, 1985, Taylor *et al.,* 1994; Branscombe & Ellemers, this volume).

Nonassertive Responses

Most of the classifications of types of responses acknowledge nonassertive responses as an important option. These responses include humor, attempts to placate a harasser, displaced aggression, and passive-aggressive defiance of the behavioral norms of the immediate social context (Feagin & Sikes, 1994; Fitzgerald *et al.,* 1995; Gruber and Bjorn, 1986; Simpson & Yinger, 1985; Swim & Hyers, 1998). There are also several nonassertive responses discussed in the literature that are of a more delayed nature, such as seeking social support from friends and family or future boycotting of an establishment (Feagin & Sikes, 1994; Fitzgerald *et al.,* 1995; Simpson & Yinger, 1985). While nonassertive responses may sometime be the result of acceptance or denial of prejudice and discrimination (Ruggiero & Taylor, 1995; Simpson & Yinger, 1985; Wright, Taylor, Moghaddam, 1990), many of the nonassertive responses imply that the nonassertive responder finds the event objectionable. Even if an individual decides to act in deference toward the perpetrator or appeases a perpetrator, this does not mean that the individual approves of the treatment (Feagin & Sikes, 1994; Fitzgerald *et al.,* 1995; Haslett & Lipman, 1997; Swim & Hyers, 1998).

Psychological Responses

Fitzgerald and colleagues (1995) have suggested that response strategies should not be categorized on a unidimensional scale of assertiveness because this simplifies the rich variation in response options, places too much emphasis on action-oriented responses, and neglects psychological responses. Fitzgerald and colleagues instead classify response styles into two general categories of internally and externally focused responses. Two important psychological responses are emotional reactions and cognitive coping strategies. Typical immediate emotional responses to prejudice are frustration and anger (Feagin & Sikes, 1994; Haslett & Lipman, 1997; Swim *et al.,* 1997). Attributing an event to prejudice rather than to something about oneself can be considered a general cognitive response (Crocker & Major, 1989). Other cognitive strategies may include adopting a more defensive self-protective stance (Feagin & Sikes, 1994; Simpson & Yinger, 1985), dissociating from one's stigmatized group or changing one's standards of social comparison from intragroup to intergroup standards (Crocker, Major, & Steele, 1998; Tajfel & Turner, 1979; Simpson & Yinger, 1985), developing a false, "illusory" sense of control over future offensive events (Fitzgerald *et al.,* 1995), and denial or relabeling of a prejudiced event as nonprejudiced (Fitzgerald *et al.,* 1995).

THE CHOICE TO PUBLICLY RESPOND

There are several reasons why targets would publicly respond to prejudice, and these reasons may not necessarily be consciously planned. For example, both assertive and nonassertive styles may serve as an emotional release, serving cathartic or revenge functions (Kowalski, 1966; Simpson & Yinger, 1985). For more assertive styles of responding, the intention may be to communicate displeasure in order to terminate the offensive behavior (Kowalski, 1996) or to educate the perpetrator and other bystanders about prejudice and discrimination (Blanchard, Crandall, Brigham, & Vaugh, 1994, Feagin, 1991; Feagin & Sikes, 1994). Finally, targets may respond in order to obtain social support and validation for their perceptions from others.

Costs and Benefits

When surveyed about how they would respond to a prejudicial incident, targets typically think that they would respond more directly than other data suggest they actually would respond (Adams *et al.,* 1983; Swim & Hyers, 1998). Thus, there is more involved in confronting than simply knowing that an offensive event has occurred and wanting to respond. While not all responses are consciously considered, a careful cost/benefit analysis may be engaged in to determine the best type of response (Haslett & Lipman, 1997; Kowalski, 1996). An assertive response may only be chosen if the individual's intended goals would be maximized (e.g., stopping the offensive behavior) and any risks are minimized (e.g., perpetrator retaliation).

Very little research has examined the cost and benefits of different response strategies to prejudice and discrimination, with most of the available studies examining women's responses to harassers in the workplace. In a study of workplace harassment, assertive responding improved the situation for about half of the targets (U.S. Merit Systems Protection Board, 1981). More grim conclusions may be drawn from a study by Loy and Stewart (1984) in which 62% of their sample of state workers reported negative effects of assertive responding, including receiving poorer job evaluations, being denied promotions, being transferred, or being fired (see also Livingston, 1982). In a participant observation examination of the effectiveness of confronting racist and sexist language, Latting (1994) found that targets who complained did have some impact upon others' use of derogatory language yet some labeled targets as "hypersensitive," "emotional," and "undereducated." Finally, in a study of "micro-inequities" Haslett and Lipman (1997) report that overt responding by most of the female attorneys in the study resulted in no change or increase in tension in relationships.

Considering the many risks of assertive responding, it is not surprising that targets often choose to make unassertive or no response at all to prejudice (e.g., Swim & Hyers, 1998). However, it should be acknowledged that there are costs to not publicly responding as well. These costs include the buildup of unreleased frustration (Feagin & Sikes, 1994), feelings of disempowerment, as well as the self-disappointment or guilt over one's failure to act on one's attitudes (Haslett & Lipman, 1997). Not publicly responding can also have physiological consequences. For instance, African American women who report being quiet rather than talking or acting in response to sexism and racism are more likely to have higher blood pressure (Krieger, 1990).

Situational Factors

An important influence on response choices are situational constraints. One aspect of the situation that may play a role in responding is the status of the perpetrator (Livingston, 1982; Haslett & Lipman, 1997), with people being less likely to confront higher status perpetrators. Further, contexts such as formal or unfamiliar settings may increase the likelihood of more polite, indirect response (Swim & Hyers, 1998). Another situational constraint may be imposed by bystanders. Targets may look to other witnesses of an event to observe their apparent reaction. This is especially likely to create pluralistic ignorance, diffusion of responsibility, or normative pressures not to respond if the others who are suspected to share the targets' attitudes are not overtly responding (Swim & Hyers, 1998).

Broader social norms can also affect response choice. Social norms for response styles can come from within the target's in group, as well as from the larger society. For African-Americans, the civil rights movement encouraged more assertive response styles, replacing an earlier norm of deference to prejudice (Feagin & Sikes, 1994). Similarly, the feminist movement may have also encouraged a more assertive norm for women (Worell, 1994). Perhaps as a result of this more assertive norm, society often holds the simplistic view that targets will complain when they are offended. For instance, courts have unfairly used whether a women publicly responds to harassment or sexual assault as indicative of how offended she was (Estrich, 1991, cited in Fitzgerald et al., 1995). However, such simplistic views fail to acknowledge that there are still many strong normative pressures for target group members not to respond.

Majority group members can be successful at stifling targets' assertive response efforts. The majority group may minimize targets' assertiveness by suggesting that targets are always complaining, that they are oversensitive, or that they are paranoid (Adams, Kottke, Padgitt, 1983; Feagin & Sikes, 1994; Essed, 1991; Haslett & Lipman, 1997; Latting, 1993; Simpson & Yinger, 1985). As a result, those who are the targets of prejudice are in a double bind between their desire to confront prejudice to promote change and the societal pressure for them to keep quiet to avoid the stigma of the "uppity oppressed person". As an African American woman described in an interview by Feagin and Sikes (1994), ". . . I get myself into difficulties because I deal with it head on. And generally, I'm considered a troublemaker, or someone who's constantly looking at race, and someone who's looking to argue . . ." (p. 282).

Individual Differences

In the face of such pressures not to respond, one might think that targets who choose to assertively confront prejudice must have special characteristics, such as strong group identification (see Branscombe & Ellemers, this volume). However, research examining individual traits that relate to group identity has revealed mixed findings. For instance, some research has shown that feminist and gender-related beliefs relate to women's assertive responding to harassment (Brooks & Perot, 1991; Jensen & Gutek, 1982; Swim & Hyers, 1998). However, similar research has not found a relationship between characteristics of the target of harassment and the response they choose to give to the harassment (Gruber & Bjorn, 1982).

There may be many reasons why individual differences in group identification do not consistently predict assertive responses. One factor that may reduce the strength of group identification as a predictor of assertive confronting is "burnout". As Feagin and Sikes (1994) have suggested, those who have a strong commitment to improving their groups' situation may become fatigued from daily confrontations with perpetrators resulting in a preference not to respond even though their group commitment has not weakened. Further, while greater group identification has been associated with greater activism and collective action (e.g., Bargard & Hyde, 1991; Branscombe & Ellemers, this volume; O'Niel, Eagin, Owen, and Murry, 1993), group identification does not necessarily make one a more assertive person. Changes in group identity may be independent of personality (Cross, 1991). Finally, situational constraints may often be powerful enough to override any individual differences in response choice (Swim & Hyers, 1998).

CONCLUSION

Our review of targets' experiences with prejudice and discrimination focused on women's experiences with sexism and African Americans' experiences with racism. While many may be able to recall incidents where they have experienced prejudice and discrimination, the nature of these encounters likely differs for the stigmatized and the nonstigmatized (Crocker *et al.,* 1998; Haslett & Lipman, 1997). For instance, while men and European Americans may be devalued in particular contexts, in most contexts within the U.S. culture they are not devalued. Thus, the implications of their particular experiences are not as wide ranging as they are for stigmatized groups such as women and many ethnic groups. We suspect that nonstigmatized individuals spend less of their time and effort anticipating the possibility of future encounters with prejudice. Further, the impact of the encounters may differ because, for instance, of the possible cumulative impact of encounters with these specific forms of daily hassles, many of which bring about emotional reactions such as feelings of anger or threat. Finally, the lessor social power of the stigmatized may result in different perceived options for responding.

While the general experience of anticipating, encountering, and deciding how to respond to prejudice and discrimination is likely shared by many targets of prejudice, differences exist in the specific content of their experiences (Swim *et al.,* 1997). Differences between and within target groups will likely emerge as a result of differences in the quality and quantity of interpersonal relationships with those who are prejudiced against their group, the visibility of one's stigmatizing condition, and the extent to which the target of prejudice identifies with her or his social group or agrees with others' prejudice against her or his group. Differences between and within groups could also affect one's emotional reactions and coping responses. For instance, some individuals may not notice or define events as prejudicial or perceive negative impact of events and, therefore, may not be disturbed by particular events. On the other hand, not noticing or defining events as prejudicial may prevent individuals from engaging in effective coping responses. Further, there may be unique aspects of experiences by people who belong to more than one stigmatized groups (St. Jean & Feagin, 1997). For instance, African American women may face unique attributional issues when encountering prejudice because the prejudice may be a result of their ethnicity, gender, or both (DeFour, 1990; Smith & Stewart, 1983). More research is needed to examine variations in experiences between and within groups of interest.

Understanding the extent to which these everyday experiences with prejudice and discrimination infiltrate within and affect people's lives and choices is a source of concrete information about what it is like to be frequently a target or potential target of prejudice. Such a focus also points to specific ways that difficulties can emerge within intergroup interactions and the ways that prejudice manifests itself in our current social climate. Thus, studying experiences with prejudice and discrimination not only provides information about targets but also provides information about prejudice in general.

APPENDIX

Please use the following scale to indicate how often during the previous semester you experienced each of the events listed below.

A. Never
B. About once during the last semester
C. About once a month during the last semester
D. About once a week during the last semester
E. About two or more times a week during the last semester

Code numbers before items, which were not included in the original survey, represent: unwanted and objectifying behaviors and comments directed at the respondent (1); traditional gender stereotypes and roles directed at the respondent (2A); traditional gender stereotypes and roles directed at women in general (2B); traditional gender stereotypes and roles directed at men in general (2C).

    1. Been treated in a sexist manner.

2A 2. Not been taken serious because of my gender.

2A 3. Been encouraged to do gender stereotypical activities or discouraged from doing activities counter to stereotypes about my gender (for example, activities such as pursuing certain majors or careers, joining certain organizations, doing certain recreational activities.)

2A 4. Been perceived gender stereotypically when the person was wrong or did not know me well enough to know what I'm like (for example, if you are male, that you are logical or you are not sensitive and if you are female, that you are sensitive or you or not logical). This could be in terms of, for example, your traits, abilities, or preferences.

2A 5. Heard someone express <u>approval</u> of me because I exhibited behavior consistent with stereotypes about my gender.

2A 6. Heard someone express <u>disapproval</u> of me because I exhibited behavior <u>inconsistent</u> with stereotypes about my gender.

1   7. Had people shout sexist comments, whistle, or make catcalls at me.

1   8. Had someone refer to me with a demeaning or degrading label specific to my gender (bitch, chick, bastard, faggot, etc.)

1   9. Had sexist comments made about parts of my body or clothing.

1   10. Heard someone make comments about sexual behavior I might do or things they would want to do with me.

1   11. Had someone do or say something that made me feel threatened sexually.

1   12. Experienced unwanted staring or ogling at myself or parts of my body when the person knew or should have known I was not interested or it was inappropriate for the situation or our relationship.

1   13. Experienced unwanted flirting when the person knew or should have known I was not interested or it was inappropriate for the situation or our relationship.

1   14. Experienced unwanted flirting when the person knew or should have known I was not interested or it was inappropriate for the situation or our relationship.

2A 15. Been excluded from a job, college, class, or organization because of gender.

2A 16. Been the victim of violence from someone of the opposite sex.

2B 17. Heard sexist jokes about women.

2C 18. Heard sexist jokes about men.

2B 19. Heard someone express general dislike or resentment of women.

2C 20. Heard someone express general dislike or resentment of men.

2B 21. Heard someone use words that exclude women (e.g., he or him to refer to people in general).

2B 22. Heard someone make stereotypical comments about women's traits, abilities, or preferences.

2C 23. Heard someone make stereotypical comments about men's traits, abilities, or preferences.

2B 24. Heard someone make stereotypical comments about work or family roles women should or should not do.

2C 25. Heard someone make stereotypical comments about work or family roles men should or should not do.

2B 26. Head someone express negative attitudes about women's equality.

REFERENCES

Adams, J. P., & Dressler, W. W. (1988). Perceptions of injustice in a Black community: Dimensions and variation. *Human Relations, 41,* 753–767.

Adams, J. W., Kottke, J. L., & Padgitt, J. S. (1983). Sexual harassment of university students. *Journal of College Student Personnel, 24,* 484–490.

Arvey, R. D., & Cavanaugh, M. A. (1995). Using surveys to assess the prevalence of sexual harassment: Some methodological problems. *Journal of Social Issues, 51,* 39–52.

Aspinwall, L. G., & Taylor, S. E. (1998). A stich in time: Self-regulation and proactive coping. *Psychological Bulletin.*

Bargard, A., & Hyde, J. S. (1991). Women's studies: A study of feminist identity development in women. *Psychology of Women Quarterly, 15,* 181–201.

Baron, R. S., Burgess, M. L., & Kao, C. F. (1991). Detecting and labeling prejudice: Do female perpetrators go undetected? *Personality and Social Psychology Bulletin, 17,* 115–123.

Blanchard, F. A., Crandall, C. S., Brigham, J. C., & Vaugh, L. A. (1994). Condemning and Condoning racism: A social context approach to interracial settings. *Journal of Applied Psychology, 79,* 993–997.

Branscombe, N. R., & Ellemers, N. (This volume). Use of individualistic and group strategies in response to perceived discrimination among the disadvantaged. In J. K. Swim & C. Stangor (Eds.), *Prejudice: The target's perspective.* San Diego: Academic Press.

Brooks, L., & Perot, A. R. (1991). Reporting sexual harassment: Exploring a predictive model. *Psychology of Women Quarterly, 15,* 31–47.

Bullock, S. C., & Houson, E. (1987). Perceptions of racism by Black medical students attending White medical schools. *Journal of the National Medical Association, 79,* 601–608.

Casas, J. M., Ponterotto, J. G., & Sweeney, M. (1987). Stereotyping the stereotyper: A Mexican-American perspective. *Journal of Cross-Cultural Psychology, 18,* 45–57.

Chatterjee, J., & McCarrey, M. (1989). Sex role attitudes of self and those inferred of peers, performance, and career opportunities as reported by women in nontraditional vs. Traditional training programs. *Sex Roles, 21,* 653–669.

Crocker, J., & Major, B. (1989). Social stigma and self-esteem: The self-protective properties of stigma. *Psychological Review, 96,* 608–630.

Crocker, J., Major, B., & Steele, C. (1998). Social stigma. In D. Gilbert, S. T. Fiske, & G. Lindzey (Eds.), *Handbook of social psychology* (4th ed.). Boston, MA: McGraw-Hill.

Cohen, L. L., & Swim, J. K. (1995). The differential effect of gender ratios on women and men: Tokenism, self-confidence, and expectations. *Personality and Social Psychology Bulletin, 21,* 876–884.

Crosby, F. (1982). *Relative deprivation and working women.* New York: Oxford University Press.

Cross, W. E. (1991). *Shades of Black: Diversity in African-American identity.* Philadelphia, PA: Temple University Press.

D'Augelli, A. R., & Hershberger, S. L. (1993). African American undergraduates on a predominantly White campus: Academic factors, social networks, and campus climate. *Journal of Negro Education, 62,* 67–81.

Deaux, K., & Major, B. (1987). Putting gender into context: An interactive model of gender-related behavior. *Psychological Review, 94,* 369–389.

DeFour, D. C. (1990). The interface of racism and sexism on college campuses. In M. A. Paludi (Ed.), *Ivory power: Sexual harassment on campus,* (pp. 45–52). SUNY series in the psychology of women. Albany, NY: State University Press.

Essed, P. (1988). Understanding verbal accounts of racism: Politics and heuristics of reality construction. *Text, 8,* 5–40.

Essed, P. (1991). *Understanding everyday racism: An interdisciplinary theory.* Sage series on race and ethnic relations: Vol. 2. Newbury Park, CA: Sage Publications.

Essed, P. (1992). Alternative knowledge sources in explanations of racist events. In M. L. McLaughlin, M. J. Cody, & S. J. Reed (Eds.), *Explaining one's self to others: Reason-giving in a social context,* (pp. 199–224). Hillsdale NJ: Lawrence Erlbaum Associates.

Feagin, J. R. (1991). The continuing significance of race: Antiblack discrimination in public places. *American Sociological Review, 56,* 101–116.

Feagin, J. R. (1992). The continuing signficance of racism: Discrimination against Black students in White colleges. *Journal of Black Studies, 22,* 546–578.

Feagin, J. R., & Sikes, M. P. (1994). *Living with racism: The black middle-class experience.* Boston, MA: Beacon Press Books.

Feldman Barrett, L., & Swim, J. (This volume). Appraisals of prejudice and discrimination. In J. K. Swim & C. Stangor (Eds.), *Prejudice: The target's perspective.* San Diego: Academic Press.

Fiske, S. T., & Taylor, S. E. (1991). *Social Cognition* (2nd ed.). New York: McGraw-Hill.

Fitzgerald, L. F., & Ormerod, A. J. (1993). Breaking silence: The sexual harassment of women in academia and the workplace. In F. Denmark and M. Paludi (Eds.), *The psychology of women: Handbook of issues and theories,* (pp. 553–581). Westport, CT: Greenwood.

Fitzgerald, L. F., & Hesson-McInnis, M. (1989). The dimensions of sexual harassment: A structural analysis. *Journal of Vocational Behavior, 35,* 309–326.

Fitzgerald, L. F., Shullman, S. L., Bailey, N., Richards, M., Swecker, J., Gold, Y., Ormerod, M., & Weitzman, L. (1988) The incidence and dimensions of sexual harassment in academia and the workplace. *Journal of Vocational Behavior, 32,* 152–175.

Fitzgerald, L. F., Swan, S., & Fischer, K. (1995). Why didn't she just report him? The psychological and legal implications of women's responses to sexual harassment. *Journal of Social Issues, 51,* 117–138.

Gelfand, M. J., Fitzgerald, L. F., & Drasgow, F. (1995). The structure of sexual harassment: A confirmatory analysis across cultures and settings. *Journal of Vocational Behavior, 47,* 164–177.

Glick, P., & Fiske, S. T. (1996). The ambivalent sexism inventory: Differentiating hostile and benevolent sexism. *Journal of Personality and Social Psychology, 70,* 491–512.

Gruber, J. E. (1982). Blue collar blues: The sexual harassment of women autoworkers. *Work and Occupations, 9,* 271–298.

Gruber, J. E., & Bjorn, L. (1986). Women's responses to sexual harassment: An analysis of sociocultural, organizational, and personal resource models. *Social Science Quarterly, 67,* 814–826.

Haslett , B. B., & Lipman, S. (1997). Micro inequities: Up close and personal. In N. V. Benokraitis (Ed.), *Subtle sexism* (pp. 34–53). Thousand Oaks, CA: Sage.

Hastie, R. (1984). Causes and effects of causal attribution. *Journal of Personality and Social Psychology, 46,* 44–56.

Inman, M. L., & Baron, R. S. (1996). The influence of prototypes on perceptions of prejudice. *Journal of Personality and Social Psychology, 70,* 727–739.

Instone, D., Major, B., & Bunker, B. B. (1983). Gender, self-confidence, and social influence strategies: An organizational simulation. *Journal of Personality and Social Psychology, 45,* 322–333.

Izraeli, D. (1983). Sex effects or structural effects? An empirical test of Kanter's theory of proportions. *Social Forces, 62,* 153–165.

Jackman, M. (1994). *The velvet glove, paternalism and conflict in gender, class, and race relations.* Berkeley, CA: University of California Press.

Jackson, J. S., McCullough, W. R., Gurin, G., & Broman, C. L. (1991), Race identity. In J. S. Jackson (Ed.), *Life in Black America* (pp. 238–253). Newbury Park, CA: Sage Publications.

Jenson, I., & Gutek, B. A. (1982). Attributions and assignment of responsibility for sexual harassment. *Journal of Social Issues, 38,* 121–136.

Junger, M. (1987). Women's experience of sexual harassment: Some implications for their fear of crime. *British Journal of Criminology, 27,* 358–383.

Kanter, R. M. (1977). *Men and women of the corporation.* New York Basic Books.

Kelley, H. H. (1967). Attribution theory in social psychology. In D. Levine (Ed.), *Nebraska Symposium on Motivation, 15* (pp. 192–240). Lincoln: University of Nebraska Press.

Klonoff, E. A., & Landrine, H. (1995). The schedule of sexist events: A measure of lifetime and recent sexist discrimination in women's lives. *Psychology of Women Quarterly, 19,* 439–473.

Koss, M. P., & Oros, C. J. (1982). Sexual experiences survey: A research instrument investigating sexual aggression and victimization. *Journal of Consulting and Clinical Psychology, 50,* 455–457.

Kowalski, R. M. (1996). Complaints and complaining: Functions, antecedents, and consequences. *Psychological Bulletin, 119,* 176–196.

Krieger, N. (1990). Racial and gender discrimination: Risk factors for high blood pressure? *Social Science Medicine, 30,* 1273–1281.

Landrine, H., & Klonoff, E. A. (1996). The schedule of racist events: A measure of racial discrimination and a study of its negative physical and mental health consequences. *Journal of Black Psychology, 22,* 144–168.

LaLonde, R. N., & Cameron, J. E. (1994). Behavioral responses to discrimination: A focus on action. In M. P. Zanna & J. M. Olson (Eds.), *The psychology of prejudice: The Ontario symposium, 7* (pp. 257–288). Hillsdale, NJ: Lawrence Erlbaum Associates, Publishers.

Latting, J. K. (1993). Soliciting individual change in an interpersonal setting: The case of racially or sexually offensive language. *Journal of Applied Behavioral Science, 29,* 464–484.

Livingston, J. (1982). Responses to sexual harassment on the job: Legal, organizational, and individual actions. *Social Issues, 38,* 5–22.

Louw-Potgieter, J. (1989). Covert racism: An application of Essed's analysis in a South African context. *Journal of Language and Social Psychology, 8,* 307–319.

Loy, P., & Stewart, L. (1984). The extent and effects of the sexual harassment of working women. *Sociological Focus, 17,* 31-43.

Malle, B. F., Knobe, J. (1997). Which behaviors do people explain? A basic actor–observer asymmetry. *Journal of Personality and Social Psychology, 72,* 288–304.

Miller, C. T., & Meyers-Parelli, A. (This volume). Compensating for Prejudice: How obese people (and others) overcome the deleterious effects of prejudice. In J. K. Swim & C. Stangor (Eds.), *Prejudice: The target's perspective.* San Diego: Academic Press.

Mowday, R. T. (1980). Leader characteristics, self-confidence, and methods of upward influence in organizational decision situations. *Academy of Management Journal, 4,* 709–724.

O'Niel, J. M., Egan, J., Owen, S., & Murry, V. M. (1993). The gender role journey measure: Scale development and psychometric evaluation. *Sex Roles, 38,* 167–185.

Ott, E. M. (1989). The effects of the male–female ratio at work. *Psychology of Women Quarterly, 13,* 41–57.

Pettigrew, T. F. (1964). *A profile of the American Negro.* Princeton, NJ: Van Nostrand.

Pettigrew, T. F., & Martin, J. (1987). Shaping the context for Black American inclusion. *Journal of Social Issues, 43,* 41–78.

Phinney, J. S., & Traver, S. (1988). Ethnic identity search and commitment in black and white eighth graders. *Journal of Early Adolescence, 8,* 265–277.

Rettew, D. C., Billman, D., & Davis, R. A. (1993). Inaccurate perceptions of the amount others stereotype: Estimates about stereotypes of one's own group and other groups. *Basic and Applied Social Psychology, 14,* 121–142.

Rosenberg, M. (1979). *Conceiving the self.* New York: Basic Books.

Rosenberg, M. (1986). Self-esteem research: A Phenomenological corrective. In J. Prager, D. Longshore, & M. Seeman (Eds.), *School desegregation research: New directions in situational analysis* (pp. 175–203). NY: Plenum Press.

Rosenberg, J., Perlstadt, H., & Phillips, W. R. (1993). Now that we are here: Discrimination, disparagement, and harassment at work and the work of women lawyers. *Gender and Society, 7,* 415–433.

Ruggiero, K. M., & Taylor, D. M. (1995). Coping with discrimination: How disadvantaged group members perceive the discrimination that confronts them. *Journal of Personality and Social Psychology, 68,* 826–838.

Schuman, H., & Hatchet, S. (1974). *Black racial attitudes: Trends and complexities.* Ann Arbor, MI: Institute for Social Research.

Sigelman, L., & Welch, S. (1991). *Black American's views of racial inequality: The dream deferred.* New York: Cambridge University Press.

Simpson, G. E., & Yinger, J. M. (1985). *Racial and cultural minorities: An analysis of prejudice and discrimination* (5th ed.). New York: Plenum.

Smith, A., & Stewart, A. (1983). Approaches to studying racism and sexism in black women's lives. *Journal of Social Issues, 39,* 1–15.

Spangler, E., Gordon, M. A., & Pipkin, P. M. (1978). Token women: An empirical test of Kanter's hypothesis. *American Journal of Sociology, 84,* 160–170.

St. Jean, Y., & Feagin, J.R. (1997). *Racial masques: Black women and subtle gendered racism.* In N. V. Benokraitis (Ed.), *Subtle sexism* (pp. 179–200). Thousand Oaks, CA: Sage.

Swim, J. K., & Cohen, L. L. (1997). Overt, covert, and subtle sexism: A comparison between the Attitudes Toward Women and Modern Sexism scales. *Psychology of Women Quarterly, 21,* 103–118.

Swim, J. K., Cohen, L. L., Hyers, L. L., Fitzgerald, D. F., & Bylsma, W. H. (1997). *Everyday experiences with prejudice: A daily diary study.* Unpublished manuscript.

Swim, J. K., & Hyers, L. L. (1998). Excuse me—What did you say?! Women's public and private response to sexist remarks. *Journal of Experimental Social Psychology.*

Tajfel, H., & Turner, J. C. (1979) An integrative theory of intergroup conflict In W. G. Austin & S. Worchel (Eds.), *The social psychology of intergroup relations* (pp. 33–47). Monterery, CA: Brooks/Cole.

Taylor, R. D., Casten, R., Finkinger, S. M., Roberts, D., & Fulmore, C. D. (1994). Explaining the school performance of African American adolescents. *Journal of Research on Adolescence, 4,* 21–44.

Terrell, F., & Terrell, S. (1981). An inventory to measure cultural mistrust among Blacks. *The Western Journal of Black Studies, 5,* 180–185.

Theberge, N. (1993). The construction of gender in sports: Women, coaching, and the naturalization of difference. *Social Problems, 40,* 301–313.

Thibaut, J. W., & Kelley, H. H. (1959). *The social psychology of groups.* New York: Wiley.

Trenholm, S., & deMancillas, W. R. T. (1978). Student perceptions of sexism. *The Quarterly Journal of Speech, 64,* 267–283.

U.S. Merit Systems Protection Board. (1981). Sexual harassment in the federal workplace: Is it a problem? Washington DC: U.S. Government Printing Office.

Warr, M. (1985). Fear of rape among urban women. *Social Problems, 32,* 238–252.

Williams, J. D., Qualls, W. J., & Grier, S. A. (1995). Racially exclusive real estate advertising: Public policy implications for fair housing practices. *Journal of Public Policy and Marketing, 14,* 225–244.

Worell, J. (1996). Opening doors to feminist research. *Psychology of Women Quarterly, 20,* 469–487.

Wright, S. C., Taylor, D. M., & Moghaddam F. M. (1990). Responding to membership in a disadvantaged group: From acceptance to collective protest. *Journal of Personality and Social Psychology, 58,* 994–1003.

Yoder, J., Adams, J., & Prince, H. (1983). The price of a token. *Journal of Political and Military Sociology, 11,* 325–418.

Yoder, J., & Sinnett, J. (1985). Is it all in the numbers? A case study of tokenism. *Psychology of Women Quarterly, 9,* 413–418.

3

No Laughing Matter

Women's Verbal and Nonverbal Reactions to Sexist Humor

Marianne LaFrance[1] and Julie A. Woodzicka[2]

Boston College

'It's only a joke.' Of course. But it's like rib-tickling with an ice pick—careful, or you'll draw blood.
—Arthur Teitelbaum, 1987

In addition to evoking amusement, humor has long been viewed as a vehicle for expressing dislike or aversion. Freud (1928), for one, asserted that humor enables individuals to express hostility that they would feel uncomfortable expressing directly. This view has been seconded by others who see in disparaging humor a "safe" avenue for the expression of hostility (McGhee, 1988; Neitz, 1980). Although the telling of disparaging jokes is acceptable in many social contexts, the impact of such humor on some recipients may be anything but innocuous.

Although women are often the butt of disparaging jokes (Cantor & Zillman, 1973; Crawford, 1995), surprisingly little research has assessed how sexist humor impacts female recipients. Humor researchers typically ask whether individuals find sexist jokes or cartoons funny with the result that other effects, such as

[1]This research was supported in part by NSF Grant SBR-9319897 to the first author. We wish to thank Nancy Alvarado for her help in coding facial expressions and Angela Paradis for assistance in running the experiment.

[2]Order of authorship was determined alphabetically.

negative affect and reductions in self-esteem have been ignored (e.g., Moore, Griffiths, & Payne, 1987). In addition, research on sexist humor has tended to rely on self-report measures that may be particularly susceptible to demand characteristics since the stimulus is supposed to be humorous. We contend that in order to better understand how sexist humor might affect women who hear it, it is necessary to tap more than verbal indicators and reactions besides funniness ratings. The present chapter aims to do this by examining women's verbal and nonverbal responses to hearing jokes that disparage women. The underlying idea is that sexist jokes are a mode through which gender prejudice is expressed and understood.

SEXIST HUMOR AS SUBTLE PREJUDICE

Sexist humor can be defined as humor that demeans, insults, stereotypes, victimizes, and/or objectifies a person on the basis of his or her gender (Woodzicka, 1994). Hence, sex and derogation are combined into material delivered as humor (Love & Deckers, 1989). For many, sexist jokes are innocuous; they are intended only to amuse. Tellers of sexist jokes claim they mean no harm and the jokes themselves are aimed at no one in particular. But from another vantage point, sexist jokes can be construed as a vehicle for the transmission of prejudice. The prejudice may be more subtle than a derogatory comment delivered without humor but it may be no less prejudicial for that. Indeed there is support for the idea that humor may mask the recognition but not the reality of prejudice. In one study, respondents were asked to rate a number of sexist incidents on how funny and how sexist they were (Bill & Naus, 1992). The investigators found that the more humorous participants found the incidents, the less sexist and more acceptable they rated them. They were also more likely to voice approval of the sexist incident if they rated it as humorous. In short, there is reason to regard sexist jokes as a subtle form of prejudice. As such, women who hear sexist jokes may feel at some level that, like the butt of the joke, they too have been targeted by the prejudice.

Because the prejudice delivered by sexist jokes is implicit, standard modes of redress may not be available to those affected even for those who feel or wish to say something. For example, Swim and Hyers (1997) found that when women were exposed to sexist remarks, only 15% directly confronted the perpetrator and less than half openly expressed displeasure through direct comments or indirect verbalizations. These public responses, however, did not seem to be indicative of the manner in which women wanted to respond. As revealed by questionnaire ratings and thought and feeling listings, participants indicated negative feelings toward the perpetrator. In addition, 45% of women who thought about making public, confrontational remarks to the perpetrator did not do so. One would expect that for more ambiguous expressions, such as sexist jokes, women might be even more hesitant to speak up. The prejudicial content of humor is masked by the very fact that the message is in the form of a joke. What is yet to be determined is whether sexist jokes have negative effects on women who hear them and what these effects might be.

SEXIST HUMOR AS GENDER HARASSMENT

In 1995, Chevron Corporation agreed to pay $2.2 million to settle sexual harassment charges that were brought by four female employees who said they had been the targets of a barrage of offensive jokes, e-mail messages and comments about their clothes and body parts (Lewin, 1995). In this case and others, employers have been held financially liable for behavior that might have been delivered as a joke but that others saw as harassment. For example, in a survey of more than 4000 individuals, 71% considered the telling of gender stereotyped jokes to be sexual harassment (Frazier, Cochran, & Olson, 1995), although women consider the telling of sexist jokes at work to be more inappropriate than do men (Hemmasi, Graf, & Russ, 1994; Smeltzer & Leap, 1988).

Sexist jokes can be construed as gender harassment because the repeated telling of them in a work setting can generate a hostile work environment (Baker, Terpstra, & Larntz, 1990; Fitzgerald, Swan, & Fischer, 1995; Gutek & Koss, 1993). Hostile environment harassment is distinguishable from quid pro quo harassment. Quid pro quo harassment, which is based on demands for sexual favors in return for particular job-related benefits, is more often directed by a single individual at another person, while hostile work environment can be experienced by any or all of those in a particular setting (Meritor Savings Bank v. Vinson, 1986).

Researchers have concentrated on two kinds of responses to being sexually harassed. The first has to do with understanding whether victims directly confront the harasser with the offending behavior or file formal complaints about it to the organization. Gruber and Bjorn (1986) found that women with less organizational power (lower job status) and fewer personal resources (lower self-esteem) responded less assertively and directly to the harasser than did women with more resources.

The second has to do with documenting the psychological and emotional effects of being harassed (Fitzgerald et al., 1995). For example, research has shown that among women who had requested assistance for sexual harassment, a significant proportion reported feeling that their self-esteem and life satisfaction had suffered as a result. They also reported feeling helpless and vulnerable as well as experiencing anger, fear, depression, anxiety, irritability, humiliation, and alienation (Gutek & Koss, 1993).

What is not known, however, is what behavioral, emotional, and/or cognitive responses are specifically linked to having been exposed to sexist jokes on the job. For example, no work has specifically asked about the degree to which sexist jokes on the job, in the absence of other kinds of harassment, lead hearers to directly confront the joke teller or file formal complaints. It may be especially difficult to report being harassed by others' joking even though it may be experienced as hostile, because the situation may not be seen as serious or unequivocal as other forms of harassment like quid pro quo harassment.

Secondly, research has not yet determined whether "hostile gender environment" harassment, which subsumes but is not limited to sexual and sexist joking, elicits the same kinds of emotional effects that quid pro quo harassment is thought to generate. For example, do sexist jokes cause hearers increased anger, fear, and anxiety and diminished self-esteem? In sum, we know next to nothing about how sexist jokes specifically affect women hearers' emotional responses. There is reason to suppose that women's emotional responses to sexist humor will depend on their preexisting gender attitudes. For example, women with more traditional attitudes were found to label fewer incidents as harassment, evidenced more self-blame when it was directed at them, and were less likely to report it than were women with more liberal attitudes (Jensen & Gutek, 1982).

INDIVIDUAL DIFFERENCES IN RESPONSES TO SEXIST HUMOR

Research has shown great variability in what people find funny (Hassett & Houlihan, 1979). One factor seems to be whether joke recipients either identify with or distance themselves from the "butt" of the joke. The dispositional theory of humor argues that humor is more likely elicited by the mischances of those who are viewed as socially undesirable or disliked than those who are regarded highly. In addition, the theory proposes that mirth increases as negative disposition toward the disparaged group increases (Zillman, 1983; Zillman & Cantor, 1976).

With respect to sexist jokes, the prediction has been that men should find jokes that disparage women to be funnier than women find them. Indeed, several studies have found that as the humorous stimuli become more sexist toward women, funniness ratings made by males increase (Chapman & Gadfield, 1976; Neuliep, 1987; Priest & Wilhelm, 1974). However, for women the results appear more complicated. While some studies indicate that women do not find female-disparaging humor funny (Chapman & Gadfield, 1976; Love & Deckers, 1989; Priest & Wilhelm, 1974), others have demonstrated that women report enjoying humor that disparages females as much as do males (Brodzinsky, Barnet, & Aiello, 1981; Cantor, 1976; Carroll, 1989; Losco & Epstein, 1975; McGhee & Duffy, 1983).

Individual differences in gender attitudes rather than group membership per se may better explain these results (Henkin & Fish, 1986; Moore, Griffiths, & Payne, 1987; Zillman, 1983). Specifically, individuals holding more sexist attitudes might enjoy sexist humor more than those holding less sexist views. Indeed, using the Attitudes toward Women Scale (AWS), Moore, Griffiths, and Payne (1987) found that more liberal people of both sexes found sexist humor less funny than those holding more traditional views of women's roles. It is worth noting, however, that both sexist and liberal subjects perceived sexist jokes as more humorous than nonsexist jokes (Moore, Griffiths, & Payne, 1987). Similar results using the AWS were obtained by Henkin and Fish (1986). Participants with more liberal scores rated cartoons that disparaged women as less amusing than did participants with more traditional attitudes. Furthermore, the more liberal the subject's AWS score, the lower the humor ratings of all sexist cartoons, irrespective of gender of cartoon victim or aggressor.

Another aspect of gender attitudes is the degree to which women identify with their own group. Women who are highly identified with women report feeling that they have much in common with women and feel that what happens to women in general affects them personally (Gurin & Marcus, 1989). Although dispositional theory predicts that women who are strongly identified with women as a group should find sexist humor less funny and enjoyable than women who are weakly identified (Zillman, 1983), no research has yet tested this idea. Furthermore, strong identification could plausibly "protect" women against the pernicious effects of exposure to sexist humor. Swim (1997) found that after exposure to sexist remarks, women who considered themselves activists (i.e., strongly identified) evidenced higher self esteem than nonactivists (i.e., weakly identified). This is attributed to activists being more likely to label remarks as sexist, thereby refusing to internalize the negative messages conveyed by the sexist remark.

In sum, various studies indicate how women regard sexist humor. The present investigation aims to extend this research in a number of ways. Specifically, the questions concern how sexist humor affects women besides measuring how funny they find it. In addition, we are interested in whether several aspects of gender attitudes affect these various responses.

NEW CONCEPTIONS AND MEASUREMENTS OF SEXISM

Research investigating how gender attitudes affect responses to sexist humor has drawn heavily on scales such as the Attitudes toward Women Scale (Spence & Helmrich, 1972) and the Sexist Attitudes toward Women Scale (Benson & Vincent, 1980). Although results have shown that greater sexism leads to greater enjoyment of sexist jokes, some concerns about the measurement of gender attitudes have been voiced of late. For example, some argue that the scales are beginning to show ceiling effects (Spence & Hahn, 1997), perhaps due to the transparency of some of the scale items (e.g., Men will always be the dominant sex; The intellectual leadership of a community should be largely in the hands of men.). In short, normative pressures may now be impeding subjects' endorsement of blatantly sexist remarks (Barker, 1994).

Secondly, current gender attitudes appear to be more complex than that captured by existing unidimensional measures (Glick & Fiske, 1996; Swim, Aikin, Hall, & Hunter, 1995; Tougas, Brown, Beaton, & Joly, 1995). For example, Glick and Fiske's (1996) Ambivalent Sexism Inventory (ASI) assesses both hostile sexism and benevolent sexism. Hostile sexism (HS) is argued to be rooted in antipathy toward females and expresses negative attitudes toward women. Examples of statements that measure HS are: "Women are too easily offended," and "Women exaggerate problem they have at work." Benevolent sexism (BS), on the other hand, is characterized by viewing women in an idealized, yet stereotypically dependent, manner. Example of items that measure BS are: "Every man ought to have a woman whom he adores," and "Women, as compared to men, tend to have a more refined sense of culture and good taste." Although benevolent sexism may appear benign, it is also considered sexist because it is based on the notions of masculine dominance and conventional stereotypes (Glick & Fiske, 1996).

Fiske and Glick (1995) have proposed that benevolent sexism and hostile sexism derive from different motivations and lead to different outcomes. For example, according to Fiske and Glick, sexual harassment motivated by hostility is rooted in dominance of the target, while sexual harassment motivated by benevolence expresses as its primary motive a desire for heterosexual intimacy. In addition, they describe subtypes of ambivalent harassment based on the degree to which hostile and benevolent motives are realized (either covertly or overtly) by the harasser. For example, in one subtype, a harasser may honestly believe that his motives for continually pursing an employee are benevolent (e.g., he desires her and wants to become intimate with her), but his persistence in spite of her refusal is based on his superior job status. Ambivalent harassment is viewed as especially dangerous in that the harasser can justify his actions as harmless. For example, what appears to be harassing is only wanting to protect a woman.

One might expect that people scoring high on hostile sexism would find sexist jokes to be more amusing than respondents scoring low on this scale and hostile sexism is likely to be a better predictor of how funny these jokes are found to be than is benevolent sexism. It is also likely that emotional reactions such as anger or fear might be differentially related to HS and BS. Women who score high on hostile sexism may express fewer negative emotions and more positive emotions to sexist jokes than do women who score low on hostile sexism because sexist jokes reflect the antipathy toward females that they feel. But because benevolent sexism is rooted in the idealization and protection of women rather than in demeaning images of them, women scoring high on benevolent sexism might experience more distress upon hearing sexist jokes than do women scoring lower on benevolent sexism. Finally, those who show neither form of sexism might find sexist jokes offensive and react to them with annoyance.

WOMEN'S VERBAL AND NONVERBAL RESPONSES TO SEXIST HUMOR

Humor is typically assessed using one dimension (funniness) and one mode (self-report). Respondents usually rate how funny they find various stimuli (Brodzinsky, Barnet, & Aiello, 1981; Chapman & Gadfield, 1976; Hassett & Houlihan, 1979; Henkin & Fish, 1986; Love & Deckers, 1989; Neuliep, 1987; Priest & Wilhelm, 1974; Prerost, 1995). More rarely, subjects indicate how much they like or dislike the humorous stimuli (Chapman & Gadfield, 1976; Groch, 1974; Young & Frye, 1966).

To the degree that sexist humor is disparaging to women, then women are likely to respond in more complex ways than simply finding it to be funny or not. Other psychological reactions, including changes in affect, mood, and self-esteem, may also be present. Consequently, in the present study, we assessed several reactions to each of the jokes immediately after they were heard (e.g, funniness, comfort, interest). In addition we measured mood and self esteem after being exposed to a entire set of jokes.

We also wanted to capture nonverbal reactions. We are aware of only one empirical study that assessed nonverbal behavior to humorous stimuli. Brodzinsly, Barnet, and Aiello (1981) coded whether participants showed a (1) a blank expression (2) a slight smile (3) a full smile, or (4) chucking or laughter in response to disparaging humor. But expressive behavior is not limited to noting whether someone smiles or laughs in response to a joke. In fact, as one of us noted elsewhere, facial expression may be a particularly apt modality for coding emotional reactions to humor because of the fine distinctions that can be made among various emotions and among various kinds of smiling (LaFrance, 1983).

Ekman and his colleagues were among the first to describe types of smiles based on which facial muscles are involved, the intensity with which these action units are manifest, the degree to which the action appears on one or both sides of the face, and various aspects of timing (Ekman, 1985; Ekman & Friesen, 1982). A key distinction for the purposes of the present study is the distinction between the Duchenne smile and the non-Duchenne smile. The Duchenne smile, which is marked by changes in both the mouth and eye regions, has been reliably related to subjectively experienced positive affect. The non-Duchenne smile, which consists of only changes in the mouth region, differs from the Duchenne smile in that it has not been consistently associated with positive affect (Ekman, Friesen, & Ancoli, 1982). But other facial actions associated with anger, contempt, and sadness may also convey something about the impact of sexist jokes. Thus the present study examined participants' facial expressions using the Facial Action Coding System (FACS; Ekman & Friesen, 1978).

METHOD

Participants

Sixty females (ages 16–59; mean age = 26.7 years) volunteered to participate, the majority of whom were European American (80%). Participants were entered into a $100 lottery from which one person was chosen as a winner.

Materials and Measures

Participants were randomly assigned to a condition in which they heard either sexist jokes or attorney jokes. The seven sexist jokes were selected from the

"Party Jokes" section of *Playboy* magazine; the seven attorney (nonsexist) jokes were taken from an electronic bulletin board. The attorney jokes were included in order to determine which responses were unique to the particular type of presented humor. It was also expected that sexism scores would predict women's reactions to sexist jokes, but not to nonsexist jokes. Jokes were selected on the basis of pretesting which showed them to be equally funny (for details on the joke selection process, see Woodzicka, 1994). All jokes were communicated by the same male speaker and were delivered via cassette audiotape.

Glick and Fiske's Ambivalent Sexism Inventory (ASI; 1996) was used to measure sexist attitudes of participants. The ASI consists of 22 statements to which respondents indicate their agreement on a 6-point scale ranging from 0 (disagree strongly) to 5 (agree strongly).

To measure identification with women as a group, three items posited by Gurin and Markus (1989) were included in the study. The three items were: "How often do you think about being a woman and what do you have in common with women and men?" " How much do you have in common with most women?" and "To what extent will what happens to women generally in this country affect what happens in your life?" These items were rated on a 4-point Likert scale, ranging from 1 (a lot) to 4 (hardly at all).

Watson, Clark, and Tellegen's (1988) Positive and Negative Affect Schedule (PANAS) Brief Form was used to measure the participants' affect after listening to all seven jokes. Participants are asked to rate the congruency of their present emotions with 10 high-arousal positive affective words (e.g., active, enthusiastic) and 10 high-arousal negative affective words (e.g., upset, hostile) on a 5-point Likert scale ranging from 1 (very slightly) to 5 (extremely). Interest in several other emotions prompted the addition of the following six affective words to the PANAS list: *angry, amused, sad, happy, disgusted,* and *surprised.*

Heatherton and Polivy's (1991) State Self-Esteem Scale (SSES) was used to measure state self-esteem. The scale consists of 20 items that are scored on a 5-point scale ranging from 1 (not at all) to 5 (extremely). The SSES has three correlated factors: performance (e.g., "I feel confident about my abilities."), social (e.g., "I feel that others respect and admire me."), and appearance (e.g., "I feel satisfied with the way my body looks right now.") self-esteem and is purportedly sensitive to manipulations designed to temporarily alter self-esteem. In addition, three items from Luhtanen and Crocker's (1992) Collective Self Esteem Scale were added to the end of the SSES. These items (e.g., "In general, I'm glad to be a woman.") were included to measure self-esteem associated with being a woman.

Procedure

The procedure consisted of two phases designed deliberately to separate the assessment of gender attitudes from the measurement of reactions to humorous stimuli. Participants were told that an undergraduate researcher was desperately trying to recruit subjects to complete a 5- to 10-minute questionnaire exploring relationships between men and women and they were asked if they would be willing to do that first. All participants agreed to complete this questionnaire. They were then introduced to the undergraduate researcher and taken to a separate room to complete the sexism and identification scales.

After completing these measures, participants were then escorted back to the original experimenter who took them to another room where they were seated in front of a computer behind which a small hidden camera was mounted. The experimenter then gave the participants instructions and left the room. Participants were randomly assigned to listen to an audiotape of either seven jokes that disparaged women (sexist) or attorneys (nonsexist). Following the audiotape delivery of each joke, participants immediately used the mouse to click on chosen ratings of joke *funniness, amusement, comfort,* and *interest.* Ratings were made on 7-point scales ranging from 1 (not at all) to 7 (extremely). After listening to the entire group of seven jokes, participants completed the mood and self-esteem measures.

Following these measures, participants in the sexist joke condition were informally interviewed by the experimenter. They were asked if they felt the jokes they heard would be considered appropriate in several settings including school, work, in a social setting among strangers, and in a social setting with friends. Lastly, they were asked if the jokes were sexually harassing and, if they answered in the affirmative, the conditions under which the sexist jokes could be considered a form of sexual harassment were elicited.

During debriefing, all participants were told that the "study of relationships between men and women" and the "joke study" were two parts of the same experiment. Furthermore, participants were informed that they were being videotaped while listening to the jokes and that their tape would be destroyed immediately if they objected to being videotaped. None of the participants in either condition objected.

Coding of Facial Expression

Two coders certified in Ekman and Friesen's (1978) Facial Action Coding System (FACS) coded participant's facial expressions for a total of 7 seconds, beginning one second prior to the end of the tape of each joke. This period was chosen to capture most if not all facial expressions associated with a particular joke. All FACS Action Units (AU's) were coded for frequency, duration, onset, and offset. In addition, coders noted eye rolls, head shakes, talking, and instances when the hand was brought up to cover the mouth after a joke. To assess inter-rater reliability, 25% of the same participants were coded. Inter-rater reliability of $r = .79$ was acceptable for this type of coding (Ekman & Friesen, 1978).

RESULTS

Overview

We were primarily concerned with two questions. The first had to do with exploring how sexist jokes affect women. We wanted to find out whether women find sexist jokes less funny than other kinds of jokes. But we also wanted to see whether sexist jokes elicit affective reactions besides amusement. To this end we draw on data from both self-report responses as well as from analysis of facial displays.

The second question explored whether individual differences differentially predicted these various reactions. One measure was the Ambivalent Sexism Inventory (Glick & Fiske, 1995), chosen because of its dual structure, namely the separate assessment of hostile sexism and benevolent sexism. Specifically, we believed that hostile sexists would find sexist jokes funnier and would show less negative affect than benevolent sexists. A second measure assessed the degree to which women identified with women as a group (Gurin & Markus, 1989). Because the sexist jokes disparage a group to which highly identified women feel they strongly belong, it was predicted that highly identified women would respond with more disgust and anger at being the target of jokes that stereotype women than those who were less female-identified.

In what follows, we present results first having to do with how women responded verbally and nonverbally to sexist as opposed to nonsexist jokes. Following that, we take up the second question and report data bearing on how individual differences predicted these various responses. When reporting significance tests, effect size r's will follow the particular test unless otherwise stated (e.g., F (1,28) = 6.20, $p < .05$, $r = .42$)

REACTIONS TO DIFFERENT KINDS OF JOKES

Comparison of Reactions to Joke Types

Verbal Reactions to Sexist Jokes

Although pretesting had indicated that sexist and attorney jokes were perceived to be equally funny, participants in the present study did not find them comparable. Thus, significant results based on differences in joke type should be viewed as tentative since the unequal funniness ratings may have had an effect on mood and self-esteem ratings. Separate scores for funniness and amusement as well as comfort and interest were created by combining ratings for each measure across the seven jokes for each individual. Results showed that respondents rated the sexist jokes significantly less funny than the nonsexist (attorney) jokes (F (1, 58) = 8.71, $p < .005$, $r = .36$) and less amusing ($F(1, 58) = 9.28$, $p < .005$, $r = .37$). Although ratings of comfort and interest did not differ significantly between those hearing sexist and nonsexist jokes, the means suggested that respondents were less comfortable and less interested in the sexist than in the nonsexist jokes. Table 3.1 provides means and standard deviations for the ratings to both sexist and nonsexist jokes immediately following each one.

Although type of joke did not affect total positive or total negative mood as indicated by composite PANAS scores, joke type did influence participant's ratings of several of the emotion words. Specifically, women hearing sexist jokes

TABLE 3.1   Mean Funniness, Amusement, Comfort, and Interest Ratings for Women Hearing
Sexist and Nonsexist Jokes

	Sexist		Nonsexist	
	M	*SD*	*M*	*SD*
Funniness*	2.10	.80	2.88	1.20
Amusement*	2.10	.89	2.93	1.20
Comfort	4.52	1.40	4.97	1.35
Interest	2.83	1.27	3.36	1.41

Note. Ratings were made on a 7-point scale ranging from 1 (*not at all funny*) to 7 (*extremely funny*). Ratings were aggregated across all seven jokes.
   *$p < .01$.

reported feeling more disgusted, $F (1, 58) = 17.54$, $p < .001$, $r = .48$; angry, F
$(1, 58) = 12.97$, $p < .001$, $r = .42$; hostile, $F (1, 58) = 8.09$, $p < .01$, $r .35$;
determined, $F (1, 58) = 4.06$, $p < .05$, $r = .25$; and surprised, $F (1, 58) = 3.79$, $p < .06$, $r = .25$, than did women hearing nonsexist jokes. Table 3.2 lists the mean
ratings of significant PANAS items and added mood items for women hearing
sexist and nonsexist jokes. Further, women hearing sexist jokes did not indicate
lower self-esteem on any of the subcomponents of the State Self-Esteem Scale or
on the three items for the Collective Self-Esteem Scale.

TABLE 3.2   Mean Ratings of PANAS and Additional Mood Items for Women Hearing Sexist
and Nonsexist Jokes

	Sexist		Nonsexist	
	M	*SD*	*M*	*SD*
PANAS items				
Hostile**	1.40	.77	1.00	0
Determined*	2.70	1.39	2.03	1.16
Total positive affect	24.50	8.01	23.43	7.00
Total negative affect	12.67	4.29	11.69	2.42
Additional items				
Disgusted***	2.27	1.36	1.17	.46
Angry***	1.90	1.24	1.07	.25
Surprised*	2.20	1.32	1.63	.89

Notes. Ratings were made on a 5-point scale ranging from 1 (*very slightly or not at all*) to 5 (*extremely*).
   ***$p<.001$.
    **$p<.01$.
     *$p<.06$.

TABLE 3.3   Occurrences of Facial Action Units (AUs) for Women Hearing Sexist and Nonsexist Jokes

Action unit (AU)	Percentage of women displaying AU		Mean total duration for all 7 jokes* (seconds)			
	Sexist	Attorney	Sexist		Attorney	
			M	SD	M	SD
6+12 (Duchenne smiles)	53	53	7.96	5.28	11.93	6.19
12 (Non-Duchenne smiles)	77	83	7.20	6.07	6.26	5.85
Unilateral 12	30	47	2.55	3.26	2.66	2.81
14 (Dimpler)	27	20	5.06	2.71	2.59	3.29
Unilateral 14	17	20	2.39	2.74	1.48	.56
24 (lip press)	43	50	3.21	1.97	3.45	2.65
10 (Upper lip raise)	27	23	3.00	2.58	5.64	7.50
15 (Lip corner depress)	30	10	3.67	4.75	4.68	4.80
1+2 (Brow raise)	37	33	4.27	4.76	2.15	1.48
28 (Lip suck)	20	10	2.08	1.39	.77	.51
4 (Brow lower)	67	50	4.86	7.02	3.62	3.32
Head shake	27	13				
Eye roll	30	3				
Hand to face	17	3				
Talks	13	3				

*Note: Mean total duration out of a possible 49-second total duration.

Nonverbal Responses to Sexist Jokes

Affective reactions were also assessed by noting changes in facial expressions during the time participants listened to either the sexist or nonsexist jokes. Table 3.3 provides a breakdown of the facial action units (AUs) shown in both conditions. Analyses are based on computing separate z scores for frequency and duration for each AU and then summing the two z scores for each participant. Thus, for each participant a z score for each facial AU was computed. This combined z score represented standardized frequency and duration of the given expression.

One might expect jokes to elicit some amount of smiling but as noted previously, smiling is not a unitary behavior. Specifically, smiles that indicate the presence of positive emotion look differently from smiles that do not. The first category, Duchenne smiles, involve two facial actions (AUs): AU 12, which results when the lip corners being are pulled up and back and AU 6, which raises the cheeks causing wrinkles to form at the outer corners of the eyes. Non-Duchenne smiles, on the other hand, only involve AU 12 and show no particular relationship to positive feelings (Ekman, Friesen, & Ancoli, 1980).

Given that women rated sexist jokes as less funny and less amusing, one might have expected that they would also display fewer Duchenne smiles than did women hearing nonsexist jokes. Such was not the case. Joke type did not influence amount of Duchenne smiling, $F (1, 58) = 1.33, p > .2$. In other words, both joke categories elicited the same amounts of the smile most strongly associated with positive affect. This raises the possibility that hearers of the sexist jokes may have found them somewhat funny even though they rated them on self-report scales as less amusing.

Smiling was not the only facial reaction to hearing jokes. Women were found to roll their eyes significantly more in response to sexist jokes than to nonsexist jokes $(F (1, 58) = 6.93, p < .05, r = .32)$. Eye rolling has been associated with feelings of contempt (Rosenberg & Ekman, 1995). Women hearing sexist jokes also displayed a gesture associated with feelings of embarrassment (Edelmann & Hampson, 1979; Keltner, 1995). Specifically, they covered their mouths with their hands more than those exposed to nonsexist jokes, although this latter effect was only marginally significant $(F (1, 58) = 3.01, p < .09, r = .22)$. In sum, sexist jokes are not merely occasions for mirth. Facial actions indicate some amusement, but other actions signal also signal the possibility of embarrassment and contempt.

Individual Differences and Responses to Sexist Jokes

To this point, we have been discussing reactions to sexist jokes as though all the women exposed to them responded in comparable fashion. But we know, of course, that women exposed to the sexist jokes do not respond as one. We turn now to a discussion of whether individual differences in gender attitudes differentially affected respondents' verbal and nonverbal responses. The thought was that individual differences in amount and type of sexism measured by the Ambivalent Sexism Inventory (ASI) would influence women's reactions to sexist jokes, as would degree of identification with women.

Ambivalent Sexism Inventory and Verbal and Nonverbal Responses

In developing their ASI scale, Glick and Fiske (1996, 1997) presented data showing that hostile sexism and benevolent sexism have different correlates: Hostile sexism correlates with negative attitudes toward women and benevolent sexism correlates with positive attitudes toward and positive stereotypes about women, although there is some indication among women that benevolent sexism is also correlated with negative views of women. In the present study, hostile sexism and benevolent sexism also had different and theoretically meaningful correlates in addition to being uncorrelated with each other $(r = .054)$.

It is worth noting that ASI scores did not differ between those women who heard the sexist $(M = 34.10, SD = 12.27)$ and those who heard the nonsexist jokes $(M = 34.67, SD = 14.44)$. Secondly, we found that scores on hostile sexism and benevolent sexism predicted reactions to the sexist jokes only. Gender attitudes did not affect reactions to the nonsexist jokes. These findings clearly show that the individual differences in the ASI pertain only to situations in which gender is made salient and do not predict general humor responses.

In this section we present results pertaining to whether hostile sexism and benevolent sexism independently predict (a) immediately resported funniness and amusement ratings of the jokes; (b) subsequent mood ratings; and (c) facial signs of affect in response to hearing the jokes. Simple regressions confirmed our guess that hostile sexism was a better predictor of women's ratings of sexist jokes on funniness and amusement immediately after hearing each one. Hostile sexism scores predicted both funniness [$r = .59$; $b = .053$, $\beta = .588$, $F (1, 28) = 14.81$, $p < .001$] and amusement [$r = .57$; $b = .056$, $\beta = .569$, $F (1, 28) = 13.42, p < .001$]. In contrast, benevolent sexism scores, did not predict either funniness [$r = .04$; $b = -.004$, $\beta = -.039$, $F < 1$] or amusement [$r = .002$; $b < -.001$, $\beta = .-.002$, $F < 1$]. Hostile and benevolent sexism scores, along with the interaction between them (hostile × benevolent), were then entered into a multiple regression. As was the case with the simple regressions, hostile sexism, but not benevolent sexism nor the interaction term, significantly predicted ratings of both funniness [$sr = .58$; $b = .053$, $\beta = .592$, $t (26) = 3.74$, $p < .001$] and amusement [$sr = .56$; $b = .057$, $\beta = .572$, $t (26) = 3.54$, $p < .005$].[3] In short, HS alone was associated with being more amused by sexist jokes.

Hostile sexism scores did not significantly predict total negative or positive affect as measured by the PANAS. Benevolent sexism and the interaction with HS also did not predict mood as measured by the PANAS. However, scores on the hostile sexism scale predicted participants' subsequent feelings of amusement [$r = .51$; $b = .069$, $\beta = .506$, $F (1, 28) = 9.64$, $p < .005$] and activity [$r = .36$; $b = .045$, $\beta = .36$, $F (1, 28) = 4.18, p < .06$].

Finally, hostile sexism and benevolent sexism independently predicted facial expressions in response to hearing sexist jokes. Results showed that hostile sexism was uniquely associated with the display of genuine smiling. Simple regressions revealed that hostile sexism scores significantly predicted amount of Duchenne smiling (AU 6 +12), $r = .56$; $b = .124$, $\beta = .564$, $F (1, 28) = 13.07, p < .01$, while benevolent sexism scores did not predict amount of Duchenne smiling, $r = .26$; $b = .064$, $\beta = .263$, $F (1, 28) = 2.08, p > .1$. A multiple regression showed the same pattern with hostile sexism scores, but not benevolent scores or the interaction between them, once again significantly predicting amount of Duchenne smiling, $sr = .55$; $b = .119$, $\beta = .541$, $t (26) = 3.56$, $p < .01$. Non-Duchenne smiles (AU 12) were not predicted by hostile [$sr = .29$; $b = .067$ $\beta = .311$, $t (26) = 1.71$, $p > .1$], benevolent [$sr = -.19$; $b = -.054$, $\beta = -.227$, $t (26) = 1.15$, $p > .2$], or hostile × benevolent scores [$sr = .09$; $b < .001$, $\beta = -.006$, $t (26) = .032, p > .9$]. In sum, women scoring higher on HS displayed genuine positive affect while those scoring high on benevolent sexism did not.

---

[3]Semi-partial correlations (sr) were computed to find the unique contributions of hostile and benevolent sexism in predicting the dependent variables.

Scores on benevolent sexism, however, predicted a negative facial expression. Benevolent sexism scores, in contrast to hostile sexism scores, predicted an expression that has been associated with feelings of disgust (Rozin, Lowery, & Ebert, 1994). The action unit in question is AU 10 and involves raising of the upper lip. Simple regressions revealed that the benevolent sexism scale predicted AU 10, $[r = .50; b = .12, \beta = .503, F (1, 28) = 9.50, p < .005]$ while the hostile sexist scale did not $[r = .001; b < .001, \beta = -.001, F < 1]$. When both scales and the interaction (hostile × benevolent) were entered into a multiple regression, benevolent sexism was the only significant predictor of the occurrence of AU 10, $sr = .50; b = .129, \beta = .542; t (26) = 2.96, p < .01$. To sum up, hostile sexism alone predicts both self reports and nonverbal displays of enjoyment of sexist jokes for women respondents. Benevolent sexism, on the other hand, is associated more with the nonverbal display of disgust.

Identification with Women as a Predictor of Verbal and Nonverbal Responses

It was expected that women who rate themselves as strongly identified with women would respond differently to the sexist jokes than did women who rate themselves as weakly identified with women. Specifically, strongly identified women were expected to express less positive emotion and more negative emotion in response to sexist jokes than did weakly identified women.

A simple regression indicated that identification with women significantly predicted joke funniness ratings, $r = -.39; b = .-227, \beta = -.385, F (1,27) = 4.70, p < .05$, and amusement ratings, $r = -.39; b = -.255, \beta = -.390, F (1,27) = 4.83, p < .05$. As level of identification with women increased, ratings of joke funniness and amusement decreased. In addition, identification with women significantly predicted AU 15 (Lip Corner Depressing), $r = .39; b = .522, \beta = .387, F (1,27) = 4.75, p < .05$. As level of identification with women increased, this expression that has been associated with sadness also increased. A multiple regression was also performed on identification scores, hostile sexism scores, and benevolent sexism scores. Again, identification with women was a significant predictor of funniness, $sr = -.34; b = -.194, \beta = -.330 , t (25) = 2.287, p < .05$ amusement, $sr = .35; b = .221, \beta = .338, t (25) = 2.29, p < .05$, and frowning, $sr = .38; b = .522, \beta = .39, t (25) = 2.33, p < .05$.

DISCUSSION

This study clearly demonstrated that amusement is not the only or even the most significant reaction that women have to sexist jokes. In contrast to nonsexist jokes, women hearing sexist jokes reported feeling less amused and more disgusted. They also reported being more angry, hostile, determined, and surprised than women hearing nonsexist jokes. Their faces also told a story of some adverse effects. Women exposed to sexist jokes displayed more eye rolling (possibility of contempt) and touched their faces more often (possibility of embarrassment) than did women exposed to nonsexist jokes.

In addition, the picture of how women respond to sexist jokes became more refined when we looked at individual differences in preexisting gender attitudes. Specifically, scores on the hostile and benevolent scales of the Ambivalent Sexism Inventory predicted responses to the sexist jokes and did not predict responses to the nonsexist jokes. Thus, the present study clearly demonstrates that individual differences in gender attitudes measured by the ASI relate how these female respondents reacted both verbally and nonverbally to hearing the jokes.

Those women who scored higher on hostile sexism enjoyed the sexist jokes more than did those who scored lower on this scale. Inherent in hostile sexism is the exploitation of women as sexual objects and the portrayal of women as not very bright. Sexist jokes get their punch by drawing on these very issues and hence it makes eminently good sense why hostile sexists, even though they too are women, would enjoy this humor more than those who subscribe less to these beliefs. Of the seven sexist jokes used in the present study, five depicted women as sexual objects, one implied that women are intellectually inferior to men, and one described physical aggression toward women if they did not conform to societal gender roles. Because hostile beliefs are endorsed by the sexist jokes, it was expected that hostile sexism scores would predict more amusement to these jokes. In the present study, this was indeed the case.

In contrast, benevolent sexism relies on gentler justifications for male dominance. Benevolent sexism encompasses feelings of affection, idealization, and protection of women (Glick and Fiske, 1996). We expected that women high in benevolent sexism would have some negative emotional reaction to the sexist jokes because they would take offense at jokes that fail to idealize women. Indeed, the present study found that benevolent sexism scores specifically predicted disgust reactions (AU 10) to sexist jokes. Recently however, Glick and Fiske (1997) assert that the benevolent dimension may not have the same meaning for women as it does for men. Specifically, they argue that such idealization does not necessarily translate into benevolent motives for women since other women may be seen as competition for men's affection. Nonetheless, subscribing to benevolent sexism even by women indicates not hostility but belief in a kind of traditional gender specialness. Consequently, one would expect that benevolent sexist women would be somewhat repulsed by jokes that disparage women. This is what happened here: Women classified as benevolent sexists displayed more disgust reactions than did ambivalent, hostile, or nonsexist women.

Identification with women also proved to be a valuable predictor of women's responses to sexist humor. Women who were strongly identified with women report finding the jokes less funny, and that they felt less amused after hearing the jokes than did less identified women. Highly identified women's mouth frowning was congruent with their self-reporting of minimal amusement. As frowning is an ambiguous expression, it is difficult to know whether feelings of anger, sadness, or guilt were present while listening to the sexist jokes. However, the presence of frowning suggests the possibility that negative affect or heightened attention were the responses of these particular women.

In using both self-report and nonverbal measures, this study advanced understanding of how women are affected by sexist humor. The self-report data on funniness ratings are compatible with other studies showing that females find sexist humor at least somewhat problematic. The findings on mood intimate that more is going on than assessment of the jokes themselves. They leave an affective aftertaste. The nonverbal data add a much needed nonreactive measurement modality. Smiling patterns, eye rolling, and hand-to-mouth gestures provide information that is not redundant with that provided through self-report.

Although the sexist and attorney jokes were pretested to be comparable in funniness, the women participating in the present study did not rate them equally. The sexist jokes were rated as less funny than the nonsexist jokes. This difference could be attributed to different ages of pretest and actual participants, although other reasons are possible. The mean age of participants in the present study was about 27 years, while that for the pretest sample was about 20 years. Analyses done on the current data set revealed that as participants' age increased, funniness ratings of the sexist jokes decreased. This was not the case for participants hearing the attorney jokes. Thus, differential ratings by older participants (as compared to those participating in pretesting) may have contributed to the unequal funniness ratings for the sexist and nonsexist jokes.

The nonequivalence of funniness ratings for participants hearing the two types of jokes makes the comparisons based on joke type somewhat guarded. Knowing that the sexist jokes were rated as less funny, care must be taken in interpreting the self-report comparisons of the sexist and attorney jokes. Consequently, perceived funniness of the jokes could be partly responsible for differences in self-reported affect. For this reason, results based on joke-type should be interpreted tentatively and focus should be placed on within joke type results (e.g., the relationship of the ASI and sexist jokes).

Scores on the ASI indicate that women vary in their levels of sexism directed toward women. Consequently, verbal and nonverbal affective responses among women after hearing sexist jokes appear to be closely aligned with their gender attitudes. For women endorsing hostile attitudes toward women, sexist jokes may not be perceived as a form of subtle sexism. However, women endorsing nonsexist or benevolent gender attitudes appear to be especially vulnerable to jokes that disparage women. For these subgroups of women, exposure to the gender prejudice inherent in sexist joking is associated with marked negative affective reactions.

CONCLUSIONS

In summary, this study explored women's reactions to sexist jokes and demonstrated that women respond to such jokes in complex and significant ways. Although sexist jokes demean women, many assert that such jokes are harmless.

The present study contradicts this notion by demonstrating that women are negatively affected by sexist jokes. The current study supports the idea that sexist joking creates a hostile working environment and, in light of the negative impact such jokes have on women, should be viewed as a form of gender harassment. If the occurrence and acceptance of sexist jokes is to be reduced, it is vital that society recognize sexist humor as a form of subtle prejudice toward women. Sexist messages should not be interpreted as innocuous simply because they are couched in humor. To the extent that sexist messages veiled in humor can and do negatively affect women, sexist humor is no laughing matter.

REFERENCES

Baker, D. D., Terpstra, D. E., & Larntz, K. (1990). The influence of individual characteristics and severity of harassing behavior on reactions to sexual harassment. *Sex Roles, 22 (5/6)*, 305–325.

Barker, K. (1994). To be PC or not to be? A social psychological inquiry into political correctness. *Journal of Social Behavior and Personality, 9 (1)*, 271–281.

Benson, P. L., & Vincent, S. (1980). Development and validation of the Sexist Attitudes Toward Women Scale. *Psychology of Women Quarterly, 5 (2)*, 276–291.

Bill, B., & Naus, P. (1992). The role of humor in the interpretation of sexist incidents. *Sex Roles, 27, 11/12*, 645–664.

Brodzinsky, D. M., Barnet, K., & Aiello, J. R. (1981). Sex of subject and gender identity as factors in humor appreciation. *Sex Roles, 7*, 561–573.

Cantor, J. R. (1976). What is funny to whom? The role of gender. *Journal of Communication, 26*, 164–176.

Cantor, J. R., & Zillman, D. (1973). Resentment toward victimized protagonists and severity of misfortunes they suffer as factors in humor appreciation. *Journal of Experimental Research in Personality, 6*, 321–329.

Carroll, J. L. (1989). Changes in humor appreciation of college students in the last twenty-five years. *Psychological Reports, 65*, 863–866.

Chapman, A. J., & Gadfield, N. J. (1976). Is sexual humor sexist? *Journal of Communication, 26*, 141–153.

Crawford, M. E. (1995). *Talking difference: On gender and language*. London: Sage.

Edelmann, R. J., & Hampson, S. E. (1979). Changes in non-verbal behavior during embarrassment. *British Journal of Social and Clinical Psychology, 18*, 385–390.

Ekman, P. (1985). *Telling lies: Clues to deceit in the marketplace, politics and marriage*. New York: W.W. Norton & Company.

Ekman, P., & Friesen, W. V. (1978). *Facial action coding system: A technique for the measurement of facial movement*. Palo Alto, CA: Consulting Psychologists Press.

Ekman, P., & Friesen, W.V. (1982). Felt, false and miserable smiles. *Journal of Nonverbal Behavior, 6*, 238–252.

Ekman, P., Friesen, W. V., and Ancoli, S. (1980). Facial signs of emotional experience. *Journal of Personality and Social Psychology, 39*, 1125–1134.

Fiske, S. T., & Glick, P. (1995). Ambivalence and stereotypes cause sexual harassment: A theory with implications for organizational change. *Journal of Social Issues, 51 (1)*, 97–115.

Fitzgerald, L. F., Swan, S., & Fischer, K. (1995). Why didn't she just report him? The psychological and legal implications of women's responses to sexual harassment. *Journal of Social Issues, 51 (1)*, 117–137.

Frazier, P. A., Cochran, C. C., and Olson, A. M. (1995). Social science research on lay definitions of sexual harassment. *Journal of Social Issues, 51 (1)*, 21–37.

Freud, S. (1928). Humour. *International Journal of Psychoanalysis, 9,* 1–6.

Glick, P., & Fiske, S. T. (1996). The ambivalent sexism inventory: Differentiating hostile and benevolent sexism. *Journal of Personality and Social Psychology, 70 (3),* 491–512.

Glick, P., & Fiske, S. T. (1997). Hostile and benevolent sexism: Measuring ambivalent sexist attitudes toward women. *Psychology of Women Quarterly, 21,* 119–135.

Groch, A. S. (1974). Generality of response to humor and wit in cartoons, jokes, stories, and photographs. *Psychological Reports, 35,* 835–838.

Gruber, J. E., & Bjorn, L. (1986). Women's responses to sexual harassment: An analysis of sociocultural, organizational, and personal resource models. *Social Science Quarterly, 67 (4),* 814–826.

Gurin, P., & Markus, H. (1989). Cognitive consequences of gender identity. In S. Skevington & D. Baker (Eds.), *The social identity of women* (pp.152–172). London: Sage.

Gutek, B. A., & Koss, M. P. (1993). Changed women and changed organizations: Consequences of and coping with sexual harassment. *Journal of Vocational Behavior, 42,* 28–48.

Hassett, J., & Houlihan, J. (1979). Different jokes for different folks. *Psychology Today, 12,* 64–71.

Heatherton, T. F., & Polivy, J. (1991). Development and validation of a scale for measuring state self-esteem. *Journal of Personality and Social Psychology, 60 (6),* 895–910.

Hemmasi, M., Graf, L. A., & Russ, G. S. (1994). Gender-related jokes in the workplace: Sexual humor or sexual harassment? *Journal of Applied Social Psychology, 24,* 1114–1128.

Henkin, B., & Fish, J. M. (1986). Gender and personality differences in the appreciation of cartoon humor. *Journal of Psychology, 120 (2),* 157–175.

Jensen, I., & Gutek, B. A. (1982). Attributions and assignment of responsibility for sexual harassment. *Journal of Social Issues, 38,* 121–136.

Keltner, D. (1995). Signs of appeasement: Evidence for the distinct displays of embarrassment, amusement, and shame. *Journal of Personality and Social Psychology, 68 (3),* 441–454.

LaFrance, M. (1983). Felt versus feigned funniness: Issues in coding smiling and laughing. In P. McGhee & J. Goldstein (Eds.), *Handbook of humor research.* New York: Springer-Verlag.

Lewin, T. (1995, February 22). Chevron settles harassment charges. *New York Times,* p. 16.

Losco, J., & Epstein, S. (1975). Humor preferences as a subtle measure of attitudes towards the same and the opposite sex. *Journal of Personality, 43,* 321–334.

Love, A. M., & Deckers, L. H. (1989). Humor appreciation as a function of sexual, aggressive, and sexist content. *Sex Roles, 20 (11/12),* 649–654.

Luhtanen, R., & Crocker, J. (1992). A collective self-esteem scale. *Personality and Social Psychology Bulletin, 18,* 312–318.

McGhee, P. E. (1988). The contribution of humor to children's social development. *Journal of Children in Contemporary Society, 20 (1–2),* 119–134.

McGhee, P. E., & Duffy, N. S. (1983). The role of identity of the victim in the development of disparagement humor. *Journal of General Psychology, 108,* 257–270.

Meritor Savings Bank v. Vinson, 106 S. Ct. 2399 (1989).

Moore, T. E., Griffiths, K., & Payne, B. (1987). Gender, attitudes towards women, and the appreciation of sexist humor. *Sex Roles, 16 (9/10),* 521–531.

Neitz, M. J. (1980). Humor, hierarchy, and the changing status of women. *Psychiatry, 43,* 211–223.

Neuliep, J. W. (1987). Gender differences in the perception of sexual and nonsexual humor. *Journal of Social Behavior and Personality, 2 (3),* 345–351.

Prerost, F. J. (1995). The influences of sexual desire on the appreciation of sexist humor: Effects of mood state. *Psychology: A Journal of Human Behavior, 32 (1),* 11–15.

Priest, R. F., & Wilhelm, P. G. (1974). Sex, marital status, and self/actualization as factors in the appreciation of sexist jokes. *The Journal of Social Psychology, 92,* 245–249.

Rosenberg, E. L., & Ekman, P. (1995). Conceptual and methodological issues in the judgment of facial expressions of emotion. *Motivation and Emotion, 19 (2),* 111–138.

Rozin, P., Lowery, L., & Ebert, R. (1994). Varieties of disgust faces and the structure of disgust. *Journal of Personality and Social Psychology, 66 (5),* 870–881.

Smeltzer, L. R., & Leap, T. L. (1988). An analysis of individual reactions to potentially offensive jokes in work settings. *Human Relations, 41,* 295–304.

Spence, J. T., & Hahn, E. D. (1997). The attitudes toward women scale and attitude change in college students. *Psychology of Women Quarterly, 21 (1),* 17–34.

Spence, J. T., & Helmreich, R. (1972). The Attitudes Toward Women Scale: An objective instrument to measure attitudes toward the rights and roles of women in contemporary society. *JSAS Catalog of Selected Documents in Psychology, 2,* 1–66.

Swim, J. K., Aikin, K. J., Hall, W. S., & Hunter, B. A. (1995). Sexism and racism: Old-fashioned and modern prejudices. *Journal of Personality and Social Psychology, 68,* 199–214.

Swim, J. K., & Hyers, L. L. (1997). Excuse me—what did you say?!: Women's public and private reactions to sexist remarks. Manuscript under review.

Tougas, F., Brown, R., Beaton, A. M., & Joly, S. (1995). Neo-sexism: Plus ca change, plus c'est pariel. *Personality and Social Psychology Bulletin, 21,* 842–849.

Watson, D., Clark, L. A., & Tellegen, A. (1988). Development and validation of brief measures of positive and negative affect: The PANAS scales. *Journal of Personality and Social Psychology, 54 (6),* 1063–1070.

Woodzicka, J. A. (1994). *The effect of distraction on sexist humor elicitation: A test of a theory based on the elaboration likelihood model of persuasion.* Unpublished master's thesis, University of Dayton, Ohio.

Young, R. D., & Frye, M. (1966). Some are laughing; Some are not—Why? *Psychological Reports, 18,* 747–754.

Zillman, D. (1983). Disparagement humor. In P. E. McGhee & J. H. Goldstein (Eds.), *Handbook of humour research, vol. 1.* New York: Springer-Verlag.

Zillman, D., & Cantor, J. R. (1976). A dispositional theory of humor and mirth. In A. J. Chapman & H. C. Foot (Eds.), *Humor and laughter: theory, research and applications* (pp. 93–116). London: Wiley.

PART

II

CONSEQUENCES OF PREJUDICE

4

STEREOTYPE THREAT AND THE ACADEMIC UNDERPERFORMANCE OF MINORITIES AND WOMEN

JOSHUA ARONSON

University of Texas, Austin

DIANE M. QUINN

University of Michigan

STEVEN J. SPENCER

University of Waterloo

"Math is hard!"
—Talking Barbie Doll (eventually recalled by the manufacturer
due to complaints).

"When I talk in class, I feel as though I'm totally on stage, like
everyone's thinking, 'oh what's the black girl going to say?' I
pretty much never speak up in class though, so I guess it's not a
big problem."
—Stanford undergraduate

"Being held up as a role model, it's a big problem. People just
want you to succeed so bad . . . but it's just too much pressure
put on you."
—Latino undergraduate (cited in Seymour, 1996)

Shortly before his death, Arthur Ashe told a reporter that dying of AIDS was difficult, but in many ways not as difficult as living with the burden of being black in American society. Ashe was quick to point out that he was not merely referring

to the obvious fact that, as an African American, he was constantly being subjected to overt acts of prejudice, but, in addition, he was referring to the fact that
he was frequently viewed as a representative of his race—athletically and
politically—both on and off the tennis court. That is, as an African American,
Ashe was troubled by never being able to tell if he or his achievements could be
evaluated independent of his race. For the past few years, our research has focused
on what we believe to be an important case of this subtler sort of burden—borne
not only by African Americans, but by anyone who is the target of stereotypes
based on race, ethnicity, gender, or physical appearance. Much of this research
has been conducted under the rubric of a theory we call "stereotype threat,"
(Spencer, Steele, & Quinn, 1997; Steele, 1997; Steele & Aronson, 1995) and has
focused on the consequences for targets contending with negative stereotypes
about their intellectual abilities. The aim of this chapter is to describe this research, and in so doing, to suggest how taking the perspective of the target can
help to explain and to ameliorate the problem of low academic achievement
among certain minorities and women.

The academic underperformance of groups that face negative stereotypes about
their academic ability is well documented. Although the precise numbers vary
somewhat from source to source and from year to year, the general pattern of the
statistics regarding the academic achievement of these groups does not: women
underperform relative to men in math and the physical sciences while African
Americans and Latinos lag behind European Americans and Asian Americans in
every domain of academic achievement. For example, the gap between the
achievement of African American and European American children widens to as
much as two grade levels by the sixth grade and persists through high school
(Alexander & Entwistle, 1988; Burton & Jones, 1982; Gerard, 1983). This pattern,
which continues from elementary school through graduate school, is parallel for
Latino students (e.g., Miller, 1996; Romo & Falbo, 1995; Valencia, 1991; 1997).

While there have been some signs of improvement in recent years, these gains
may be more apparent than real. For example, the percentage of African American
students obtaining high school diplomas has risen to nearly that of European
American students (77% vs. 82%, respectively), but they appear to be graduating
with significantly lower GPAs and college entrance exam scores (Nettles, 1988;
Miller, 1996). Moreover, compared to their European American counterparts,
African American and Latino students who graduate from high school are much
less likely to apply to college and are far more likely to drop out after entering
(American Council on Education, 1995–1996; Hurtado et al., 1997). The picture
does not improve at the postgraduate level where women are notoriously under
represented in math and science programs, and African Americans and Latinos
are scarce in nearly all programs (e.g., Evangelauf, 1993).

The underperformance of women takes a slightly different pattern but is troubling nonetheless. From elementary school through middle school, boys and girls
score approximately equally on tests of math computation and problem-solving
(Hyde, Fennema, & Lamon, 1990). Yet, starting around the time of junior high

(in the age range of 13 to 15) and continuing and increasing through high school and college, women tend to underperform on mathematical problem-solving tests—particularly standardized tests of math ability (Armstrong, 1981; Hyde *et al.,* 1990).

Most commentators agree that statistics like these point to a crisis of great proportions, not only for members of underperforming groups, but for the nation as a whole (e.g., Fullilove & Treisman, 1990; Herrnstein & Murray, 1994). Precisely what causes underlie the underachievement of these groups is, on the other hand, a matter of dispute. Explanations have run the gamut, citing obstacles such as socioeconomic disadvantage (e.g., Bereiter & Engelman, 1966; White, 1982), cultural differences (e.g., Boykin, 1986; Ogbu, 1986), low teacher expectations (e.g., Feagin & Sikes, 1994; Sadker & Sadker, 1994), and genetic differences in intelligence (e.g., Benbow & Stanley, 1980; Hernstein & Murray, 1994; Jensen, 1969).

Our view is that these explanations hold more intuitive appeal than they offer in substantive explanation for these problems. Moreover, any explanation that attributes the underperformance of women or minorities solely to differences in skill or intelligence cannot sufficiently account for a very well-established fact: The gap in school achievement between minority students and European Americans is as wide for highly skilled and prepared students (as measured by standardized tests and earlier grades) as it is for those with low skills and preparation (Jensen, 1980), and for the most part, this holds for the gap that exists between men and women in mathematics (Strenta, Adair, Scott, & Matier, 1993). This means, for example, that an African American student with a given SAT score will earn lower grades in college than a European American student with the same score, even when the scores they share are extremely high, say, at the 98th percentile. Because the achievement of these students is lower at every level of skill and preparation, factors such as genetic differences and socioeconomic disadvantage cannot be the sole causes of their underachievement. Some other factor or factors must play a role.

The central thesis behind our research is that an important, but unappreciated factor in this underperformance is the psychological burden posed by stereotype-based suspicions of inferiority in achievement domains. We refer to this burden as stereotype threat. Stereotype threat, we argue, undermines academic achievement both by interfering with performance on mental tasks, and, over time, by prompting students to protect their self-esteem by disengaging from the threatened domain.

STEREOTYPE THREAT DEFINED

Stereotype threat can be thought of as the discomfort targets feel when they are at risk of fulfilling a negative stereotype about their group; the apprehension that they could behave in such a way as to confirm the stereotype—in the eyes of others, in their own eyes, or both at the same time. If the threat is strong enough, it can interfere with social interaction and intellectual performance. Consider the African American student trying to solve difficult items on a test, or a woman called upon in math class to answer a complex question. As for anyone, low performance in such situations brings with it the risk of discouragement or shame about not doing well. But members of stereotyped groups face an extra threat because of the long-standing and widely proliferated cultural stereotypes alleging a group-based limitation of ability. The mere existence of such stereotypes poses for targets the additional risk of being seen and treated stereotypically, of having their access to and belongingness in the domain limited by stereotype-driven perceptions and treatment—and of calling their own abilities into question. For those among the stereotyped group who are identified with the domain in which the stereotype applies, this threat can be upsetting. It threatens something that they care about and that is critical to their self-image. And, in situations where the stakes are high, it may cause enough distress to interfere with their performance and enjoyment of the activity. The experience of this threat over the long run, we propose, may cause a chronic disidentification with the domain, a dropping of the domain as a basis of self-esteem.

ELEMENTS OF THE
STEREOTYPE-THREAT MODEL

Although it is a new model, stereotype threat—and its role in the academic underachievement of women and minorities—is founded on three links between stereotypes and underachievement that are well established in social psychology.

First, we start with a simple assumption about the self-esteem threatening nature of negative stereotypes. It is based on one of the least controversial generalizations in social psychology—that most people like to think well of themselves and have others share that view. A host of self-esteem and self-presentational theories share this assumption, and a spate of research has shown what can occur when self-esteem or public image is threatened. In general, people become concerned, upset, agitated, and, as a result, motivated to compensate for the threat (e.g., Baumeister, 1982; Higgins, 1987; Jones & Pittman 1982; Steele, 1988; Swann, 1983). Various theorists have written about the role of stigma in creating interpersonal discomfort and psychological stress (Allport, 1954; Goffman, 1963; Jones, Farina, Hastorf, Markus, Miller, & Scott, 1981; Stangor & Sechrist, this volume), and some have drawn a link between this sort of anxiety and the low academic performance of African Americans (e.g., Howard & Hammond, 1985; S. Steele, 1990).

Stereotype threat has two points of departure from these other models. First, it is conceptualized primarily as a situational pressure rather than as something arising from acceptance of the stereotype. From our perspective, targets need not see the stereotype as valid in order to experience stereotype threat. Mere awareness of the stereotype and its alleged relevance to one's performance in a given situation is sufficient, we believe, to arouse the apprehension that disrupts performance and adds anxiety to intellectual pursuits. Second, if our reasoning is correct, stereotype threat is likely to have its strongest effects among those who are least likely to internalize or accept the stereotype—those who are heavily invested in the domain. Those who are most invested—most "identified"—are also most likely to be concerned about poor performance in the domain. Ironically, because people tend to identify with pursuits for which they have talent, this means that stereotype threat has the potential to be most acutely felt by the very members of the stereotyped group who are justified in having high hopes for achieving in a domain—the potential Arthur Ashe or Tiger Woods—who, in the case of school domains, we would expect to have the least reason to internalize stereotype-related doubts about their ability. This is not to say that the smarter one is, the more one will be vulnerable to stereotypes about lacking intelligence. Rather, what we are suggesting is that all other things being equal, the more a person cares about being good at something, the greater will be his or her distress about stereotypes alleging a lack of ability. More will be said about this later.

The second link between stereotypes and academic achievement is the well-documented performance-debilitating effect of not wanting to perform badly. Studies of "test-anxiety," for example, show how the fear of low performance can spoil performance on difficult cognitive tasks, either by simply diverting attention (e.g., Bond, 1982; Carver & Scheier, 1981; Sarason, 1972; Wine, 1971), or by prompting a self-protective withdrawal of effort (e.g., Hormuth, 1986; Geen, 1985). Indeed, as Pittner and Houston (1980) have demonstrated with studies examining people's responses to ego threat or threat of electric shock, threats to the self-concept (such as stereotype threat) can be every bit as debilitating to cognitive functioning as threats to physical well-being.

The final link is disidentification, the psychological disengagement from achievement that helps students cope with the persistence of stereotype threat in a domain. Disidentification can be said to occur when one defines or redefines the self-concept such that a threatened domain (be it academic, social, or moral) is not used as a basis of self-evaluation. William James (1890) was probably the first to describe this process as a method of maintaining self-esteem, but many researchers have provided evidence for his view that one sustains a positive self view either by triumphing in a given domain—if one can—or by divesting the self from the domain if success is elusive or the struggle to succeed is too unpleasant (e.g., Aronson, Blanton, & Cooper, 1995; Major & Schmader, 1997; Major, Spencer, Schmader, Wolfe, & Crocker, 1998; Pelham, 1995; Pelham & Swann, 1989; Steele, 1992, 1997). There is increasing evidence that ability-stigmatized groups, like African Americans, are more prone than their nonstigmatized counterparts to disidentify from academics (Major, 1995; Osbourne, 1995). Because identification with academics—the extent to which one is affected by one's outcomes in school—is assumed to be crucial for significant levels of achievement

(Steele, 1997), the protective disengagement from academics constitutes a serious barrier to the sustained motivation required for high achievement.

However, this concept of disidentification or disengagement should be distinguished from the similar concept of devaluing (see Major & Schmader, this volume). Devaluing, as Major and Schmader (1998) have conceptualized it, occurs when people no longer see a domain as important. While ability-stigmatized groups tend to be higher in disidentification—that is, they do not base their self-evaluation on their performance in a domain where they are stigmatized—they are not higher in devaluing. African Americans, for example, show more evidence of disidentification than their European American counterparts in that they are less likely to base their self-esteem on performance on intelligence tests, but they show less evidence of devaluing than their European American counterparts in that they are more likely to see good performance on these tests as important (Major, 1997; Stangor & Sechrist, 1998).

Theoretically, these three elements—the self-threatening nature of negative stereotypes, the effect of self-threat on intellectual performance, and the tendency to disidentify with chronically threatened domains—interact to undermine the performance and motivation of women and minorities.

SUPPORT FOR THE STEREOTYPE-THREAT MODEL

If it is the case that apprehension over confirming stereotypes causes stereotype targets to underperform, and, ultimately, to disidentify with academics, then it is reasonable to assume that reducing this apprehension should hold the key to improving their performance and sustaining their identification. This has been the overarching hypothesis of our research. Let us now turn to a fairly detailed description of research testing specific factors hypothesized to either increase or decrease stereotype threat.

TEST DIAGNOSTICITY

Perhaps most basic to the stereotype threat definition is the idea that low performance means something special for members of stereotyped groups. For them, not doing well can validate the stereotype about them. Thus, when members of a stereotyped group encounter frustration and difficulty with a test problem, they also must deal with the additional significance of their performance in relation to the stereotype. One way to examine whether it is the meaningfulness of the test—what it signifies about ability—that affects performance is to alter the perceived purpose of the test.

Quinn and Spencer (1996) manipulated the level of stereotype threat in a test-taking situation for women by altering the perceived diagnosticity of a math test. Explicitly describing a test as nondiagnostic of ability, it was hypothesized, would reduce stereotype threat by taking away the possibility of fulfilling the negative stereotype. That is, if women believe that the test cannot assess their mathematical ability, then a negative judgment of competency and a further fulfillment of the negative stereotype is not possible. Such nondiagnostic instructions, the reasoning went, should reduce the apprehension about performance on the test, and allow women to perform equally to men taking the same math test.

In order to test these hypotheses, men and women college students were brought into the lab to take a math test. In this case, the test was composed of word problems taken from Graduate Management Admissions Test (GMAT). All participants had equal math backgrounds as measured by their SAT scores and calculus grades. Half of the participants read the "diagnostic" instructions stating that the test they were about to take was specifically designed to assess people's mathematical abilities and limitations, and that the test had been shown to be an excellent indicator of mathematical aptitude. In the nondiagnostic instructions, participants read that the purpose of the test was to examine the way people solve problems and use problem-solving strategies, and that their particular scores on the test were not meaningful. Thus, for half of the participants, the situation of taking a math test was altered such that their ability could not be judged within the bounds of the negative stereotype.

The results showed that when participants believed the test to be diagnostic of their abilities, women underperformed in comparison to men. However, when participants believed the test to be nondiagnostic, men and women performed equally well on the test. In addition, women in the diagnostic condition performed significantly worse than all other groups. Thus, by simply changing the testing situation such that performance could not be stereotypically judged, women's and men's test performances were equalized.

Using similar methods Steele and Aronson (1995) examined the role of diagnosticity in mediating stereotype threat in African American students on a challenging test of verbal aptitude. Rather than varying the description of the test, the experimenters changed the purported aim of the study. Half of the African American and European American undergraduates taking the difficult version of the verbal GRE were told that the study was aimed at understanding verbal ability (diagnostic condition), whereas the other half were told that the purpose of the study was to better understand the psychology of problem solving (nondiagnostic condition). The results were identical to those in the Quinn and Spencer (1996) study: the African Americans performed just as well as the European Americans in the nondiagnostic condition, where stereotype threat was presumed to be eliminated, but their performance was significantly lower than all other groups in the diagnostic condition, where stereotype threat was made acute by the evaluative scrutiny implied by the description of the study. Aronson and Salinas (1997) have found parallel results with Latino college students taking a GRE verbal exam.

Each of these studies replicate the seminal work conducted by Irwin Katz and his associates more than three decades ago. In one study, Katz, Roberts, and Robinson (1965) found that African American children performed better on an IQ subtest when it was presented as a test of hand–eye coordination than when it was said to be a test of intelligence. Although these researchers had a very different view about the source of the children's apprehension (worry over the tester's anger should they exceed his low performance expectations), it is clear that, then as now, test diagnosticity is a powerful factor in evoking stereotype-related concerns, and as a result, undermining intellectual performance.

Of course, these studies by no means force the conclusion that performance is hampered by a concern with fulfilling a stereotype. Perhaps it is some other factor in the testing situation. That is, in the diagnostic/nondiagnostic studies, it may be that what we are altering is general test anxiety (which may certainly be a part of stereotype threat) that is unrelated to the stereotype itself. A variety of manipulations and measures have addressed the role played by the stereotype.

APPLICABILITY OF THE STEREOTYPE

In a subsequent study conducted by Spencer, Steele, and Quinn (1997) stereotype threat was reduced by taking the relevance of the stereotype out of the test taking situation—by portraying the test as one in which gender differences do not occur.

Again, equally prepared men and women were brought into the lab to take a difficult math test. Half of the participants were told that the test they were about to take had shown gender differences in the past. The rest of the participants were told that the test had never shown gender differences in the past. Thus, this study examined the effects of making the stereotype applicable or inapplicable to the participants. That is, for the participants who were told the test had never shown gender differences, when they experienced difficulty with the test, the stereotype should no longer be relevant to interpreting their difficulty with the test or their performance. It is no longer a stereotype-threatening situation. However, for those women taking a test purportedly known to show gender differences, underperformance would have a distinct meaning—that the stereotype regarding gender differences in ability was relevant to, and therefore confirmable by, their performance. Results of this study followed the predictions. When the stereotype was not applicable, in the "no-gender-differences condition," women and men did equally well on the test. However, when the stereotype was made applicable, in the "gender-differences condition," women significantly underperformed in comparison to men. Thus, this study directly tested and supported the premise that it is the threatening implications of the stereotype that interfere with performance in the testing situation.

In a similar vein, Aronson and Salinas (1997) induced stereotype threat in Latino undergraduates taking a difficult GRE verbal test by merely raising the issue of test bias. Latino and European American (male and female) undergraduates took a 30-minute test that was divided in half. After completing the first half of the test, participants filled out a brief questionnaire pertaining to their experience with the test items. Half the participants received questionnaires containing an extra question: "Tests of this sort are sometimes considered to be biased against certain groups of people (e.g., women, minorities). How biased do you think tests like this are?" After answering the question (a Likert-scale rating), participants moved on to the second half of the test. The results were dramatic. For the Latinos, those who received the question about test bias performed significantly worse on the second half of the test than those who did not. The bias question, on the other hand, had no effect on the performance of the European American students.

In a third study, Broadnax, Crocker, and Spencer (1997) told half of their European American and African American participants that a standardized English literature exam was a test on which African Americans and European Americans performed equally. To validate this claim several of the test items required knowledge of noted African American authors (e.g., James Baldwin, Ralph Ellison). The other half of the participants were given the standard directions for the test. The results suggested that removing the applicability of the stereotype—by saying that African Americans and European Americans performed equally—also removed the stereotype threat; African Americans in the "no-race-difference" condition performed just as well as their European American counterparts and significantly better than when they thought they were taking the standard version of the test.

Thus for African Americans, women, and Latinos, the implied unfairness of a test—whether it is capable of revealing ethnic or gender differences—seems to play a role in whether or not an evaluative task will be stereotype threatening and disrupt performance. Interestingly, exactly how the perception of fairness or bias translates into lower performance may be different for the different groups, a point that will be discussed shortly.

THE SITUATIONAL INDUCEMENT OF STEREOTYPE THREAT

We have elsewhere argued (Spencer *et al.,* 1997; Steele & Aronson, 1995) that because stereotype threat is a situational predicament, it can, in theory, befall the member of any group. So long as a person is identified with—that is, cares enough about—a domain to be bothered by a stereotype that alleges shortcomings in that domain, he or she is capable of experiencing the kind of performance decrement that we have been discussing. The fact that we have demonstrated this now with women, African Americans, and Latinos encourages this situationist view of minority underperformance. Still, one might argue, these are groups with a long-standing history with the stereotype, people who, because of their group membership, may have been nursing doubts about their abilities well before entering the stereotype-threatening situation. Thus, the argument would go, they have internalized the stereotype about their group's inferiority and our stereotype threat manipulations undermine their performance simply by bringing this deep-seated sense of inferiority to the surface.

Some recent evidence suggests, however, that although frequent exposure to and internalization of stereotypes about one's group may be sufficient to arouse stereotype threat, it is by no means necessary. Aronson, Lustina, Keough, Brown, and Steele (1997) tested this hypothesis by recruiting European American male college students who were highly proficient in and identified with math. Half of them were given a very challenging math test and told the purpose of the test was to gauge their math ability. The remaining males were given the same test and same rationale, but were given a further, stereotype-threatening, reason for the test: they were told that the purpose of the test was to better understand why Asian Americans so frequently outperformed European Americans on such tests. As in the studies involving African Americans, women, and Latinos, these stereotype-threatened participants performed significantly worse on the test.

This result suggests that what drives stereotype threat is a concern—at least a momentary one—about being limited. It is highly unlikely that these European American males spent many of their waking hours thinking themselves at risk of confirming the stereotype that "white men can't do math." The opposite is almost certainly true. But they were, for a moment, forced by the specter of the Asian stereotype to contend with the possibility that there were problems on the test they could not solve that perhaps the stereotypic Asian American student could, thus confirming for them and anyone else present their relative inferiority. It is this sense of limitation, of prospects potentially narrowed by either perceived or real shortcomings in a cherished domain, we believe, that makes contending with the stereotype upsetting and disruptive. But we think this apprehension is a *state,* not a trait.

Our research—the studies we have been discussing and the pilot testing conducted in conjunction with them—give us an indication of the type of situation likely to evoke this state. First, stereotype threat is likely to emerge when the test itself pushes ability to the limit. There are two reasons for this. First, the kind of disruption involved these studies (i.e., the effects of test anxiety or cognitive interference) tend mainly to get in the way of performance of very complex tasks. If the task is well within the bounds of a person's abilities, performance is unlikely to be hampered. Second, if an individual is doing well on a test, his or her performance should in itself discredit the stereotype and reduce stereotype threat. Spencer, Steele, and Quinn (1997) found evidence for this hypothesis manipulating the difficulty of a math test they gave to talented male and female undergraduates. When the test was difficult (the advanced GRE in mathematics), the typical stereotype threat effect emerged—women underperformed relative to men. But when the test was easier (the general GRE mathematics section), there was no evidence of stereotype threat—women performed just as well as men.

Second, stereotype threat appears to be most likely to emerge when the testing situation is one in which ability is submitted to evaluative scrutiny, as the research on test diagnosticity above demonstrates. Third, as in the above research on the applicability of the stereotype, we have shown that it is the situation in which a negative stereotype is directly applicable to a student's performance that provokes stereotype threat. Finally, stereotype threat is most likely to affect individuals who are highly identified with the domain in question, and least likely to bother individuals who care lttle about the domain. For example, in the study by Aronson and colleagues involving the male math majors exposed to the stereotype about Asians' math superiority, the stereotype threat manipulation disrupted the performance of only those who cared a great deal about being good at math. Those who were equally talented, but less deeply identified, actually performed *better* on the task when they thought they were being evaluated in light of the Asian stereotype. For the mildly identified, thinking about a devaluing stereotype can be an energizing challenge. For the deeply identified, it can be a debilitating threat.

These four factors—task difficulty, ability evaluation, stereotype applicability, and domain identification—all appear to be important conditions in the research linking stereotypes with underperformance. It is primarily under conditions where all these factors are present that stereotype threat poses the most serious obstacle to relaxed concentration, and thus to high performance.

MEDIATION OF STEREOTYPE THREAT

While the above studies have been directed at showing the type of situation in which people's performances are affected by negative stereotypes, the studies have not shown *how* performance is affected. What is psychologically mediating the relationship between stereotype threat and performance?

MEASURING STEREOTYPE ACTIVATION

Steele and Aronson (1995) examined the mediation of stereotype threat by looking for independent evidence that stereotype-threatening situations (e.g., taking a diagnostic ability test) induce targets to think about stereotypes. If African Americans underperform because they are psychologically contending with a stereotype alleging lower ability, then perhaps participants would demonstrate heightened cognitive activation of stereotypes when in the midst of a stereotype threat situation. The study was a variant of the diagnostic/nondiagnostic studies described above. After receiving the test characterization (either diagnostic or nondiagnostic) and perusing a sample test item (a difficult analogy from the verbal GRE) participants were given a stereotype activation measure.

This measure was comprised of a long series of word fragments (e.g., _ _ C E). The participant's task was to quickly fill in the blanks to form an English word, which previous research indicates is good way of measuring constructs either recently encountered or self-generated (Gilbert & Hixon, 1991; Tulving, Schacter, & Stark, 1982). On several of the items the fragment could be completed to form, among several other possibilities, a word related to stereotypes about African Americans. Thus, using the above fragment as an example, if one filled out the measure not long after eating in a Chinese restaurant, it would increase the likelihood of completing the fragment to form the word RICE. If one was thinking about a very kindhearted person, it would increase the odds of completing the word NICE. And, as we hypothesized would be the case for African American participants in the diagnostic condition of the experiment, if one was psychologically contending with the stereotype regarding their intellectual abilities, this would increase the chances of filling in the blanks to form the word RACE. And this is precisely what happened. These participants completed significantly more of the critical items—the dozen or so stereotype-related items—in this manner than the participants in any other group. These results strongly suggest that the evaluative scrutiny implied by the diagnostic condition arouses thoughts about the stereotype for individuals targeted by the stereotype.

Interestingly, however, explicit evaluation may not be necessary to activate stereotypes and undermine performance. The mere difficulty of an intellectual task may be enough to bring the stereotype to mind. McGlone and Aronson (1996) tested this hypothesis by giving African American and European American undergraduates two versions of the stereotype activation task descibed above. Half of the subjects were given a difficult version of the task, half were given an easier version. Thus, in the difficult version participants had to solve items that looked like this: _ _ T A P _ _ _ _ , whereas participants in the easy condition got items that looked like this: T A _ _ . Each version, however, contained the same race-related fragments. Relative to all other conditions, blacks in the difficult condition completed significantly more "critical" word fragments in a way that formed a race-related word, suggesting that their frustration with the items made them think about the stereotype alleging the inferiority of their group. Moreover, these same subjects completed fewer total items than subjects in all other groups, suggesting that at least one reason African Americans underperformed on this task—and on perhaps on extremely challenging tasks more generally—is that task difficulty encumbers them with the additional apprehension about confirming negative stereotypes.

The connection between the mere activation of stereotypes and underperformance is further supported by a subsequent study reported in Steele and Aronson (1995). All of the African American and European American undergraduates in this study took a challenging verbal GRE test under the nondiagnostic conditions described earlier, conditions shown to produce equivalent performance for both groups. However, just prior to beginning the test half the participants were "primed" to think about their race by a questionnaire that asked them to indicate their ethnicity. The effect of this reminder on the performance of the African Americans was dramatic; they performed significantly worse than the test-takers in all of the other conditions.

STEREOTYPE AVOIDANCE

Some evidence that stereotype threat involves not simply the mere activation of stereotypes, but also a desire to disconfirm them, can be found in Steele and

Aronson's (1995) measures of stereotype avoidance. Participants who thought they were about to take a challenging standardized test (described as diagnostic or nondiagnostic) rated their enjoyment of a variety of activities and types of music, and indicated the degree to which several adjectives were self-descriptive. Several of these items were associated with stereotypes about African Americans (e.g., enjoying rap music, liking basketball, being lazy). As predicted, there was a significant trend for the African American participants to rate the stereotypically African American items as less applicable to themselves when they were in the diagnostic condition of the experiment, and thus expected to be evaluated with a difficult standardized test. In the same study there was further evidence that diagnosticity aroused apprehension about confirming a negative racial stereotype. Participants filled out a demographic questionnaire that asked them to provide their race, but gave them the option of not doing so. Almost uniformly, African American participants in the diagnostic condition opted not to indicate their race, whereas nearly all of the African American participants in the nondiagnostic condition—like the European American participants in both conditions—complied with the request.

Experimental evidence that women similarly avoid feminine stereotypes when their math abilities are under scrutiny await the completion of studies in progress (e.g., Aronson, Good, & Harder, 1997). But, there is some compelling survey and ethnographic work suggesting a corresponding process. Seymour and Hewitt (1996), for example, report a trend among female math majors to "dress down"—that is, to dress less femininely—in their math classes than in their humanities classes. This suggests that in situations where women feel at-risk of confirming a negative gender stereotype, they take steps to avoid projecting stereotypically feminine traits, thereby reducing the risk that will be viewed through lens of the stereotype and treated accordingly.

These findings, we believe, show stereotypes—and the desire to deflect their negative implications—at work in the underperformance of these groups. How exactly they do so is not clear. We now consider research examining some possible mediators, processes whereby the desire not to confirm negative stereotypes may undermine cognitive functioning.

ANXIETY AND EVALUATION APPREHENSION

Research on test performance has shown that evaluation apprehension (Geen, 1991; Schlenker & Leary, 1982) and generalized test anxiety (Sarason, 1972; Wigfield & Eccles, 1989) can both negatively affect performance. Given that stereotype threat has its greatest impact in testing situations in which ability is being judged, it would make sense that anxiety and evaluation apprehension would be especially high in members of stereotyped groups. Another possibility is that members of stereotyped groups have lower performance expectations in stereotype threat situations. That is, perhaps their feelings of self-efficacy are lower, and these lowered feelings negatively affect performance. It is possible, for example, that when told a test had shown no gender differences in the past, women, instead of seeing the stereotype as inapplicable, simply experienced heightened performance expectancies for the test. In order to test these possible mediators and alternative explanations, another study was conducted.

In this study (Spencer *et al.*, 1997) men and women college students with equal math background were brought into the lab. As in the previous study, half of the participants read that the test they were about to take had shown no gender differences in the past. These directions were expected to take away the stereotype threat in the situation by making the stereotype inapplicable to women's performance on this particular test. The other half of the participants simply read that they were taking a math test. No mention of gender or gender differences was made. This condition was meant to be similar to the usual standardized testing situation where no mention of the stereotype is made, yet the stereotype imbues the situation. Once all the participants read the test instructions, they then saw a difficult practice problem, similar to those on the test. Having participants try a practice problem presumably gives rise to the feelings associated with stereotype threat. After the practice problem, all participants filled out measures of evaluation apprehension (e.g., "people will look down on me if I do not do well on this test"); self-efficacy (e.g., "I am uncertain I have the mathematical knowledge to do well on this test"); and anxiety (e.g., "I feel nervous"). After filling out these potential mediator measures, all participants took the same difficult math test based on the GMAT.

The results of this study replicated the basic stereotype threat affect reported above; women in the "no-gender-differences condition" performed equally to the men in both conditions, whereas the women in the control condition underperformed in comparison to the other three groups. Again, when the applicability of the stereotype was removed, women did not underperform. Mediation was tested by means of a series of regression equations for each of the potential mediators—efficacy, evaluation apprehension, and anxiety (Baron & Kenny, 1986). The results showed that although efficacy was positively related to the stereotype threat manipulation, it was not related to test performance, nor did it reduce the direct relationship between the stereotype threat manipulation and test performance. Thus, efficacy feelings do not appear to mediate stereotype threat. Likewise, although evaluation apprehension was significantly related to test performance, it was not related to the stereotype threat manipulation, nor did it reduce the direct relationship between the manipulation and test performance. Hence, evaluation apprehension does not appear to mediate the stereotype threat and performance. The final potential mediator was anxiety. Anxiety was related both to the threat manipulation and to test performance. That is, women in the control condition experienced more anxiety, and more anxiety was related to lower test performance. In addition, including anxiety as a predictor of test performance reduced the direct effect of the threat manipulation on test performance. Thus, anxiety was a partial mediator of the stereotype threat-test performance relationship.

We have also examined evaluation apprehension and self-efficacy as mediators of stereotype threat in African Americans. In the (Broadnax, Crocker, & Spencer, 1997) study described earlier that manipulated whether an English literature test had produced race differences in the past, the authors examined evaluation apprehension and self-efficacy as mediators of the underperformance of African Americans. After reading the characterization of the test ("no-race-differences" or standard instructions) participants completed a practice item, then completed mediational items designed to measure evaluation apprehension (e.g., "People will look down on me if I do not do well on this test") and self-efficacy (e.g., "I can handle this test"). The results suggested that evaluation apprehension (and not self-efficacy) mediated African Americans' performance. The sense that others might look down on them and think less of their intellectual ability explained why African Americans did worse when given the standard instruction than when given the no-race-difference instructions.

These last two studies suggest that the mediation of stereotype threat manipulations may take a different form for African Americans than for women. African Americans seem to be quite conscious that others may be stereotyping them and they wish to avoid these stereotypes, and thus they are concerned about others evaluating them stereotypically. The stereotype threat manipulation seems to have little affect on women's concern that others will view them negatively, but they do decrease women's anxiety. One possible explanation for this pattern of findings is that African Americans may be more conscious of the fact that others will stereotype them and apprehension arising from this concern undermines their performance. Women may be less conscious of these concerns, but removing the stereotype as a relevant interpretation of their performance may unconsciously lower anxiety and thus increase their performance.

REDUCING STEREOTYPE THREAT
AND DISIDENTIFICATION

If stereotype threat disrupts targets by forcing them to contend with the possibility that they are limited or that others will think they are, then perhaps blocking that attribution might reduce the threat. Several studies offer support for this reasoning, and suggest practical ways of reducing stereotype threat in educational contexts. We now turn to a brief description of these studies.

Josephs and Schroeder (1997) successfully reduced the underperformance of women taking a math test by manipulating these women's performance on a prior unrelated task. Women in this condition were given problems and feedback on their performance that emphasized that they had made substantial gains in skill improvement throughout the course of this first task. Awareness of this "learning curve" appears to have inoculated these participants from the deleterious effects of stereotype threat. Women given this prior experience completed a later math test with performance equal to a male control group and better than women who completed the same set of problems and who got just as many correct but who were not given the impression that their performance was improving. Thus in this study the attribution that participants could improve their performance seemed to reduce stereotype threat.

In a similar vein, Aronson and Tichy (1997) manipulated whether a GRE verbal test was introduced as a measure of a malleable or fixed intelligence (Dweck & Legget, 1988), reasoning that one would experience more anxiety if the test measured an ability upon which a person had little hopes of improving. As predicted, the African Americans—as well as the European Americans— performed much better and reported lower performance anxiety when the test was said to diagnose an ability that could be expanded with practice.

The usefulness of thinking of ability as malleable was further underscored in two additional studies conducted by Aronson and Fried (1997). In one study, undergraduates were led to believe they had either performed well or poorly on a test measuring their speed-reading ability. Prior to receiving the feedback, the test-takers had been led to believe either that speed-reading was a highly improvable skill, or that it was an endowed ability that could not be improved much with practice. At issue was how the feedback and the conception of the ability would interact to influence how much students ultimately valued the importance of speed-reading. The results were quite clear. When speed-reading was presented as a trait that could not be improved, test-takers who received positive feedback gave it high ratings ("speed-reading is an extremely valuable skill"), however, test-takers who received negative feedback did not believe that speed-reading was an important skill. This devaluing did not occur when the test-takers were led to believe that they could get better at speed-reading. In this condition, those who received positive feedback and those who receive negative feedback alike said that speed-reading was an important skill.

A larger scale intervention (Aronson & Fried, 1997) built upon these two findings. A program involving African American and European American college students employed numerous tactics of attitude change to get them to adopt—and make highly accessible—the belief that intelligence was improvable. Attitudes toward academic achievement and actual performance were assessed 4 months later and at the end of the school year. The results were highly encouraging. Not only did the African American students who took part in the intervention (relative to a control group who did not) report enjoying and feeling more identified with academics, their GPA at year's end reflected these positive attitudes. On average these African American students improved their grades (overall GPA) by four-tenths of a grade.

A more multifaceted approach to reducing stereotype threat was undertaken by Steele, Spencer, Hummel, Carter, Harber, Schoem, and Nisbett, (1998). These researchers designed a comprehensive program for first-year students at the University of Michigan. This program sought to reduce stereotype threat through three means: (1) Students were honorifically recruited by emphasizing that they had already met the tough admission standards at the University of Michigan.

(2) Students participated in weekly seminars through the first semester that allowed students to get to know one another and to learn some of the common problems they shared. (3) Students participated in subject master workshops in one of their courses that exposed the students to advanced material that went beyond material in the class. These elements sought to convey the message that instructors and peers thought they could excel academically, would not stereotype them, and believed they belonged at the University.

Four years of the program have been completed and the results demonstrate that the program leads to a substantial increase in African Americans performance in school. On average African Americans randomly assigned to the program do four-tenths of a grade better than African Americans randomly assigned to a control group. In addition, this increase in performance, although it diminishes, is evident throughout the college years and leads to higher retention rates. Why is the program effective? Analysis of survey data collected from the program participants and the control group suggests that the program decreases stereotype threat which in turn promotes identification with school which leads to better grades.

These interventions—as well as the laboratory research we have reported here—give us reason to be optimistic about the success of programs aimed at reducing the negative effects of stereotype threat. Our analysis stresses that there is nothing special about the personalities, the belief systems, or the values of women and minorities that undermines their performance. Rather, we argue that they fall victim to a situation that undermines their performance. This situation, which we have labeled stereotype threat, arises when negative stereotypes are available as a possible explanation for performance. What is hopeful about this analysis is that situations can be changed. Although we cannot eradicate the negative stereotypes that devalue the intellectual abilities of the groups we have been discussing, we can change other important features of the situation. Stereotype threat is reduced when people think their ability is not being evaluated (as in our test diagnosticity studies), when people think the stereotype is not relevant in the situation (as in our stereotype relevance studies), when people think the ability in question is malleable (as in the Aronson & Fried intervention), and when people think they are in an environment where they will not be treated stereotypically (as in the Steele *et al.,* intervention). Each of these factors is highly modifiable.

And this list is far from exhaustive. There have been numerous interventions that have yielded impressive gains in the academic achievement of minority youth by structuring classroom or study environments, in a way that minimizes the performance-undermining processes akin to those we have discussed here. E. Aronson and colleagues' "Jigsaw Classroom" (Aronson & Patnoe, 1997) and Uri Treisman's (e.g., Treisman, 1992) work with African American math students are outstanding examples in this regard. In the future other interventions and the mechanisms of the current interventions will undoubtedly be uncovered. It is our view that our prospects for progress on this front will be brightest if we fully embrace the philosophy emphasized by social psychologists in the tradition of Kurt Lewin: to most effectively understand and address the problems of human beings, the best place to start is by taking the perspective of the human beings in question.

REFERENCES

Alexander, K. L., & Entwistle, D. R. (1988). Achievement in the first two years of school: Patterns and processes. *Monographs of the Society for Research in Child Development, 53*(2).

Allport, G. (1954). *The nature of prejudice.* New York: Doubleday.

Armstrong, J. M. (1981). Achievement and participation of women in mathematics: Results of two national surveys. *Journal for Research in Mathematics Education, 12*(5), 356–372.

Aronson, E., & Patnoe, S. (1997). *The jigsaw classroom.* New York: Longman.

Aronson, J., Blanton, H., & Cooper, J. (1995). From dissonance to disidentification: Selectivity in the affirmation process. *Journal of Personality and Social Psychology, 58,* 1062–1072.

Aronson J., & Fried, C. (1997). *Belief in the malleability of intellectual ability: An intervention to increase the performance of African-American college students.* Unpublished manuscript, University of Texas.

Aronson, J., Lustina, M., Keough, K., Brown, J. L., & Steele, C. M. (1997). *Inducing stereotype threat in the non-stereotyped.* Unpublished manuscript, University of Texas.

Aronson, J., & Salinas, M. F. (1997). *Stereotype threat, attributional ambiguity, and Latino underperformance.* Unpublished manuscript, University of Texas.

Aronson, J., Tichy, J. C., & Croteau (1997). *Conceptions of ability and stereotype threat.* Unpublished manuscript, University of Texas.

American Council on Education (1995–1996). *Minorities in higher education.* Washington, DC: Office of Minority Concerns.

Baron, R. M., & Kenny, D. A. (1986). The moderator-mediator variable distinction in social psychological research: Conceptual, strategic, and statistical considerations. *Journal of Personality and Social Psychology, 51,* 1173–1182.

Baumeister, R. (1982). A self-presentational view of social phenomena. *Psychological Bulletin, 91,* 3–26.

Benbow, C. P., & Stanley, J. C. (1980). Sex differences in mathematical ability: Fact or artifact? *Science, 210,* 1262–1264.

Bereiter, C., & Engleman, S. (1966). *Teaching disadvantaged children in the preschool.* Englewood Cliffs, NJ: Prentice-Hall.

Bond, C. F. (1982). Social facilitation: A self-presentation view. *Journal of Personality and Social Psychology, 42,* 1042–1050.

Boykin, A. W. (1986). The triple quandary and the schooling of Afro-American children. In U. Neisser (Ed.), *The school achievement of minority children.* Hillsdale, NJ: Lawrence Earlbaum.

Broadnax, S., Crocker, J., & Spencer, S. (1997). *African-Americans and academic performance: The mediational role of stereotype vulnerability.* Unpublished manuscript, State University of New York at Buffalo.

Burton, N. W., & Jones, L. V. (1982). Recent trends in achievement levels of Black and White youth. *Educational Researcher, 11,* 10–17.

Carver, C. S., & Scheier, M. F. (1981). *Attention and self-regulation: A control-theory approach to human behavior.* New York: Springer-Verlag.

Dweck, C. S., & Legget, E. L. (1988). A social cognitive approach to motivation and personality. *Psychological Review, 95,* 256–273.

Evangelauf, J. (1993). Number of Minority Students in Colleges Rose by 9% from 1990 to 1991, U.S. Reports; Fact File: State-by-State Enrollment by Racial and Ethnic Group, Fall 1991. *Chronicle of Higher Education, 39,* 20, 30–31.

Feagin, J. R., & Sikes, M. P. (1994). *Living with racism: The black middle-class experience.* Boston: Beacon.

Fullilove, R., & Treisman, P. (1990). Mathematics achievement among African American undergraduates the University of California Berkeley: An evaluation of the mathematics workshop program. *Journal of Negro Education, 59,* 463–479.

Geen, R. G. (1985). Evaluation apprehension and response withholding in solution of anagrams. *Personality and Individual Differences, 6,* 293–298.

Geen, R. G. (1991). Social motivation. *Annual Review of Psychology, 42,* 377–399.

Gerard, H. (1983). School desegregation: The social science role. *American Psychologist, 38,* 869–878.

Gilbert, D. T., & Hixon, J. G. (1991). The trouble of thinking: Activation and application of stereotypic beliefs. *Journal of Personality and Social Psychology, 60,* 509–517.

Goffman, E. (1963). *Stigma: Notes on the management of a spoiled identity.* New York: Touchstone.

Herrnstein, R. J., & Murray, C. (1994). *The bell curve. Intelligence and class structure in American life.* New York: Free Press.

Higgins, E. T. (1987). Self-discrepancy: A theory relating self and affect. *Psychological Review, 94,* 319–340.

Hormuth, S. E. (1986). Lack of effort as a result of self-focused attention: An attributional ambiguity analysis. *European Journal of Social Psychology, 16,* 181–192.

Howard, J., & Hammond, R. (1985, September 9). Rumors of inferiority. *New Republic, 72,* 18–23.

Hurtado, S. (1996, November). *It was the best of times, it was the worst of times: Evidence regarding diverse students and diverse student outcomes.* Paper presented to the Diversity and Student Outcomes Conference, Austin, TX.

Hyde, J. S., Fennema, E., & Lamon, S. J. (1990). Gender differences in mathematics performance: A meta-analysis. *Psychological Bulletin, 107*(2), 139–155.

James, W. (1890/1950). *The principles of psychology.* New York: Dover.

Jensen, A. R. (1969). How much can we boost I.Q. and scholastic achievement? *Harvard Educational Review, 39,* 1–123.

Jensen, A. R. (1980). *Bias in mental testing.* New York: Free Press.

Jones, E. E., Farina, A., Hastorf, A. H., Markus, H., Miller, D. T., & Scott, R. A. (1984). *Social stigma: The psychology of marked relationships.* New York: Freeman.

Jones, E. E., & Pittman, T. (1982). Toward a general theory of strategic self-presentation. In J. Suls (Ed.), *Psychological perspectives on the self.* Hillsdale, NJ: Erlbaum.

Josephs, R., & Schroeder, D. (1997). *The self-protective function of the learning curve.* Unpublished manuscript, University of Texas at Austin.

Katz, I., Roberts, S. O., & Robinson, J. M. (1965). Effects of task difficulty, race of administrator, and instructions on digit-symbol performance of Negroes. *Journal of Personality and Social Psychology, 2,* 53–59.

Major, B. (1995, August). *Academic performance, self-esteem, and race: The role of disidentification.* Paper presented at the annual meeting of the American Psychological Association, New York, NY.

Major, B., & Schmader, T. (This volume). Coping with stigma through psychological disengagement. In J. K. Swim & C. Stangor (Eds.), *Prejudice: The target's perspective.* San Diego: Academic Press.

Major, B., Spencer, S. J., Schmader, T., Wolfe, C., & Crocker, J. (1998). Coping with negative stereotypes about intellectual performance: The role of psychological disengagement. *Personality and Social Psychology Bulletin, 24(1),* 34–50.

McGlone, M., & Aronson, J. (1996). *The role of task-difficulty and stereotype activation in the underperformance of African Americans.* Paper Presented at the 76th Meeting of the Western Psychological Association, San Jose, CA.

Miller, L. S. (1996). *Promoting high academic achievement among non-Asian minorities.* Paper presented at the Princeton University Conference on Higher Education, Princeton, NJ.

Nettles, M. T. (1988). *Toward undergraduate student equality in American higher education.* New York: Greenwood.

Ogbu, J. U. (1986). The consequences of the American caste system. In U. Neisser (Ed.), *The school achievement of minority children.* Hillsdale, NJ: Lawrence Earlbaum.

Osbourne, J. W. (1995). Academics, self-esteem, and race: A look at the underlying assumptions of the disidentification hypothesis. *Personality and Social Psychology Bulletin, 21,* 449–455.

Pelham, B. W. (1995). Self-investment and self-esteem: Evidence for a Jamesian model of self-worth. *Journal of Personality & Social Psychology, 69,* (6) 1141–1150.

Pelham, B. W., & Swann, W. B. (1989). From self-conceptions to self-worth: On the sources and structure of global self-esteem. *Journal of Personality & Social Psychology, 57,* 672–680.

Pittner, M., & Houston, B. (1980). Response to stress, cognitive coping strategies, and the Type A behavior pattern. *Journal of Personality & Social Psychology, 39,* 147–157.

Quinn, D. M., & Spencer, S. J. (1996, August). *Stereotype threat and the effect of test diagnosticity on women's math performance.* Paper presented at the annual American Psychological Association conference, Toronto, Canada.

Romo, H., & Falbo, T. (1995). *Latino high school graduation: Defying the odds.* Austin, TX: University of Texas Press.

Sadker, M., & Sadker, D. (1994). *Failing at fairness: How our schools cheat girls.* New York: Touchstone.

Sarason, I. G. (1972). Experimental approaches to test anxiety: Attention and the uses of information. In C. D. Spielberger (Ed.), *Anxiety: Current trends in theory and research, 2.* New York: Academic Press.

Schlenker, B. R., & Leary, M. R. (1982). Social anxiety and self-presentation: A conceptualization and model. *Psychological Bulletin, 92,* 641–669.

Seymour, E. (1996, November). *Persistence difficulties that White and non-White S.M.E. students do and do not share.* Paper presented to the Diversity and Student Outcomes Conference, Austin, TX.

Seymour, E., & Hewitt, N. (1996). *Talking about leaving. Why undergraduates leave the sciences.* Boulder, CO: Westview Press.

Spencer, S. J., Steele, C. M., & Quinn, D. M. (1997). *Stereotype vulnerability and women's math performance.* Unpublished manuscript, University of Waterloo.

Stangor, C., & Sechrist, G. B. (This volume). Conceptualizing the determinants of academic choice and task performance. In J. Swim and C. Stangor (Eds.), *Stigma: The target's perspective.* San Diego: Academic Press.

Steele, C. M. (1988). The psychology of self-affirmation: Sustaining the integrity of the self. In L. Berkowitz (Ed.), *Advances in experimental social psychology,* (Vol. 21). New York: Academic Press.

Steele, C. M. (1992, April). Race and the schooling of Black Americans. *The Atlantic Monthly.*

Steele, C. M. (1997). A threat in the air: How stereotypes shape intellectual identity and performance. *American Psychologist, 52,* 613–629.

Steele, C. M., & Aronson, J. (1995). Stereotype threat and the intellectual test performance of African Americans. *Journal of Personality & Social Psychology, 69,* 5, 797–811.

Steele, C. M., Spencer, S. J., Hummel, M., Carter, K., Harber, K., Schoem, D., & Nisbett, R. (1998). African-American college achievement: A "wise" intervention. In C. Jencks & M. Phillips (Eds.), *Test score differences between Blacks and Whites.* Cambridge, MA: Harvard University Press.

Steele, S. (1990). *The content of our character.* New York: St. Martin's Press.

Strenta, A., Elliott, R., Adair, R., Scott, J., & Matier, M. (1993). *Choosing and leaving science in highly selective institutions.* A report submitted to the A. P. Sloan Foundation.

Swann, W. B., Jr. (1983). Self-verification: Bringing social reality into harmony with the self. In J. Suls & A. G. Greenwald (Eds.), *Social psychological perspectives on the self* (Vol. 2, pp. 33–66). Hillsdale, NJ: Erlbaum.

Treisman, U. (1992). Studying students studying calculus: A look at the lives of minority mathematics students in college. *College Mathematics Journal, 23*(5), 362–372.

Tulving, E., Schacter, D. L., & Stark, H. A. (1982). Priming effects in word-fragment completion are independent of recognition memory. *Journal of Experimental Psychology: Learning, Memory, and Cognition, 8,* 336–342.

Valencia, R. R. (1991). The plight of Chicano students: an overview of schooling conditions and outcomes. In R. R. Valencia (Ed.), *Chicano school failure and success: Research and policy agendas for the 1990s* (pp. 3–26). The Stanford Series on Education and Public Policy. London, England: Falmer Press.

Valencia, R. R. (1997). Latinos and education: An overview of sociodemographic characteristics and schooling conditions and outcomes. In M. Barrera-Yepes (Ed.), *Latino education issues: Conference proceedings.* Princeton, NJ: Educational Testing Service.

White, K. R. (1982). The relation between socioeconomic status and academic achievement. *Psychological Bulletin, 91,* 3, 461–481.

Wigfield, A., & Eccles, J. S. (1989). Test Anxiety in Elementary and Secondary School Students. *Educational Psychologist, 24*(2), 159–183.

Wine, J. (1971). Test anxiety and direction of attention. *Psychological Bulletin, 76,* 92–104.

5

CONCEPTUALIZING THE DETERMINANTS OF ACADEMIC CHOICE AND TASK PERFORMANCE ACROSS SOCIAL GROUPS

CHARLES STANGOR
GRETCHEN B. SECHRIST

University of Maryland, College Park

One social phenomenon that has continued to intrigue social scientists and to frustrate members of the affected groups is the fact that, despite an unmistakable loosening of gender roles and a reduction of overt gender and racial stereotyping in the United States, substantial differences in academic and vocational choices, as well as success in these chosen domains, continue to exist between men and women and across racial groups (see Aronson, Spencer, & Quinn, this volume; Crocker, Major, & Steele, 1997; Eccles, 1994; Herrnstein & Murray, 1994; Jones, 1997; Major & Schmader, this volume; Neisser, 1986; Steele, 1992, for some relevant reviews). Such differences produce marked inequities in income and social status (cf. Crosby, 1984; Herrnstein & Murray, 1994) across social groups as individuals use their academic experiences to propel them into occupations.

Because differences in academic and occupational choice and subsequent achievement in these domains clearly have a host of causes, and because these causes are to a large part individual and social in nature, psychologists have long been interested in attempting to classify and isolate them. We review in this chapter current models of how young adults make academic choices, and corresponding models of academic performance, with a particular concern for explaining differences across social groups. This literature is drawn from a wide variety of sources in counseling, developmental, educational and social psychology.

This review will show that in large part these models propose, and empirical data confirm, that such outcomes are determined by social expectations—and particularly by stereotypes held by one group about another group or by the internalization of culturally defined stereotypical beliefs. We focus particularly on literature showing that individuals make career choices—and particularly those involving college admission and college major—on the basis of their perceptions about their likely success in the domain, the extent to which the domain seems appropriate and interesting to them, as well as the perceived likelihood of being stereotyped by others in the domain.

Although it would be possible to expand our review to include occupational as well as academic choices and to compare decisions across other relevant social groups, we will focus in this review on the factors that may lead women to avoid majors and careers in math and the physical sciences and lead African Americans to avoid (and to be more likely than European American students to fail at) academic pursuits more generally. Of course the specific variables that influence academic choices for women and for African Americans may not be the same, and these influences may not necessarily be generalizable to the influences on task choice and performance of other social groups. Nevertheless, considering the determinants of academic choice across more than one social group provides a method for comparing influences and of triangulating on the underlying causes, and there is a large body of literature concerning the academic choices of women and African Americans. We believe that this literature provides an appropriate base for drawing conclusions about the influences of these variables on academic choice and performance.

The data we will present in this regard are far from conclusive. We know much less than we need to about these important issues. Yet, taken together they provide a relatively coherent picture of the variables that impact the choices and eventual performance of college students. Before developing our approach, however, let us briefly consider the magnitude of existing differences in academic achievement among these groups.

DIFFERENCES AND THEIR MAGNITUDE

Differences between men and women and between African Americans and European Americans have been found in many areas of academic achievement. In high school, African American students are three times more likely to be suspended, three times more likely to be placed in classes for the mildly mentally handicapped, and more than twice as likely to drop out of school as are European American students (Cardenas & First, 1985). Furthermore, the national dropout rate for all college students (those who begin college but do not finish within 6 years) is 40% as compared to the national dropout rate of 62% for African American college students, and African American students who do graduate have substantially lower GPAs (cf. Nettles, 1988). Differences between men and women among fields of study with high degrees of math content have also been found. Women continue to avoid college majors and occupations that have moderate amounts of math, even though they perform just as well or better in high school math and science courses as do men (Boli, Allen, & Payne, 1985; Deboer, 1986; Hyde, Fennema, & Lamon, 1990; Lefevre, Kulak, & Heymans, 1992). In the early years of college, women are 2.5 times more likely to leave fields of mathematics, engineering, and physical sciences than are men (Crocker, Major, & Steele, 1997). And although European American women comprise 43% of the U.S. population, they earn only 22% of all BS degrees and 13% of all Ph.D.'s in the physical sciences, mathematics, and engineering (Hewitt & Seymour, 1991).

These differences also extend to occupational choices. Fitzgerald and Crites (1980) found that not only do women select occupations that require less than moderate amounts of math, but women also tend to choose occupations or careers that are unrealistically low in terms of their abilities and interest. Despite efforts to increase women's participation in advanced educational training and high-status professional fields, the differences between men's and women's career and college major choices continue to exist, especially in the fields of physical science, mathematics, and engineering, where women occupy only about 10% of the jobs and are paid about 75% of the salary earned by men (Eccles, 1987; Eccles, 1994; Hewitt & Seymour, 1991; Vetter, 1981).

EXISTING MODELS

Taken together, then, it is clear that there are rather substantial differences in academic choices and academic success between men and women and between European Americans and African Americans. These differences are naturally multidetermined, and this complexity is reflected in the existing models designed to account for how academic career paths are chosen. For instance, in one comprehensive model, O'Brien and Fassinger (1993) have proposed that *ability, agentic characteristics,* and *gender role attitudes* are predictors of the academic and career choices of adolescent women. Supporting this model, O'Brien and Fassinger (1993) found that adolescent women who have high ability, liberal attitudes toward gender roles, and high degrees of self-efficacy in mathematics tend to value their career pursuits more than women lacking these qualities. In another comprehensive approach to accounting for sex differences in educational and occupational choices, Eccles and her colleagues (Eccles, 1994) have developed a model that includes such factors as the individual's *aptitude, personal efficacy, previous experiences in the domain,* as well as his or her internalization of *gender role stereotypes* and *self-schemata.* This model has also been quite successful in predicting women's choices of academic majors (See Eccles, 1994, for a review).

Within the domain of African American academic performance, a number of important models have been proposed. For instance, Boykin (1986) argues that African American students are hampered in their academic studies because of the difficulties of simultaneously meeting the conflicting role requirements imposed by the majority culture and by their own African American culture. And Ogbu (1986; Fordham & Ogbu, 1986) suggests that African Americans frequently have academic difficulty as a result of peer pressure from other ingroup members—the perception of being perceived as "White" by other African Americans if they study too hard or do well academically. Finally, there is the influential disidentification model of Steele and his colleagues (Aronson *et al.*, this volume; Steele, 1992). This approach argues that the academic choices and performance of African American students are frequently undermined because of their perception of the stereotype that African Americans are not good at academics (*stereotype threat*) and that these beliefs may lead to both poor academic performance and eventual disidentification with academics and academic achievement. Although such disidentification may buffer the self-esteem of African American students against potential academic failure, it has clear negative outcomes for academic success (see Major & Schmader, this volume).

FOUR SOURCES OF INFLUENCE ON TASK CHOICE

One notable aspect of each of the existing models concerning academic choice and performance of women and African Americans is that a great proportion of the variables proposed to be relevant involve the potential impact of stereotypes held by the students. For instance, within the O'Brien and Fassinger (1993) model, gender role orientation is a measure of the extent to which the woman has internalized gender stereotypes, and agentic characteristics can be considered a measure of the extent to which the individual has internalized traditionally "masculine" gender roles (Bem, 1981). Similarly, the predictor variables of gender role stereotypes and self-schemata within the Eccles *et al.* model are based on the internalization of gender-role appropriate expectations. The Fordham and Ogbu and the Steele models are also based on knowledge of the existing cultural stereotypes about the academic ability of African Americans. For instance, Steele's model proposes that disidentification with academics can be the result of the perception of cultural stereotypes about likely task performance on academically related tasks.

That these diverse models of task choice, derived within different subdisciplines and designed to explain differences in academic choice across different social groups have all found stereotypes and the internalization of stereotypic perceptions to be important suggests that a specific focus on the impact of stereotypes on academic and occupational choice is in order. These models also validate to a large extent the traditional interest within the social psychological literature on stereotyping (cf. Macrae, Stangor & Hewstone, 1996; Spears, Oakes, Ellemers, & Haslam, *et al.*, 1996), which has been based upon the assumption that stereotypes do indeed have a (frequently negative) impact on their targets.

TABLE 5.1   Four Influences on Task Choice and Task Performance, With Prototypical Examples

	Source of influence	
Type of influence	Internal	External
Direct	Competence; ability; task preferences	Prejudice, discrimination, sexual harassment; self-fulfilling prophecies
Indirect	Expectations about task performance; self-efficacy	Inaccurate perceptions of discrimination; cultural mistrust

Although current models of academic decision making have been successful in accounting for variance in the career paths of both women and African Americans, they have each also tended to be rather unidimensional in their own right. For instance, regarding women's achievement, although the Eccles and the O'Brien and Fassinger models both suggest that differences in aptitude are important, they have generally controlled for these variables, focusing instead on the extent to which stereotypes have been internalized by the target person—for instance, the influence of gender role identity and self-schemas. And they have not taken into consideration the extent to which actual gender discrimination or sexism, or the perceptions of potential sexism, might influence task choice and performance. Conversely, the models of academic choice and achievement of African Americans have not generally taken into consideration the potential importance of initial differences in aptitude, interests or abilities between African Americans and European Americans, and have focused almost entirely on the impact of stereotyping and prejudice. Because existing models are each somewhat limited in terms of the variables they consider important, an approach that simultaneously considered all of the variables assumed to be important within each of these existing models could be useful to the extent that it provided a clearer focus on the many potential influences on academic choices.

Table 5.1 organizes the potential influences on task choice and performance specified by these existing models into four different domains, formed on the basis of two dichotomous distinctions. One of these distinctions is between influences that are *direct* in the sense that they are not mediated by the individuals' perceptions or interpretations and those that are *indirect* in the sense that they are driven by an internalized perception or expectation. The second distinction involves a division into *external sources* (those effects that emanate from others) and *internal sources* (those that located within the target individual).

In brief, *direct internal influences* are those in which internal differences in intelligence, abilities or competence, general personality characteristics, or personal preferences influence an individual's choice to engage in or to avoid an activity, whereas *indirect internal influences* are those in which an individual's expectation about one's task skills—for instance in the form of perceived task confidence or self-efficacy—impacts choice above and beyond any true differences in aptitude or ability. *Direct external influences* include, for example, such overt behaviors as sexual harassment or racial discrimination as well as more subtle responses such as differential behavior of instructors including behavioral confirmation (self-fulfilling prophecy) effects. *Indirect external influences* occur when a target perceives him- or herself as possessing a characteristic that is stigmatizing (for instance an ascribed characteristic such as race or sex or an achieved characteristic such as being a male nurse or a female firefighter) and this perception leads to an expectation of being stereotyped by others. These perceptions then lead the individual to change behavior to avoid or overcome this expected discrimination (cf. Miller and Myers, this volume, Swim *et al.,* this volume).

Of course, the four types of influences are not entirely independent, and thus the effects of each must be carefully partialled from estimates of the effects of the others, both conceptually and empirically. For instance, indirect internal influences such as task confidence can impact actual task ability (cf. Aronson *et al.,* this volume) and actual abilities impact task confidence (Campbell & Hackett, 1986). We will discuss these complexities in the sections to come. Finally, we should note that the current approach to conceptualizing the impact of stereotypes on target individuals is not completely different from previous analyses. For instance, the distinction between internal (cf. aptitude; ability) and external (cf. nutritional; cultural) influences is a basic distinction in this literature (Fraser, 1995; Herrnstein & Murray, 1994; Ogbu, 1986). And in their comprehensive review, Crocker, Major, and Steele (1997) differentiate the influence of indirect sources (e.g., "stereotype threat") and direct sources (e.g., experience with prejudice). It is our hope that a focus on the source of each of the influences will be heuristic not only in organizing the potential influences, but may also provide a foundation for a comparison of the relative impact of each. In the following sections we review each of the four influences in more detail.

DIRECT INTERNAL INFLUENCES

Perhaps the most obvious explanations for differences in academic choice and subsequent performance are those based upon differences in skills, competence, aptitude, or initial task interest. Individuals would naturally not be expected to choose to engage in activities in which they are not skilled. And failure rates for unqualified individuals who do enter such activities should be high. There is at least some evidence for true differences in task aptitude between men and women and across racial groups on abilities that are relevant to academic pursuits.

One area in which differences between men and women are well documented is in spatial skills. There is a substantial body of data to suggest that women have poorer spatial skills than do men (Liben, 1978; 1991; Liben & Golbeck, 1984).

Men have significantly higher scores on both physical and nonphysical versions of tasks that assess how people represent horizontals and verticals, such as the water jar problem (Liben, 1978). And Battista (1990) found that high school girls had significantly lower performance than high school boys on geometry and spatial visualization tasks. Because geometry is one of the main sections of standardized aptitude tests, observed differences across sex on these tests may be due in part to differences in spatial abilities. Although some reviews have documented decreases in the relative advantage for men on these tests over time (Feingold, 1988), one recent review (Halpern, 1989) found that women scored about 46 points (that is, almost one-half of a standard deviation) lower on the mathematical section of the SAT than men who had taken the same math courses and received the same or higher grades in them (cf. Callahan, 1991; Wainer & Steinberg, 1992).

There is also evidence for IQ and aptitude differences between African Americans and European Americans on academically related tasks. In their review of the literature, Herrnstein & Murray (1994) report finding, across a wide variety of intelligence and aptitude tests, that African Americans score about one standard deviation lower than European Americans, and the existence of this difference has generally been confirmed in the literature (Fraser, 1995).

In short, then, there is at least some evidence that differences in academic achievement across social groups are determined in part by actual differences in aptitude and ability among the groups. The etiology of such differences is of course a question of much controversy (Herrnstein & Murray, 1994; Jensen, 1969; see Ogbu, 1986 for a review), with some arguing for the contribution of innate cognitive or neurological differences (cf. Benbow & Stanley, 1980; Connor, Schackman, & Serbin, 1978) and others for the role of social factors such as nutrition, parenting, education and socialization (cf. Gould, 1995; Nisbett, 1995). Considering the merits of such arguments is beyond the scope of our review, but we should point out that, regardless of their etiology, because intelligence and aptitude remain fairly stable after infancy, these differences—no matter how they are initially created—involve the direct effects of actual ability on task choice.

Despite its intuitive appeal, the idea that differences in intelligence or aptitude are the major determinant of academic task choice or performance across gender or race is probably not correct. For one thing, although virtually all predictive models find aptitude test scores to be significant predictors of academic performance, aptitude measures tend to have much less direct, and frequently insignificant, influence when other contributing variables are controlled (cf. Tracey & Sedlacek, 1987). Second, the relationship between aptitude test scores and college GPA is much stronger in the first year in college, and declines dramatically thereafter (Tracey & Sedlacek, 1987). Since many students choose their final majors after their first year in school, it seems unlikely that aptitude is playing a large part in determining them. There is also evidence that the observed differences in college performance between men and women (cf. Aronson *et al.,* this volume) and between African and European Americans (Herrnstein & Murray, 1994) are found at all ability levels. Finally, it is not unlikely that influences normally interpreted as direct aptitude effects are frequently overestimated because the scores on the tests may themselves be influenced by student's expectations about their task skills (see Aronson *et al.,* this volume). In this case the true effect is an indirect, rather than a direct one.

There is another direct internal influence—namely the task interest, motivations, and goals of the individual—that may play a more important role in task choice. For instance, girls name their favorite school subjects as English, music, and drama, whereas boys rate physical sciences, sports and athletics, and mathematics higher (Benbow, 1988; Benbow & Minor, 1986; Benbow & Stanley, 1984). These differences, and particularly those in mathematics, are usually quite large. Girls also place much more emphasis on family, friends, and quality of life in comparison to boys (see Eccles, 1994), and these values influence academic and vocational choice. These findings provide a nice example of the difficulty and yet also the importance of determining the interrelationships among the different influences, because while such interests are commonly assumed to be produced by the impact of cultural sex stereotypes and sex roles on the individual (external sources), it is also possible that they represent to a large extent the internalized motivations of the child to conform to existing social structures rather than the direct influence of others on the child (cf. Stangor & Ruble, 1987). In any case, once they are internalized such interests, motivations and goals become direct internal influences.

DIRECT EXTERNAL INFLUENCES

There are a wide variety of potential direct external influences that may operate to keep individuals from choosing given tasks or that may influence their subsequent performance on those tasks (see for instance Miller & Myers, this volume). For instance, even though direct prejudice and discrimination may no longer operate to as large an extent on an overt basis as they once did, they have certainly not been eliminated entirely. Sexual harassment is still found in organizational climates (Pryor & McGinney, 1995; Stockdale, 1993; Tinsley & Stockdale, 1993) and this harassment has been shown to have negative psychological outcomes on its targets (Fitzgerald, Drasgow, Hulin, Gelfand, & Magley 1997). Furthermore, sexual harassment is more likely in cases where the distribution and power of men and women is unequal (Fitzgerald *et al.,* 1997; Kanter, 1977). College frequently represents such a situation for African Americans, whereas many college majors may also do so for women (or potentially men) if the majority of instructors and students within the major are men (or women).

It is difficult to document the extent to which direct prejudice, discrimination, and harassment play a role in task choice, particularly since there are so many possible sources of such impacts (for instance, Jones, 1997, documents independent effects of individual, institutional and cultural racism on African Americans). Nevertheless, some research is now beginning to attempt to quantify the impact of overt sexism and racism. For instance, Swim and her colleagues (this volume) have shown that some individuals perceive sexism and racism on an almost daily basis, and Landrine and colleagues (Landrine & Klonoff, 1996; Landrine, Klonoff, Gibbs, Manning, & Lund, 1995) have found that these perceptions are related to negative self-reported psychological states (cf. Allison, this volume). However, these data are still very limited in terms of the information they provide about the causal impact of such perceptions on psychological states or behavior. Furthermore, as we will consider in more detail below, this research has not generally investigated the extent to which such perceptions are accurate reflections of actual prejudice or discrimination (cf. Feldman Barrett *et al.*, this volume).

Another common form of direct external influence, and one that clearly has a large impact on academic decision making, is that of guiding adults who preferentially direct adolescents into certain activities over others. It has been found that parents (and especially mothers) frequently have gender role stereotypic beliefs about their children's abilities such that they overestimate the ability of sons and underestimate the ability of daughters in math and science (Eccles, Jacobs, & Harold, 1990). For instance, Eccles & Jacobs (1986) found that parents' perceptions of the difficulty of math for their child and parents' attitudes about the value of math both influenced childrens' confidence in their ability and the likelihood that the child would enroll in advanced math classes. Eccles (1987) found that students of parents who have high estimates of their child's ability are more confident in math and more likely to continue taking math courses. Parental beliefs will also have a direct influence on children, for example when they select courses of study that differentially prepare (or underprepare) them for academic careers. High school academic advisors also play an important role in such decision making. They may direct girls out of math classes and potentially even keep African Americans from applying to college.

Still another source of direct external effects are self-fulfilling prophecies (cf. Feagin & Sikes, 1994; Jussim, 1989, 1991; Jussim & Fleming, 1996; Miller & Myers, this volume; Sadker & Sadker, 1994). Teachers' perceptions of their students have long been known to play a role in producing differences in academic achievement. Studies have demonstrated that teachers interact differently with male and female students in math courses, such that the teachers pay more attention to and give more praise to male than female students (Eccles, 1987). And Midgley, Feldlaufer, and Eccles (1989) demonstrated that students had higher expectancies and perceptions of their performance and ability and rated math as less difficult when they had teachers who believed in their ability, as compared to students with low-efficacious teachers. Furthermore, teacher efficacy beliefs had a stronger impact on low-achieving students as compared to those who were high achievers.

Thus, although we may hope that the direct external influences are decreasing in contemporary society, given laws designed to prevent differential treatment as well as changes in individual attitudes, because there are wide variety of such sources, they may play rather substantial roles overall. Perhaps most disconcerting is that external effects do not always emanate from outside of the impacted group. For instance, peer pressure on African American students stemming from cultural stereotypes held by the ingroup may keep African American students from doing well in high school and even enrolling in college (cf. Boykin, 1986; Fordham & Ogbu, 1986; Ogbu, 1986). Such influences are going to be difficult to eliminate. And, even though they represent a potentially large source of impact, because they do not fall under the traditional rubric of intergroup attitudes they are not being given the research attention they deserve.

INDIRECT INTERNAL INFLUENCES

Internal influences occur when target individuals have developed perceptions of their own abilities or competencies, and when these expectations influence task choice or task performance independently of measures designed to assess actual aptitude or ability. These effects are common and form the basis of much research on academic choice. For instance, Deboer (1986) found that students' ratings of their abilities in science predicted the number of science courses they took in college above and beyond the number of courses they had taken in high school and their grades in those courses (see also Parsons, 1983). Furthermore, despite performing *better* in high school science courses than men, women still rated their ability in science as being lower than that of men (Deboer, 1986). Similarly, Dwinell and Higbee (1991) found that rated math anxiety predicted students' grades in the first quarter in college above and beyond the effects of aptitude as assessed by high school GPA and SAT-Q score, although women did not show greater anxiety than men. Furthermore, people with high degrees of math anxiety have been found to avoid mathematical majors and courses (Lefevre, Kulak, & Heymans, 1992), and Hollinger (1983) found that there was a strong relation between gifted girls' confidence in their math abilities and their aspirations to enter vocations such as engineering and computer science (see also Betz & Fitzgerald, 1987; Betz & Hackett, 1986).

In terms of differences in academic choice and performance between African Americans and European Americans, it has long been argued that the abilities of African Americans are undermined by their uncertainty about their academic skills (see Ogbu, 1986 for a review). Recently, in a provocative line of research, Steele and his colleagues (1992; Aronson *et al.*, this volume) have convincingly demonstrated such effects in a series of laboratory experiments. And this research suggests that the impact of the perception of stereotypes is not limited to academic choice or performance, but can even affect scores on aptitude tests, because activating racial stereotypes relevant to academic skills prior to performing aptitude tests was found to reduce the task performance of African American students (who are stereotypically expected to be poor on these tasks), evidently by undermining task confidence and increasing anxiety. Similar indirect internal effects are found for women when stereotypes about mathematics abilities undermine performance on aptitude tests of mathematics.[1]

---

[1]As we will argue later, the research on stereotype threat (see Aronson *et al.*, this chapter) actually represents a case where an indirect external source (perceptions of the likelihood of being stereotyped by others) produces an indirect internal effect (changes in perceived competence).

Still another potential direct internal source involves higher level internal variables such as self-esteem, optimism, self-confidence, and self-efficacy. It has long been known that such variables play an important role in behavioral choice (Aspinwall & Taylor, 1997; Atkinson, 1964; Bandura, 1977, 1986; See Eccles, 1994; Weiner, 1974, for reviews) and research has generally supported the assumption that these variables can in some cases impact individual performance above and beyond actual ability. Students with high levels of self-efficacy, for instance, earn higher grades, are more academically persistent, and have a wider perception of career options available to them, as compared to those individuals low in self-efficacy (Lent, Brown, & Larkin, 1986).

However, although such global individual difference variables have an influence on career choice overall, they do not seem to be able to provide a convincing account for differences in academic choice across social groups. Research tends to find few differences on these variables between men and women or across racial groups (cf. Coleman *et al.,* 1966; Crocker & Major 1989; Eccles, 1994; Porter and Washington, 1979; and Rosenberg & Simmons, 1972, for reviews; but for some evidence of differences on self-esteem see Major, Barr, Zubek & Babe, 1996; Skaalvik, 1986). And initial task confidence in academic achievement does not appear to be lower for African Americans. In fact in most data, African Americans show every bit as high task confidence and predictions of task success in college as do European American students (Mickelson, 1990; Stangor, Carr & Taylor, 1997).

Although it seems to us possible that at least some differences in task choice and performance are driven by expectations about one's own ability, and particularly so for confidence about specific academic tasks, there are ambiguities in these data that must still be resolved before any firm conclusions can be drawn about their impact. For instance, it has been found that women score significantly higher grades than men in introductory psychology statistics courses, math courses, algebra courses, and accounting courses (Brooks & Mercincavage, 1991; Struik & Flexer, 1984) even though women are less likely to continue to take classes in these fields. And it is not clear why perceptions of cultural stereotypes would produce differences on scores on standardized tests, such as those found by Steele and Aronson (1995), but would not cause corresponding differences on grades in stereotype-related courses.

INDIRECT EXTERNAL INFLUENCES

The last potential source of influence in our model—indirect external influences—are those that occur when a person's beliefs or expectations of being stereotyped, by either ingroup or outgroup members, influence their task choice above and beyond any direct external effects of prejudice or discrimination. In short, external indirect influences involve an individual's perceptions of how others are perceiving the self and how the behavior of others will impact the self. Although such influences have been extensively studied in other domains (cf.

Goffman, 1963; Jones, Faring, Hastorf, Markus, Miller, and Scott, 1984), they have not been considered as determinants of academic choice between social groups. Such effects could occur, for instance when an African American drops out of college because of a perception that the university system is discriminating against his racial group, or when a woman believes that she will not be able to perform well in a math class because she will be singled out as a female by her professor. Thus, just as indirect internal effects involve the perception of ability rather than effects of ability per se, indirect external effects involve the perceptions of stereotyping, prejudice or discrimination.

One line of research that represents indirect external influences is the Major and Crocker (1989) model of attributional ambiguity (see Major & Schmader, this volume; Rosenberg and Simmons, 1972). This model proposes that stigmatized individuals explicitly consider the possibility, at least in cases when self-relevance is high because the individual is making attributions about performance on important self-relevant tasks, that others may be judging them on the basis of their category memberships. This leads them to perceive that other's judgments are based on prejudice, and this perception then allows them to make attributions that protect their self-esteem. For instance, stigmatized individuals who have failed on a self-relevant task might attribute that failure to discrimination rather than to internal factors (Crocker et al., 1997).

In cases where they are likely to be accurate, perceptions of being the potential target of prejudice seem adaptive. For instance, proactive coping (Aspinwall & Taylor, 1997) involves the anticipation of stressful events and preparations to prevent the effects of the stressor (see Swim, Cohen, & Hyers, this volume). However, if perceptions are inaccurate target individuals may unnecessarily or unreasonably change their behavior. For instance, individuals may avoid activities when they think they are likely to be the target of prejudice (cf. Pettigrew & Martin, 1987; Heilman, 1979) even if that prejudice might never actually materialize. And these perceptions may even develop into a general dislike and mistrust of others (Terrell, Terrell & Miller, 1993; Watkins, Terrell, Miller, and Terrell, 1989)—a potentially false negative stereotype held by the stigmatized group about the nonstigmatized group.

But individuals do not always perceive that others are prejudiced against them. In fact, an extensive line of research by Ruggiero, Taylor, and colleagues (cf. Ruggiero & Taylor, 1995) suggests that individuals often do not perceive themselves to have been the target of discrimination, even when the actual likelihood that they have been is quite high. Although seemingly inconsistent with the findings of Major and her colleagues, these two sets of findings do highlight two important issues. First, they demonstrate the extent to which target individuals are actively construing their social environment, denying discrimination when it is not beneficial to perceive it, but perceiving it when doing so has beneficial outcomes for the self. The factors that determine whether one is able and motivated to deny discrimination are under extensive investigation. Second, these findings suggest that it will be useful to study the extent to which individual's perceptions of discrimination are accurate or biased (Feldman Barrett & Swim, this volume). If individuals underestimate the occurrence of discrimination they may not adequately prepare for it (cf. Miller & Myers, this volume). But if they overestimate the extent of discrimination they may end up unnecessarily avoiding activities. In any case, these influences all fall under the rubric of indirect external influences, because they involve the perception of discrimination, controlling for actual discrimination.

COMPARISONS AND INTERRELATIONS AMONG THE INFLUENCES

To this point we have considered the four potential influences on academic choice and achievement largely as if they produce only independent main effects. Indeed, such an approach is typical within the literature in the sense that virtually all existing analyses of differences in academic choices and performance across gender and racial groups have focused primarily on one of the four proposed influences. For instance, the models of Eccles (1994), O'Brien and Fassinger (1993), and Steele (1992) deal primarily with internal effects in the form of aptitude and internal beliefs and expectations. On the other hand, other approaches (cf. Fitzgerald *et al.,* 1997; Jones, 1997; Ogbu, 1986) have focused on direct external effects such as racism, prejudice, and sexual harassment. And even when more than one type of influence is considered and measured in the same research (cf. Tracey & Sedlacek, 1987), the regression analyses do not test for the possibility of interactive effects.

It is our expectation that complete models of academic choice and achievement will require the development of comprehensive models that take into consideration the simultaneous impact of the various sources of influence. There are at least two types of questions that seem important and that could be addressed in empirical studies. One question involves comparisons of the relative magnitude of each type of effect, and the other involves considering the potential interrelations among the influences.

RELATIVE IMPACT

Questions about the relative impact of external and internal effects (such as the relative impact of genetics versus environment) are frequently considered central to an adequate understanding of social behavior. According to our approach, such an analysis will be extremely important for providing a full understanding of task choice and performance, and yet our literature review has uncovered virtually no studies addressing this question. We can, however, speculate at least to some extent on the likely relative impact of different influences.

Most generally, we expect (as it usually turns out to be when analyzed from a social psychological perspective) that indirect effects will have a more powerful impact overall in comparison to direct effects. There are several reason to think this might be the case. For one, direct effects, both internal and external, seem to be decreasing over time. In terms of external effects, overt racism and sexism are declining, and beliefs about the appropriate behaviors across social groups, held by parents and other guiding adults, should also be so. Furthermore, in terms of internal influences, aptitude differences (particularly between men and women) are also closing (but see Herrnstein & Murray, 1994, and Fraser, 1995, for contradictory positions regarding the convergence of aptitude differences between African Americans and European Americans). These changes suggest that direct effects may be becoming increasingly less important as determinants of academic choice.

However, perceptions of the corresponding internal and external effects may take longer to erase. For instance, many individuals might still have perceptions that racism and sexism are prevalent even though overt instances have declined. And perceptions of the differences in abilities across social groups may well lag behind actual changes in such differences. In short, because indirect effects involve an active construction of social reality they are not bound by objective differences across social groups, but may instead develop a life of their own. As with other social expectations, these perceptions may in many cases be inaccurate and biased. Furthermore, because they are social constructions, indirect effects are likely to be resistant to disconfirmation. Indirect influences also come from a broader set of sources and this may lead them to have a greater impact. For example, just as a member of a majority group may perceive that all or most members of a minority group have similar characteristics, an individual from a stigmatized group may perceive that all or most members of a powerful outgroup are prejudiced against his or her social group (cf. Rettew, Billman, & Davis, 1993).

INTERACTIONS AMONG THE INFLUENCES

A second important consideration concerns potential interrelationships among the sources of influence. It would be important to study such interactive effects in several ways. For one, it would appear that full models of academic choice should consider the causal sequences among the various influences. For instance, to what extent do indirect internal influences, such as expectations about likely task performance actually produce true aptitude differences (direct internal effects) in everyday life? And, through what mechanisms are social stereotypes about group differences internalized to develop into internal effects on behavior? The stereotype threat model of Steele and his colleagues (see Aronson *et al.*, this volume) is a nice example of such an approach. In this model external influences (the perception of being stereotyped) produce internal influences (undermining of confidence; anxiety) that may then impact task choice and performance.

Another relevant question concerns the extent to which different sources of influence may serve to buffer or to undermine the influence of competing sources. For instance, a buffering effect might be observed if students with low actual ability are nevertheless able to perform well if they have high expectations about their skills. In this case, the indirect internal effect buffers negative direct internal effects. On the other hand, true ability may be undermined by poor expectations. For instance, the expectations of being the target of prejudicial behavior may lead a student to avoid given tasks, even if they have strong task skills.

There is a small but growing body of research testing such interactive effects. In an experimental study Cohen and Swim (1995) tested the hypothesis that an internal influence (the extent to which one was confident that they had high ability at a task) would buffer the negative impact of external effects (expecting to be stereotyped because one was a solo in a group). This research showed that both men and women expected to be stereotyped to a greater extent when they were going to be a solo, but that this tendency was reduced when the individuals had confidence about their task abilities.

Stangor and Carr (1997) extended this line of research by investigating individuals' perceptions of their likely performance on, and their expressed desire to change the task as a function of task confidence and solo versus majority group status. However, rather than producing a buffering effect, this research found that solo status undermined the effects of task feedback. Individuals who expected to work in dissimilar groups (different sex and major) reported expecting to perform poorly and wanting to change the task even if the feedback had led them to perceive that they were quite good at the task. Future research will undoubtedly continue to study such interactive effects.

IMPACTING CHANGES

Given we can continue, in future research, to more fully determine the relative and interactive impact of these different sources of influence upon task choice and performance, we are left with the lingering question of how teachers, parents, and policymakers can reduce these discrepancies, and in fact whether such attempts are even desirable. We believe that considering each of the potential sources together can potentially provide some new insights in this regard. This approach makes it clear that a full understanding of the determinants of academic and career choice and success will involve considering the perceptions of both the group under study as well as the perceptions of members of other groups. This approach thus explicitly suggests that changing intergroup relations can be accomplished either from the point of view of the perceiver or from the point of view of the target person, or from a focus on the interaction between the two (cf. Branscombe & Ellemers, this volume).

Although it is traditionally assumed that differences in academic and career choices across social groups are unnatural and thus should be eliminated, such a decision is not necessarily valid. For instance, if there are aptitude or interest differences between men and women or across racial groups that are not determined by social stereotypes (but that rather are direct internal effects) then we should perhaps expect and allow such differences to continue. It is not unreasonable to expect that individuals should self-select into activities for which they are most skilled or most inherently interested. Of course, if these differences continue to be associated with occupational choice, status and income, such an approach may not appear desirable because it would maintain such differences.

On the other hand, if choices and performance are primarily determined by direct external effects such as sexism and racism then it would appear that targets are being unfairly and differentially directed into activities, or prevented from succeeding in them, and thus that we should attempt to make changes. If it turns out that the primary determinants are external effects, the focus will necessarily be on the perpetrators, rather than the targets. We might propose that teachers, parents, school admission members, policymakers, and counselors continue to attempt to reduce prejudice, but also that stigmatized individuals be trained to cope with the impact of these behaviors. On the other hand, if the determinants are by and large indirect and internal, then members of the stigmatized groups should themselves be the focus. Women must be encouraged to recognize the career options that they have available to them in the mathematical and scientific domains, and to move beyond stereotypical expectations about appropriate task choices. In any case, we hope that the present approach to addressing these issues, which suggests that a full understanding of group differences in academic choice and performance will involve considering the simultaneous, interactive, influence of many different sources of impact, will provide a foundation for addressing these questions.

REFERENCES

Aspinwall, L. G., & Taylor, S. E. (1997). A stitch in time: Self-regulation and proactive coping. *Psychological Bulletin, 121*, 417–436.

Atkinson, J. W. (1964). *An introduction to motivation*. Princeton, NJ: Van Nostrand.

Bandura, A. (1977). Self-efficacy: Toward a unifying theory of behavior change. *Psychological Review, 84*, 191–215.

Bandura, A. (1986). *Social foundations of thought and action: A social cognitive theory*. Englewood Cliffs, NJ: Prentice-Hall.

Battista, M. T. (1990). Spatial visualization and gender differences in high school geometry. *Journal for Research in Mathematics Education, 21*, 47–60.

Bem, S. L. (1981). Gender schema theory: A cognitive account of sex typing. *Psychological Review, 88*, 354–364.

Benbow, C. P. (1988). Sex differences in mathematical ability in intellectually talented preadolescents: Their nature, effects, and possible causes. *Behavioral and Brain Sciences, 11*, 169–232.

Benbow, C. P., & Minor, L. L. (1986). Mathematically talented males and females and achievement in high school sciences. *American Educational Research Journal, 23*, 425–436.

Benbow, J., & Stanley, J. C. (1980). Sex differences in mathematical ability: Fact or artifact? *Science, 210*, 1262–1264.

Benbow, C. P., & Stanley, J. C. (1984). Gender and the science major: A study of mathematically precocious youth. In M. W. Steinkamp & M. L. Maehr (Eds.), *Women in Science*. Greenwich, CT: JAI Press.

Betz, N. E., & Hackett, G. (1986). Applications of self-efficacy theory to understanding career choice behavior. *Journal of Social and Clinical Psychology, 4*, 279–289.

Betz, N. E., & Fitzgerald, L. F. (1987). *The career psychology of women.* Orlando, FL: Academic Press.

Boli, J., Allen, M. L., & Payne, A. (1985). High-ability women and men in undergraduate mathematics and chemistry courses. *American Educational Research Journal, 22,* 605–626.

Boykin, W. (1986). Reading achievement and the socio-cultural frame of reference of Afro-American children. *Journal of Negro Education, 53,* 464–473.

Brooks, C. I., & Mercincavage, J. E. (1991). Grades for men and women in college course taught by women. *Teaching of Psychology, 18,* 47–48.

Callahan, C. (1991). An update on gifted females. *Journal for the Education of the Gifted, 14,* 284–311.

Campbell, N. K., & Hackett, G. (1986). The effects of mathematics task performance on math self-efficacy and task interest. *Journal of Vocational Behavior, 28,* 149–162.

Cardenas, J., & First, J. M. (1985). Children at risk. *Educational Leadership, 43,* 4–8.

Cohen, L. L., & Swim, J. K. (1995). The differential impact of gender ratios on women and men: Tokenism, self-confidence, and expectations. *Personality and Social Psychology Bulletin, 21,* 876–884.

Coleman, J. S., Campbell, E. Q., Hobson, G. J., McPartland, J., Mood, A. M., Weinfield, F. D., & York, R. L. (1966). *Equality of educational opportunity.* Washington, DC: Office of Education, US Government Printing Office.

Connor, J. M., Schackman, M., & Serbin, L. (1978). Sex-related differences in response to practice on a visual-spatial test and generalization to a related test. *Child Development, 49,* 24–29.

Crocker, J., & Major, B. (1989). Social stigma and self-esteem: The self-protective properties of stigma. *Psychological Report, 96,* 608–630.

Crocker, J., Major, B., & Steele, C. (1997). Social Stigma. In D. Gilbert, S. T. Fiske, & G. Lindzey (Eds.), *Handbook of social psychology* (4th ed.). Boston: McGraw Hill.

Crosby, F. (1984). Relative deprivation in organizational settings. *Research in Organizational Behavior, 84,* 651–693.

Deboer, G. E. (1986). Perceived science ability as a factor in the course selections of men and women in college. *Journal of Research in Science Teaching, 23(4),* 343–352.

Dwinell, P. L., & Higbee, J. L. (1991). Affective variables related to mathematics achievement among high-risk college freshman. *Psychological Reports, 69,* 399–403.

Eccles, J. S. (1987). Gender roles and women's achievement-related decisions. *Psychology of Women Quarterly, 11,* 135–172.

Eccles, J. S. (1994). Understanding women's educational and occupational choices. *Psychology of Women Quarterly, 18,* 585–609.

Eccles, J. S., & Jacobs, J. E. (1986). Social forces shape math attitudes and performance, *Signs, 11,* 367–380.

Eccles, J. S., Jacobs, J. E., & Harold, R. D. (1990). Gender-role stereotypes, expectancy effects, and parents' role in the socialization of gender differences in self perceptions and skill acquisition. *Journal of Personality, 46,* 182–201.

Feagin, J. R., & Sikes, M. P. (1994). *Living with racism: The Black middle-class experience.* Boston: Beacon.

Feingold, A. (1988). Cognitive gender differences are disappearing. *American Psychologist, 43,* 95–103.

Fitzgerald, L. F., & Crites, J. O. (1980). Toward a career psychology of women: What do we know? What do we need to know? *Journal of Counseling Psychology, 27,* 44–62.

Fitzgerald, L. F., Dragow, F., Hulin, C. L., Gelfand, M., & Magley, V. J. (1997). The antecedents and consequences of sexual harassment in organizations: A test of an integrated model. *Journal of Applied Psychology, 82,* 578–589.

Fordham, S., & Ogbu, J. U. (1986). Black students' success: Coping with the "burden of acting White." *Urban Review, 18,* 176–206.

Fraser, S. (1995). *The Bell Curve Wars.* New York: BasicBooks.

Goffman, E. (1963). *Stigma: Notes on the management of spoiled identity.* Englewood Cliffs, NJ: Prentice-Hall.

Gould, S. J. (1995). Curveball. In S. Fraser (Ed.), *The bell curve wars.* New York: BasicBooks.

Halpern, D. F. (1989). The disappearance of cognitive gender differences: What you see depends on where you look. *American Psychologist, 44,* 1156–1158.

Heilman, M. E. (1979). High school students' occupational interest as a function of projected sex ratios in male-dominated occupations. *Journal of Applied Psychology, 64,* 275–279.

Herrnstein, R. E., & Murray, C. A. (1994). *The Bell Curve.* New York: The Free Press.

Hewitt, N. M., & Seymour, E. (1991). Factors contributing to high arrition rates among science Hewitt, N. M., & Seymour, E. (1991). Factors contributing to high arrition rates among science and engineering undergraduate majors. Report to the Alfred P. Sloan Foundation.

Hollinger, C. L. (1983). Self-perception and the career aspirations of mathematically talented female adolescents. *Journal of Vocational Behavior, 22,* 49–62.

Hyde, J. S., Fennema, E., & Lamon, S. J. (1990). Gender differences in mathematics performance: A meta-analysis. *Psychological Bulletin, 107,* 139–155.

Jensen, A. R. (1969). How much can we boost IQ and scholastic achievement? *Harvard Educational Review, 39,* 1–123.

Jones, E. E., Farina, A., Hastorf, A. H., Markus, H., Miller, D. T., & Scott, R. A. (1984). *Social stigma: The psychology of marked relationships.* New York: Freeman.

Jones, J. (1997). *Prejudice and Racism.* New York: The McGraw-Hill Companies, Inc.

Jussim, L. (1989). Teacher expectations: Self-fulfilling prophecies, perceptual biases, and accuracy. *Journal of Personality and Social Psychology, 57,* 469–480.

Jussim, L. (1991). Social perception and social reality: A reflection-construction model. *Psychological Review, 98,* 54–73.

Jussim, L., & Fleming, C. (1996). Self-fulfilling prophecies and the maintenance of social stereotypes: The role of dyadic interactions and social forces. In C. N. Macrae, C. Stangor, & M. Hewstone (Eds.), *Stereotypes and stereotyping* (pp. 161–192). New York: The Guilford Press.

Kanter, R. M. (1976). The impact of hierarchical structures on the work behavior of women and men. *Social Problems, 23,* 415–430.

Landrine, H., & Klonoff, E. A. (1996). The schedule of racist events: A measure of racial discrimination and a study of its negative physical and mental health consequences. *Journal of Black Psychology, 22,* 144–168.

Landrine, H., Klonoff, E. A., Gibbs, J., Manning, V., & Lund. (1995). Physical and psychiatric correlates of gender discrimination: An application of the Schedule of Sexist Events. *Psychology of Women Quarterly, 19,* 473–492.

Lefevre, J., Kulak, A. G., & Heymans, S. L. (1992). Factors influencing the selection of university majors varying in mathematical content. *Canadian Journal of Behavioural Science, 24,* 276–289.

Lent, R. W., Brown, S. D., & Larkin, K. C. (1986). Self-efficacy in the prediction of academic performance and perceived career options. *Journal of Counseling Psychology, 33,* 265–269.

Liben, L. S. (1978). Performance on Piagetian spatial tasks as a function of sex, field dependence, and training. *Merrill Palmer Quarterly, 24,* 97–110.

Liben, L. S. (1991). Adults' performance on horizonality tasks: Conflicting frames of reference. *Developmental Psychology, 27,* 285–294.

Liben, L. S., & Golbeck, S. L. (1984). Performance on Piagetian horizontality and verticality task: Sex-related differences in knowledge of relevant physical phenomena. *Developmental Psychology, 20,* 595–606.

Macrae, C. N., Stangor, C., & Hewstone, M. (1996). *Stereotypes and stereotyping.* New York: The Guilford Press.

Major, B., Barr, L., Zubek, J., & Babe, S. (1996). *Gender and self-esteem: A meta-analysis.* Manuscript in preparation.

Mickelson, R. A. (1990). The attitude-achievement paradox among Black adolescents. *Sociology of Education, 63,* 44–61.

Midgley, C., Feldlaufer, H., & Eccles, J. S. (1989). Change in teacher efficacy and student self- and task-related beliefs in math during the transition to junior high school. *Journal of Educational Psychology, 81,* 247–258.

Neisser, U. (1986). *The school achievement of minority children.* Hillsdale, New Jersey: Lawrence Erlbaum Associates, Publishers.

Nettles, M. T. (1988). *Toward undergraduate student equality in American higher education.* New York: Greenwood.

Nisbett, R. (1995). Race, IQ, and scientism. In S. Fraser (Ed.), *The bell curve wars.* New York: BasicBooks.

O'Brien, K. M., & Fassinger, R. M. (1993). A causal model of the career orientation and career choice of adolescent women. *Journal of Counseling Psychology, 40,* 456–469.

Ogbu, J. (1986). The consequences of the American caste system. In U. Neisser (Ed.), *The school achievement of minority children: New perspectives.* Hillsdale, NJ: Erlbaum.

Parsons, J. E. (1983). Expectancies, values, and academic behaviors. In J. T. Spence (Ed.), *Achievement and achievement motives: Psychological and sociological approaches.* San Francisco: W. H. Freeman.

Pettigrew, T. F., & Martin, J. (1987). Shaping the organizational context for Black American inclusion. *Journal of Social Issues, 43,* 41–78.

Porter, J. R., & Washington, R. E. (1979). Black identity and self-esteem: A few studies of black self-concept, 1968–1978. *Annual Review of Sociology, 5,* 53–74.

Pryor, J. B., & McKinney, K. (1995). Research on sexual harassment: Lingering issues and future directions. *Basic and Applied Social Psychology, 17,* 605–611.

Rettew, D. C., Billman, D., & Davis, R. A. (1993). Inaccurate perceptions of the amount others stereotype: Estimates about stereotypes of one's own group and other groups. *Basic and Applied Social Psychology, 14,* 121–142.

Rosenberg, M., & Simmons, R. G. (1972). *Black and White self-esteem: The urban school child.* Washington, DC: American Sociological Association.

Ruggiero, K. M., & Taylor, D. M. (1995). Coping with discrimination: How disadvantaged group members perceive the discrimination that confronts them. *Journal of Personality and Social Psychology, 68,* 826–838.

Sadker, M., & Sadker, D. (1994). *Failing at fairness: How our schools cheat girls.* New York: Touchstone.

Skaalvik, E. M. (1986). Sex differences in global self-esteem: A research review. *Scandinavian Journal of Educational Research, 30,* 167–179.

Spears, R., Oakes, P. J., Ellemers, N., & Haslam, S. A. (1996). *The social psychology stereotyping and group life.* Oxford: Blackwell.

Stangor, C., & Carr, C. (1997). *Influence of solo status and task performance feedback on expectations about task performance in groups.* Manuscript submitted for publication.

Stangor, C., Carr, C., & Taylor, D. M. (1997). *Social determinants of academic achievement.* Manuscript in preparation.

Stangor, C., & Ruble, D. N. (1987). Development of gender role knowledge and gender constancy. In L. Liben, & M. Signorella, (Eds.). *Children's gender schemata* (pp. 5–22). San Francisco: Jossey-Bass.

Steele, C. M. (1992). Race and the schooling of Black Americans. *The Atlantic Monthly, April.*

Steele, C. M., & Aronson, J. (1995). Stereotype vulnerability and the intellectual test performance of African-Americans. *Journal of Personality and Social Psychology, 69,* 797–811.

Stockdale, M. S. (1993). The role of sexual mispreceptions of women's friendliness in an emerging theory of sexual harassment. Special Issue: Sexual harassment in the work place. *Journal of Vocational Behavior, 42,* 84–101.

Struik, R. R., & Flexer, R. J. (1984). Sex differences in mathematical achievement: Adding data to the debate. *International Journal of Women's Studies, 7,* 336–342.

Terrell, F., Terrell, S. L., & Miller, F. (1993). Level of cultural mistrust as a function of educational and occupational expectations among Black students. *Adolescence, 28,* 573–578.

Tinsley, H. E. A., & Stockdale, M. S. (1993). Sexual harassment in the workplace. *Journal of Vocational Behavior, 42,* 1–4.

Tracey, T. J., & Sedlacek, W. E. (1987). Prediction of college graduation using noncognitive variables by race. *Measurement and Evaluation in Counseling and Development,* January, 177–184.

Vetter, B. M. (1981). Women scientists and engineers: Trends in participation. *Science, 214,* 1313–1321.

Wainer, H., & Steinberg, L. S. (1992). Sex differences in performance on the mathematics section of the scholastic aptitude test: A bidirectional validity study. *Harvard Educational Review, 62,* 323–336.

Watkins, C., Terrell, F., Miller, F. S., & Terrell, S. L. (1989). Cultural mistrust and its effects on expectational variables in Black client-White counselor relationships. *Journal of Counseling Psychology, 36,* 447–450.

Weiner, B. (1974). *Achievement motivation and attribution theory.* Morristown, NJ: General Learning Press.

6

VULNERABILITY TO THE AFFECTIVE CONSEQUENCES OF THE STIGMA OF OVERWEIGHT

DIANE M. QUINN AND JENNIFER CROCKER

University of Michigan

Overweight people suffer from a variety of negative outcomes linked to their weight status, beginning with childhood teasing and derogation and following through to professional and social discrimination in adulthood (Allon, 1982; DeJong & Kleck, 1986; Larkin & Pines, 1979; Karris, 1977; Richardson, Goodman, Hastorf, & Dornbusch, 1961). Moreover, because overweight people are considered personally responsible for their condition, strangers and acquaintances are more likely to openly express their prejudice and dislike toward the overweight than toward stigmatized individuals who are not considered personally responsible for their stigma (DeJong, 1980; Crandall, 1994). Stereotypes about overweight people depict them as lazy, gluttonous, and both mentally and physically slow (Allon, 1982). Whereas open derogation of other stigmatized groups is seen as morally objectionable—or at least in bad taste—belittling jokes directed toward the overweight can be seen any night of the week on prime-time television (Coleman, 1993). Thus, the overweight learn repeatedly that they possess an attribute that discredits their persons, brands them as different, and declares that they are deserving of lesser outcomes.

Although both men and women are stigmatized for being obese, negative reactions and consequences may apply more strongly and at lower levels of overweight for women (Fallon, 1990). Unlike the cultural ideal for men, which includes a body shape quite similar to the natural body shape of men, the cultural ideal for women includes a practically unreachable standard of thinness, quite different from the natural body shape of most women (Rodin, Silberstein, & Striegel-Moore, 1984). Failure to realize this thinness standard may make certain groups of American women vulnerable to being stigmatized at weight levels that are below the medical criteria for obesity. In fact, Rodin *et al.* (1984), assert that constant worrying about weight, and chronic dieting, have become the norm for women in America.

It has long been hypothesized that social stigmatization leads to negative feelings about the self. Symbolic interactionists, such as Cooley (1956) and Mead (1934), proposed that people come to view themselves the way that others view them. Feelings about the self reflect and develop out of others' responses to the self. Given the seemingly constant and pervasive devaluation of those who are overweight, clinicians and researchers have long assumed that people who are overweight or obese would exhibit increased psychological distress, particularly low self-esteem. However, the relationship between being a member of a stigmatized group and self-regard has not been as straightforward as expected. Recent reviews have shown that for many stigmatized groups, global levels of self-esteem are consistently as high or higher than the self-esteem of nonstigmatized group members (Crocker & Major, 1989). Empirical research comparing levels of psychological distress between those who are overweight and those who are not has revealed mixed results—some studies find that the overweight have lower self-esteem and higher rates of depression compared to the normal weight, whereas other studies do not find any mean differences between the two groups (for reviews, see Downey & Miller, 1996; Friedman & Brownell, 1995; Jarvie, Lahey, Graziano, & Framer, 1983). Based on these inconsistent findings, some researchers have concluded that the stigma of overweight may not have any direct negative psychological consequences, in spite of its overwhelmingly negative connotations.

Instead of searching for direct negative psychological consequences, Friedman and Brownell (1995) have suggested that individual differences in levels of psychological distress among those who are overweight may be so great that the variability overwhelms any between-group effects. These researchers have called for a more complex approach to studying the psychological correlates of overweight. They suggest developing a model of risk factors to predict who will be vulnerable to psychological distress due to their overweight status. This approach suggests that there may be both demographic variables such as age, race, and geographical location, as well as psychological variables, which will raise or lower a person's vulnerability to the psychological distress related to being overweight.

Alternatively, the psychological consequences of stigma may be context-specific, rather than internalized. That is, stigmatized individuals may be vulnerable to distress and low self-esteem in some, but not all, circumstances. Thus, one approach searches for traitlike vulnerability factors while the other focuses on statelike vulnerability contexts. Research in our laboratory has begun to investigate both approaches to the understanding of the stigma of overweight and its affective consequences. Although we have been looking at these variables separately, it is likely that both individual differences and specific contexts play a part in explaining why some overweight people are vulnerable to negative feelings about the self while others are not.

INDIVIDUAL VULNERABILITY FACTORS

REFLECTED APPRAISALS

Self-concept theorists point to several ways in which self-regard may be affected by being a member of a stigmatized group (i.e., Crocker & Major, 1989; Goffman, 1963; Steele, 1988; Cooley, 1956; Harter, 1993; Shrauger & Schoeneman, 1979). First, most individuals base their feelings about the self on a number of different competencies and areas of importance. Family attachment, appearance, and achievement are just a few of the areas upon which a person may base his or her self-esteem. One basis of self-esteem that we have begun to explore as a vulnerability factor is the amount a person bases his or her self-regard on the opinions or evaluations of others. Individuals whose self-esteem is highly dependent on receiving praise and approval from others, or "reflected appraisals" in Cooley's (1956) terms, may be vulnerable to low self-esteem when they fail to receive those positive evaluations. Given the normal fluctuations in others' opinions and evaluations, basing one's self-regard on approval from others is a risky strategy for any person. However, because an overweight person is especially likely to be stigmatized and devalued, basing self-esteem on reflected appraisals may be a particularly damaging strategy. Thus, one of our goals was to examine the relationship between basing self-esteem on reflected appraisals and level of self-esteem for both normal weight and overweight people.

DISLIKE OF THE OVERWEIGHT

A second vulnerability factor, similar to the original views of symbolic interactionists, is the possibility that some stigmatized people have internalized the negative cultural view of their group. Thus, those overweight people who agree with negative stereotypes of the overweight may be most vulnerable to negative views of the self. The stigma of overweight is a somewhat unique stigma in that many of those in the stigmatized group consider their status temporary. There is no reason for them to develop group consciousness or attempt to change the way society views their weight because most members believe that they will be able to leave the group through weight loss. Therefore, a person may profess great dislike and disgust toward overweight others even though he or she may be overweight. Indeed, research by Crandall (1994; Crandall & Biernat, 1990) on "anti-fat attitudes" shows that normal weight and overweight people are equally high in dislike of the overweight. Although neither normal nor overweight people express extreme negative views of overweight people, the negativity they do express does not differ by personal weight status. It may seem odd that those who categorize themselves as overweight express negative views toward other overweight people, but these negative views may have a number of positive benefits for the overweight: It may feel normative (with the culture as a whole), motivational (for attempting weight loss), and even mood enhancing (to think of the self

as separate from, and one day no longer a part of, the overweight group). However, disliking overweight people when one is a member of the group seems risky
for self-esteem, especially given the actual difficulty of ever leaving the group.
Recent research has shown that maintaining a weight loss (after dieting) is extremely difficult, with some putting the percentage of people re-gaining weight
(after a loss) as high as 90 to 95 percent (National Center for Health Statistics,
1991). These figures suggest that once a person is substantially overweight, he or
she will remain in that weight group permanently. Over time and with repeated
failures at dieting, disliking overweight others may come to be synonymous with
disliking the self.

CONSERVATIVE IDEOLOGICAL BELIEFS

Another possible vulnerability factor is the extent to which overweight people
hold conservative ideological beliefs, such as belief in the Protestant work ethic
(Katz & Hass, 1988), or belief in a just world (Lerner, 1980). These beliefs emphasize personal responsibility and control for life outcomes—both positive and
negative. Given that the overweight experience many negative outcomes due to
their stigma, believing that they are personally responsible could be harmful.
Crandall (1994) has found that dislike toward the overweight is predicted by
conservative ideological beliefs about personal responsibility and deservingness
of outcomes, such that the more people endorse conservative ideology beliefs, the
more they dislike the overweight. Crandall suggests that the link between conservative ideology and dislike of the overweight is mediated by beliefs about the
controllability of weight. Specifically, conservative ideological leanings are strongly
related to the belief that weight is controllable, which in turn leads to dislike of the
overweight because the overweight are held responsible for their condition. Thus,
holding a set of conservative ideological beliefs may be particularly harmful to
feelings of self-worth for the overweight if they interpret their overweight status
to mean personal failure at weight control and deservingness of negative outcomes.
Conversely, the relationship between ideology and self-regard may be positive for
the normal weight. Those normal weight persons who hold these conservative
ideological beliefs can feel personally responsible (and perhaps morally superior)
for maintaining their normal weight status and deserving of any positive outcomes
they receive as a result of it. In short, believing in an ideology of personal responsibility may lead to feelings of decreased self-worth and increased negative affect
for the overweight and feelings of increased self-worth for the normal weight.

EXAMINING INDIVIDUAL
VULNERABILITY FACTORS

As an initial step in examining reflected appraisals, dislike, and conservative
ideology as vulnerability factors for overweight people, we conducted a survey

TABLE 6.1   Means (and Standard Deviations) for Normal Weight and Overweight Women

	Perceived normal weight	Perceived overweight	
Psychological well-being			
Rosenberg self-esteem	3.35 (0.51)	3.18 (0.51)	$p < .05$
CES-D	1.77 (0.53)	1.89 (0.49)	$p = .06$
Anxiety	2.09 (0.46)	2.20 (0.45)	$p = .05$
Vulnerability factors			
Dislike of overweight	2.26 (1.32)	2.38 (1.34)	ns
Belief in weight controllability	4.41 (1.28)	4.70 (1.22)	$p = .06$
Reflected appraisals	5.60 (1.32)	5.74 (1.23)	ns
Protestant ethic	4.25 (0.66)	4.39 (0.64)	$p = .09$

study of 257 college women. The survey contained the Protestant ethic scale (Katz & Hass, 1988) as an *ideology* measure, measures of feelings of *dislike* toward the overweight and beliefs in the *general controllability* of weight, both based on Crandall (1994), a *reflected appraisals* scale (Crocker & Wolfe, 1996), a global *self-esteem* scale (Rosenberg, 1965), a *depression* symptomology scale (Center for Epidemiological Studies—Depression Scale), and a trait *anxiety* scale (Spielberger, Gorsuch, & Lushene, 1970). In order to look at the different relationships for normal and overweight women, we used a measure of self-perceived weight status on which participants ranked themselves from "extremely underweight" to "extremely overweight."

In our sample of college women there were mean differences in the psychological well-being of those who perceived themselves as normal weight and those who felt overweight (see Table 6.1 for means). The women who felt overweight had significantly lower self-esteem than the normal weight women. In addition, overweight women had higher levels of anxiety and marginally higher levels of depression. Thus, in this particular sample, perceiving the self to be overweight was itself a vulnerability factor for negative affect and self-regard. However, consistent with Crandall's (1994) findings, there were no mean differences between the overweight and the normal weight for amount of dislike toward the overweight. There were marginally significant differences between the overweight and normal weight in belief in the Protestant ethic and belief in the controllability of weight, with overweight women being slightly more likely to hold conservative ideological beliefs and to believe that weight is controllable.

The results of the survey replicated Crandall's (1994) findings. There was a strong relationship between belief in the Protestant ethic ideology and dislike of overweight people ($r = .27$, $p < .001$), as well as significant correlations between ideology and belief in the general controllability of weight ($r = .38$, $p < .001$), and belief in the general controllability of weight and dislike of the overweight ($r = .43$, $p < .001$). In addition, Crandall (1994) found that belief in the general controllability of weight mediated the relationship between ideology and dislike. In order to test whether our survey results replicated this finding, we conducted a hierarchical regression predicting dislike, with ideology entered on the first step and controllability entered on the second step. The beta for ideology was reduced from .27 to .12 when controllability was entered, although it remained significant at $p < .04$. Thus, although there was partial mediation by belief in controllability of weight, in this sample there remained a direct relationship between ideology and dislike of the overweight.

DISLIKE OF THE OVERWEIGHT
AND CONSERVATIVE IDEOLOGY

Next, we examined each of the possible vulnerability factors—dislike, ideology, and reflected appraisals—for each of our psychological outcomes (self-esteem, depression, and anxiety). We regressed each psychological outcome variable on self-perceived weight status and the vulnerability factor in the first step, and the interaction of the two on the second step. We found that for self-esteem there was a main effect of dislike ($\beta = -.13$, $p < .05$) and weight status ($\beta = -.15$, $p < .05$), indicating that greater dislike of the overweight (regardless of one's weight status) and feeling overweight were related to lower self-esteem. More importantly, however, there was also an interaction between the two ($\beta = -.19$, $p < .01$). Specifically, the more overweight women felt, the more

TABLE 6.2   Main Effects and Interactions for Each Vulnerability Factor on Self-esteem, Anxiety, and Depression

	Self-esteem	Anxiety	Depression
Dislike			
Dislike	$\beta = -.13$*	$\beta = .12$*	$\beta = .10^r$
Weight status	$\beta = -.15$*	$\beta = .12$*	$\beta = .10$
Dislike × weight status	$\beta = -.19$*	$\beta = .12$*	$\beta = .08$
Conservative ideology			
Conservative ideology	$\beta = .04$	$\beta = -.10$	$\beta = -.05$
Weight status	$\beta = -.16$*	$\beta = .14$*	$\beta = .11^r$
Cons. ideology × weight status	$\beta = -.10^r$	$\beta = .12$*	$\beta = .16$*
Reflected appraisals			
Reflected appraisals	$\beta = -.37$*	$\beta = .30$*	$\beta = .14$*
Weight status	$\beta = -.13$*	$\beta = .10^r$	$\beta = .10$
Ref. appraisals × weight status	$\beta = -.10^r$	$\beta = .04$	$\beta = -.01$
Belief in general controllability of weight			
Controllability beliefs	$\beta = .05$	$\beta = -.09$	$\beta = -.05$
Weight status	$\beta = -.16$*	$\beta = .13$*	$\beta = .11^r$
Controllability × weight status	$\beta = -.13$*	$\beta = .11^r$	$\beta = .08$

*$p \le .05$; ^{r} $p < .10$

TABLE 6.3   Relationship between Dislike of the Overweight and Self-Esteem, Anxiety, and Depression, for the Overweight and Normal Weight

	Self-esteem	Trait anxiety	Depression
Self-perceived overweight	$\beta = -.24, p < .01$	$\beta = .22, p = .01$	$\beta = .17, p < .05$
Self-perceived normal weight	$\beta = .004$, ns	$\beta = .02$, ns	$\beta = .02$, ns

strongly dislike of overweight people was related to low self-esteem. Therefore, although normal weight and overweight women had similar levels of dislike, the dislike presented a risk factor for low self-esteem for the overweight women only. A similar interaction between weight status and dislike occurred for state anxiety ($\beta = .12$, $p < .05$) (see Table 6.2 for a complete listing of all main effects and interactions). For overweight women only, greater dislike was related to greater anxiety. For the depression variable, there was not a significant interaction between weight status and dislike. In order to clarify the meaning of the interactions, separate analyses were run for self-perceived overweight women and self-perceived normal weight women. The relationships between dislike and the psychological outcomes variables for each group of women is shown in Table 6.3. For women who perceive themselves as overweight, holding negative feelings toward the overweight as a group is a vulnerability factor for decreased self-esteem and increased anxiety.

Probing the interactions between weight status and conservative ideology showed a slightly different pattern of results. Examination of the interaction between belief in the Protestant ethic and self-perceived weight status resulted in the following: The interaction between ideology and self-perceived weight was marginally significant for self-esteem ($\beta = -.10$, $p = .09$), significant for trait anxiety ($\beta = .12$, $p < .05$), and significant for depression ($\beta = .16$, $p < .01$). However, the pattern of these interactions is not as clear as was the case for the dislike variable. As can be seen in Table 6.4, when the analyses were run separately for each weight group, the effects of belief in a conservative ideology on psychological well-being were consistently in opposite directions for overweight and normal weight women. However, ideology was significantly related to higher self-esteem and lower depression and anxiety for the normal weight women, whereas it was

TABLE 6.4   The Relationship between Conservative Ideology and Self-Esteem, Anxiety, and Depression, for the Overweight and Normal Weight

	Self-esteem	Trait anxiety	Depression
Self-perceived overweight	$\beta = -.09$, ns	$\beta = .06$, ns	$\beta = .13$, ns
Self-perceived normal weight	$\beta = .15, p = .08$	$\beta = -.21, p < .05$	$\beta = -.23, p < .05$

TABLE 6.5   The Relationship between Belief in the Controllability of Weight and Self-Esteem, Anxiety, and Depression, for the Overweight and Normal Weight

	Self-esteem	Trait anxiety	Depression
Self-perceived overweight	$\beta = -.10$, ns	$\beta = .04$, ns	$\beta = .04$, ns
Self-perceived normal weight	$\beta = .15$, p = .10	$\beta = -.18$, p < .05	$\beta = -.12$, ns

not significantly related to self-esteem, depression, or anxiety for the overweight women.

A more specific and focused type of belief in personal responsibility is the measure of belief in the general controllability of weight. Whereas conservative ideology, as measured by the Protestant ethic scale, measures a broad belief system, the measure of belief in the general controllability of weight examines the extent to which people believe that weight is controlled by each person and each person is responsible for weight status. Thus, belief in the controllability of weight could be seen as a more proximal form of conservative ideology. When weight controllability beliefs, weight status, and their interaction were entered in a hierarchical regression, there was a significant interaction between controllability and weight status on self-esteem ($\beta = -.13$, $p < .05$), and a marginally significant interaction for anxiety ($\beta = .11$, $p = .08$). No interaction effect was found for depression. Examining the relationships separately for each group shows a similar pattern to conservative ideology. As can be seen in Table 6.5, believing in the controllability of weight has opposite effects on self-esteem, anxiety, and depression for normal weight and overweight women, with the stronger relationships occurring for normal weight women.

In sum, the dislike variable presented a clear vulnerability factor for overweight women. It was strongly negatively related to self-esteem and positively related to anxiety and depression. For normal weight women, however, dislike of the overweight had virtually no relationship with self-esteem, depression, or anxiety. Thus, not surprisingly, disliking one's own group—perhaps internalizing the negative cultural view—has a negative relationship with psychological well-being, whereas disliking a stigmatized group one is not a member of has no relationship to psychological well-being. The relationships for conservative ideology and belief in the controllability of weight were more complex. Conservative ideology seems to serve as a resiliency factor for normal weight women. The more normal weight women believed that people are responsible for their outcomes, the lower their depression and anxiety, and the higher their self-esteem. However, for overweight women, belief in conservative ideology did not have these positive outcomes. Although belief in conservative ideology was not significantly negatively related to the psychological outcomes among the overweight, believing that one is personally responsible for one's outcomes certainly did not lead overweight women to feel better about themselves.

REFLECTED APPRAISALS

The last individual vulnerability factor we were interested in exploring was basing self-regard on others' opinions. We measured reflected appraisals using a recently developed scale (Crocker & Wolfe, 1996). The scale includes items such as, "It's important to me to be well thought of by others," "I can't respect myself if others don't respect me," and "What I think about myself is unrelated to how other people view me." Normal weight and overweight women did not differ in how much their self-regard was based on reflected appraisals. A regression analysis showed a main effect for basing self-regard on reflected appraisals, such that it was highly negatively related to self-esteem for *both* normal weight and overweight women ($\beta = -.37$, $p < .001$). However, even with the reflected appraisals variable held constant, there was a main effect for weight status on self-esteem ($\beta = -.13$, $p < .05$). In addition, the interaction between weight status and reflected appraisals was marginally significant ($\beta = -.10$, $p = .07$). Examining the relationship between reflected appraisals and self-esteem separately for the overweight and normal weight women showed that although basing self-esteem on reflected appraisals was negatively related to self-esteem for normal weight women ($\beta = -.28$, $p < .01$), it was even more strongly and negatively related for overweight women ($\beta = -.46$, $p < .001$). For both depression and anxiety there was a main effect for reflected appraisals ($\beta = .14$, $p < .05$, $\beta = .30$, $p < .001$, respectively), but no significant interaction between reflected appraisals and weight status. Thus, depending on reflected appraisals as a basis for self-esteem can be considered a vulnerability factor for all women and especially risky for overweight women.

THE STIGMA OF OVERWEIGHT AND VULNERABILITY FACTORS FOR MEN

Our analysis thus far has focused on vulnerability factors for women who perceive themselves to be overweight. Our research has focused on women for several reasons. Weight concerns seem to be much more salient and pressing for women than for men (Rodin *et al.,* 1984). Women feel more stigmatized at lower levels of overweight than men (Fallon & Rozin, 1985). Women experience eating disorders—the extreme outcomes of concern with weight—at much higher rates than men (Drewnowski, Hopkins, & Kessler, 1988; Lucas, Beard, O'Fallon, & Kurland, 1991), making the stigma of overweight for women both a psychological and a physiological problem. Also, there is some evidence that concerns with the shape and size of their bodies affects women in unique and negative ways, including interfering with concentration and introducing body shame (Fredrickson & Roberts, 1996). However, this is not to say that overweight men do not feel stigmatized, or that excess weight is a stigma only for women. Although men may not place themselves within the overweight category at the same levels of overweight as women, it may be that those men who do perceive themselves as overweight have the same vulnerability factors for negative psychological outcomes as women. Whether this is the case or not, to gain a full understanding of the stigma of overweight, it is important to study all people who feel stigmatized.

In order to examine the question of whether men have the same vulnerability factors as women, we gave a sample of male college students the same survey given to the women. Unfortunately, our sample is quite lopsided—we have only 40 self-perceived overweight men and approximately 160 self-perceived normal weight men. Keeping these sample limitations in mind, we conducted parallel analyses to those conducted with the female participants. Normal weight and overweight men did not differ on mean levels of self-esteem, depression, or anxiety. They also did not differ in levels of conservative ideology or on basing their self-esteem on reflected appraisals. Normal weight men, however, did express significantly more dislike toward the overweight than did the overweight men ($Ms = 3.1, 2.4$, respectively, $p < .05$). Perhaps not surprisingly then, there were no weight by vulnerability factor interactions for any of the psychological outcome measures. That is, neither dislike, conservative ideology, nor reflected appraisals were differentially related to psychological outcomes for overweight men as compared to normal weight men. However, as was found for women, basing self-esteem on reflected appraisals was negatively related to global self-esteem and positively related to depression and anxiety for all of the men, regardless of weight status. Because of our sample limitations, it is difficult to make a strong statement about the vulnerability factors for overweight men. However, from this college sample, it seems that men do not experience the stigma of overweight in a psychologically similar manner to women who feel overweight.

RACE DIFFERENCES: REFLECTED APPRAISALS

Although in our survey sample we found that basing self-esteem on reflected appraisals was a risk factor for all of the women and men, it must be noted that the majority of the sample were European Americans, and all were college age. There may be some groups which differ substantially in the amount they base their self-esteem on reflected appraisals. Crocker and Major (1989) have theorized that some stigmatized groups learn to protect their self-regard by recognizing that many of the negative outcomes they receive are a result of prejudice and discrimination against their group. These group members can then attribute negative outcomes and evaluations to an external source—discrimination—instead of an internal source—their selves. In short, some stigmatized individuals may learn to discount or ignore negative appraisals from others, and in return protect their self-esteem. Crocker and Major (1989) suggest that this is one reason why African Americans, even with their long history of cultural devaluation, tend to have self-esteem equal to or higher than European Americans. One interesting question is whether *not* basing self-esteem on reflected appraisals is protective for African Americans not only in the realm of race, but also in the realm of overweight. If African Americans are less likely to base their regard on other's opinions, will that serve as a protector of self-esteem for overweight African Americans as compared to overweight European Americans? Kerr, Crocker, and Broadnax (1995) conducted a survey study to explore this question.

Kerr and colleagues (1995) had 90 African American women and 82 European American women complete a survey. The women were approached in an urban shopping mall and were paid to fill out a survey that included their self-perceived weight status, self-esteem (Rosenberg, 1965), a depression scale (Beck Depression Inventory), and a short measure of our reflected appraisals scale. The average age of the women was in their early 30s. The women were a diverse sample in both income and education.

Contrary to the women in our college sample, the overweight and normal weight women in this sample did not differ in self-esteem or depression. Also, there were no race differences on these variables. However, there was an significant interaction indicating that overweight European American women had higher depression scores than the other three groups. Thus, feeling overweight had more negative consequences for the well-being of European American women than for the African American women. There was also a mean difference in reflected appraisals, with European American women more likely to base their self-esteem on reflected appraisals than African American women. In a series of regression equations, which controlled for demographic variables such as age, education, and socioeconomic status, Kerr and colleagues found that the weight group by race interaction on depression was partially explained by the race differences in basis of self-esteem. The overweight European American women were more likely to be depressed than the overweight African American women in part because they based their self-esteem to a greater extent on reflected appraisals. Thus, the lowered likelihood of African Americans to base their self-esteem on reflected appraisals does seem to be a general protective factor against psychological distress.

INDIVIDUAL DIFFERENCE VULNERABILITY FACTORS: CONCLUSIONS AND SPECULATIONS

The work reviewed above suggests a number of possible vulnerability factors for the psychological well-being of the overweight. Perhaps the easiest initial classifications for who is most vulnerable (or resilient) are gender and race. In our college age sample, overweight women had significantly lower self-esteem than their normal weight peers, while no such difference existed between overweight and normal weight men. In addition, European American women seem to be more vulnerable than African American women to the psychological consequences of the stigma of overweight. In our community survey sample, European American women who felt overweight also felt depressed, while this was not the case for African American women.

Although demographic variables such as gender and race make it easy to predict who may be more vulnerable to the stigma of overweight, such categories do not give much insight into *why* certain people are more vulnerable or more resilient to stigma. The "why" question might be answered by examining how gender and race are related to a number of concepts, including cultural standards for beauty and size, individual differences in personality characteristics (i.e., level of basing self-worth on reflected appraisals, and level of dislike for the overweight group), and ideology (i.e., conservative ideology emphasizing personal responsibility and deservingness).

Women in American culture are continually exposed to impossibly thin beauty standards. Although the standards for men include that they be physically fit and attractive, it is unlikely that they have the same psychological effects that the beauty standards have for women (Fallon, 1990). Recent theorizing by Fredrickson and Roberts (1996) suggests that the focus on women's bodies in America is so intense that both men and women tend to objectify women's bodies, making body parts separate from, and perhaps more important than, women as whole, complex, individuals. Women may even come to chronically view their own bodies from the third person perspective, with a constant emphasis on evaluating their appearance and comparing it to the ideal. In addition, women are more likely to equate a positive evaluation of how they look with a positive evaluation of their self than men are (Lerner, Orlos, & Knapp, 1976). Therefore, although extreme obesity may be stigmatizing for both men and women, the cultural beauty standards for women combined with the constant scrutiny of women's bodies may lead to feelings of stigmatization at much lower levels of overweight for women.

However, the cultural standard for beauty and thinness that saturates American media tends to depict primarily European American women. Not all subgroups of American women aspire to the same ideal of thinness. It has been suggested that African Americans have a much more realistic, rounded shape as their female body standard (Heatherton, Kiwan, & Hebl, 1996; Cunningham, Roberts, Barbee, Druen, & Wu, 1995). Women within these groups may be less vulnerable to psychological distress because their weight status does not carry the same stigmatization. Recent work by Heatherton and colleagues (1996) showed that African American and European American women have very different evaluations of overweight women. Heatherton and colleagues showed European American and African American female study participants photos of both normal weight and overweight women and had the participants rate the women in the photos on a number of dimensions. Whereas the European Americans denigrated the overweight women in the photos—assigning them lower scores on attributes such as intelligence, happiness, and relationship success—the African Americans did not denigrate the overweight women in the photos—particularly if they were photos of African American women. Thus, African American women may be less vulnerable to the stigma of overweight because they hold different standards for body shape and size, and they do not attach negative stereotypes to large bodies.

Another way in which the differing relationship between overweight, race, and vulnerability may be explained is through differences in the amount individuals base their self-esteem on others' evaluations. Crocker and Major (1989) suggested that one way members of stigmatized groups can protect their self-esteem is to disregard others' evaluations of them. Or, more specifically, to view others' evaluations as tainted by prejudice and discrimination, and, therefore invalid for judging the self. However, it may not always be clear whether others' evaluations are due to discrimination or not, thereby placing members of stigmatized groups in a state of attributional ambiguity. For African Americans there may be less ambiguity. They may learn from other group members, as well as through their own experience, that negative evaluations and outcomes are often determined by race. Thus, African American women, as a group, may be less likely to base their self-evaluations on the evaluations of others. European American women, however, may not be as likely to view their negative outcomes in terms of discrimination. Instead, when they are experiencing attributional ambiguity about their outcomes, they may be more willing to accept others' evaluations and to focus attributions (and blame) on the self. Thus, European American women may be more apt to use reflected appraisals as a basis of self-esteem. In fact, recent work by Crocker and Wolfe (1996) showed mean differences in the amount African Americans and European Americans based their self-esteem on reflected appraisals. Our data show that using reflected appraisals as a basis of self-esteem can make women more vulnerable to negative psychological well-being—particularly women who feel overweight. Thus, African American women's decreased likelihood of basing self-esteem on reflected appraisals may be one factor explaining the race differences in the vulnerability to the stigma of overweight.

The final two vulnerability factors are dislike of the overweight group and conservative ideological leanings. Both of these variables may also partially explain the relationships between gender, race, and vulnerability. As noted, if African American women have different beauty standards and greater acceptance of bigger body shapes (Heatherton *et al.*, 1996), they are also less likely to have dislike and negative affect toward overweight others. European American women may be more vulnerable to the psychological effects of the stigma of overweight because they feel greater dislike of overweight others than African American women feel. Thus, although disliking the overweight may feel normative for European-American women, repeated failure to actually lose weight might lead the dislike of overweight others to turn into greater dislike of the self (i.e., lower self-esteem).

The final individual vulnerability factor we examined was conservative ideology. Those women who believe that people generally are responsible for their outcomes may be most likely to feel they deserve the negative outcomes they receive from being overweight. Interestingly, in our college sample, although we did find an interaction between belief in a conservative ideology and weight status on psychological well-being, a closer examination of the pattern of relationships showed that normal weight women seem to be particularly benefited (psychologically) by belief in a conservative ideology. That is, it was normal weight women holding conservative beliefs who had higher self-esteem and lower depression and anxiety. Although the pattern was reversed for overweight women, the relationships were not as strong. Thus, in agreement with the literature on belief in a just world (Lerner, 1980) and perceived control (i.e., Taylor & Brown, 1988), normal weight women who believe they are in control of, and responsible for, their outcomes have more positive psychological well-being. However, this leaves open the question of what happens when overweight women believe they are responsible for their outcomes, yet those outcomes are consistently negative (i.e., chronic diet failure and stigmatization). There is also evidence that African Americans are less likely to agree with the tenets of the Protestant ethic or the belief in a just world (Crocker & Sung, 1995; Smith & Green, 1984). If this is the case, overweight African Americans may be less likely to hold themselves (or overweight others) responsible for negative outcomes received due to their stigma.

CONTEXT-DEPENDENT VULNERABILITY: DATING STUDIES

A different way to resolve the contradictory findings between weight status and psychological well-being is to argue that the psychological consequences of stigma are context-specific, rather than internalized. There may be certain events or circumstances in which stigmatized individuals are vulnerable to distress, while in many other contexts, their stigma has no bearing on affect and feelings about the self. This view is consistent with evidence that the self-concept is dynamic and responsive to challenges from the environment (Markus & Kunda, 1986; Markus & Wurf, 1986). Instead of being passive internalizing agents of the negative cultural view, overweight people may be temporarily affected by negative outcomes in certain contexts, but overall they will respond in ways that protect their self-regard.

In order to begin to investigate these possibilities, two studies were conducted in a context in which weight and appearance are particularly salient: a dating context. In a study by Crocker, Cornwell, and Major (1993), overweight and normal weight college women came into the lab for a study of dating relationships. All participants first filled out a trait self-esteem scale. Participants believed that they would be exchanging information with an attractive male college student who was ostensibly in the next room. All women filled out a form with information about themselves, including height and weight. The women then received feedback from the male about how much he wanted to get to know the participant, to date her, and to get into a long-term relationship with her. Half of the women received feedback from the male that was positive—he was very interested in dating her. The other half of the women received negative feedback—he was not interested in dating her. Participants then answered questions about why the male did or did not want to date them. Attributions to his personality, the participant's personality, his concern with appearance, and the participant's weight were assessed. Participants also completed measures of mood, depression, anxiety, hostility, and state self-esteem. Crocker and colleagues (1993) found that the overweight women were more likely to attribute the man's negative feedback to their weight than the normal weight women were, but they were *not* more likely to attribute the negative feedback to the man's concern with appearance. Thus, it seems that while the overweight women did recognize that they received a negative outcome from the man because of their weight, they did not blame him for that negative outcome. For the overweight women who received negative feedback, levels of negative mood, depression, and hostility were all significantly higher than for either overweight women who received positive feedback, or normal weight women who received either positive or negative feedback. Likewise, the state self-esteem of overweight participants who received negative feedback was lower than the other three groups. However, there were no significant changes in trait self-esteem from before to after the feedback for any of the women. Apparently overweight women are vulnerable to negative affect in certain contexts, such as when rejected in a dating context, but the negative affect and feelings about the self may be only temporary reactions to a particular event—not a vulnerability that is perpetually salient in all contexts.

Although the overweight women were not asked to state explicitly how much they deserved the negative reaction they received, their responses suggest that the overweight women did not blame the male participant for his negative reaction. It seems that, at least in this particular context, overweight women who receive a negative outcome which they attribute to their weight do not feel that they are being unjustly discriminated against. Instead, they seem to feel that they are deserving of the negative outcome because of their weight status. There are at least two possible reasons for this outcome. First, it may be that overweight people feel that discrimination based on their weight is deserved only in contexts in which appearance is considered a relevant, legitimate basis of evaluation. This study was designed to emulate a dating/attraction context, in which appearance is considered by many people to be highly relevant. It is possible that had the situation been one in which appearance was not perceived as a legitimate basis of evaluation—such as a hiring context or evaluation of job competence—overweight people might have seen the negative feedback as completely illegitimate and undeserved. If this were the case, the affective reactions might be quite different. Because we have only examined one context, it remains for future research to investigate the effects of varied contexts.

However, a second possibility is that overweight people are vulnerable to negative outcomes only when they feel that they are in control of the attribute upon which they are being evaluated. Specifically, when overweight people feel that their weight is personally controllable, they may also feel that discrimination based on their weight is deserved. Although believing that weight is controllable may be partially an individual difference (as tested in the survey study), it is possible that the controllability of one's weight may be made more or less salient within a context. Thus, it may be only during those events, or contexts, in which overweight people feel the most responsible for their weight status, that they are the most vulnerable.

In order to take a closer look at this question, Amato and Crocker (1995) conducted a study that replicated the negative feedback condition of the study by Crocker and colleagues (1993) for overweight and normal weight women. In this study, the researchers manipulated beliefs about the controllability of weight. Amato and Crocker hypothesized that if women believe that weight is not controllable—that they are not responsible for their weight—then they should also feel that receiving negative outcomes based on such an uncontrollable attribute is unfair. Belief in the controllability of weight was manipulated by having all subjects read a passage that supposedly came from the Surgeon General. The passage convincingly stated the evidence that weight is controllable (for half the subjects), or is not controllable (for the remaining subjects). Participants in this study had a similar cover story to that of Crocker and colleagues (1993); they believed that the study was one in which they would be exchanging information with a potential male dating partner. However, in this study, subjects read the passage about the controllability of weight as part of a test of "cognitive abilities" ostensibly for use on a later "judgment" part of the study. Thus, after reading the controllability manipulation, all participants received negative dating feedback from the supposed male participant. After the negative feedback, all participants completed a series of questionnaires, including a manipulation check of belief in the controllability of weight, attributions for the male's feedback, a deservingness scale about how deserved and justified the male's feedback was, state self-esteem, trait self-esteem, and a mood scale.

The manipulation checks showed that women who read that weight was controllable did believe that weight was more controllable than women who read that weight was not controllable. As predicted, overweight women in the weight-uncontrollable condition made more attributions to the male's prejudice than overweight women in the weight-controllable condition, and more than normal weight women in both conditions. Although the pattern of means for the deserving scale followed a similar pattern—overweight women in the weight-uncontrollable condition saw the negative feedback as least justified and least deserved—the interaction did not reach significance. In addition, when initial trait self-esteem was controlled for, post-feedback self-esteem was affected by the weight-controllability manipulation. There was a significant interaction such that overweight women in the weight-controllable condition had the lowest self-esteem of all three groups. Surprisingly, however, negative mood was also affected, such that overweight women in the weight-*uncontrollable* condition had the highest amount of negative mood.

Thus, it seems that believing that weight is not controllable allowed the overweight women to make attributions to prejudice that protected trait self-esteem. However, these same attributions did not protect mood. How vulnerable overweight people are to different events may depend on the extent to which they are made to feel responsible for their weight status. In this study, the combination of a "Surgeon's General" report asserting weight is controllable with a social rejection placed overweight women in a context that resulted in negative feelings about the self. In addition, these results reaffirm one of the suggestions stated earlier about why it is so difficult to changes people's feelings of responsibility and control of their weight: These beliefs enhance people's mood, probably by allowing the overweight person to remain optimistic about one day changing his or her weight and leaving the overweight group.

CONCLUSIONS

For those who feel overweight, vulnerability to psychological distress may be precipitated by certain contexts, beliefs, and/or bases of self-esteem. The research presented in this chapter is an initial attempt to examine some of these risk factors. Although we have examined contextual effects and individual differences separately, in the everyday life of those who feel stigmatized, the two doubtless interact to determine how people evaluate themselves and their outcomes.

Research on the stigmatized may be criticized for focusing too much on what to change about the stigmatized, and not enough on how to change the culture. Although we would like to see the culture changed such that being overweight and feeling overweight is no longer stigmatizing, there is little evidence that our culture is moving in that direction. In fact, given the current multibillion dollar diet and weight loss industry's economic stake in promoting the thin ideal, it is doubtful that cultural standards and beliefs are going to change in the near future. Although we have focused on who may be vulnerable to distress and when they may be vulnerable, it may be useful at this point to look at the flip side of the research. That is, we can begin to paint a picture of people who feel that they are overweight, but who are *resilient* to psychological distress due to the stigma of overweight.

First, those people who are most resilient may not view the overweight group with dislike or disgust. They have not internalized the negative stereotypes about the overweight group. Second, they do not base their self-regard on others' evaluations and opinions of them. Maybe they base their self-regard on their own accomplishments or on the love and support of their family. We cannot be sure, but we know that these resilient people do not depend on others' approval to feel good about themselves. Third, resiliency may be increased by not endorsing a conservative ideology, but, instead realizing that not all outcomes are deserved and not all things (including weight) are under personal control. Finally, these resiliency factors may interact with certain types of situations. If the situation is one where outcomes are not linked to weight status, then overweight people may not need to draw on these resiliencies at all. However, if the situation is one where a social rejection occurs, it might be momentarily painful, but resilient people have the resources to cope with the rejection and not experience any long-lasting psychological distress. This may be particularly true if they solidly believe that their weight is not controllable. Thus, although we have presented our research with a focus on who is vulnerable, it also possible to think about who is resilient, and how the stigma of overweight can be reduced. Viewed in this way, those who feel overweight are not passive victims of stigma, but active individuals, working like all people to feel good about themselves and their world.

REFERENCES

Allon, N. (1982). The stigma of overweight in everyday life. In B. Wolman (Ed.), *Psychological aspects of obesity: A handbook* (pp. 130–174). New York: Van Nostrand Reinhold Co.

Amato, M., & Crocker, J. (1995). *The stigma of being overweight and self-esteem: The role of controllability.* Paper presented at the annual American Psychological Association convention, New York, New York.

Brownell, K. D. (1991). Dieting and the search for the perfect body: Where physiology and culture collide. *Behavior Therapy, 22,* 1–12.

Coleman, J. A. (1993, August 2). Discrimination at large. *Newsweek, 122*(9).

Cooley, C. H. (1956). *Human nature and the social order.* New York: Free Press.

Crandall, C. S. (1994). Prejudice against fat people: Ideology and self-interest. *Journal of Personality and Social Psychology, 66*(5), 882–894.

Crandall, C. S. (1995). Do parents discriminate against their heavyweight daughters? *Personality and Social Psychology Bulletin, 21*(7), 724–735.

Crandall, C. S., & Biernat, M. (1990). The ideology of anti-fat attitudes. *Journal of Applied Social Psychology, 20*(3), 227–243.

Crocker, J., Cornwell, B., & Major, B. (1993). The stigma of overweight: Affective consequences of attributional ambiguity. *Journal of Personality and Social Psychology, 64*(1), 60–70.

Crocker, J., & Major, B. (1989). Social stigma and self-esteem: The self-protective properties of stigma. *Psychological Review, 96,* 608–630.

Crocker, J., & Sung. (1995). Unpublished data.

Crocker, J., & Wolfe, C. T. (1996). *Bases of self-esteem.* Unpublished data and manuscript.

Cunningham, M. R., Roberts, A. R., Barbee, A. P., Druen, P. B., & Wu, C. (1995). Their ideas of beauty are on the whole the same as ours: Consistency and variability in the cross-cultural perception of female physical attractiveness. *Journal of Personality and Social Psychology, 68,* 261–279.

DeJong, W. (1980). The stigma of obesity: The consequences of naive assumptions concerning the causes of physical deviance. *Journal of Health and Social Behavior, 21*(1), 75–87.

DeJong, W. (1993). Obesity as a characterological stigma: The issue of responsibility and judgments of task performance. *Psychological Reports, 73*(3), 963–970.

DeJong, W., & Kleck, R. E. (1986). The social psychological effects of overweight. In C. P. Herman, M. P. Zanna, & E. T. Higgins (Eds.), *Physical Appearance, stigma, and social behavior: The Ontario Symposium, Volume 3* (pp. 65–87). Hillsdale, NJ: Lawrence Erlbaum.

Downey, K., & Miller, C. T. (1996). *A meta-analysis of obesity and self-esteem: Implications for the role of stigma controllability.* Manuscript under review.

Drewnowski, A., Hopkins, S. A., & Kessler, R. C. (1988). The prevalence of bulimia nervosa in the U.S. college student population. *American Journal of Public Health, 78,* 1322–1325.

Fallon, A. (1990). Culture in the mirror: Sociocultural determinants of body image. In T. F. Cash & R. Prozinsky (Eds.), *Body images: Development, deviance, and change* (pp. 80–109). New York: The Guilford Press.

Fallon, A. E., & Rozin, P. (1985). Sex differences in perceptions of desirable body shape. *Journal of Abnormal Psychology, 94,* 102–105.

Fredrickson, B. L., & Roberts, T. (1997). Objectification theory: Toward understanding women's lived experiences and mental health risks. *Psychology of Women Quarterly, 21,* 173–206.

Friedman, M. A., & Brownell, K. D. (1995). Psychological correlates to obesity: Moving to the next research generation. *Psychological Bulletin, 117*(1), 3–20.

Goffman, E. (1963). *Stigma: Notes on the management of spoiled identity.* Englewood Cliffs, NJ: Prentice-Hall.

Harter, S. (1993). Causes and consequences of low self-esteem in children and adolescents. In R. F. Baumeister (Ed.), *Self-Esteem: The puzzle of low self-regard* (pp. 87–116). New York: Plenum Press.

Heatherton, T. F., Kiwan, D., & Hebl, M. R. (1996). *The stigma of obesity in women: The difference is Black and White.* Manuscript under review.

Jarvie, G. J., Lahey, B., Graziano, W., & Framer, E. (1983). Childhood obesity and social stigma: What we know and what we don't know. *Developmental Review, 3,* 237–273.

Katz, I., & Hass, R. G. (1988). Racial ambivalence and American value conflict: Correlational and priming studies of dual cognitive structures. *Journal of Personality and Social Psychology, 55*(6), 893–905.

Karris, J. (1977). Prejudice against obese renters. *Journal of Social Psychology, 101,* 159–160.

Kerr, K., Crocker, J., & Broadnax, S. (1995). *Thinking you're fat and feeling depressed: Race differences.* Paper presented at the annual American Psychological Association convention, New York, New York.

Larkin, J. C., & Pines, H. A. (1979). No fat persons need apply: Experimental studies of the overweight stereotype and hiring preferences. *Sociology of work and occupation, 6*(3), 312–327.

Lerner, M. (1980). *The belief in a just world: A fundamental delusion.* New York: Plenum.

Lerner, R. M., Orlos, J. B., & Knapp, J. R. (1976). Physical attractiveness, physical effectiveness, and self-concept in late adolescents. *Adolescence, 11*(43), 313–326.

Lucas, A. R., Beard, C. M., O'Fallon, W. M., & Kurland, L. T. (1991). 50-year trends in the incidence of anorexia nervosa in Rochester, Minn: A population-based study. *American Journal of Psychiatry, 148,* 917–922.

Mead, G. H. (1934). *Mind, self, and society.* Chicago: University of Chicago Press.

Richardson, S. A.; Goodman, N; Hastorf, A. H.; & Dornbusch, S. M. (1961). Cultural uniformity in reaction to physical disabilities. *American Sociological Review,* 241–247.

Rodin, J., Silberstein, L., & Striegel-Moore, R. (1985). Women and weight: A normative discontent. In T. B. Sonderegger (Ed.), *Nebraska symposium on motivation: Volume 32. Psychology and gender* (pp. 267–307). Lincoln: University of Nebraska Press.

Shrauger, J. S., & Schoeneman, T. J. (1979). Symbolic interactionist view of self-concept: Through the looking glass darkly. *Psychological Bulletin, 86,* 548–573.

Smith, K. B. & Green, D. N. (1984). Individual correlates of the belief in a just world. *Psychological Reports, 54,* 435–438.

Spielberger, C. D., Gorsuch, R. L., & Lushene, R. E. (1970). *Manual for the State-Trait Anxiety Inventory.* Palo Alto, CA: Consulting Psychologist Press.

7

STRESS AND OPPRESSED SOCIAL CATEGORY MEMBERSHIP

KEVIN W. ALLISON

Virginia Commonwealth University

Available research indicates that members of cultural, sexual, religious and other minorities continue to face experiences of prejudice and discrimination (APA, 1996; Berrill, 1992; Gaertner & Dovidio, 1986; Swim, Aikin, Hall, & Hunter, 1995; Swim, Cohen, & Hyers, this volume). Tangible costs to targets of prejudice and discrimination have been demonstrated and proposed to involve direct effects on life outcomes, as well as potential indirect effects (wherein the impact of prejudice operates through a range of mediating variables) on rates and experiences of unemployment and underemployment, income level and social status, infant mortality, physical health and injury, emotional distress, and psychopathology, as well as access to housing, education, and a range of social, mental and other health services (e.g., Anderson, 1995; Belle, 1990; Bulhan, 1985; Flack *et al.,* 1995; Russo, 1995; Swim *et al.,* 1995; Turner & Kramer, 1995). The present chapter examines the conceptual and empirical linkage of prejudice and discrimination to stress.

Psychological theory and research have utilized a variety of conceptual ideas to define groups that are the targets of prejudice and discrimination. For example, these groups have been identified as "stigmatized" (e.g., Crocker & Major, 1989), or as "non-culture defining groups" (Tyler, Brome, & Williams, 1991). At base, this body of work underlines that members of these groups are subject to experiences of prejudice and discrimination based not on the characteristics, qualities, actions, or abilities of the individual, but rather to being cognitively classified into a stereotyped social category or group. In our common language, we find a number of terms that identify prejudice and related behavior linked to the characteristics or groups that are targeted for discrimination (e.g., cultural or racial bias or op-pression, ethnocentrism, racism, sexism, homophobia, heterosexism, ageism, xeno-phobia, and religious persecution). An examination of stress processes relevant to these targeted groups in the current American context would involve a focus on ethnic minorities, including African Americans, Native American Indians, Chi-canos, Puerto Ricans, Asian Americans and Pacific Islanders, as well as women, gays, lesbians, and bisexuals, individuals with sensory and motor impairment, and members of specific religious groups such as Jews. This is clearly not an exhaus-tive list of groups and an attempt to articulate an all-inclusive list of members of oppressed groups is plagued with our current and historical lack of adequate language and questionable precision in and utility of conceptual constructs under-lying membership within specific groups (e.g., see Anderson, 1995 or Jones, 1991b for discussions of the concepts of race, ethnicity and culture).

While the nature of prejudice (Gaertner & Dovidio, 1986; Swim *et al.*, 1995) and the specific suspect classes or stigmatized groups that are the focus or target of prejudice may change over historical time and with geopolitical focus, there may be both general and specific components of stress processes linked to the experience of prejudice and discrimination that an inclusive perspective provides an opportunity to analyze, articulate, and compare. Consequently, the present examination of the role of prejudice and discrimination on stress will use an inclusive approach, broadly focusing on "oppressed groups," (Clatterbaugh, 1986), those members of social groups or categories that have experienced histo-ries of prejudice, discrimination, negative stereotyping, and devaluation within the broader twentieth-century American sociocultural context. Such an inclusive approach is further supported by Moritsugu and Sue's (1983) argument that any group difference may be utilized as a cue for prejudice and discrimination. In utilizing such an inclusive approach, it is necessary to acknowledge the challenges and limitations presented by the variable, distinctive, and specific histories of oppression and discrimination experienced by members of different social cate-gorical groups.

This chapter will present a conceptual analysis of available literature examin-ing individuals' experiences of stress as the result of prejudice based on member-ship in a specific social or demographic category associated with oppression. While there has been considerable variability in the definition and conceptualiza-tion of stress, Cohen, Kessler, and Underwood-Gordon (1995) broadly define stress as, "A process in which *environmental demands tax or exceed the adaptive capacity of an organism resulting in psychological and biological changes that may place the individual at risk for disease.*" The chapter will focus on the principal question: How are experiences of prejudice and discrimination and their outcomes related to stress and what are the potential pathways and processes relevant to understanding the impact of prejudice on stress experiences of mem-bers of targeted groups?

Several authors (Meyers, 1982; Peters & Massey, 1983; Slavin, Rainer, McCreary, & Gowda, 1991) have provided useful models that conceptually integrate the experience of prejudice into the stress process. These examinations, however, have generally focused on one of the three predominate conceptual and research traditions utilized within the stress literature. Recent work by Cohen and colleagues (1995) provides a useful comprehensive model based on the integration of these three historical emphases in stress research and conceptualization: (a) stress as an environmental experience; (b) stress as a psychological experience; and (c) stress experienced biologically as a physical or emotional response. The present review builds on this model to examine and conceptualize the role of prejudice within the stress process.

Using this integration of perspectives on stress and extending it to examine prejudice, one can consider that prejudice may result in stress as an event in the environment: (1) through major or chronic experiences of prejudice (e.g., Root, 1992; Swim *et al.,* this volume); (2) through normative developmental events or non-normative stressors that are specifically linked with membership in an oppressed social group (e.g., Berrill, 1992; Cross; 1991); (3) because members of oppressed groups may experience unique or different types of life events linked to their social status (e.g., Billings & Moos, 1981; 1984); or (4) because members of oppressed groups may experience greater general stress due to the indirect impact of discrimination on its contextual sequelae (e.g., income and residence, social role). The psychological experience of stress that results from these prejudice-linked events may be determined by a range of cognitive factors (e.g., an individual's psychological appraisal of the event, linked for example, to her categorical-group self-schema and the consequent meaningfulness of a specific experience) that lead to the event being experienced as a threat, as causing harm, or as resulting in loss (i.e., Lazarus and Folkman's "primary appraisal"). In addition, an individual's perception of having the resources available to handle these prejudice-linked stresses (i.e., Lazarus and Folkman's "secondary appraisal") may influence whether the event is experienced as stressful or not. In considering the impact of prejudice on stress processes, it is important to consider that the access to such resources may be determined, in part, by a range of contextual factors (e.g., access to financial resources with which to handle a job loss rooted in discriminatory practice) that are themselves direct outcomes of prejudice. Prejudice may also shape cognitive factors relevant to an individual's perception of having resources to handle a stressful experience (e.g., social definitions of gender role may shape socialization practices, leading to an individual's greater likelihood of developing a specific style of responding to stressful events, which consequently affect the individual's appraisal of the availability of relevant personal resources with which to respond to stress). The experience of prejudice-related events and their psychological impact may also lead to changes in an individual's social cognitions (e.g., one's sense of self). It is also important to note that contextual factors (such as categorical group cultural norms, role expectations, and related socialization) may shape the physical and emotional outcomes of stress (Slavin *et al.,* 1991). These physical and emotional outcomes of stress may, in turn, influence both cognitions (e.g., how a person perceives her

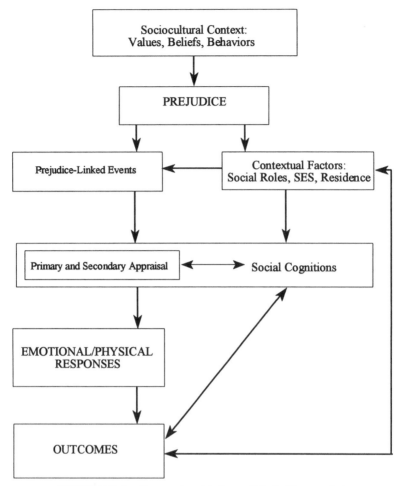

FIGURE 7.1   Integrated model of stress linked with categorical status.

self-efficacy in handling stressful situations based on her assessment of her well-being) and the individual's context (e.g., an individual's psychological and physical functioning may affect her income and access to resources). This analysis is based, in part, on the assumption that the experience of prejudice and discrimination is generated within a sociocultural context that has a set of broad cultural norms and beliefs, including some that support a range of prejudicial beliefs and behaviors. These experiences of prejudice may take various forms, and occur across different levels of social context. Building largely on the work of Cohen and colleagues (1995), the basic integration of this model is presented in Figure 7.1. The chapter further expands on the model presented by reviewing and integrating the literature relevant to prejudice within each of the three research and theoretical traditions articulated.

STRESS AS ENVIRONMENTAL DEMAND: PREJUDICE-LINKED EVENTS

The first general research tradition, rooted in the early work of Meyer (1951), Hawkins (Hawkins, Davies, & Holmes, 1957), and Holmes and Rahe (1967), conceptualizes stress as an environmental demand, and focuses on the examination of stressful life experiences. Research from this perspective has linked the experience of major life changes or stressors and, more recently, daily hassles and chronic strains, with a range of physical and psychiatric distress (Cohen *et al.,* 1995; Coyne & Downey, 1991; Lazarus & Folkman, 1984; Kessler, Price, & Wortman, 1985). Early work within this general tradition was based in an underlying assumption that cumulative life change was the central factor in the impact of stress on pathology, while more recent work has focused on specifying the characteristics of stress experiences relevant to health disruption (Cohen *et al.,* 1995).

Our available research and conceptual literature suggests that there are several ways in which prejudice and membership in an oppressed group may be linked to the environmental experience of stress. This section examining stress from an event perspective will consider: (a) the ways in which prejudice may be experienced as a major event (e.g., a discrete experience of discrimination) or in the form of a chronic daily experience; (b) perspectives emphasizing normative and non-normative stress experiences as a means of conceptualizing unique stressors experienced by members of categorical groups; (c) the possibility that social roles create different "structural" types of stress for oppressed and nonoppressed groups; and (d) findings that suggest oppressed groups experience higher rates of "generic" events (i.e., life events not specifically linked to an overt experience of prejudice or discrimination). In addition, this section will examine the methodological implications of this work.

PREJUDICE AS A MAJOR OR CHRONIC, DAILY EVENT

In examining event perspectives, stress can be linked to actual experiences of prejudice. Prejudice can be made manifest in many forms including antilocution or "verbal rejection," avoidance, discrimination, physical attack, and extermination (Allport, 1954; see also Feagin, 1994; Swim *et al.,* this volume). These experiences have been identified differentially in the literature based on the targeted social category and type of prejudicial behavior [e.g., "disability harassment" (Holzbauer & Berver, 1996); heterosexism or homophobia (Kitzinger, 1996)]. From an event perspective considering major and daily life events, one can utilize Root's (1992) conceptual work that suggests that membership in an oppressed social group may result in the experience of three types of traumatic life events: direct, indirect, and insidious. Direct traumas are those life events that occur to a target individual, such as interpersonal experiences of violence (e.g., Lenard Clark, an African American adolescent being attacked in a Southside Chicago neighborhood). Indirect, or secondary traumas are those events or injuries that occur to others and impact members of their social networks, the witnessing of trauma, or experiencing reports of trauma (e.g., an African American male viewing a television report of the Rodney King beating). Finally, Root defines insidious traumas as those chronic events linked to the social structure and institutionalized and ubiquitous forms of oppression experienced in every day life. This description of insidious trauma is more conceptually similar to the ideal of chronic strains or daily hassles, and to Peters and Massey's (1983) discussion of the mundane stress experienced by African Americans. Peters and Massey (1983), building on the ideas of Myers (1977) and Pierce (1975), suggest that Blacks live in a *mundane, extreme environment,* "that is an environment where racism and subtle oppression are ubiquitous, constant, continuing, and mundane as opposed to an occasional misfortune" (p. 195). These authors suggest that mundane stress adds an additional source of stress, in the form of racially based, chronic limitations in access to opportunities and resources. (For a further discussion of mundane stressors, see Swim *et al.,* this volume). (For other reviews examining prejudice or discrimination as a stressor, see Harrell, 1997; Slavin *et al.,* 1991.)

NORMATIVE AND NON-NORMATIVE EVENTS

In addition to examining prejudice as a chronic or major life event, a number of stress researchers have also made distinctions between stress associated with normative developmental processes (e.g., identity development) or transitions (e.g., pair bonding, childbearing, school socialization), as opposed to stressful events that are "non-normative" (e.g., being attacked, being fired, becoming seriously ill) (Jensen, Richters, Ussery, Bloedau, & Davis, 1991; Simmons, Burgeson, Carlton-Ford, & Blyth, 1987). The intersection of sociocultural and developmental factors may play a role in the creation or experience of a range of normative stressors or transitions that are specific to members of oppressed groups. For example, stress may be associated with processes of "coming out" among gays and lesbians (Escoffier, 1975), and with the general process of sexual identity discovery and development (Cass, 1984). Several models of ethnic and gender identity development specifically implicate the role of stress in the normative developmental process. For example, Cross' (this volume; 1991; 1978) theory of psychological Nigrescence specifically suggests that African Americans encounter an experience or set of circumstances that represents their differential treatment from European Americans. It is hypothesized that this "Encounter" results in a state of disequilibrium and distress, and plays a central role in the identity development process. This process of identity development has been extended to other oppressed groups such as women (Downing & Roush, 1985). Prejudicial attitudes operating within the social context play a clear and important role in these developmental processes, most often by presenting negative images of identities linked with categorical group membership. It is also important to note that biological and other cultural differences between groups may result in members of oppressed groups having different types of normative stressors than those encountered by non-oppressed groups (e.g., menarche). In attempting to understand the unique contribution of prejudice to the stress experiences of members of oppressed groups, research and conceptual work must appreciate and take into account that all group differences are not rooted in oppression and discrimination.

There may also be a range of "non-normative" transitions and life stresses experienced by members of categorical groups. Accidents that result in the loss of sensory or motor abilities and consequent processes of the development of new skills and self-conceptions present specific stresses. Physical attack such as domestic abuse experienced by women (Ucko, 1994), or gay bashing (Berrill, 1992) are also among non-normative experiences specifically linked to prejudicial attitudes and discrimination.

Many American minorities also face the non-normative stressors precipitated by migration or immigration, including acculturation. While processes of acculturation do not necessitate the experience of prejudice, models of acculturation and stress have included premigration experiences of trauma, and postmigration acculturative experiences, including experiences of prejudice and discrimination (Liebkind, 1996). In addition, research has clearly suggested that perceptions and experiences of prejudice are a central component of the acculturation process and experiences of acculturative stress within the United States and other countries (Gil, Vega, & Dimas, 1994; Sanchez & Fernandez, 1993; Smart & Smart, 1995). For example, Sandhu and Asrabadi's (1994) factor analysis of their Acculturative Stress Scale for International Students produced a dimension labeled perceived discrimination (which included items such as, "Others are biased toward me").

STRUCTURAL DIFFERENCES

In addition to potential differences in experiences of overt prejudice, and specific normative and non-normative events, there may be other factors that contribute to the experience of different kinds of life events between members of oppressed and non-oppressed groups. For example, there may be differences in the "types" of life events experienced by members of different categorical groups because of different social structures (e.g., social roles, social status). This type of variability in the experience of life stress has been identified as "structural." Related research has suggested that men and women may experience different types of stressful experiences, with women reporting more health-, child-, and family-related stressors and men reporting greater work and economic stressful experiences (Billings & Moos, 1981, 1984; Folkman & Lazarus, 1980; Murphy, Beaton, Cain, & Pike, 1994; Porter & Stone, 1995). MacIntosh, Keywell,

Reifman, and Ellsworth (1994) suggest that such patterns of gender differences are linked to role strain.

In considering these structural differences in stress we can utilize Pearlin's (1989) work suggesting that stress is generated from multiple sources, including social roles, social status, and aspects of the physical environment. An individual, for example, may experience conflict between two social roles (e.g., being a mother and an employee), or someone might face too many demands within a single role (e.g., high levels of demands in housekeeping and family management). Related research has suggested that working women experience greater role conflict than men (Beutell & Greenhaus, 1986; Gutek, Repetti, & Silver, 1988). Meyer (1995) notes that these structural differences in stress experiences may be linked to the cost of care-taking roles socially ascribed to women. It is important to note, however, that not all research has strongly supported structural gender differences in stress (Deater-Deckard & Scarr, 1996; Geller & Habfoll, 1994; Ptacek, Smith, & Zanas 1992). Across these studies on gender variability in stress experiences, unfortunately, authors have not largely addressed the specific developmental, historical, and contextual factors that may contribute to the similarities or differences in stress experiences across different samples.

If structural differences do exist, it is also necessary to consider whether they are specifically or necessarily rooted in prejudice and discrimination. This is a conceptual, empirical, and, in part, political question. For example, these structural differences in stress experiences, including the findings of gender differences in role conflict, may be rooted in broader sociocultural stereotypes of male and females social roles. Research indicates that despite historical changes in some aspects of women's social status, there are continued discrepancies in the distribution of adult work and family role demands (e.g., Beutell & Greenhaus, 1986; Gutek *et al.,* 1988). When these social constructions of men's and women' gender roles and related stereotypes operate through cultural socialization and lead to the construction of subordinate social roles, prejudice may be a factor in the creation of specific types of stress for women and men.

GROUP DIFFERENCES IN THE EXPERIENCE
OF GENERIC EVENTS

Up to this point, our review has largely suggested that members of oppressed groups may experience different life stressors than members of nonoppressed groups. It is also possible that members of these categorical groups may experience differential rates of "generic" life events (i.e., events not specifically related to prejudice). For example, research examining such general life stressors has indicated that African Americans experience more stress (Dohrenwend & Dohrenwend, 1970; Askenasy, Dohrenwend, & Dohrenwend, 1977; Dohrenwend, 1973 a,b) than do European Americans. Jung and Khasla (1989) reported that African American college students, while rating specific life events at similar levels of intensity, report a greater frequency and severity of life hassles than their European American peers. Greater stress, in turn, was associated with higher levels of depression. Similarly, Hamilton and Fagot (1988) reported that women experience a greater range and frequency of stressful events than college men.

Some research has suggested that it may not be categorical group membership per se that results in higher levels of general stress, but the contextual (e.g., socioeconomic) consequences of prejudice and discrimination that are relevant to higher levels of stress among oppressed group members. Research generally suggests that individuals with fewer economic resources face greater life stress (Dohrenwend, 1970). Garrison, Schoenbach, Schulchter, and Kaplan (1987) found that African American adolescents, in comparison to their European American peers, more often reported experiencing specific types of life events (e.g., the divorce or separation of parents; death of a friend; birth of a sibling; parental job loss; decreased parental income; school failure and suspension; juvenile court involvement). Many of these experiences might be specifically linked with the impact of prejudice on socioeconomic status (SES) (e.g., parental underemployment may, because of limited economic resources, result in residence in more anomic and violent neighborhoods). In fact, when SES was taken into account in the study by Garrison and colleagues (1987), race did not produce a main effect on reports of undesirable life events. The association between social class and life stress, however, was more pronounced for African Americans than for European Americans. Other research on adolescents (Gad & Johnson, 1980) similarly suggests that socioeconomic status, not race, is important in the differential experience of life stress across different ethnic groups.

While there was not a main effect for race in these studies, some empirical work suggests that members of oppressed groups may experience "differential vulnerability" to stress. For example, ethnicity appears to interact with SES, such that lower income African Americans show the highest levels of vulnerability to stress (operationalized as undesirable life events and economic problems) when compared to low-income European American, and middle-income African Americans and European Americans (Ulbrich, Warheit, & Zimmerman, 1989). In this work, lower SES African Americans were more likely to experience psychological distress and symptomatology linked to stress experiences than members of other racial and socioeconomic groups. In general, it has been demonstrated that adults at lower income levels (McLeod & Kessler, 1990) and relatedly, adolescents from lower income families, and single-parent households (Gore, Aseltine, & Colton, 1992), show greater vulnerability to life stress. Conceptual work on life stress also suggests that experiencing high levels of life stress exacerbates the impact of subsequent stress (Pearlin, Menahgan, Liebermann, & Mullan, 1981). An examination of vulnerability and stress exacerbation might also be linked to findings that women in male-dominated careers who report experiences of sexual harassment also report higher levels of job stress, sexual stereotyping, and violence than women who do not report sexual harassment (Rossell, Miller, & Barber, 1995).

It is possible that increased vulnerability might also be linked to the specific contextual (e.g., socioeconomic) impact of prejudice on stress via the process of stress exacerbation. This idea fits with Pearlin's (1989) conceptual work noting that some aspects of stress may be linked to an individual's physical environment. Limited economic resources rooted in discrimination may result in fewer housing options, poor housing quality, and the greater likelihood of exposure to ambient stress (e.g., noise, smells, etc.). Research has linked residence in poor, urban areas to the experience of violence (Fitzpatrick & Boldizar, 1993; Gladstein *et al.,* 1992), and, in turn, exposure to traumatic violent events has been linked to higher ratings of depression among urban children (Freeman *et al.,* 1993) and to symptoms of posttraumatic stress disorder (PTSD) in both children and adolescents (Berton & Staubb, 1996; Fitzpatrick & Boldizar, 1993). Recent work by Allison and colleagues (1997) suggests that residence in specific urban contexts results in higher levels of stress. Most often in these examinations, African American youth comprised the majority of the samples. There may also be residential factors associated with oppressed group membership that moderate stress experiences. Research by Caspii and colleagues (1987) found that perceptions of chronic neighborhood stress exacerbated the impact of daily stress on mood among urban women. The possibility that the differential impact of stress on members of oppressed groups operates through environmental factors is further supported by Wilson's (1987) work, which indicates that poor African Americans more often live in neighborhoods characterized by poverty than poor European Americans. These data raise the possibility that the contextual outcomes of prejudice may create an indirect path through which prejudice effects (i.e., mediates) the experience of stress, but might also alter (i.e., moderate) the impact of stress on members of oppressed categories.

METHODOLOGICAL IMPLICATIONS

This examination raises the question as to whether researchers have largely underestimated the stress experienced by members of oppressed groups because they omit or ignore important, but "categorically specific" sources of stress (i.e., daily and major experiences of prejudice, categorical specific normative and non-normative events, and specific structural events). In face of the broader range of articulated events and experiences that may be specific to different categorical groups, a number of new measures have been developed. This would include the Schedule of Racist Events (Landrine & Klonoff, 1996), the Schedule of Sexist Events (Klonoff & Landrine, 1994), the Gay Life Events Scale (Rosser, & Ross, 1989) and the African American Women's Stress Scale (Watts-Jones, 1990). For a review of these scales, see Landrine and Klonoff, (1994). Research based on these and similar measures assessing stress specific to ethnic minority status have suggested that different ethnic groups of college students experience different levels of stress associated with ethnic minority status (Prillerman, Myers, & Smedley, 1989). In the current analysis, it has been argued that gender roles are, in part, undergirded by prejudice; consequently, one could also consider the use the Feminine Gender-Role Stress Scale (Gillespie & Eisler, 1992) to assess components of stress linked to prejudice. This measure consists of five factors (fear of unemotional relationships, physical unattractiveness, victimization, behaving assertively, and not being nurturant). Specifically, the ideas on which this measure is based suggest that women who hold strongly to gender-role stereotypes may experience stress when their experiences or behaviors do not conform to these expectations. Pilot work suggests that women who have high levels of fearing unattractiveness and of not being nurturant have higher levels of depression (Gillespie & Eisler, 1992). Related cross-cultural work has also suggested that high levels of masculine and feminine role stress are associated with higher levels of mental and physical health problems within a Chinese sample (Tang & Lau, 1995).

The current review also suggests that when estimating the effect of prejudice on the stress experienced by members of oppressed groups, it is important to consider the interaction of group membership and socioeconoimc status. In addition, it is important to examine the potential impact of prejudice on an individual's exposure to a range of additional environmental and contextual stressors. Finally, research specifically examining life stress linked to prejudice should differentiate between group differences in life stress linked to prejudice and those differences linked to cultural and biological group differences not associated with prejudice or its contextual outcomes.

PSYCHOLOGICAL TRADITION: PRIMARY AND SECONDARY APPRAISAL

This second section of the chapter utilizes the stress and coping framework of Lazarus and Folkman (1984) to examine the ways in which *primary and secondary appraisal* are affected by membership in groups that experience prejudice. Lazarus and Folkman define psychological stress as, "a relationship between the person and the environment that is appraised by the individual as taxing or exceeding his or her resources and endangering his or her well being" (p.21). These authors suggest that when an event or experience occurs, an individual makes two cognitive appraisals of the experience. First, the individual must determine if the experience is a possible cause of harm or loss, a threat, or a challenge. This assessment is referred to as Primary Appraisal. Simultaneously, an individual must consider whether they have the resources with which to respond to the event experienced. This is referred to as Secondary Appraisal.

PRIMARY APPRAISAL

The linkage of primary appraisal to experiences of prejudice and discrimination are clear. An individual's may appraise that a specific prejudice-linked experience will lead to injury or damage to their person, their self-concept, or to a loved one, or the individual may anticipate that the event will result in loss or harm. An individual may perceive a range of acts as threatening (e.g., an employer's oversight may be seen as a risk to promotion and lead to loss of potential income). In addition, events may be perceived as a challenge that calls for the individual to mobilize coping efforts (e.g., a bisexual college student may find the lack of library holding on issues of sexual orientation to be an impetus for engaging college administrators as a way of increasing access to informational resources).

As part of this appraisal process, Lazarus and Folkman indicate that a range of *person* factors may influence appraisals. For example, it is crucial that the event or experience be seen as personally relevant and meaningful, that is, the individual must have a personal "commitment" linked to the experience. This suggests an individual's self-schema or their level of identity development and self-attitudes related to membership in an oppressed social category may be relevant to whether an incident is perceived as stressful or not. Considering Cross' (1991; 1978) perspectives on ethnic identity development, we might anticipate that individuals at different stages of identity development might perceive potential acts of prejudice in very different ways. In the first stage, Preencounter, where an individual might minimize issues of ethnic difference, an event may not be perceived as potentially prejudicial or discriminatory. At a later stage of development, individuals early in the Immersion/Emersion Stage (where there is an initial strong identification with one's ethnic group and a rejection of the majority culture), may find issues of ethnicity, race, and relatedly discrimination, more salient. This would suggest that individuals engaged in the process of identity development, particularly prior to the later integration of identity (according to Cross, the stage of "Internalization"), may be at greater risk of perceiving and therefore experiencing stress related to prejudice or discrimination. Related research by Hammen and Goodman-Brown (1990) suggests that when stress is more self-relevant, there is a greater risk of negative outcomes. (See in addition, Swim, Cohen, Hyers Fitzgerald, & Bylsma, 1997).

While self-conceptions may be related to whether an individual perceives a specific experience as stressful or not, the perception of prejudice may also result in an individual altering their self-concept (Crocker & Major, 1989; Ogbu, 1978). Such an analysis is implicated in the conceptual work of Steele (1992) on the processes of disidentification. Here members of oppressed groups react to subtle and overt negative messages regarding their performance or membership within counterstereotypic domains of performance (e.g., math and engineering for women and African Americans) by minimizing their investment and sense of personal identification with that specific domain or related identities. This perspective suggests that these experiences of prejudice may lead to or predict changes in self-concept and change individual's commitments linked to their perception of experiences as relevant and stressful (see Aronson, Quinn, & Spencer, this volume; Major & Schmader, this volume). Consequently, a circular or bidirectional process may exist whereby stressful experiences of prejudice that have an impact on the self-concept, may also subsequently result in lower commitment and reductions in stress within that domain. It is notable that such processes, in addition to precipitating changes in the self-concept as a protection from stress, may reduce behavioral efforts and have an impact on structural outcomes (e.g., academic motivation, educational attainment, and subsequent employment and income).

It may be particularly important when considering identity development and prejudice's effects on commitment among different groups to consider that the boundaries of the self may vary across cultural groups (e.g., Markus & Kitayama, 1991). Consequently, it may not only be the personal or direct experiences of prejudice or discrimination that have an impact on these self-processes, but vicarious experiences as well. The social and psychological processes implicated in "basking in reflected glory," may also be implicated in "soaking in shared oppression." This fits with Root's (1992) suggestion that the vicarious experience of prejudice may be important to the experience of oppression linked trauma and discrimination-based life stress. It may also be important to consider that individual life events may also have broader, real-life implications for and impact on the social group [(e.g., an individual's job loss may have a widespread impact on an extended family) Slavin *et al.,* 1991].

In addition to person factors, Lazarus and Folkman (1984) suggest that *situational characteristics,* (i.e., properties of events) are relevant to individuals' primary appraisals of stress. For example, the novelty, predictability, or uncertainty of an event may be relevant to an individual's appraisal of whether the experience is stressful or not, or how stressful the event is. In the situational appraisal of a stressful event, an individual may also make attributions as to whether the event occurred because of a some internal (i.e., personal) or external (i.e., environmental) cause, whether the cause of the event was a temporary or stable contributor to such life experiences, and whether the cause of the event was based on general (i.e., global) or a set of specific contributing factors. Such attributions regarding the event situation have been linked to its subsequent level of negative impact. For example, the attribution of internal (vs. external), stable (vs. temporary), and global (vs. domain-specific) causes of controllable events has been linked to the greater negative impact of stressful events on depression (Brown & Siegel, 1988). Uomoto (1986) suggests that experiences of prejudice involve this set of situational attributions. He consequently hypothesizes that an employee who attributes not getting a promotion to a lack of openings (i.e., an external, temporary, and specific cause) may experience less stress than an individual who attributed not getting a job to their ethnicity (an internal, stable, and global cause). Such an analysis is relevant to the question of whether attributions of experiences occurring as the result of prejudice reduce or lead to greater stress. Dion, Dion, and Pak (1992) argue that "Experiencing discrimination is stressful because it elicits cognitive appraisals of threat, such that an attribution of discrimination by the victim leads him or her to impute stable, malevolent motives and intentions to the antagonist(s) and to see him/herself as the deliberate target of discriminatory behavior by the antagonist(s)." In contrast to the perspectives of Uomoto and Dion and colleagues, Perloff (1983) suggests that in some cases, perceptions of *universal vulnerability* (which may occur when an individual perceives that they have been discriminated against, not as a person, but as a member of a group, in contrast to attributions of *unique vulnerability,* where one feels that he or she is unique in their experience of misfortune) may lead to external attributions and consequently, less negative outcomes. (For a further discussion of the primary appraisal of threat and prejudice, see Feldman Barrett & Swim, this volume, and Slavin *et al.,* 1991).

SECONDARY APPRAISAL

Within Lazarus and Folkman's framework, secondary appraisal is also important to the perception of an experience as stressful. Here the individual asks whether they have resources that can be brought to bear on this experience. This raises questions as to whether sociocultural factors (e.g., an African American's access to fictive kin as "family," or a culture's philosophy of acceptance) or group identity affects an individual's sense of coping efficacy (Slavin *et al.,* 1991). There may be also contextual factors in the access to and appraisal of coping resources (Banyard & Graham-Bermann, 1993). Blockage to tangible, instrumental coping resources may decrease perceptions of coping efficacy. For example, limited access to financial resources may decrease options for problem-focused coping. In addition, membership in specific oppressed groups may present particular challenges in the development of and access to relevant coping strategies. Gay-lesbian youth or individuals with disabilities may lack developmental models and socialization resources for coping, and in addition, may be wary of utilizing "available" family/community resources.

RECENT RESEARCH AND IMPLICATIONS

When we consider the empirical work relevant to the impact of stress appraisal processes and membership in an oppressed group, research has examined the potential variability of the primary and secondary stress appraisals between oppressed and nonoppressed groups. Jorgensen and Johnson (1990) found women to perceive life events as having greater potential to produce stress than men did. In addition, as compared to men, women reported experiencing greater stress, and less perceived control over outcomes, and perceived less effectiveness in coping (Ptacek, Smith, & Zanas, 1992). In contrast, Porter and Stone (1995) report no overall differences in appraisal of severity, chronicity, or control among married men and women; however, women did appraise problems that focus on the self as more chronic than did men. These gender differences again raise questions as to whether these possible gender variations in appraisals are rooted in differences in prejudice, differences in the sociocultural meaning of events and being exposed to different types of events, or gender differences in cognitive appraisal style, which are potentially rooted in socialization or biologically based gender differences. Similar to the conclusions from the analysis of coping by Banyard and Graham-Bermann (1993), at present, unfortunately, we have limited evidence with which to respond to this question.

While specifying the bases of group differences in appraisal is challenging, this question is important is our understanding the potential role of prejudice within the stress process. Work in this area has largely focused on gender differences and should be expanded to examine differences between other oppressed and nonoppressed groups. The review of research and conceptual work relevant to understanding the impact of psychological appraisals of stressful events underlines the importance of considering individual differences in primary appraisals rooted in the process of identity development, the dynamic role that experiences of prejudice may play in self-understanding and identity development, and the potential role that contextual outcomes of prejudice may play in secondary appraisals. There is, in addition, the need for further work clarifying the effect of situational attributions of intentional discrimination on the impact of prejudice-linked events. (For a related discussion of primary and secondary appraisal and coping, see Miller & Myers, this volume.)

"BIOLOGICAL" TRADITION: EMOTIONAL AND PHYSICAL RESPONSES AND OUTCOMES

The final perspective on stress emphasizes *stress as an organismic response.* A range of conceptual and empirical work has considered the possibility that negative physical and mental health outcomes are associated with the experience of prejudice and related stress. Within such an analysis of stress outcomes, it is important to consider and specify the emotional and physical stress-related disease processes implicated in the experience of prejudice and discrimination. In considering the impact of prejudice on its victim, Allport (1958) suggested that there may be a range of ego defenses that develop into traits. Among these are a potentially maladaptive set of reactions, including obsessive (suspicion-based) concern, withdrawal, self-hate and aggression toward one's own group. Early research by Dion and Earn (1975) indicates that attributions of discrimination are associated with greater aggression, sadness, and anxiety. In this study, Jewish male undergraduates were placed in a ticket exchange task where they failed in comparison to their three competitors. Participants were randomly assigned to two contrived interpersonal conditions: one in which three other participants were reported to be Christian and were aware of the participant's religious membership, and a control condition in which religious affiliation was not made available to the participant or their fictional task opponents.

Recent research by Swim and colleagues (1997) found anger to be the most frequent response of women and African American women and men to events they perceived as being based in prejudice. Additional evidence for the role of anger as an affective consequence of the experience of prejudice comes from anecdotal responses to discrimination simulations. One set of college students who were the targets of discrimination in a mock simulation reported,

> I felt one of two emotions, one of helplessness and one of anger. . . The funny thing is, after the discrimination starts, you start to believe what others say . . . I can't imagine what it would be like to face something like this every day of your life. . . I felt like a big zero . . . I was angry, antagonistic, resentful, and even bordered on hate for brown eyes. I was shocked at how quickly I felt those feelings. (Byrnes & Kiger, 1990; p. 347).

Related research suggests that African Americans, younger, unemployed individuals, and women experience higher number of stressful life events, which, in turn were linked to greater feelings of anger (Bronan & Johnson, 1988). The ways in which one responds to these potential affective consequences of stress in general, and prejudice in particular, may also be important in understanding outcomes associated with stress based in prejudice. In general, hostile expressions of anger have been linked with high levels of cardiovascular reactivity (Burns & Katkin, 1993), a risk factor for cardiovascular disease. However, African American male adolescents who reported higher levels of anger suppression had higher levels of cardiovascular symptoms and greater sleep disturbance (Johnson & Greene, 1991). Similarly, while Kreiger (1990) found that there were comparable rates of self-reported hypertension in a sample of African American and European American women, African American respondents who demonstrated acceptance in the face of discrimination were more than four times as likely to report hypertension as were African American women who took action or talked to others. In addition, African American women who did not report experiencing sexism or racism were at 2.6 times greater risk of high blood pressure than were African American women who perceived and reported having such experiences.

In considering the sequelae of discrimination, researchers have often looked to social categorical differences in mental and physical health outcomes, largely with the assumption that group differences, particularly those not attributable to cultural differences, are linked with prejudice. Research has considered both physical and mental health outcomes. Results from the Epidemiologic Catchment Area Study (Robins & Regier, 1991) indicate that women have higher rates of major depressive episodes, somatization disorder, and obsessive-compulsive disorder. It is important to note however that men have a higher lifetime prevalence of having any psychiatric disorder, and also have higher rates of alcohol abuse and antisocial personality disorder. Ethnic differences in lifetime risk for disorder are limited to the 45-and-older age group and were largely related to higher rates of cognitive impairment of African Americans. In addition, somatization was more prevalent in African Americans, but this occurred overall at low levels. In the area of physical health, Flack and colleagues (1995) report that African Americans have shorter life expectancies, higher levels of impairment linked to chronic health conditions, higher levels of heat disease, infant mortality, and death by homicide, and lower survival rates for prostrate and breast cancers than do European Americans. Available data related to health outcomes for Asian/Pacific Islanders and Hispanics is noted to be quite poor. Among Hispanics in the 15-to-44 age group, there are higher death rates, and among Native American, data suggest overall higher rates of violence and alcohol-related death, but there is notable variability among tribal groups.

While the overall data on categorical group differences in health outcomes are more compelling, the minimal ethnic differences in mental health outcomes have led some to question the role of categorical status and related stressors in the etiology of psychosocial disorder. In response to the lack of a main race effect, Kessler and Neighbors (1986) reanalyzed data from eight epidemiological studies and indicated that socioeconomic status and ethnicity interact to predict psychological distress, specifically suggesting that members of ethnic minority groups low in socioeconomic status are disproportionately represented among individuals with mental disorders. In addition, several studies specifically link the experience of discrimination to emotional distress and health outcomes. Meyer (1995) found internalized homophobia, stigma, and experiences of prejudice linked to sexual orientation to be associated with demoralization, guilt, suicidal ideation, and AIDS Traumatic Stress Response (which includes preoccupation with HIV infection, associated with avoidance, nightmares, panic, and general problems in daily functioning). McKirnan and Peterson (1988) also found discrimination attributable to sexual orientation to predict alcohol and drug use problems. This was especially true for men who saw substances as a means of reducing tension.

Landrine, Klonoff, Gibbs, and Manning (1995) report that sexist discrimination accounted for more of the variance in premenstrual, depressive, obsessive compulsive, somatic, and total psychiatric and physical symptoms than generic stress (i.e. traditional indices of major life events and daily hassles). Ethnic differences were important, for while generic stress was a better predictor of outcomes for European American women, sexist discrimination, not generic stress, was associated with physical and emotional symptoms for women of color. In related work examining racist events, Landrine and Klonoff (1996) found the experience of racist events to be associated with somatic and stress-related symptoms as well as smoking in a sample of African American adults. In addition, racist events were more likely to be reported by African Americans who were less "acculturated" into mainstream American society and were more immersed in African culture.

When attempting to understand differences between oppressed and nonoppressed groups in the manifestations of stress outcomes, it is important to consider that these outcomes may in part be rooted in sociocultural norms and expectations specific to the individual group (Slavin et al., 1991). For example, high interpersonal stress was related to high self-reported depression and suicidality among women, while achievement events demonstrated stronger association with suicidality among men (Waelde, Silvern, & Hodges, 1994). Adolescent females in schools with higher rates of violence achieve high scores on indices tapping PTSD symptoms, while males at these same schools report low to moderate levels of

PTSD symptoms (Berton & Stabb, 1996). Such results further support the suggestion that sociocultural constructions of social role and the impact of sociocultural
meaning define our stress experiences and reactions to them. Recent work indicates that gender differences in depression may be linked to women's greater
likelihood of rumination, which may be based in certain aspects of gender role
socialization (Nolen-Hoeksema, Parker, & Larson, 1994), and raises concerns that
sexism is implicated in the socialization of women's use of less adaptive coping
strategies. Other work suggests that several factors linked to prejudice and discrimination (e.g., the feminization of poverty, childhood sexual and adult domestic abuse) are linked to women's higher incidence and prevalence of depression
(Belle, 1990; Liebenluft, 1996; Nolen-Hoeksema,1990; Russo, 1995). Such an
analysis also raises the question as to whether there may be costs to "nonoppressed" groups in their experience of the other side of the discriminatory coin, such
as the case of men's greater anger-linked blood pressure reactivity (Burns &
Katkin, 1993), and higher overall levels of psychopathology in general, and substance abuse in particular (Robins & Reiger, 1991).

Research has also indicated that the manifestation of physical and mental
health compromise may be specifically linked to the interaction of contextual
outcomes (e.g., access to educational and economic resources and residence in
anomic neighborhoods) and cognitive beliefs about one's self-perceived efficacy
in controlling the environment. It is notable that these contextual outcomes may
be associated with experiences of prejudice and discrimination and provide an
additional mechanism through which prejudice may impact stress processes. For
example, work by James (James, Hartnett, & Kalsbeek, 1983) suggests that individual differences in education and cognitive beliefs systems reflected in John
Henryism, are related to African American men's experience of cardiovascular
risk. John Henryism is described specifically as a behavioral orientation that
involves coping actively with behavioral stressors in the environment, and moreover, the belief that the individual can control such stressors through a combination of hard work and determination. James, Hartnett, and Kalsbeek (1983)
examined the relationship between John Henryism (JH) and cardiovascular risk
factors in a sample of Southern, working class, Black men. While education and
blood pressure were inversely correlated overall, with controls for age, body mass,
time of day, and smoking, individuals at low levels of educational attainment and
high levels of JH had the highest levels of diastolic blood pressure. Related research on a European sample of Dutch adults suggests that these effects are not
race specific, but that lower access to educational resources in face of high John
Henryism is more generally linked to cardiovascular risk. In this sample of 100
Caucasian males and 100 Caucasian females, John Henryism was found to be
related to systolic blood pressure for men after controlling for age, alcohol consumption, physical activity, and overweight (Duijers, Drijver, Kromhout, &
James, 1988). These effects were apparent for men at lower educational levels,
but not for men with high levels of education. There were no effects for women

after age, alcohol consumption, physical activity, and overweight were controlled. In contrast, research with 162 male and 259 female first-year African American college students found no association between John Henryism and blood pressure (Jackson, & Adams-Campbell, 1994). It is important to note, however, that this group had lower levels of John Henryism overall that James' samples, that these individuals have greater access to resources, and were at a different developmental stage (i.e., they may not be primary economic providers for their families) as compared to members of James' samples. The general pattern of these studies, however, suggests that a belief system supporting an individual's active persistence to overcome environmental stressors, despite limited resources [(that may have resulted from contextual outcomes of prejudice and discrimination (i.e., education and income)], may place members of oppressed categorical groups with few resources at particular risk.

In this analysis of physical and emotional outcomes, it is important to note that stress and coping are dynamic and interactive processes. The effectiveness of coping within the proposed model is relevant to the continued experience of stress and further risk for health compromise. In addition, the limited access to relevant supports and the limited availability of appropriate services that members of oppressed categorical groups may experience, and the cultural variation in the meaning and activation of help seeking behaviors for members of these groups may play an important role in understanding the ongoing experience of physical and mental health compromise. Physical and mental health outcomes may also be linked to the effects of discrimination and prejudice on a range of performance factors (e.g., academic motivation, energy and attention directed away from task performance toward affective and behavioral regulation in reaction to an episode of discrimination), which may, in turn, lead to limited access to instrumental resources (e.g., poorer job performance and consequent lower income). There may also be important genetic and physiological group variations or cultural factors that contribute to the differential experience of mental and physical health outcomes between oppressed and nonoppressed groups. As the focus of the present work is to consider experiential (i.e., prejudice-linked) contributions to stress, a review of these contributions, in face of the lack of consensus in articulating the specific contributions of biology to stress outcomes and group differences (Anderson, 1989; Liebenluft, 1996; Nolen-Hoeksema, 1990), and the wide range of specific cultural contributions to the expression of physical illness and psychopathology (e.g., Jones, 1991a), are considered beyond the scope of the present work. In attempting to fully understand the specific contributions of prejudice to differences in group outcomes, however, it is important to recognize and address the potential confound that cultural and biological factors present. The present review further suggests that it is important to consider both the potential direct (i.e., oppressed group membership) and moderational effects of prejudice (e.g., influence operating in relation to socioeconomic status) on the physical and emotional outcomes of prejudice.

SUMMARY, COMMENTS, AND INTEGRATION

While it has not been possible in the current chapter to cover the unique sociocultural factors relevant to the stress experiences of members of different categorical groups, the present chapter does provide a conceptual departure point from which to consider the impact of prejudice in the experience of stress by members of oppressed social groups. As with many examinations of the experience of membership in an oppressed social group, the majority of available empirical and conceptual work focuses on one or two dimensions of group membership (e.g., gender and ethnicity). People, however, inhabit real life spaces that emphasize the multidimensionality of group membership and relevant effects. Our empirical work has not yet evolved to the point of fully appreciating the stress experiences of a Jewish, African American, lesbian with a visual impairment. Work considering the differential experiences of disabled women (Holzbauer & Berver, 1996) and single and partnered Hispanic professional women (Amaro, Russo, & Johnson, 1987) begins to provide a rich understanding of prejudice-related stress processes in context.

The present chapter emphasizes the importance of considering (1) the experience of prejudice-linked life events; (2) the appraisal processes relevant to experiencing a life event rooted in prejudice; and (3) the specific stress outcomes linked with prejudice in understanding stress associated with membership in an oppressed social group. In addition, the model and literature review presented provide a useful heuristic for conceptualizing the multiple pathways through which prejudice and discrimination play a role in these stress experiences. To date, few studies have approached an examination of the full model produced from the current integration. Such examinations, however, will be important in furthering our understanding of the linkage between prejudice and stress.

REFERENCES

Allison, K. W., Burton, L., Marshall, S., Perez-Febles, A., Yarrington, J., Kirsh, L. B., & Merriwether-deVries, C. (1997). *Life experiences among urban adolescents: Measurement and the role of context.* Unpublished manuscript.

Allport, G. W. (1954). *The nature of prejudice.* Reading, MA: Addison-Wesley Publishers.

Amaro, H., Russo, N. F., & Johnson, J. (1987). Family and work predictors of psychological well-being among Hispanic women professionals. Special Issue: Hispanic women and mental health. *Psychology of Women Quarterly, 11,* 505–521.

American Psychological Association (1996). Basic behavioral science research for mental health: Sociocultural and environmental processes. *American Psychologist 51,* 722–731.

Anderson, N. B. (1995). Summary of task group research recommendations. *Health Psychology, 14,* 649–653.

Anderson, N. B. (1989). Racial differences in stress-induced cardiovascular reactivity and hypertension: Current status and substantive issues. *Psychological Bulletin 105,* 89–105.

Askenasy, A. R., Dowhrenwend, B. P., & Dowhrenwend, B. S. (1977). Some effects of social class and ethnic group membership on judgements of the magnitude of stressful life events: A research note. *Journal of Health and Social Behavior, 18,* 432–439.

Banyard, V. L., & Graham-Bermann, S. A. (1993). Can women cope? A gender analysis of theories of coping and stress. *Psychology of Women Quarterly, 17,* 303–318.

Belle, D. (1990). Poverty and women's mental health. *American Psychologist, 45,* 385–389.

Berrill, K. T. (1992). Anti-gay violence and victimization in the United States: An overview. In G. M. Herek & K. T. Berrill (Eds.), *Hate crimes: Confronting violence against lesbians and gay men* (pp. 19–45). Newbury Park, CA: Sage.

Berton, M. W., & Staubb, S. D. (1996). Exposure to violence and post-traumatic stress disorder in urban adolescents. *Adolescence, 31,* 489–498.

Beutell, N., & Greenhaus, J. (1986). Balancing acts: Work-family conflict and the dual career couple. In L. L. Moore (Ed.), *Balancing acts: Work-family conflict and the dual career couple* (pp. 149–162). Lexington, MA: D. C. Health..

Billings, A. G., & Moos, R. H. (1981). The role of coping responses and social resources in attenuating the stress of life events. *Journal of Behavioral Medicine, 4,* 139–157.

Billings, A. G., & Moos, R. H. (1984). Coping, stress, and social resources among adults with unipolar depression. *Journal of Personality and Social Psychology, 46,* 881–891.

Bronan, C. L., & Johnson, E. H. (1988). Anger expression and life stress among Blacks: Their role in physical health. *Journal of the National Medical Association, 80,* 1329–1334.

Bronfenbrenner, U. (1977). Toward an experimental ecology of human development. *American Psychologist, 32,* 513–531.

Brown, J. D., & Siegel, J. M. (1988). Attributions for negative live events and depression: The role of perceived control. *Journal of Personality and Social Psychology, 54,* 316–322.

Bulhan, H. A. (1985). *Franz Fanon and the psychology of oppression.* New York: Plenum Press.

Burns, J. W., & Katkin, E. S. (1993). Psychological, situational, and gender predictors of cardiovascular reactivity to stress: A multi variate approach. *Journal of Behavioral Medicine, 16,* 445–465.

Byrnes, D. A., & Kiger, G. (1990). The effect of a prejudice-reduction simulation on attitude change. *Journal of Applied Social Psychology, 20,* 341–356.

Caspii, A., Bolger, N., & Eckenrode, J. (1987). Linking person and context in the daily stress process. *Journal of Personality and Social Psychology, 52,* 184–195.

Cass, V. C. (1984). Homosexual identity formation: Testing a theoretical model. *Journal of Sex Research, 20,* 143–167.

Clatterbaugh, K. (1986, Winter). Are men oppressed? *Changing Men,* 17–18.

Cohen, S., Kessler, R. C., & Underwood-Gordon, L. (1995). Strategies for measuring stress in studies of psychiatric and physical disorders. In S. Cohen, R. C. Kessler, & L. Underwood-Gordon (Eds.), *Measuring stress: A guide for health and social scientists.* New York: Oxford University Press.

Coyne, J. C., & Downey, G. (1991). Social factors and psychopathology: Stress, social support, and coping processes. *Annual Review of Psychology, 42,* 401–425.

Crocker, J., & Major, B. (1989). Social stigma and self-esteem: The self-protective properties of stigma. *Psychological Review, 96,* 608–630.

Cross, W. E. (1978). The Thomas and Cross models of psychological nigrescence: A review. *Journal of Black Psychology, 5,* 13–31.

Cross, W. E. (1991). *Shades of black: Diversity in African-American identity.* Philadelphia: Temple University Press.

Deater-Deckard, K., & Scarr, S. (1996). Parenting stress among dual-earner mothers and fathers: Are there gender differences? *Journal of Family Psychology, 10,* 45–59.

Dion, K. L., Dion, K. K., & Pak, A. W. (1992). Personality-cased hardiness as a buffer for discrimination-related stress in members of Toronto's Chinese Community. *Canadian Journal of Behavioural Science, 24,* 515–536.

Dion, K. L., & Earn, B. M. (1975). The phenomenology of being a target of prejudice. *Journal of Personality & Social Psychology, 32,* 944–950.

Dohrenwend, B. S. (1973a). Life events as stressors: A methodological inquiry. *Journal of Health & Social Behavior, 14,* 167–175.

Dohrenwend, B. S. (1973b). Social status and stressful life events. *Journal of Personality and Social Psychology, 28,* 225–235.

Dohrenwend, B. S. (1970). Social class and stressful events. In E. H. Hare & J. K. Wing (Eds.), *Psychiatric epidemiology.* London: Oxford University Press.

Dohrenwend, B. S., & Dohrenwend, B. P. (1970). Class and race as status related sources of stress. In S. Levine & N. A. Scotch (Eds.), *Social stress* (pp.111–140). Chicago: Aldine.

Dohrenwend, B. S., & Dohrenwend, B. P. (1984). Life stress and illness: Formulations of the issues. In B. S. Dohrenwend, & B. P. Dohrenwend (Eds.), *Stressful life events and their contexts.* New Brunswick, NJ: Rutgers University Press.

Downing, N. E., & Roush, K. L. (1985). From passive acceptance to active commitment: A model of feminist identity development for women. Special Issue: Cross-cultural counseling. *Counseling Psychologist, 13,* 695–709.

Duijkers, T. J., Drijver, M., Kromhout, D., & James, S. A. (1988). "John Henryism" and blood pressure in a Dutch population. *Psychosomatic Medicine, 50,* 353–359.

Escoffier, J. (1975). Stigmas, work environment, and economic discrimination against homosexuals. *Homosexual Counseling Journal, 2*(1), 8–17.

Fitzpatrick, K. M., & Boldizar, J. P. (1993). The prevalence and consequences of exposure to violence among African-American youth. *Journal of the American Academy of Child and Adolescent Psychiatry, 32,* 424–430.

Flack, J. M., Amaro, H., Jenkins, W., Kunitz, S., Levy, J., Mixon, M., & Yu, E. (1995). Panel I: Epidemiology of minority health. *Health Psychology, 14,* 592–600.

Folkman, S., & Lazarus, R. S. (1980). An analysis of coping in a middle-aged community sample. *Journal of Health & Social Behavior, 21,* 219–239.

Freeman, L. N., Mokros, H., & Poznanski, E. O. (1993). Violent events reported by normal urban school-aged children: Characteristics and depression correlates. *Journal of the American Academy of Child and Adolescent Psychiatry, 32,* 419–423.

Gad, M. J., & Johnson, H. H. (1980). Correlates of adolescent life stress as related to race, SES, and levels of perceived social support. *Journal of Clinical Child Psychology, 9,* 13–16.

Gaertner, S. L., & Dovidio, J. F. (1986) . The aversive form of racism. In J. F. Dovidio & S. L. Gaertner (Eds.), *Prejudice, discrimination, and racism* (pp. 61–89). Orlando, FL: Academic Press.

Garrison, C. Z., Schoenbach, V. J., Schluchter, M. D., & Kaplan, B. H. (1987). Life events in early adolescence. *Journal of the American Academy of Child and Adolescent Psychiatry, 26*(6), 865–872.

Geller, P. A., & Habfoll, S. E. (1994). Gender differences in job stress, tedium and social support in the workplace. *Journal of Social and Personal Relationships, 11,* 555–572.

Gil, A. G., Vega, W. A., & Dimas, J. M. (1994). Acculturation stress and personal adjustment among Hispanic boys. *Journal of Community Psychology, 22,* 43–54.

Gillespie, B. L., & Eisler, R. M. (1992). Development of the feminine gender role stress scale. *Behavior Modification, 16,* 426–438.

Gladstein, J., Slater Rusonis, E. J., & Heald, F. P. (1992) A comparison of inner-city and upper-middle class youths' exposure to violence. *Journal of Adolescent Health, 13,* 275–280.

Gore, S., Aseltine, R. H., & Colton, M. E. (1992). Social structure, life stress and depressive symptoms in a high school-aged population. *Journal of Health & Social Behavior, 33,* 97–113.

Gutek, B., Repetti, R. L., & Silver, D. L. (1988). Nonwork roles and stress at work. In C. L. Cooper, & R. Payne (Eds.), *Causes, coping and consequences at work* (pp. 141–174). New York: Wiley.

Hamilton, S., & Fagot, B. I. (1988). Chronic stress and coping styles: A comparison of male and female undergraduates. *Journal of Personality & Social Psychology, 55,* 819–823.

Hammen, C., & Goodman-Brown, T. (1990). Self-schemas and vulnerability to specific life stress in children at risk for depression. *Cognitive Therapy and Research, 14*(2), 215–227.

Harrell, S. P. (1997). *Direct, vicarious and collective experinces of racism: Implcations for mental health.* Paper presented at the 6th Biennial Conference on Community Research and Action, Society for Community Research and Action (Division 27–American Psychological Association), Columbia, SC.

Hawkins, N. G., Davies, R., & Holmes, T. H. (1957) . Evidence of psychosocial factors in the development of pulmonary tuberculosis. *American Review of Tuberculosis and Pulmonary Diseases, 75,* 68–780.

Holmes, T. H., & Rahe, R. H. (1967). The social readjustment rating scale. *Journal of Psychosomatic Research, 11,* 213–218.

Holzbauer, J. J., & Berven, N. L. (1996). Disability harassment: A new term for a long-standing problem. *Journal of Counseling & Development, 74,* 478–483.

Jackson, L. A., & Adams-Campbell, L. L. (1994). John Henryism and blood pressure in Black college students. *Journal of Behavioral Medicine, 17,* 69–79.

James, S. A., Hartnett, S. A., & Kalsbeek, W. D. (1983). John Henryism and blood pressure differences among Black men. *Journal of Behavioral Medicine, 6,* 259–278.

Jensen, P. S., Richters, J., Ussery, T., Bloudau, L., & Davis, H. (1991). Child psychopathology and environmental influences: discrete life events versus ongoing adversity. *Journal of the American Academy of Child and Adolescent Psychiatry, 30,* 303–309.

Johnson, E. H., & Greene, A. (1991). The relationship between suppressed anger and psychosocial distress in African American male adolescents. *The Journal of Black Psychology, 18,* 47–65.

Johnson, K. W., Anderson, N. B., Bastida, E., & Kramer, B. J. (1995). Panel II: Macrosocial and environmental influences on minority health. *Health Psychology, 14,* 601–612.

Jones, A. C. (1991a). Psychological functioning in African Americans: A conceptual guide for use in psychotherapy. In R. L. Jones (Ed.), *Black psychology* (3rd ed.). Berkeley, CA: Cobb and Henry.

Jones, J. M. (1991b). Psychological models of race: What have they been and what should they be? In J. D. Goodchilds (Ed.), *Psychological perspectives on human diversity in America.* Washington, DC: American Psychological Association.

Jorgensen, R. S., & Johnson, J. H. (1990). Contributions to the appraisal of major life changes: Gender, perceived controllability, sensation seeking, strain, and social support. *Journal of Applied Social Psychology, 20,* 1123–1138.

Jung, J., & Khalsa, H. K. (1989). The relationship of daily hassles, social support, and coping to depression in Black and White students. *Journal of General Psychology, 11,* 407–417.

Kessler, R. C., & Neighbors, H. W. (1986). A new perspective on the relationships among race, social class, and psychological distress. *Journal of Health & Social Behavior, 27,* 107–115.

Kessler, R. C., Price, R. H., & Wortman, C. B. (1985). Social factors in psychopathology. *Annual Review of Psychology, 36,* 531–72.

Kitzinger, C. (1996). Speaking of oppression: Psychology and the language of power. In E. D. Rothblum & L. A. Bond (Eds)., *Preventing heterosexism and homophobia.* Thousand Oaks, CA: Sage Publications.

Klonoff, E. A., & Landrine, H. (1995). The Schedule of Sexist Events: A measure of lifetime and recent sexist discrimination in women's lives. *Psychology of Women Quarterly, 19,* 439–472.

Krause, N. (1992). Stress, religiosity, and psychological well-being among older Blacks. *Journal of Aging & Health, 4,* 412–439.

Kreiger, N. (1990). Racial and gender discrimination: Risk factors for high blood pressure? *Social Science and Medicine, 30,* 1273–1281.

Landrine, H., Klonoff, E. A., Gibbs, J. & Manning, V. (1995). Physical and psychiatric correlates of gender discrimination: An application of the Schedule of Sexist Events. *Psychology of Women Quarterly, 19,* 473–492.

Landrine, H., & Klonoff, E. A. (1996). The Schedule of Racist Events: A measure of racial discrimination and a study of its negative physical and mental health consequences. *Journal of Black Psychology, 20,* 144–168.

Landrine, H., & Klonoff, E. A. (1994). The African American Acculturation Scale: Development, reliability, validity. *Journal of Black Psychology, 20,* 104–127.

Lazarus, R. S., & Folkman, (1984). *Stress, appraisal, and coping.* NY: Springer.

Leal, L., Weise, S. M., & Dodd, D. K. (1995). The relationship between gender, symptoms of bulimia, and tolerance for stress. *Addictive Behaviors, 20,* 105–109.

Liebenluft, E. (1996). Sex is complex. *American Journal of Psychiatry, 153,* 969–972.

Liebkind, K. (1996). Acculturation and stress. *Journal of Cross-Cultural Psychology, 27,* 161–180.

MacIntosh, D. N., Keywell, J., Reifman, A., & Ellsworth, P. C. (1994). Stress and health in first-year law students: Women fare worse. *Journal of Applied Social Psychology, 24,* 1474–1499.

Mansfield, P. K., Koch, P. B., Henderson, J., Vicary, J. R., Cohn, M., & Young, E. W. (1991). The job climate for women in traditionally male blue-collar occupations. *Sex Roles, 25,* 63–79.

Markus, H., & Kitayama, S. (1991). Culture and the self: Implications for cognition, emotion, and motivation. *Psychological Review, 98,* 224–253.

McKirnan, D. J., & Peterson, P. L. (1988). Stress, expectancies, and vulnerability to substance abuse: A test of a model among homosexual men. *Journal of Abnormal Psychology, 97,* 461–466.

McLeod, J. D., & Kessler, R. C. (1990). Socioeconomic status differences in vulnerability to undesirable life events. *Journal of Health and Social Behavior, 31,* 162–172.

Meyer, I. H. (1995). Minority stress and mental health in gay men. *Journal of Health & Social Behavior, 36,* 38–56.

Meyer, A. (1951). The life chart and the obligation of specifying positive data in psychopathological diagnosis. In E. E. Winters (Ed.), *The collected papers of Adolph Meyer, Vol 3: Medical teaching.* Baltimore: The Johns Hopkins University Press.

Meyers, H. F. (1982). Stress, ethnicity, and social class: A model for research with Black populations. In E. E. Jones, & S. J. Korchin (Eds.), *Minority Mental Health.* New York: Praeger.

Mirowsky, J., & Ross, C. (1989). *Social causes of psychological distress.* New York: Aldine de Gruyter.

Moritsugu, J., & Sue, S. (1983). Minority status as stressor. In R. D. Felner, L. A., Jason, J. Moritsugu, & S. S. Farber (Eds.), *Preventive psychology: Theory, research and practice.* New York: Praeger.

Myers, H. F. (1977). *Cognitive appraisal, stress, coping, and Black health: The politics of options and contingencies.* Los Angeles, CA: Fanon R and D Center, Charles R. Drew Postgraduate Medical School.

Neighbors, H. W., Jackson, J. S., Bowman, P. J., & Gurin, G. (1983). Stress, coping, and Black mental health: Preliminary findings from a national study. *Prevention in Human Services, 2,* 5–29.

Newcomb, M. D., Huba, G. J., & Bentler, P. M. (1986). Desirability of various life change events among adolescents: Effects of exposure, sex, age, and ethnicity. *Journal of Research in Personality, 20,* 207–227.

Nolen-Hoeksema, S. (1990). *Sex differences in depression.* Stanford, CA: Stanford University Press.

Nolen-Hoeksema, S., Parker, L. E., & Larson, J. (1994). Ruminative coping with depressed mood following loss. *Journal of Personality & Social Psychology, 67,* 92–104.

Ogbu, J. (1978). *Minority education and caste.* New York: Academic Press.

Pearlin, L. I. (1989). The sociological study of stress. *Journal of Health and Social Behavior, 30,* 241–256.

Pearlin, L. I., Menaghan, E. G., Lieberman, M. A., & Mullan, J. T. (1981). The stress process. *Journal of Health and Social behavior, 22,* 337–356.

Perloff, L. S. (1983). Perceptions of vulnerability to victimization. *Journal of Social Issues, 39,* 41–62.

Peters, M. F., & Massey, G. (1983). Mundane extreme environmental stress in family stress theories: The case of Black families in White America. *Marriage and Family Review, 6,* 193–218.

Pierce, C. (1975). The mundane extreme environment and its effects on learning. In S. G. Brainard (Ed.), *Learning disabilities: Issues and recommendations for research.* Washington, DC: National Institute of Education.

Porter, L. S., & Stone, A. A. (1995). Are there really gender differences in coping? A reconsideration of previous data and results from a daily study. *Journal of Clinical and Social Psychology, 14,* 184–202.

Prillerman, S. L., Myers, H. F., & Smedley, B. D. (1989). Stress, well-being, and academic achievement in college. In G. Berry & J. Asmen (Eds.), *Black students psychosocial and academic achievement.* Beverly Hills, CA: Sage.

Ptacek, J. T., Smith, R. E., & Zanas, J. (1992). Gender, appraisal, and coping: A longitudinal analysis. *Journal of Personality, 60,* 747–770.

Reifman, A., Biernat, M., & Lang, E. L. (1991). Stress, social support and health in married professional women with small children. *Psychology of Women Quarterly, 15,* 431–445.

Robins, L. N., & Regier, D. A. (1991). *Psychiatric disorders in American: The Epidemiologic Catchment Area Study.* New York: Free Press.

Root, M. P. (1992). Reconstructing the impact of trauma on personality. In L. S. Brown & M. Ballou (Eds.), *Personality and psychopathology: Feminist reappraisals* (pp. 229–266). New York: Guildford.

Rosell, E., Miller, K., & Barber, K. (1995). Firefighting women and sexual harassment. *Public Personnel Management, 24,* 339–350.

Rosser, B. S., & Ross, M. W. (1989). A Gay Life Events Scale (GALES) for homosexual men. *Journal of Gay & Lesbian Psychotherapy, 1,* 87–101.

Ruggiero, K. M., & Taylor, D. M. (1995). Coping with discrimination: How disadvantaged group members perceive the discrimination that confronts them. *Journal of Personality & Social Psychology, 68,* 826–838.

Russo, N. F. (1995). Women's mental health: Research agenda for the Twenty-first century. In C. V. Willie, P. P. Rieker, B. M. Kramer, & B. S. Brown (Eds.), *Mental health, racism, and sexism.* Pittsburgh: University of Pittsburgh Press.

Sanchez, J. J., & Fernandez, D. M. (1993). Acculturative stress among Hispanics: A bidimensional model of ethnic identification. *Journal of Applied Social Psychology, 23,* 654–668.

Sandhu, D. S., & Asrabadi, B. R. (1994). Development of an acculturative stress scale for international students: Preliminary findings. *Psychological Reports, 75,* 435–448.

Simmons, R. G., Burgeson, R., Carlton-Ford, S., & Blyth, D. A. (1987). The impact of cumulative change in early adolescence. *Child Development, 58,* 1220–1234.

Slavin, L. A., Rainer, K. L., McCreary, M. L., & Gowda, K. K. (1991). Toward a multicultural model of the stress process. *Journal of Counseling & Development, 70,* 156–163.

Smart, J. F., & Smart, D. W. (1995). Acculturative stress of Hispanics: Loss and challenge. *Journal of Counseling and Development, 73,* 73–396.

Steele, C. (1992) Race and the schooling of Black Americans. *The Atlantic, 269,* 68–72.

Swim, J. K., Aikin, K. J., Hall, W. S., & Hunter, B. A. (1995). Sexism and racism: Old-fashioned and modern prejudices. *Journal of Personality & Social Psychology, 68,* 199–214.

Tang, C. S., & Lau, B. H. (1995). The assessment of gender role stress for Chinese. *Sex Roles, 33,* 587–595.

Turner, C. B., & Kramer, B. M. (1995). Connections between racism and mental health. In C. V. Willie, P. P. Rieker, B. M. Kramer, & B. S. Brown (Eds.), *Mental health, racism, and sexism.* Pittsburgh: University of Pittsburgh Press.

Tyler, F. B., Brome, D. R., & Williams, J. E. (1991). *Ethnic validity, ecology, and psychotherapy: A psychosocial competence model.* New York: Plenum Press.

Ucko, L. G. (1994). Culture and violence: The interaction of Africa and America. *Sex Roles, 31,* 185–204.

Ulbrich, P. M., Warheit, G. J., & Zimmerman, R. S. (1989). Race, socioeconomic status, and psychological distress: An examination of differential vulnerability. *Journal of Health and Social Behavior, 30,* 131–146.

Uomoto, J. M. (1986). Examination of psychological distress in ethnic minorities from a learned helplessness framework. *Professional Psychology: Research and Practice, 17,* 448–453.

Waelde, L. C., Silvern, L., & Hodges, W. F. (1994). Stressful life events: Moderators of the relation-
    ships of gender and gender roles to self-reported depression and suiciality among college students.
    Sex Roles, 30, 1–22.
Wagner, B. M., Compas, B. E., & Howell, D. C. (1988). Daily and major life events: A test of an
    integrative model of psychosocial stress. *American Journal of Community Psychology, 16,*
    189–205.
Watts-Jones, D. (1990). Toward a stress scale for African-American women. *Psychology of Women
    Quarterly, 14,* 271–275.
Wilson, W. J. (1987). *The truly disadvantaged: The inner city, the underclass, and public policy.*
    Chicago: University of Chicago Press.
Yee, B. W. K., Castro, F. G., Hammond, W. R., John, R., Wyatt, G. E., & Yung, B. R. (1995). Panel IV:
    Risk-taking behavior and abusive behaviors among ethnic minorities. *Health Psychology, 14,*
    622–631.

8

UNDERMINED?
AFFIRMATIVE ACTION
FROM THE TARGETS'
POINT OF VIEW

KATHRYN TRUAX AND DIANA I. CORDOVA[1]

Yale University

AURORA WOOD, ELISABETH WRIGHT,
AND FAYE CROSBY[1]

Smith College

Not every American gives enthusiastic support to affirmative action. Some Americans admit that they are unclear about what the policy entails but nonetheless dislike the words "affirmative action." Others are well informed and still find fault with the practice or the policy.

Past studies have shown support for affirmative action to be greater among women than among men and to be greater among African Americans, Hispanics, and Asian Americans than among European Americans. Yet even some members of targeted groups express dislike of many of the practices and even of the policy of affirmative action. Indeed, some of the most eloquent detractors of affirmative action have been African American and Hispanic American men (Winkelman & Crosby, 1994).

A major criticism of affirmative action is that the policy undermines those who are intended to be its direct beneficiaries. When an organization has a strong commitment to affirmative action, some women and minority group members may think that other people in the organization question their competencies. Even if the women and the minority group members do not internalize the stigma,

---

[1]Corresponding authors.

171

such suspicions could erode anyone's confidence and jeopardize interpersonal relations.

Our chapter focuses on affirmative action and its direct consequences for the target. We are especially concerned about the potential for unintended undermining effects of affirmative action. We start with a brief definition of terms. We then review the arguments and the empirical evidence concerning how beneficiaries might feel undermined. Empirical evidence fails to show that affirmative action has an undermining effect in actual employment situations. On the contrary, affirmative action has been documented to have positive effects on morale and work commitment (Ayers, 1992; Taylor, 1994). Quite possibly, students are more vulnerable to the unintended ill effects of affirmative action than are employed people. After all, students are typically younger than employed people, and they live in a highly evaluative world. Surprisingly, while many scholars have conducted analog studies of preferential treatment using college students, no one has published a survey of actual minority students' reactions to affirmative action in which one can see if minority students do in fact like or dislike the policy and whether or not they feel undermined by it. At the core of our chapter is a survey conducted at Yale University and at Smith College. Our study shows that ethnic minority students are, indeed, susceptible to what Steele (1991) calls "racial doubt" and Major, Feinstein, and Crocker (1994) call "the suspicion of inferiority," but that they endorse affirmative action nonetheless. Noticing the persistence of discrimination, minority students in our sample perceive that others stereotype them, but they do not identify affirmative action as the source of the stigma.

DEFINITIONS

Affirmative action means many things to many people. The multiplicity of meanings was noted by George Stephanopoulos and Christopher Edley in the report they prepared for President Clinton (Stephanopoulos & Edley, 1995). The reigning confusion regarding the actual meaning of the term may be one of the reasons why the policy is as controversial as it is (Golden, Crosby, & Hinkle, in press; Tomasson, Crosby, & Herzberger, 1996). In the interest of clarity, we begin by defining our terms.

Like the American Psychological Association, we see affirmative action as occurring whenever "an organization expends energy to make sure there is no discrimination in employment or education" (American Psychological Association, 1996, p. 5). Affirmative action employers differ from equal opportunity employers (Crosby, 1994). Whereas the equal opportunity employer assumes that in the absence of intentional discrimination, fairness exists in hiring and promotion, the affirmative action employer assumes that unintended biases can persist unless corrective actions are taken. Both types of employers wish to avoid discrimination, but only the affirmative action employer devotes resources to accomplishing employment parity. Similarly, the educational institution that endorses affirmative action is one that applies energy to its desires for justice. Rather than remaining passively nondiscriminatory, schools that endorse affirmative action devote time and effort to removing unjust barriers that, by force of habit or as a consequence of former prejudices have come to block the progress of meritorious individuals who are not European American males.

In employment and educational situations, one can further distinguish between classical affirmative action and newer forms of affirmative action (Crosby & Cordova, 1996). Classical affirmative was instituted in 1965 by Executive Order 11246. It affects one in four American workers. Newer affirmative action programs have influenced only a fraction of those affected by classical affirmative action, but have received a disproportionate amount of attention (Crosby & Cordova, 1996). During the 1970s and 1980s, for example, some regulations and laws allowed for price adjustments in the bids submitted by minority construction firms. These practices do not always withstand legal scrutiny, and President Clinton has enjoined the Justice Department to eliminate them (Stephanopoulos & Edley, 1995).

Classical affirmative action is essentially a monitoring system by which institutions (especially those that hold contracts with the federal government) make sure that they utilize talent in proportion to its availability within designated groups. The methods for determining availability vary, of course, for different jobs in different locations and different industries, but the Office of Federal Contract Compliance Programs (OFCCP) makes available to companies its time-tested methods of calculation.

Under classical affirmative action, if an affirmative action employer determines that it is underutilizing people from one of the designated categories (e.g., women) for some job classification, it then devises legal remedies. The remedies usually involve goals for hiring and promotion according to sensible timetables. Never are strict quotas allowed, and never should the remedies involve the hiring or retention of unqualified people.

One standard technique for rectifying underutilization is what Crosby and Herzberger call "justified preferential treatment" (Tomasson *et al.*, 1996). Justified preferential treatment occurs when a person from the target group is selected rather than a comparable person from the majority group in an attempt to correct a documented imbalance. Justified preferential treatment was deemed legal by the Supreme Court in 1987 when it decided the case of *Johnson v. Transportation* agency (Newman, 1989).

Another common corrective technique is to devote extra effort to the recruiting and retaining of members of underrepresented groups. Resources may be spent in an effort to attract African Americans, Hispanic Americans, Native Americans, Asian Americans, and European American women that are not spent on attracting European American men to an organization. Resources may also be spent dispelling an image of an organization as hostile to women and/or minorities. Such efforts, which can be more or less costly, pose no challenge to and suggest no bending of the existing standards, but they are like justified preferential treatment in that they involve differential apportioning of organizational resources.

Affirmative action operates in education much as it does in employment. The educational analog to classical affirmative action policies in employment would dictate that a public university system make sure that the incoming freshman class reflects the gender and ethnic balance among high school graduates with specified qualifications (e.g., a certain grade-point average). Justified preferential treatment occurs in education when a candidate for admission who is from an underrepresented category is granted admission rather than an equally qualified candidate from a majority category.

Affirmative action in education also means taking steps to correct for the biases of entrance tests. With affirmative action, one might scrutinize the gate-keeping tests to make sure that they do accurately predict scholastic performance. If tests are not accurate enough for all groups, they can be revised or eliminated (Crosby & Blanchard, 1989). When tests cannot be eliminated or revised, the option remains to correct numerically for biases by, for example, adding points to the scores of groups whose abilities are underestimated by the test. After a gender bias was discovered in one of the SAT tests, for example, at least one prestigious technical school announced that it would still use SAT scores in determining admission but would make the appropriate scoring adjustments until such time as the SAT were revised to be more gender-neutral (Rosser, 1996).

THE CLAIM

People criticize affirmative action on many grounds. Some people dislike the attention paid to categorical factors and believe that it would be better to live in a world that is "gender blind" and "color blind." Others think that today's European American males are being asked to pay for the bad behavior of their forefathers. Still others see the policy as driving an economic wedge between better-off and worse-off African Americans.

Some of the most eloquent and vociferous detractors of affirmative action have been African American and Hispanic American men who feel that affirmative action undermines the intended beneficiaries. Speaking autobiographically (at least in part) several well-known commentators have pointed out that affirmative action can make those in the targeted categories worry that they have been accorded special privilege or, more realistically, that those in power make the assumption of special privilege. Among the critics are Thomas Sowell, Stephen J. Carter, and Shelby Steele (Winkelman & Crosby, 1994).

Shelby Steele (1991) writes in passionate and captivating prose about how affirmative action harms those whom it is meant to help. Equating affirmative action with arbitrary preferences, Steele decries affirmative action on many grounds. Echoing Martin Luther King, Jr., Steele asks that people judge African Americans by "the content of our character" and not "the color of our skin."

Focusing on the experiences of African Americans, Steele argues that "one of the most troubling effects of racial preferences for Blacks is a kind of demoralization, or put another way, an enlargement of self-doubt" (p. 116). Intertwined with the self-doubt is what Steele calls "racial doubt." Even if an African American person does not originally think of herself or himself as inferior, when affirmative action is in place, she or he will sense the doubt of European Americans and will begin to internalize it. According to Steele, "under affirmative action the quality that earns us preferential treatment is an implied inferiority" (p. 116). From the status of being a victim a faulty sense of power develops among African Americans— and especially young African Americans. Or at least, so says Steele.

Terry Eastland (1996) agrees with Steele that affirmative action stigmatizes its direct beneficiaries. Eastland maintains that everyone in an organization will know if the organization has an affirmative action policy, but few will know the qualifications of those hired. European Americans will think of people from other groups as having been chosen for jobs because of affirmative action and will assume that standards have been lowered to comply with affirmative action goals. Eastland believes that such generalizations are common and that they undermine the successes of minorities who could have met standards without affirmative action being in place.

A similar line of thought is found in Tomasson's critique of affirmative action. According to Tomasson, European American college students see their non-White peers as having been admitted to college as "affirmative action babies" (Tomasson et al., 1996, p. 194). To end the patronizing and demeaning ways of viewing minority group members, one would—according to Tomasson—need to put an end to affirmative action. Tomasson's focus is less on the direct beneficiaries of affirmative action and more on others in the environment, but his point is that life is unpleasant for the minority group when its members think the majority group undervalues them. From the targets' perspective, Tomasson's arguments are important if we remember that what Major and colleagues (1994) call the "suspicion of inferiority" or what Steele (1991) calls "racial doubt" can perturb peaceful existence quite apart from internalized self-doubt.

THE EVIDENCE

The arguments of the opponents of affirmative action, compelling as they may be on first blush, contain some flaws. One problem is the unthinking equation of affirmative action with arbitrary preferential treatment (Winkelman & Crosby, 1994). No official document defines affirmative action in the terms used by Steele, Eastland, or Tomasson. Indeed, according to a report produced by the Congressional Research Service for then Senator Dole, only a small fraction of federal laws and regulations involve arbitrary preferences on the basis of ethnicity or gender (Crosby & Cordova, 1996).

Another problem is the lack of empirical evidence to support their assertions (Crosby & Clayton, 1990). While Steele and others have every right to assume that their personal experiences are as legitimate as anyone else's, they cannot assume that they are more legitimate. For every anecdote showing stigma one can find other anecdotes showing the opposite (Clayton & Crosby, 1992).

It is possible the some writers have identified a real problem but made misattributions about the source of the problem. Responding to the autobiographical account of Stephen J. Carter (1991), the African American law professor at Yale who resented being "the best Black," Barbara Bergmann writes,

> In thinking about this issue, we have to ask whether African Americans would be a less stigmatized group if there were fewer Black undergraduates at Yale, fewer Black Yale graduates, and fewer Black members of the Yale faculty. We also have to ask about those doing the stigmatizing. Has affirmative action created derogatory feelings about Blacks in people who would otherwise have had perfectly friendly feelings toward them? . . . what is the evidence for all this extra stigmatizing? (Bergmann, 1996, p. 28)

STIGMATIZING EFFECTS
OF PREFERENTIAL TREATMENT

That it is common for individuals to feel stigmatized by preferential treatment has been amply and beautifully demonstrated by Madeline Heilman and her colleagues (Heilman, 1994). In a long and thematic program of laboratory research, Heilman has shown that women feel insecure about their own abilities and unhappy with their assigned roles when they have been told that they gained their good position through preferential treatment rather than through merit. When women were given information that they had been preferentially selected but were not given information that they were competent, they assumed themselves to be incompetent. Nor were the women the only ones to make the assumption. In one line of studies, Heilman (1994) demonstrated that men react negatively to women who they deem to be the direct beneficiaries of preferential selection procedures.

In much of her writing, Heilman tacitly or explicitly equates affirmative action with unjustified preferential treatment (e.g., Heilman, Kaplow, Amato, & Stathatos, 1993; Heilman, Lucas, & Kaplow, 1990; Heilman, Rivero, & Brett, 1991; Heilman, Simon, & Repper, 1987).[1] In this assumption Heilman resembles Steele, Sowell, Carter, and Tomasson.

In her laboratory studies, Heilman typically assigns research participants to a leadership position on the basis of their merit or sex. In addition, those research participants assigned to the coveted position based on their group membership are explicitly told that the preferential assignment was based solely on the fact that not enough subjects of their sex had signed up to take part in the study. This selection method is problematic because it is not equivalent to the procedures employed in actual affirmative action programs, where organizations attempt to

---

[1]The same assumption is sometimes made by Nacoste (1985, 1987, 1989) who has done laboratory work similar to Heilman's.

hire or admit a member of a targeted group from a pool of qualified applicants.

For the effects that Heilman demonstrates in the laboratory to generalize outside the laboratory, it would need to be the case that most Americans hold the same assumptions about affirmative action as does Heilman. Heilman believes the match to exist. She claims, for example, that "affirmative action has come to be seen as involving preferential selection and treatment based solely on group membership" (Heilman, 1994, p. 125); that "affirmative action has increasingly come to be seen by the public as involving preferential selection and treatment of women and minorities" (p. 127); and that "affirmative action is widely assumed to be little more than preferential selection without regard to qualifications" (p. 159).

Surveys show that the majority of Americans do not see affirmative action as arbitrary preferential treatment on the basis of group membership. In 1991, Louis Harris conducted two public opinion polls related to the issue (Harris, 1992). In the first, he found that less than half of the people favored federal laws requiring "racial preference programs" but that 70% favored federal laws requiring "affirmative action programs." The same split appeared in the second study, and even more dramatically. When citizens were asked to respond to the words "racial preference," more than 80% of their associations were negative, being phrases like 'hiring minorities who are unqualified." When asked to respond to the words "affirmative action," the same sample produced positive associations. This time, more than 80% gave answers like "doing something good for people who have not had an equal chance," which were coded as positive.

An academic study conducted in Chicago and environs in May and June of 1993 substantiated the findings of Harris (Golden, Crosby, & Hinkle, in press). A stratified random sample of approximately 1000 people was interviewed concerning a number of policy issues. One question in the interview asked: "Which of the following two statements come closer to defining the policy of Affirmative Action for you? The first definition is: Affirmative action occurs when an organization monitors itself to make sure that it employs and promotes qualified minorities and White women in proportion to their numbers. The second definition is: Affirmative Action occurs when the government forces organizations to meet quotas for minorities and White women." Fifty-six percent of the European American participants and 51% of the non-European American participants who answered the question saw affirmative action as a monitoring system, not as a quota system.

EVIDENCE CONCERNING RACIAL DOUBT
IN EMPLOYMENT

Given that at least half of Americans do not equate affirmative action with unjustified preferential treatment and over 80% have positive associations with affirmative action, it would seem likely that the undermining effects of preferential treatment shown in laboratory situations might not generalize to people in

everyday situations outside the laboratory. One might wonder how many adults
have experienced the kind of self-doubt that Steele, Sowell, and Carter confess
to have felt. One might also wonder if the majority of European American
women and ethnic minority women and men agree more with Steele that affirmative action produces stigma or more with Bergmann that the stigma has a life of
its own.

Only a few studies have tried to test systematically the notion that the recipients
of affirmative action experience either self-doubt or racial doubt in an employment context. One early study was conducted by Lea Ayers (1992). Ayers interviewed in-depth 13 African American, Hispanic American, and Asian American
women who had participated in and personally benefited from programs that were
known to be affirmative action programs. Only one of the 13 felt that the program
undermined her in the eyes of other people or in her own eyes. The rest of the
women felt that any stigma that others attached to them would have been attached
in the absence of affirmative action.

While Ayers probed in depth with a small sample, Marylee Taylor looked at a
few items with a large sample: the 1990 General Social Survey. Taylor (1994)
found that African Americans working for affirmative action employers expressed
less cynicism and more ambition than their counterparts working for other firms.
Affirmative action was thus found empirically to create positive rather than negative effects for one minority group.

Similar results were obtained by a 1995 Gallup poll (Gallup Short Subjects,
1995). More than 700 African American, Hispanic American, Native American
and Asian American men and women, in addition to European American women,
participated in the survey. Among them only 8% of the European American
women, 19% of the minority women, and 29% of the minority men indicated
gender or racial doubt of the type that Steele worries about in response to the
question "Have you ever felt that your colleagues at work or school privately
questioned your abilities or qualifications because of affirmative action or have
you never felt this way?"

EVIDENCE CONCERNING YOUTH

In Ayers' study of African American, Hispanic, and Asian American women,
the one person who expressed doubts was among the youngest in the sample. It is
possible, likely in fact, that insecurities about one's capabilities are greatest when
one is young. People who have been in the paid work force for years probably
have developed ways of assessing self-worth that do not depend primarily on the
opinions of nonspecific others. College students who are young and who live in a
highly evaluative environment might be more susceptible to doubts than are ma-
ture adults.

What do the data show? From the myriad studies that have addressed this
question (e.g., Crocker, Luhtanen, Blaine, & Broadnax, 1994; Rowley, Sellers,
Chavous, & Smith, in press), we know that African American, Hispanic Ameri-

can, Asian American, and Native American students do not tend to have lower self-esteem than European American students. Might they have even higher self-esteem if colleges and universities did not embrace affirmative action? We do not know. Despite high self-esteem, are minority students troubled by how others view them? Steele and others would say so, but we were not able to find any systematically collected information on the issue.

Having discovered no surveys that documented in a systematic way the feelings of minority students about affirmative action, we decided to conduct our own. We selected two different sites to increase the generalizability of our findings. We wish to see if we can find in the responses of college students the same level of doubt that is evident in the self-revelations of a few famous professors.

OUR SURVEY

In the first semester of the 1996–1997 academic year, we conducted a questionnaire study of African American, Hispanic American, Asian American and Native American students at Yale University and Smith College. For purposes of comparison, we also included European American students in the survey. Our study specifically addressed three questions:

1. To what extent do minority students believe that others in the environment question their abilities?[2]
2. How strongly do minority students endorse affirmative action?
3. What is the association between the belief that others question abilities, on the one hand, and attitudes toward affirmative action, on the other? Are students who endorse affirmative action relatively unsusceptible to the idea that others doubt their abilities? Or do students endorse affirmative action even when they believe that others question their abilities?

SURVEY METHODS

Participants

Participants were 351 undergraduate students at Yale University and Smith College who filled out a survey during the fall of 1996. Students over the age of 23 were eliminated from the study. The participants were primarily first- and second-year students. Sampling proceeded in similar manners at the two locations.

---

[2]There are a number of reasons why we did not ask the students in our survey directly about their own feelings of either global or academic self-esteem. Given the work of Crocker and her associates and of Seller and his associates, we thought there would be very little variation in the answers to simple questions. We also thought that a lengthy set of questions designed to elicit variations in self-esteem could jeopardize respondent willingness to complete our survey. We did not want to risk having an unrepresentative sample. Nor did we wish to eliminate any of the questions that tapped the respondents' attitudes toward either the policy or the practice of affirmative action.

At Smith students came from two sources: the subject pool of the introduction to psychology course and from a list of minority students. Some introductory students were from ethnic minority groups, but most were European American. The introductory students were given the questionnaire to fill out at their leisure either for credit or for a chance to win a $50 lottery. This method yielded 121 participants. A list of minority students was obtained from the registrar and questionnaires were mailed to 195 first- and second-year students with a cover letter. These individuals had a chance to win a lottery prize of $150. Seventy-five students did return the mailed questionnaires and, under separate cover, their informed consent sheets.

Yale students came from two sources: two classes (108 from introductory psychology and 42 from a motivation course) and a list of Yale's ethnic minority students (5 students). The students from the introductory class had an opportunity to win a $50 lottery as did the students from the motivation class. The students from the list were each paid $5.00 for filling out the questionnaire.

One of the last items in the questionnaire asked the respondent to check one of the following options: African American; Hispanic; Native American; Asian American; Caucasian; Pacific Islander; Blended; and Other. We then collapsed categories into: Asian Americans, European Americans, and Underrepresented. In the Asian American category were those students who self-labeled as either Asian American or Pacific Islander. In the European American group were those students who self-labeled as Caucasian; in the Underrepresented Group were those students who self-labeled as African American, Native American or Hispanic American.

For the purposes of this chapter, we parse the total sample of 351 along two dimensions: Ethnicity (Asian American, European American, Underrepresented) and School-Group (Smith Women; Yale Women; Yale Men). Smith is a women's college with an undergraduate student body of about 2500. Yale's undergraduate student body numbers about 4000, of whom roughly half are male and half are female.

The Instrument

Wherever possible, we used items that had appeared on other surveys. Most of these items had to do with opinions or feelings about affirmative action. Some asked about affirmative action in general. One item, for example, asked respondents to select a definition of affirmative action as either a monitoring system or a quota system. Another asked respondents how much they endorsed the policy of affirmative action. Following Winkelman and Crosby (1994), we created four 7-item scales to measure respondents' opinions about affirmative action as an educational policy, affirmative action as an employment policy, affirmative action plans in education, and affirmative action plans in employment. The 7-point Likert scales were scored so that the higher the value, the greater the endorsement of affirmative action. Table 8.1 presents the scale for affirmative action policies in education. The same items were edited (e.g., substituting the word "employment"

TABLE 8.1   Attitude Scale: Attitudes Toward the Policy of Affirmative Action in Education

Reverse scored?	Question number	Item
yes	5	As a policy, affirmative action is a form of reverse discrimination in education.
yes	7	As a policy, affirmative action unfairly stigmatizes minorities in education
no	9	As a policy, affirmative action enhances the opportunity for people to succeed based on their own merits in education.
no	11	As a policy, affirmative action eliminates preferential treatment and unfair advantage in education.
no	13	As a policy, affirmative action does not give opportunities to less qualified rather than more qualified people in education.
yes	15	As a policy, affirmative action overemphasizes membership in a group rather than individual merit in education.
no	17	As a policy, affirmative action continues to be needed to help women and minorities overcome discrimination in education.

For each item, respondents were given a 7-point Likert scale with "Strongly disagree" on the left and "Strongly agree" on the right.

for the word "education") and used in the three other scales. All of the scales were reliable. All had Cronbach alphas of .85.

We supplemented the standard attitude items with items especially designed to measure the feelings of minority students. Several questions aimed directly at gauging the extent to which students lived under "the suspicion of inferiority." We did not ask students directly about their own confidence in their academic abilities. Other researchers have found and have explained robust self-esteem among minority students (Crocker & Major, 1989), and so we did not expect to find any differences between the minority students and the European American students. Nor would we have interpreted a lack of difference as proof that the minority students had somehow escaped from the poisonous effects of what Steele (1990) calls "racial doubt." If minority students imagine that their peers or their professors think they were admitted to college on the grounds of ethnicity rather than ability, they experience "racial doubt," that is, they believe that others hold some reservations about their academic capabilities and potential given the weight assigned to group membership in the admissions process. "Racial doubt" can become "self-doubt" if these students proceed to internalize the set of beliefs held by their peers and/or professors.

We also assessed the students' views of the extent of sexual and racial discrimination in America. Two items asked about discrimination against women. Two items asked about discrimination against minorities.

TABLE 8.2   Support for Affirmative Action

	Mean scores of students on four scales and one single-item measure			
	Asian American	White	Underrep.	F
1. Affirmative action policy in education	4.0$_a$ SD = 1.12	4.0$_a$ SD = 1.12	5.2$_b$ SD = 1.27	14.3
2. Affirmative action policy in employment	4.0$_a$ SD = 1.10	3.9$_a$ SD = 1.14	5.3$_b$ SD = 1.16	15.9
3. Affirmative action plans in education	3.7$_a$ SD = 1.05	3.6$_a$ SD = 1.06	4.8$_b$ SD = 1.39	17.4
4. Affirmative action plans in employment	3.6$_a$ SD = 1.04	3.6$_a$ SD = 1.07	4.9$_b$ SD = 1.28	17.8
5. Attitudes toward affirmative action	5.3$_a$ SD = 2.62	5.5$_a$ SD = 2.62	7.7$_b$ SD = 2.41	8.3

Numbers 1 through 4 are scales composed of 7 items each with possible values going from 1 (anti-affirmative action) to 7 (pro affirmative action). Number 5 is a single item with a possible range from 0 (dislike affirmative action) to 10 (like affirmative action).

Mean scores that have different subscripts are significantly different from each other.

FINDINGS OF THE SURVEY

We analyzed our data according to the three theoretical questions that guide our research.[3]

The Cloud of Suspicion

Do minority students at Smith College and Yale University think that they are stigmatized in the eyes of their peers and professors? Two questions from the survey allow us to answer the question. The answer is that in our survey, yes, they certainly do. Nearly three-quarters (73%) of the African American, Hispanic American, and Native American students indicate that they have wondered whether their *peers* think they (the respondents) were admitted to college because of their ethnicity and not their intellectual abilities. Significantly fewer Asian American (18%) and European American (4%) students express this belief. Interestingly, underrepresented students appear to be less worried about what their *professors* imagine than about what their peers imagine. About half (47%) of the African American, Hispanic American, and Native American students believe that their professors are suspicious about the reasons for their admittance. Only 15% and 2% of the Asian American and European American students, respectively, express this belief.

[3]With the exception of two interactions noted below, there were no significant main effects or interactions with our sample (Smith women, Yale women, and Yale men) for all the analyses reported. Due to the small number of men in our sample, we were unable to check for gender differences.

Support for Affirmative Action

Support for Affirmative Action Scales

Given that our sample of students appears to feel the kind of second-guessing or racial doubt predicted by conservative commentators and some social scientists as well, it seems logical to wonder if they support or oppose affirmative action. Previous polls have found both the policy and the practice to be more strongly supported by minority group members than European Americans and more strongly supported by women than men (Tomasson, Crosby, & Herzberger, 1996). Would we find the same split or would we find that minority students at Smith and at Yale dislike the policy?

To chart support for affirmative action among the various groups in our sample, we have conducted a series of Analyses of Variance (ANOVAs) in which there are three levels of ethnicity (Asian American, European American and Under-represented) and three levels of gender and school grouping (Smith Women, Yale Women, Yale Men). As noted in Table 8.2, African American, Hispanic American and Native American students are more supportive of policies and plans associated with affirmative action in education and employment relative to Asian American and European American students.[4] Further, the same pattern of results are found for a single-item scale assessing "To what extent do you favor or oppose the policy of affirmative action ($0 =$ dislike; $10 =$ like)." Clearly, students who are African American, Hispanic American, and Native American, strongly endorse affirmative action.

Categorical Variables

Another item taken from the Chicago survey asked respondents to choose one of two definitions of affirmative action. Eighty-four percent of the underrepresented students select the definition "Affirmative action occurs when an organization monitors itself to make sure that it employs and promotes qualified minorities and white women in proportion to their number," while 16% choose "Affirmative action occurs when the government forces organizations to meet quotas for minorities and white women." Among the European American students, the percentages are 60% and 40% for the monitoring and quota definitions. Among Asian Americans, the percentages are 68% and 32%, respectively.

Four other categorical items show the same pattern. For instance, we asked "What is the best thing to do with affirmative action programs in education

---

[4]Significant interactions were obtained with regard to students' attitudes about the practice of affirmative action in education and employment (in education, F (4, 270) = 3.61, $p<.01$; in employment, $F(4, 270) = 3.28$, $p<.02$). The pattern of effects for the interactions do not alter the interpretation of the findings. In addition, to make sure that some items were not pulling along an entire scale, we conducted a series of 28 ANOVAs for each of the items separately. We were especially eager to know if there would be strong minority support for items like "affirmative action unfairly stigmatizes minorities" or "affirmative action enhances the opportunity for people to succeed based on their own merits." In fact, on 27 of the 28 tests, the highly significant main effects for ethnicity show underrepresented students endorsing affirmative action more strongly than the other groups.

[employment]?'' For both items, the response options were (a) change them; (b) do away with them entirely; (c) leave them as they are; and (d) no opinion. About half of the African American, Hispanic American, and Native American participants who have an opinion are in favor of leaving the programs as they are in education (48%) and employment (55%). A minority of European American students and Asian American students feel the same about programs in education (23% and 19%, respectively) and employment (19% and 39%).

Another set of questions asked "Do you favor or oppose strengthening affirmative action laws for women [Black people and other ethnic minorities]?" The options were favor, oppose, and no opinion. Sixty-three percent of the African American, Hispanic American, and Native American students favor strengthening the laws for women and 66% favor strengthening the laws for minorities. Among European Americans, the figures are 31% and 27%. Among Asian-Americans, they are 39% and 33%.

In sum, those students who come from underrepresented minorities at Yale University and at Smith College strongly endorse affirmative action. No matter whether the question is phrased in terms of education or employment, in terms of policy or practice, African American, Hispanic American, and Native American students like affirmative action even more than European American and Asian American students do.

Possible Connections

Distinct Subsamples Explanation

How can it be that the African American, Hispanic American, and Native American students in our study endorse as strongly as they do affirmative action while simultaneously acknowledging in no uncertain terms the existence of the suspicion of inferiority? Three explanations come to mind.

The first explanation is that the sample of students might contain distinct subsamples. It may be that some African American, Hispanic American and Native American students endorse affirmative action while others feel undermined by it. It could be, furthermore, that what the underrepresented students perceive about their own experiences relates in systematic ways to their attitudes about affirmative action. Perhaps the students who think that others second-guess their abilities dislike affirmative action while those who feel that others do not second-guess their abilities like affirmative action.

To test the merit of the first explanation, we looked again at the answers given in response to the questions, "Have you ever wondered whether your peers [professors] think that you have been admitted to X [Smith or Yale] because of your ethnicity and not because of your intellectual abilities?" We divided the sample into those who felt questioned by both their peers *and* their professors, those who felt questioned by either their peers *or* their professors, and those who did not feel questioned by their peers or their professors. We then compared the mean scores of those who felt questioned by their peers and professors to those who felt questioned by their peers or professors and those who did not feel questioned on their overall attitudes toward affirmative action. If the first explanation were valid, we should find those who feel questioned by their peers and their professors to be less supportive of affirmative action than those who do not feel questioned. We find the opposite. Those who felt questioned by their peers and professors were more supportive of affirmative action ($M = 7.6$, $SD = 2.0$, $n = 34$) than those who felt questioned by either their peers or professors ($M = 6.0$, $SD = 3.1$, $n = 32$) and those who did not feel questioned ($M = 5.6$, $SD = 2.6$, $n = 269$; $F(2,332) = 8.41$, $p<.001$). Further analyses reveal reliable correlations between the belief that others question one's ability (measured on a 3-point scale) and support for affirmative action ($r = .21$) generally, support for the policy in education ($r = .28$), support for the policy in employment ($r = .29$), support for affirmative action plans in education ($r = .32$) and support for affirmative action plans in employment ($r = .30$).

On the basis of these analyses we can safely discard the first explanation. It is certainly not the case that the nonstigmatized subgroup endorses affirmative action while the stigmatized subgroup opposes it. Indeed, the very opposite pattern of results obtains.

Cost/Benefit Explanation

A second explanation is that ethnic minority respondents may be engaging in a cost–benefit analysis. Even while acknowledging personal costs in terms of stigma, African American, Hispanic American, and Native American students may endorse affirmative action because it brings great personal benefits. In general, we found that those students who felt that they had benefited from affirmative action were more likely to endorse the policy ($r = .19$, $p < .005$). Furthermore, three questionnaire items allow us to test the cost–benefit explanation more directly; and they show the plausibility of this explanation.

One item in the questionnaire included the prompt "Affirmative action affects me in ways that are" and then included a 7-point Likert scale that ranged from very negative (1) to very positive (7). A 3×3 ANOVA revealed only a main effect for ethnicity, $F(2, 210) = 5.06$, $p<.01$. Students from the underrepresented category score significantly higher ($M = 4.9$, $SD = 1.12$) than European Americans ($M = 4.1$, $SD = 1.22$) or Asian-Americans ($M = 4.0$, $SD = 1.33$). Underrepresented and Asian American students are also more likely than European Americans to feel that affirmative action "played a role" in their admission to college. The mean scores on the 7-point scale were 3.8 ($SD = 1.64$), 3.4 ($SD = 1.75$), and 1.6 ($SD = 1.10$), respectively. Finally, compared to European Americans or Asian Americans, underrepresented students envisioned affirmative action as giving them more access to opportunities. The questionnaire item asked "Do you believe that affirmative action gives you access to more opportunities?" Response options included "Yes, a great deal" (5), "Yes, some" (4), "Don't know" (3), "No" (2), and "No, it gives me less" (1). Average scores for the underrepresented students, European Americans, and Asian Americans were 4.1 ($SD = .63$), 2.6 ($SD = 1.09$), and 3.1 ($SD = 1.12$), respectively.

Cynicism about Racial Attitudes

Related to the cost–benefit explanation is the idea that underrepresented students are cynical about racial attitudes in the United States. African American, Hispanic American, and Native American students may acknowledge that others doubt their abilities, but they may feel that the others would doubt their abilities even if affirmative action were not around as a convenient excuse for prejudice. We asked the students "Do you ever wonder whether others judge your academic ability based upon stereotypes about your ethnic group?" Overall, 58% of the underrepresented and 91% of the Asian American students answer in the affirmative. In contrast, just 24% of the European American students agreed. Further analyses reveal a positive correlation between the belief that others judge one's academic abilities based upon stereotypes about one's ethnic group and support for the policy of affirmative action ($r = .16$, $p<.02$). When we examine the correlations for each one of our student groups separately, we find marginally significant positive correlations in the case of the African American, Hispanic American, and Native American respondents ($r = .30$, $p<.07$) and Asian American students ($r = .20$, $p<.08$). The correlation was not significant in the case of the European American students ($r = -.06$, $p<.60$).

In general, the students in our study seem to be reasoning in the fashion suggested by Major and Crocker (1989). They see that affirmative action allows others to second-guess them, but they seem to define the problem as existing in the eye of the beholder and not in themselves.

PARTING WISHES

In the current debates about affirmative action, some critics of the policy have claimed that it undermines the direct beneficiaries. More specifically, affirmative action is thought to create a suspicion among people of color that others question or second-guess their abilities. Laboratory studies in which preferential treatment was said to be operating have shown that the recipients of preferential treatment do, in fact, feel undermined by undeserved rewards. Thus far, no one has demonstrated that affirmative action causes problems in the world outside the laboratory. Indeed, with respect to employment, affirmative action has been shown not to undermine individuals.

The self-reports of our samples accord with the notion that young people in an educational setting may feel more susceptible to racial doubt than do employed individuals. About three-quarters of the students who are African American, Hispanic American, or Native American feel that other students question their admission to college. Approximately half also think that professors second-guess them.

Should we, then, abandon affirmative action? Conservatives like Shelby Steele (1990) would say yes. We say: emphatically no! The direct beneficiaries of affirmative action certainly endorse both the policy and the practice of affirmative action. Minority students know that it is not the policy that causes the stigmatizing.

Looking at the situation from the targets' point of view, we ought to educate the majority. Education has been recommended before (American Psychological Association, 1996; Turner & Pratkanis, 1994). Surely the time has come to put the plan into action.

REFERENCES

American Psychological Association (1996). *Affirmative action: Who benefits?* Washington, DC: American Psychological Association.

Ayers, L. (1992). Perceptions of affirmative action among its beneficiaries. *Social Justice Research, 5,* 223–238.

Bergmann, B. R. (1996). *In defense of affirmative action.* New York: Basic Books.

Carter, Stephen J. (1991). *Reflections of an affirmative action baby.* New York: Basic Books.

Clayton, S., & Crosby, F. J. (1992). *Justice, gender, and affirmative action.* Ann Arbor, MI: University of Michigan Press.

Crocker, J., Luhtanen, R., Blaine, B., & Broadnax, S. (1994). Collective self-esteem and psychological well-being among White, Black, and Asian college students. *Personality and Social Psychology Bulletin, 20,* 503–513.

Crocker, J., & Major, B. (1989). Social stigma and self-esteem: The self-protective properties of stigma. *Psychological Review, 96,* 608–630.

Crosby, F. J. (1994). Understanding affirmative action. *Basic and Applied Social Psychology, 15,* 13–41.

Crosby, F. J., & Blanchard, F. A. (1989). Introduction: Affirmative action and the question of standards. In F. A. Blanchard & F. J. Crosby (Eds.), *Affirmative action in perspective* (pp. 3–7). New York: Springer-Verlag.

Crosby, F. J., & Clayton, S. (1990). Affirmative action and the issue of expectancies. *Journal of Social Issues, 46* (2), 61–79.

Crosby, F. J., & Wyche, K. F. (1996). Coming together. In K. F. Wyche & F. J. Crosby (Eds.), *Women's ethnicities: Journeys through psychology* (pp. 1–4). New York: Harper Collins.

Crosby, F. J., & Cordova, D. I. (1996). Words worth of wisdom: Toward an understanding of affirmative action. *Journal of Social Issues, 52,* 33–49.

Eastland, T. (1996). *Ending affirmative action.* New York: Basic Books.

Gallup Short Subjects (July, 1995). *Gallup Poll Monthly, 358,* 34–61.

Golden, H., Crosby, F. J., & Hinkle, S. (In press). Affirmative action: Semantics vs substance. *The New England Journal of Public Policy.*

Harris, L. (1992, January–February). Unequal terms. *Columbia Journalism Review, 30* (5), 20.

Heilman, M. (1994). Affirmative action: Some unintended consequences for working women. *Research in Organizational Behavior, 16,* 125–169.

Heilman, M. E., Kaplow, S. R., Amato, M. A. G., & Stathatos, P. (1993). When similarity is a liability: Effects of sex-based preferential selection on reactions to like-sex and different-sex others. *Journal of Applied Psychology, 78,* 917–927.

Heilman, M. E., Lucas, J. A., & Kaplow, S. R. (1990). Self-derogating consequences of sex-based preferential selection: The moderating role of initial self-confidence. *Organizational Behavior and Human Decision Processes, 46,* 202–216.

Heilman, M. E., Rivero, J. C., & Brett, J. F. (1991). Skirting the competence issue: Effects of sex-based preferential selection on task choices of women and men. *Journal of Applied Psychology, 76,* 99–105.

Heilman, M. E., Simon, M. C., & Repper, D. P. (1987). Intentionally favored, unintentionally harmed? Impact of sex-based preferential selection on self-perceptions and self-evaluations. *Journal of Applied Psychology, 72,* 62–68.

Major, B., Feinstein, J., & Crocker, J. (1994). Attributional ambiguity of affirmative action. *Basic and Applied Social Psychology, 15,* 113–141.

Nacoste, R. W. (1980). Affirmative action and self-evaluation. In F. A. Blanchard & F. J. Crosby (Eds.), *Affirmative action in perspective* (pp.103–109). New York: Springer-Verlag.

Nacoste, R. W. (1985). Selection procedure and responses to affirmative action: The case of favorable treatment. *Law and Human Behavior, 9,* 225–242.

Nacoste, R. W. (1987). But do they care about fairness? The dynamics of preferential treatment and minority interests. *Basic and Applied Social Psychology, 8,* 117–191.

Newman, J. D. (1989). Affirmative action and the courts. In F. A. Blanchard & F. J. Crosby (Eds.), *Affirmative action in perspective* (pp. 31–49). New York: Springer-Verlag.

Rosser, P. (1996, September). *The SATS and gender bias.* Paper delivered at Smith College, Northampton, MA.

Rowley, S. A., Sellers, R. M., Chavous, T. M., & Smith, M. A. (In press). The relationship between racial identity and self-esteem in African American college and high school students. *Journal of Personality and Social Psychology.*

Steele, S. (1991). *The content of our character.* New York: St. Martin's Press.

Stephanopoulos, G., & Edley, C., Jr., (1995) *Affirmative action review: Report to the President.* Washington, DC: Government Printing Office.

Taylor, M. C. (1994). Impact of affirmative action on beneficiary groups: Evidence from the 1990 general social survey. *Basic and Applied Social Psychology, 15,* 143–178.

Tomasson, R., Crosby, F. J., & Herzberger, S. (1996). *Affirmative action: The pros and cons of policy and practice.* Washington, DC: American University Press.

Turner, M. E., & Pratkanis, A. R. (1994). Affirmative action: Insights from social psychological and organizational research. *Basic and Applied Social Psychology, 15,* 1–121.

Winkelman, C., & Crosby, F. J. (1994). Affirmative action: Setting the record straight. *Social Justice Research, 7,* 309–328.

COPING WITH
PREJUDICE

9

COMPENSATING

FOR PREJUDICE

HOW HEAVYWEIGHT PEOPLE
(AND OTHERS)
CONTROL OUTCOMES
DESPITE PREJUDICE

CAROL T. MILLER AND ANNA M. MYERS

University of Vermont

WHY HEAVYWEIGHT PEOPLE (AND OTHERS)
NEED TO COMPENSATE

When stigmatized people can neither eliminate prejudice nor live with its consequences, they may use compensatory strategies to prevent its adverse effects on the outcomes they receive. Thus far researchers have concentrated attention on two main classes of responses stigmatized people make to prejudice. The first is that stigmatized people may act individually or collectively to eliminate or reduce prejudice and discrimination or to redress injustices that result from prejudice (Lalonde & Cameron, 1994). The second is that once negative outcomes due to prejudice have occurred, stigmatized people may use a number of strategies to change the way they think and feel about these outcomes and their role in producing them (Crocker & Major, 1989). We will refer to the latter strategies as *secondary compensation* because their goal is to protect the stigmatized person from the psychological consequences that would otherwise follow from the diminishment of interpersonal outcomes that result from the prejudice of others.

There is another major class of responses, which we refer to as *primary compensation,* that has not received sufficient attention. We define primary compensation as a specific form of coping which reduces the threats posed by prejudice by enabling the stigmatized person to achieve desired interpersonal outcomes despite the existence of prejudice in a particular situation. When successful, primary compensation can reduce the need for secondary compensation strategies. Primary compensation may circumvent the occurrence of negative outcomes, for example, being ignored in a social situation, that would otherwise have to be handled through a secondary compensation strategy such as blaming prejudice for the social slight or reducing the perceived attractiveness or importance of the people who subjected the stigmatized person to the slight.

Our research has focused on the stigma of being heavyweight. This stigma has received increasing attention recently, in part because it is a condition so stigmatizing that Crandall (1994) calls it one of the last remaining socially acceptable prejudices. Heavyweight people are faced with overwhelming disapproval and prejudice (DeJong & Kleck, 1981; Millman, 1980). This chapter examines strategies heavyweight people and other stigmatized people may use to compensate for the prejudice they face. It also considers the effectiveness and possible unintended consequences of compensation.

SIMILARITIES BETWEEN PREJUDICE AND IMPAIRMENTS AS CHALLENGES TO SUCCESSFUL FUNCTIONING

Our model of compensation is derived from theories of compensation for physical, cognitive, and psychological impairments and losses, especially Bäckman and Dixon's (1992) general model of psychological compensation and Schulz and Heckhausen's (1996) theorizing about the role of compensation in successful aging.

Every social situation requires a certain level of skill from participants in order for them to achieve the outcomes they desire from the interaction. Some situations are more difficult than others because they require a higher level of skills. Prejudice increases the difficulties of interpersonal situations. A normative level of skills that would be sufficient to produce an efficacious interaction in a nonprejudiced situation is no longer adequate. Thus, prejudice creates a discrepancy between the skills that stigmatized people have available and the skills required to negotiate the demands of social situations. In this way, the problems posed by prejudice are functionally similar to the problems faced by people with cognitive or physical impairments, who also confront situations that require more skills than they have available (Bäckman & Dixon, 1992).

This analogy is useful because it draws attention to processes by which people in general deal with obstacles to reaching desired goals. Compensation is a key variable in both Bäckman and Dixon's (1992) model of functioning with impairment and Schulz and Heckhausen's (1996) model of functioning across the life span. They define compensation as a strategy aimed at making amends for a lack, loss, or deficit in ability or personal characteristics that threatens to block attainment of expected or desired goals. Compensation occurs when desired goals cannot be achieved with ordinary efforts or skills. Ordinary efforts and skills may be insufficient because there is some impairment or loss in the individual's abilities, as in the case of age-related declines in physical and cognitive abilities. Ordinary efforts and skills also may be insufficient because the demands of the situation that must be met to achieve the goal have increased and thus exceed the individual's unimpaired abilities (Bäckman & Dixon, 1992). Either scenario creates the mismatch between skill levels and situational demands that must be remedied by compensation.

EFFECTS OF PREJUDICE ON SITUATIONAL DEMANDS

One important difference between the problems resulting from stigma and those resulting from impairments is that stigma can affect both skill level and situational demands, whereas impairments by definition represent a loss or deficiency in normative skill levels. For example, a person with failing eyesight faces task demands that exceed that person's new (and lower) ability level. The situational demands have not changed. With stigma, the demands of the situation have changed. For example, since the turn of the century biological factors that affect women's ability to maintain a given level of thinness have not changed, but the standard for being thin has become more demanding (Rodin, Silberstein, & Streigel-Moore, 1985). Consequently, increasing numbers of women find themselves in the "too fat" category.

Results of several studies illustrate how prejudice can increase the difficulties encountered by heavyweight people in interpersonal interactions. For example, college men's beliefs about whether women they spoke to by telephone were heavyweight or nonheavyweight affected the men's treatment of the women (Snyder and Haugen, 1994; 1995). The men's beliefs were manipulated by showing them standard photographs of a heavyweight or nonheavyweight woman and informing them that the photograph represented the woman with whom they were about to speak. Ratings made by naive judges of the men's contributions to the conversation indicated that the men behaved in a less positive manner toward supposedly heavyweight women. In addition, when the women were motivated by preconversation instructions to try to get along with the men, supposedly heavyweight women reacted to the differential treatment they received from the men by confirming the men's negative expectations (Snyder & Haugen, 1995). In this study, the increase in situational demands caused by prejudice produced poorer interaction outcomes for supposedly heavyweight women than they otherwise would have had.

Surveys of heavyweight people show that they believe prejudice against heavyweight people increases the difficulty of the situations they face. Heavyweight people report more employment discrimination and school victimization (e.g., teasing by other children) than do nonheavyweight people (Rothblum, Brand, Miller, & Oetjen, 1990). A survey of gastric-bypass surgery patients showed that these heavyweight people overwhelmingly reported that people at work had a negative attitude toward them because of their weight, that they had experienced weight discrimination in hiring, and that they avoided being seen in public and especially in fast food restaurants, where the prevalence of fatty foods often exposes fat people to the censure of others (Rand & MacGregor, 1990).

Myers and Rosen (1996) used an open-ended questionnaire to ask heavyweight people about what types of stigmatizing situations they face because of their weight. From these responses they developed a measure of 11 types of situations in which people experience fat prejudice. This was administered to heavyweight people who were candidates for gastric-bypass surgery ($n = 112$) or who had participated in weight loss treatment programs ($n = 34$). Virtually all study participants were quite heavyweight. Most had a Body Mass Index greater than 40 ($n = 109$; M weight = 333 lbs, M BMI = 55) and even those with a BMI less than 40, most of whom were from weight loss treatment programs, were quite heavy ($n = 35$, M weight = 209 lbs, M BMI = 34). The three most frequently reported types of stigmatizing situations were comments from children, unflattering assumptions made about the person based upon his or her weight, and encounters with physical barriers such as seats in public places that are too small to accommodate heavyweight people. Reports about the frequency of these situations indicated that they occurred on average between several times per year to several times in the respondents' lives. Less prevalent stigma situations included, in order of frequency, being stared at, inappropriate comments from physicians, nasty comments from family and from others, being avoided, excluded, or ignored, embarrassing loved ones, job discrimination, and physical violence. In addition, the more heavyweight the participants were, the more frequently they said they encountered stigma situations.

Experimental evidence also indicates that heavyweight people believe that their weight affects how others respond to them. Heavyweight college women who received negative feedback from a man attributed his response to their weight (Crocker, Cornwell, & Major, 1993). In an experiment in which heavyweight and nonheavyweight students interacted with a nice, nasty, or neutral confederate, heavyweight students overwhelmingly attributed the confederate's behavior to their weight (Rodin & Slochower, 1974). Nonheavyweight students gave a variety of explanations for the confederate's behavior.

EFFECTS OF PREJUDICE ON SKILL LEVELS

Some (but by no means all) stigmatized conditions can include elements of impairment. For example, heavyweight people suffer some physical ailments such as heart disease, hypertension, diabetes, and respiratory difficulties that may diminish their ability to meet the physical demands of some situations. Similarly, people who are stigmatized because of their addiction to drugs or alcohol also suffer from some cognitive and physical impairments that result from substance abuse. However, our interest is *not* on physical or cognitive impairments that may be part of a stigmatizing condition. Our focus is on the possibility that the skills of stigmatized people may be reduced or remain underdeveloped because prejudice affects their opportunities for developing certain skills. For example, in social interactions between stigmatized people and others, stigmatized people may be avoided or their contributions to the interaction minimized or negated. Thus, stigmatized people's opportunities for developing effective social skills are limited.

Goldman and Lewis (1977) reasoned that because others dislike and avoid physically unattractive people, unattractive people will have little opportunity to develop and practice social skills. They conducted a study in which attractive and unattractive college students conversed by telephone and rated their impressions of each other after the conversation was over. Results showed that attractive students were perceived more positively than unattractive people even though their partners never saw them.

In a similar study, heavyweight women who conversed by telephone with another person were rated both by the other person and by naive raters as being less socially skilled and less likable than nonheavyweight women were (Miller, Rothblum, Barbour, Brand, & Felicio, 1990). Because neither the telephone partners nor the raters saw the women, these findings suggest that the cumulative impact of prejudice might be reduced opportunities to develop social skills.

There also is evidence that heavyweight people are less likely than similarly qualified nonheavyweight people to be admitted to prestigious colleges (Canning & Mayer, 1966) or to receive equivalent financial support from their parents (Crandall, 1995). Consequently, they may not become as skilled or qualified for employment as nonheavyweight people. Heavyweight people also may face discrimination in hiring and in the workplace, which further circumscribes opportunities for skill development (Heatherton, Kiwan, & Hebl, 1996; Rothblum et al., 1990; Rothblum, Miller, & Garbutt, 1988). This may contribute to the relatively low socioeconomic status and downward social mobility that has been documented among fat people (Kral, Sjostrom, & Sullivan, 1992; Sobal & Stunkard, 1989).

REDUCING MISMATCHES BETWEEN SKILLS
AND SITUATIONAL DEMANDS

Stigmatized people often face more barriers to achieving goals than do others, but obstacles can be overcome by a variety of compensatory strategies. Just as a person who experiences the loss of vision learns how to function without sight, so too might stigmatized people learn to function with prejudice. The key to functioning is to compensate for the disadvantages posed by the impairment of one's own abilities or by the impairment of others' ability to treat one without prejudice.

Figure 9.1 depicts the theoretical relationship between prejudice and use of compensatory strategies to achieve desired outcomes. As prejudice increases from low to high levels, the bars representing obstacles or barriers to successful functioning grow increasingly higher. If the skills the individual brings to bear on the situation remain stable (as represented by the horizontal line), the individual will be able to function in situations where demands are small due to the absence of

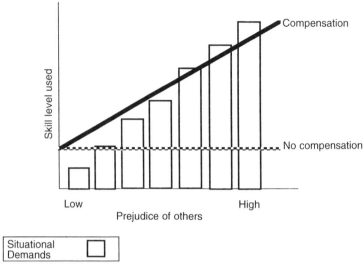

FIGURE 9.1   Compensation, situational demands, and prejudice.

prejudice. This might include, for example, situations in which the person's stigmatized status is not known to the other. As prejudice increases, the individual's skills will fall below the level required to clear the bar. Without compensation, therefore, the stigmatized person's skills are not adequate for the task at hand. However, if the individual is able and willing to increase the skills used in a situation, it may be possible to clear bars of increasing height. Thus, even in situations in which prejudice poses considerable barriers to successful functioning, the stigmatized person's skill level may be adequate for the task.

In this illustration, the meaning of skill is very broad. It includes any social, behavioral, cognitive, or other skill that affects functioning in social interactions, as well as increases in effort or persistence that might make skills more effective in a particular situation.

AN EXPERIMENTAL DEMONSTRATION OF COMPENSATION

The hypothesis that stigmatized people may compensate for prejudice has not as yet received much attention because until recently social interactions were seldom examined from the perspective of the stigmatized person (see Swim & Stangor, this volume). In taking this perspective in our own research, our first assumption was that the motivations and goals that stigmatized people bring to social situations are often the same as those of anyone else. For example, one strategy people use to maintain a positive self-image is to compensate for deficiencies in one area by bolstering other aspects of the self (Steele, 1988). Research on nonstigmatized people has shown that people who believed that another had negative information about one aspect of their personalities did not try to refute this information, but instead presented themselves more positively on other personality dimensions (Baumeister, 1982). Similarly, people who received criticism from another were more likely to volunteer for a worthy cause than people who received no criticism, even though the criticism was irrelevant to volunteering (Steele, 1975). These studies suggest that people who believe they have or are perceived to have a shortcoming in one area may change their behavior (or their behavioral descriptions) in other areas to overcome the potential negative impact of that shortcoming.

We have already described how college men's beliefs about whether the women they spoke to by telephone were heavyweight or not heavyweight affected their behavior toward the women, and how the women believed to be heavyweight reacted by confirming the men's negative expectations. This pattern of expectancy confirmation occurred only when the men were instructed to try to form a stable impression of the women and the women were instructed to try to get along with the men (Snyder & Haugen, 1994; 1995). Thus, the goals of the interaction participants were important in whether prejudice against heavyweight women affected the outcome of the interaction.

Although these results suggest that heavyweight women may be unable or unmotivated to overcome the effects of their weight on others' reactions to them, there are two features of Snyder and Haugen's (1994; 1995) experiments that must temper this conclusion. The supposedly heavyweight women were unaware that they had been portrayed as stigmatized to the men and they were not actually stigmatized (because there was no actual correspondence between the women's weight and how they were portrayed to the men).

Hilton and Darley (1985) demonstrated that people who are aware of others' negative expectations about them (that they had a cold personality) acted to disconfirm rather than confirm the expectation by behaving in an especially friendly manner. Only people who were unaware of the negative expectation behaved consistent with it. Because stigmatized people are well aware that they are the targets of prejudice, this finding suggests they may therefore be motivated and able to disconfirm expectations arising from stereotypes.

In addition, Graham (1992) and Harris and colleagues (1992) have pointed out that people who actually are stigmatized often are not included in research—even in studies of how stigmatized people react to others' treatment of them. One of the best-known demonstrations of behavioral confirmation of stereotyped expectations was an experiment in which college women were randomly assigned to be portrayed as a physically attractive or unattractive during their telephone conversations with college men (Snyder, Tanke, & Berscheid, 1977). In another often cited study, European American male college students were randomly assigned to interact with a confederate interviewer who had been trained to adopt the nonverbal behaviors that naive European American interviewers had previously displayed when they interviewed a European American or African American confederate (Word, Zanna, & Cooper, 1974). It is perhaps not surprising that the nonstigmatized people who were the recipients of prejudice-inspired behavior were at a loss to know what to do. They were being confronted, perhaps for one of the few times in their lives, with what it is like to be stigmatized. For example, Farina, Allen, and Saul (1968) reported that one of the European American male Ivy League undergraduates who participated in an experimental condition in which he thought his partner in a task had been informed that he was a homosexual became "obviously alarmed" when his partner put his arm around his shoulders to assist him in operating the apparatus required for the task.

The above considerations suggest that it is important to examine the reactions of people who actually are stigmatized to situations in which they know others are prejudiced against them. We (Miller, Rothblum, Brand, & Felicio, 1995) did that in a study of the impressions heavyweight women created during a telephone conversation with another person. We varied whether or not the person with whom they interacted could see them on a television monitor, and thus become aware of their stigma. This manipulation effectively alters the demands of the situation (depicted in Fig. 9.1 as bars of increasing height). When the heavyweight women can be seen, they face a potentially more difficult interaction than when they are not visible to their partners.

The women's perception of the potential of prejudice to affect the interaction also was manipulated by informing the women that the person with whom they conversed either could or could not see them on a television monitor. If heavyweight women try to overcome others' prejudice against them, their behavior should create different impressions when they think they are visible than when they think they are not visible.

Participants in this experiment were 77 heavyweight women (at least 20% over "ideal" weight, $M = 46\%$) and 78 nonheavyweight women (within 10% of ideal weight, $M = 2\%$ under ideal weight) who were recruited through newspaper advertisements. Most participants were middle-aged (average age was 44 for heavyweight women and 40 for nonheavyweight women).

When a woman arrived at the experiment a female experimenter met her in a room located in an area where the woman's telephone partner would not encounter her. The woman was told that she would have a conversation by telephone with another person, and that both parties would be rating their impressions of each other before and after it occurred. In all experimental conditions, there was a videocamera in the room. The women were always told that they would be videotaped so that the experimenters could examine their behavior later on. Half the women (chosen at random) were told that their partner could see them on a television monitor. The other women were told that they were being videotaped but that their partners could not see them. In this way we were able to vary whether the heavyweight women believed that they (and their stigmatizing condition) were visible or not visible to the person with whom they were about to interact without confounding this manipulation with the experience of being videotaped.

We also varied whether the partner actually could see the women on a television monitor. In the conditions in which the partners could see the women, the partner first saw the woman before the telephone conversation began under the pretext of checking that the equipment was functioning. Once the conversation began, the women in this condition continued to be visible for the entire duration of the conversation.

Having completed these preliminaries, the woman called the partner and began the conversation. The partner was a man or woman (average age about 39) who also had been recruited through advertisements in a local newspaper. The women and their partners conversed for 5 minutes about whatever they liked.

Prior to the conversation the women completed questions about how likable and socially skilled they thought they would be and after the conversation they rated how likable and socially skilled they had been during the conversation. The partners made similar ratings of the women. Questions about the women's physical attractiveness also were included. Analysis of the partners' ratings of the women's attractiveness confirmed that both before and after the conversation, heavyweight women were eveluted as less attractive than nonheavyweight women only when the women actually were visible to their partners.

Telephone partners' postconversation ratings of the women's social skills showed that heavyweight women received more negative ratings than nonheavyweight women only when prejudice actually was a factor in the interaction (because the partners could see the women) but the women did not know this (because they had been told that they were not visible to their partners). Heavyweight and nonheavyweight women who knew their partners actually could see them were rated similarly, even when the partners could actually see the women, and thus may have been prejudiced against the heavyweight women.

It is important to keep in mind that partners knew nothing about what the women had been told about their visibility to the partners. Thus, when partners rated the heavyweight women who thought they were visible as more socially skilled than the heavyweight women who thought they were not visible, the partners were reacting to some difference in the *behavior* of heavyweight women in these two conditions. In other words, the women's beliefs about whether they could be seen produced some alteration in their behavior that was obvious enough to the partners that it affected the partners' impressions of their social skills.

Our explanation for this finding is that heavyweight women who thought they were visible assumed that they might be interacting with a person who was prejudiced against them, and hence needed to deploy their social skills more effectively to compensate for this impediment to an efficacious social interaction. Ratings made by the women provided additional support for this view. When the women thought they were visible to their partners, heavyweight women who spoke to female (but not male) telephone partners reported both before and after the conversation began that they would be/were more likable and socially skilled than nonheavyweight women did. Heavyweight and nonheavyweight women's ratings did not differ when they thought their partners could not see them.

The results of this study suggest that heavyweight women are aware of the need to compensate for prejudice and have the skills necessary to overcome others' reactions to their weight. Stigmatized people have a great deal of experience with situations in which prejudice creates difficulties, and it should not be surprising that they have developed strategies and skills for dealing with these difficulties. In the next sections we explore the different forms that compensation may take and review research that illustrates these different types of compensation.

DIMENSIONS OF COMPENSATION

In common parlance, compensation can refer to pursuing a goal with greater zeal or with external assistance, pursuing a different or substitute goal, or denying the value of the original goal (English & English, cited in Bäckman & Dixon, 1992). Such definitions imply the existence of two important dimensions underlying different forms of compensation.

One distinction that occurs in virtually all descriptions of compensation is the distinction between original goals and alternative goals. Difficulties in achieving the original goal may lead to the development of alternative or substitutable goals (see Fig. 9.2). A person who has difficulty making friends, for example, may concentrate on academic pursuits, developing creative talents, or becoming proficient in employment-related skills. The shift from original to alternative goals involves two components. The first is abandoning the original goal and the second is embracing an alternative goal. Both components can involve cognitive and/or affective processes, for example, devaluing or valuing a goal and identifying or disidentifying with it. Both components also may involve goal-relevant behaviors. In abandoning the original goal stigmatized people may cease activities directed toward obtaining it. In embracing an alternative goal they may engage in activites to pursue it. The abandonment and selection of different goals may occur sequentially or simultaneously. For example, a heavyweight college woman may place greater emphasis on academic achievement at the same time that she withdraws her efforts to win popularity with her peers. Alternatively, she might first abandon the pursuit of popularity before discovering that academic achievement is a satisfactory substitute.

Another dimension that can be used to describe different types of compensatory strategies is whether they are primary or secondary compensation. Primary compensation is aimed at preventing the occurrence of negative outcomes, whereas secondary compensation is aimed at alleviating the psychological damage that the occurrence of negative outcomes would otherwise produce. This distinction is based on Heckhausen and Schulz's (1995; Schulz & Heckhausen, 1996) distinction between primary and secondary control processes. Primary control focuses mainly on changing the situation or environment, usually through a behavior that enables the individual to achieve desired outcomes. Secondary control occurs when the individual cannot successfully exert control over the environ-

Type of Goal

	Original Goal	Alternative Goal
Type of Control	Self-protective attributions	
	Selective social comparison	Value alternative
Secondary	(downward or in-group)	Identify with alternative
Compensation	Devalue goal	
	Disidentify with goal	
	Use normal skills	
Primary	Increase effort	
Compensation	More persistence	Actively pursue
	Use latent skills	alternative goal
	Use new skills	

FIGURE 9.2   Compensation by control type and goal type.

ment, and thus must protect the self from the consequences of adverse outcomes mainly by altering cognitions and/or affect.

Figure 9.1, which depicts the relationship between compensation and the ability to overcome barriers posed by prejudice, can be understood specifically as a depiction of the role of primary compensation in social interaction. Primary compensation is an effort to actually overcome the obstacles that prejudice creates. For example, a person who is prejudiced against heavyweight people might ignore a heavyweight person in a social situation. If the heavyweight person attempts to overcome this neglect by being more outgoing and charming, she may be able to overcome the prejudiced person's initial distaste and create a good impression and perhaps even develop a new friendship. The bar to these desired outcomes was higher than it would have been had she not been heavyweight, but she achieved the desired outcomes anyway.

Compensatory strategies to exert primary control include exerting more effort and being more persistent in using existing skills to achieve the goal, using latent skills to achieve the goal, and using newly acquired skills to achieve the goal (Bäckman & Dixon, 1992). For example, in Myers and Rosen's (1996) study of coping with weight stigma, heavyweight people reported that they would sometimes have to be especially assertive in obtaining medical care from doctors who insisted that they lose weight before being treated for a medical condition. This is an example of using an existing or latent skill (assertiveness) to achieve a goal (obtaining medical care). Others reported becoming socially outgoing and friendly (developing a new skill) in order to "head off" people who might be tempted to criticize them for their weight.

Sometimes heavyweight people may lack the necessary skills to use primary compensation, may be unmotivated to employ such skills, or may face situations so contaminated by prejudice that even though they are highly skilled, the other's prejudice is so strong that it cannot be overcome. When this occurs, heavyweight people may be unable to achieve the outcomes they desire. In a social interaction, for example, the other would maintain a prejudice-based negative impression of the heavyweight person and/or the prospects of developing a new friendship would remain poor.

Having been unable to achieve desired goals, the heavyweight person may use secondary compensatory strategies to mitigate the psychological damage that would otherwise occur. These might include devaluing the original goal (e.g., not caring about the other person's reaction), attributing the others' reaction to prejudice, and comparing interaction outcomes to those of other heavyweight people (see Crocker & Major, 1989). For example, women tend to compare their pay and working conditions with other women, thereby avoiding the painful conclusion that they are underpaid and overworked (Bylsma & Major, 1994; Major, 1989).

If a goal is very highly valued, it may become a core feature of the individual's self-concept (Linville, 1987; Markus, 1977). Devaluing this type of goal requires that individuals cease basing their self-concepts on it, a process referred to as disidentification (see Major & Schmader, this volume). For example, Quinn and Crocker (this volume) suggest that an important individual difference among heavyweight women is how much they base their self-concept on adherence to normative weight standards. Those whose self-concepts are based on appearance norms are especially likely to suffer from low self-esteem as a consequence of their weight, but those who have disidentified with body weight as a component of self-concept are less likely to have low self-esteem.

These secondary compensatory strategies are cognitive/affective processes that do not actually alter the outcome that has occurred, but do make the person feel better about the outcome. In the example above in which a heavyweight woman may devalue the goal of being popular in favor of being an accomplished student, the process of changing the importance of these domains has not actually altered how popular she is or how well she is doing academically. Instead she may now take greater pride in what she has accomplished academically and shrug off her unpopularity. Of course, these changes in how she values the two domains are likely to lead to changes in her behavior. Whereas before she might have tried to initiate friendships and be included in social events, she may now instead devote more of her time to studying. When this happens her actions can be conceptualized as primary compensation.

When stigmatized people first shift to an alternative goal they may value it and identify with it as anyone else would and they may use ordinary levels of efforts and skills to pursue it. The shift to an alternative goal is a form of compensation, but the manner in which it is embraced and pursued may be no different from the way a nonstigmatized person does so. However, prejudice-caused obstacles can occur with respect to both original and alternative goals, and even in the absence of overt prejudice, stigmatized people's expectations may lead them to anticipate difficulties (a compensation strategy in itself). Shifting to an alternative goal is no guarantee that prejudice will not be a threat to achieving the outcomes desired. When this happens, the alternative goal begins to function in the same way as the original goal, and the arsenal of compensatory strategies shown on the left side of Fig. 9.2 may be deployed to compensate for the effects of prejudice on pursuit of the alternative goal. It is unlikely that any one strategy will be successful in every instance, and so stigmatized people may learn to shift from primary to secondary compensation strategies and from goal to goal to achieve the best outcomes they can.

Myers and Rosen's (1996) survey of heavyweight gastric-bypass surgery patients and weight loss program participants provides one indication of the type of compensatory strategies heavyweight people may use. In the first phase of this study, an open-ended survey queried heavyweight participants about the types of responses they typically employed when they encountered fat stigma. From this open-ended survey, 21 types of responses, including both primary and secondary compensatory strategies, were identified. A close-ended survey comprising 99 examples representing the 21 response types was then administered to another sample of heavyweight patients. Participants indicated how frequently they used each response on 10-point scales with endpoints labeled "never" (scored as zero) and "daily" (scored as nine). Responses heavyweight participants said they used the most ($Ms = 4.5$) were those that Myers and Rosen called *positive self-talk* and *heading off*. Positive self-talk is a secondary compensatory strategy because it involves reaffirming that the self is of value even in the face of others' prejudice. An example of a question assessing this response is, "I think, 'It's who I am on the inside that matters.' " Heading off is a primary compensatory strategy. Heading off involves offering a verbal or nonverbal signal of friendliness at the first sign that the other may express fat prejudice. One of the questions that assessed this strategy is, "I make eye contact and say 'hi' to people who might be staring." Preemptive friendliness prevents the other from producing the overt prejudiced response.

Other primary compensatory strategies included using humor, witty comebacks, or joking ($M = 3.4$), refusing to hide one's body or making a point of being visible ($M = 3.2$), responding positively or being nice ($M = 2.7$) and educating people about fat stigma ($M = 1.4$). Refusing to camouflage one's body serves a compensatory function similar to heading off, because it may communicate to potentially prejudiced people that the heavyweight person is comfortable with his or her body. Similarly, responding by using humor, ignoring remarks, or responding with friendliness can be a way of reestablishing primary control. These responses enable heavyweight people to demonstrate superiority of social skills by not being flustered or wounded by a belittling remark. Responding to prejudice by educating the person about fat stigma takes control of a potentially damaging social encounter by turning it into an opportunity to advance fat acceptance.

It is interesting that these heavyweight participants did not report frequent use of the strategy most often recommended to heavyweight people, losing weight ($M = 1.4$). Moreover, dieting was less frequently endorsed as a way of dealing with fat prejudice than was refusing to diet ($M = 3.5$) even though all of the study participants were seeking professional assistance to lose weight, and many of them were considering relatively extreme measures (gastric-bypass surgery).

One implication of the Myers and Rosen's (1996) study is that heavyweight people employ both primary and secondary compensatory strategies in dealing with fat stigma. Prior research has focused on secondary compensation strategies that heavyweight people use in an effort to maintain self-esteem in spite of the prejudice (Crocker *et al.,* 1993). Meyers and Rosen's survey highlights the fact that heavyweight people also employ primary compensatory strategies in order to maintain control in social interactions and thereby achieve their original goals.

EVIDENCE OF PRIMARY COMPENSATION BY STIGMATIZED PEOPLE

Our focus in the review that follows is on evidence that stigmatized individuals may use primary compensation strategies. We are especially interested in studies of heavyweight people, but included any study that was relevant to the question of whether stigmatized people may use increased effort, greater persistence, and new or latent skills to achieve their objectives despite the existence of prejudice.

EVIDENCE OF INCREASED PERSISTENCE OR EFFORT

Dion and Stein (1978) studied the social influence strategies of physically attractive and unattractive elementary school children. Children were asked to try to persuade another child to eat crackers that were coated with a bitter-tasting substance. Results showed that unattractive girls were the most persistent and used the most influence strategies, while attractive girls were the least persistent. Unattractive boys used more commands and were the only ones to use physical threat. These findings suggest that unattractive children may be beginning to develop a relatively assertive or dominant interpersonal style.

According to equity theory, people evaluate the fairness of their relationships by comparing the ratio of their contributions and benefits to their partners' (Walster, Walster, & Berscheid, 1978). Contributions include behaviors (e.g., being more loving, doing more for the partner) as well as characteristics that influence perceived status or desirability of the individual. Because physically unattractive people are stigmatized, partners who differ in physical attractiveness make unequal contributions in the appearance domain. The relationship may still be equitable if the less attractive person compensates for the lesser value of his or her appearance by providing other contributions. Research shows, for example, that people who are less attractive than their partners may compensate for this by having a better sense of humor or better personality (Feingold, 1981) or by being more loving and submissive to their partners (Critelli & Waid, 1980).

EVIDENCE OF NEW OR LATENT SKILLS

The hypothesis that stigmatized people have developed new skills or new uses for previously acquired skills to combat prejudice suggests that stigmatized people may have some skills that surpass those of nonstigmatized people. Assertiveness may be one example of such a skill. We have already seen that unattractive boys and girls seem to use assertive social influence strategies. Reis and his colleagues's studies in which college students keep diaries about their social interactions indicate that this tendency may evolve into an assertive social style (Reis, Wheeler, Spiegel, Kernis, Wezlek, & Perri, 1982). They found that for women physical attractiveness was negatively correlated with social assertiveness and that social assertiveness was positively correlated with having satisfying social relationships. They also found that physically attractive and unattractive women reported equally satisfying social relationships. Reis and colleagues suggested there are two different paths by which attractive and unattractive women achieve satisfying relationships. Attractive women rely on their looks; unattractive women use assertiveness.

Other research indicates that attentiveness to nonverbal cues or other subtle cues about interactions is an important skill for stigmatized people. For example, women are more accurate in decoding nonverbal communication than men are, which may be the result of gender differences in status and power (Hall, 1978; DePaulo, 1992). Those who lack power must be attentive and knowledgeable about the moods and likely reactions of the dominant group in order to achieve their goals (Fiske, Morling, & Stevens, 1996). Stigmatized people also may use nonverbal behavior as a way to establish greater status in a relationship. For example, Stier and Hall (1984) concluded that women initiate touch toward high-status people to enhance their relative power in an interaction. Touching generally is the prerogative of those with greater power, and so the initiation of touch by low-status people may be a bid to level the playing field, and thus touching becomes a primary compensatory strategy. Similarly, in a workplace setting, the manner in which women spoke to bosses conveyed more competence than did their speech to peers (Steckler & Rosenthal, 1985). The reverse was true for men. This suggests that women may have been compensating for the stereotype that they are not as competent as men in work settings by speaking in an especially competent manner.

A PRIMARY COMPENSATION INTERPRETATION
OF RESEARCH ON THE
OBESITY/EXTERNALITY HYPOTHESIS

One interesting aspect of research on stigma is that the behavior of people who actually are stigmatized has not often been the focus of research (see Swim & Stangor, this volume). One noteworthy exception to this trend is research on the externality hypothesis about the origins of obesity (the term used in this research) (Nisbett, 1968; Schachter, 1968; Schachter & Rodin, 1974). This once lively but now largely defunct area of research tested the hypothesis that heavyweight people eat in response to external, situational cues (for example, whether food is difficult or easy to eat and whether it is meal-time) rather then in response to internal cues such as a growling stomach.

This hypothesis resulted in numerous experiments in which researchers compared the reactions of heavyweight and nonheavyweight people to an astounding number of different external stimuli. Although this research is one of the few research areas in which people who actually were stigmatized participated, the perspective of the stigmatized person was not given much attention. The reactions of nonheavyweight people, who were often referred to as normals, were taken as the norm against which the reactions of heavyweight people, who were often referred to as deviants, were compared. Our point is not to castigate the sensitivities of the people who conducted this research, who operated within the norms prevailing at the time, but rather to suggest that had the perspective of the stigmatized person been considered more carefully, researchers may have interpreted their data a bit differently than they did (see also Krantz, 1978, for a discussion of this issue).

Proponents of the externality hypothesis thought that responsiveness to external cues is a general trait of heavyweight people. Research on responsiveness to external non-eating-related cues showed that heavyweight people are influenced more than nonheavyweight people by a variety of cues including auditory and visual cues. Heavyweight people also respond more quickly to external cues, are more distracted by them, and remember them better (Pliner, 1973; 1976; Rodin & Singer, 1976).

For our purposes, it is interesting that many of the external cues that were used to test heavyweight people's responsiveness were social or evaluative cues. This raises the possibility that the distractibility and responsiveness of heavyweight people to external cues may in part be the result of a need to closely attend to situations to determine how to counteract prejudice.

For example, Rodin and Singer (1976) found that the physical location of a "potentially evaluative confederate who simply sat and watched" (p. 607) had more effect on whether heavyweight people looked at the confederate while trying to answer reflective questions than it did on nonheavyweight people. Rodin and Singer suggested that this resulted from heavyweight people's inability to screen out salient external stimuli when engaged in tasks with internal processing demands. This may be accurate, but ignores the possibility that heavyweight people had more reason to react to the potentially evaluative other than did nonheavyweight people.

Results of other experiments that were interpreted as demonstrating the supposed distractibility of heavyweight people may also be understood as a consequence of heavyweight people being more concerned about the role of prejudice in interactions than about the experimental tasks. For example, Rodin and Slochower (1974) examined heavyweight and nonheavyweight male students' responsiveness to three different manipulations of external cues. The experiment involved having the students read a word list to a confederate who supposedly was trying to learn them. The external cue manipulations were that the confederate was overweight or normal weight, the confederate acted in a nice, nasty, or neutral fashion during the interaction, and the participants were given one of three sets of instructions designed to manipulate distraction from the word list. Instructions were to simply read the word list (no distraction), to concentrate on their role as teacher while reading the list (moderate distraction), or to concentrate on the learner's nonverbal cues (high distraction).

When surprised with a recall test of the words, heavyweight students showed considerable declines in memory for difficult to remember words as distraction increased. Nonheavyweight students were unaffected by distraction. A second major dependent measure was that after the learning task was completed, the confederate asked the participant for a favor. Heavyweight participants helped the nonheavyweight confederate more than the heavyweight confederate, whereas nonheavyweight participants were unaffected by the confederate's weight. Rodin and Slochower (1974) interpreted both findings as evidence that heavyweight students were "bound by salient stimuli" and thus more affected than nonheavyweight students by the experimental manipulations.

An alternative explanation for the influence of distraction and the confederate's weight on heavyweight students is that they perceived being heavyweight as a potential difficulty for a smooth interaction. In fact, postexperimental interviews revealed that heavyweight students overwhelmingly indicated that their weight was a factor in how the other person treated them, while nonheavyweight students gave a variety of reasons for their treatment. This suggests that heavyweight students' recall of words was adversely affected by distraction because they were devoting more of their resources to handling the interpersonal interaction. As the demands of that interaction increased because of the instructions they had received, they had to concentrate more of their efforts on the interaction with the confederate. Similarly, heavyweight students may have helped the nonheavyweight confederate more than the heavyweight confederate because they assumed they needed to be more ingratiating toward a nonstigmatized person.

Put in this context, being stimulus bound and responsive to external cues seems less like a defect and more like a pragmatic reaction to prejudice. In fact, responsiveness to situational cues is the basis for Snyder's theory of self-monitoring (see Snyder, 1979). One of the hallmarks of high self-monitoring people is that they are responsive to cues in the situation that indicate what the appropriate behavior is. This contributes to the high level of social skills that high self-monitoring individuals employ in interpersonal interactions. It is noteworthy therefore that Younger and Pliner (1976) found that heavyweight male high school and university students scored higher on Snyder's (1974) self-monitoring scale than did nonheavyweight students. Younger and Pliner suggested that one explanation for this finding is that people who are deviant may need to attend more closely to situational cues about what behaviors are acceptable.

This interpretation is consistent with results of Frable, Blackstone, and Scherbaum's (1990) study that showed that college women who were deviant (for example, at least 60 pounds overweight, African American, physically attractive, or wealthy) were more mindful during a social interaction with another, as demonstrated by the frequency with which the women took their partners' perspective during the interaction and the accuracy of their recall of details about the interaction. The trade-off for being mindful of prejudice-relevant situational demands may be that there are fewer cognitive resources available to process information relevant to other aspects of the situation. For example, Lord and Saenz (1985) found that people occupying the uncomfortable role of being a token representative of their group in a social situation (as stigmatized people often do) had poorer memories about what occurred than did people who thought they were one of several group members. This may be a consequence of the tokens' need to marshall resources to adopt self-presentation strategies that ward off the effects of the extra attention from others that their token status garners. In sum, consideration of the perspective of the stigmatized person suggests that there may be good reasons why stigmatized people, including heavyweight people, may not react to situations in the same way nonstigmatized people do.

OUTCOMES OF COMPENSATION

EFFECTIVENESS

Compensation may not be successful, either because the person lacks the skills to overcome the barriers or because the barriers are so high that there is no reasonable chance that they can be overcome. In the social influence study described earlier (Dion & Stein, 1978), unattractive children had mixed success in influencing another child to consume bitter-tasting crackers. Attractive boys, who used a variety of influence strategies, were successful with girls, and unattractive boys were successful with boys. Attractive girls, who in effect did little and said little were successful with boys. Unattractive girls were not successful with anyone even though they had been quite persistent.

Successful compensation should enable stigmatized people to avoid problems in psychological adjustment that prejudice might otherwise create. Findings on this issue with respect to heavyweight people are mixed. Miller, Rothblum, Brand, and Felicio (1995) found that heavyweight and nonheavyweight women did not differ on measures of social support, social networks, social skills, or social self-esteem. Moreover, friends and co-workers of these heavyweight and nonheavyweight women who completed these same measures about the women indicated that heavyweight and nonheavyweight women did not differ. Recent meta-analytic reviews indicate that being heavyweight is not correlated with general psychological adjustment (Friedman & Brownell, 1995), but it is negatively correlated with self-esteem (Downey & Miller, 1996; Friedman & Brownell, 1995). Similarly, in Crocker and colleagues' (1993) study of secondary compensation among heavyweight women, the attribution of negative feedback to fat prejudice did not protect heavyweight college students from the esteem-damaging effects of that feedback. These findings suggest that heavyweight people escape some, but not all, of the negative consequences fat prejudice may be expected to have.

Myers and Rosen's (1996) survey of compensatory strategies used by heavyweight people provides one of the only attempts to examine the relationship between compensation and psychological adjustment. They found that both low self-esteem and frequent mental health symptoms were correlated with the frequency with which heavyweight people experienced stigma situations. Moreover, those who experienced more stigma reported more efforts to cope with stigma. This may explain why coping was also correlated with poorer psychological adjustment (low self-esteem and frequent symptoms). Some specific compensatory strategies were correlated with psychological adjustment. Positive self-talk, seeing prejudice as the other's problem, self-acceptance, and refusing to hide were positively correlated with self-esteem. Avoiding the situation, negative self-talk, crying or getting depressed, seeking therapy, and seeking social support from other fat people were correlated with more frequent symptoms and low self-esteem. Responding with physical violence or insult were correlated with frequent mental health symptoms.

Of course, these are correlational data, and so it cannot be inferred that stigmatizing situations and/or strategies used to deal with these situations result in more frequent symptoms or lower self-esteem. It is equally possible that the reverse is true: that lower self-esteem or more frequent mental health symptoms affect the perception of stigma situations and/or the type of compensatory strategies used in these situations. More research is needed in order to determine the extent to which compensatory strategies mediate the relationship between stigma and psychological adjustment.

It is likely that there are individual differences that moderate the use and effectiveness of compensatory strategies. Friedman and Brownell (1995) argued that simple comparisons of the psychological adjustment of heavyweight and nonheavyweight people are not likely to yield useful results because there are a number of factors, such as gender, age, dieting history, and childhood experiences with social disapproval, that may put some heavyweight people at greater risk for the damaging effects of stigma. We believe that there also are likely to be invulnerability factors that promote the effective use of compensation. For example, the strategy of shifting from the original goal to alternative goals should be easier for stigmatized people whose self-concepts are relatively complex or differentiated (Linville, 1987; Showers & Ryff, 1996). This is consistent with Schulz and Heckhausen's model (1996), which suggests that one of the most important tasks across the life span is to select goals that strike the correct balance between spreading oneself too thin and putting all of one's eggs in one basket. For stigmatized people, diversity of goals may facilitate efforts to compensate for prejudice.

It also is important to remember that our model suggests that when the level of prejudice is high enough, the stigmatized person is unlikely to be able to compensate for it no matter what the level of skill and effort is employed. Moreover, as we discuss next, compensatory strategies, even when successful, can have some negative outcomes.

UNINTENDED CONSEQUENCES

One of the very heavyweight women who participated in Myers and Rosen's (1996) study of what heavyweight people say they do to cope with fat prejudice commented, "If I were not overweight, I wouldn't have to deal with any negative reactions." This statement summarizes one of the drawbacks of compensation. Stigmatized people who try harder or use new or latent skills to counteract prejudice may fail to recognize the level of effort or skills needed in situations in which prejudice is not a factor, a phenomenon we call *slacking off*.

Because prejudice explains poor outcomes in many situations, efforts and skills become less plausible explanations for outcomes in *any* situation. Thus, slacking off may result from an overgeneralized application of the attributional principle of discounting. Figure 9.3 shows how discounting of effort and skill as explanations for outcomes received can produce slacking off. The horizontal line represents the skill levels employed if no compensation occurs. The s-shaped curve is a conceptual representation of the relationship between perceived prejudice and compensatory responses. At high levels of prejudice (for example, conditions in which a heavyweight woman knows that she is visible to another), the line representing the deployment of effort and/or skills falls above the line representing no compensation. The lower portion of the s-shaped curve represents responses in situations where no or low levels of prejudice are suspected, as for example, when

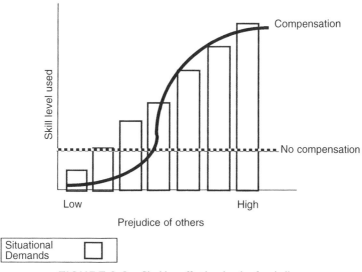

FIGURE 9.3   Slacking off at low levels of prejudice.

a heavyweight woman knows that her stigma is not visible to anyone. The skill level employed actually falls below the line representing the normal skill levels that are required for appropriate functioning in these situations.

Slacking off was demonstrated in Miller and colleagues' (1990, 1995) telephone conversation studies of the social skills of heavyweight and nonheavyweight women. In the first study (Miller *et al.*, 1990) the women were audiotaped during the conversation but there was no actual or perceived possibility that the other or anyone else could actually see them. Similarly, in Miller and colleagues' (1995) most recent study, there was a control condition in which women were not videotaped as they were in all the experimental conditions in which the women's actual and perceived visibility to the partners were manipulated. In the control condition the women were audiotaped, but they knew that they were not visible to their partners or to anyone else. In both studies, heavyweight women who knew nobody could see them received more negative ratings from telephone partners than nonheavyweight women did. One explanation for this finding is that it represents the effects of prejudice on heavyweight women's opportunities to develop social skills. However, recall that results from the experimental conditions in Miller and colleagues' (1995) study showed that heavyweight women who knew they were visible to others had the skills needed to interact in ways that created impressions that were as positive as those created by nonheavyweight women. In fact, their skills appear to have been so well developed that they received comparable ratings to nonheavyweight women even when their partners knew they were heavyweight (because the partner could actually see the women). It appears therefore that when heavyweight women know that there is no possibility that prejudice can affect how they are evaluated by others, their deployment of social skills may suffer.

These results suggest that one consequence of stigmatized people's awareness of the need to compensate may be a misperception of the skills required when their interactions are safe from prejudice. Others have pointed out that attribution of outcomes to prejudice can have adverse consequences on the motivation and performance of stigmatized people (Major & Crocker, 1993). Prejudice severs the link between performance and outcomes by creating ambiguity about whether a stigmatized person's performance or the other's prejudice is responsible for the outcomes. This attributional ambiguity can decrease the motivation of stigmatized people. The consequences of attributional ambiguity described in previous research (Crocker *et al.,* 1991; 1993; Major and Crocker, 1993) arise in situations in which the stigmatized person knows or thinks that prejudice is a plausible explanation for the outcomes received. Slacking off occurs in situations in which prejudice is not a plausible explanation for outcomes. Although it results from the attributional ambiguity caused by prejudice, it occurs in situations in which the perceived threat of prejudice is low.

OVERCOMPENSATION

The notion that people may try harder or use extraordinary skills to overcome a problem is often associated with the notion that such efforts can lead to *overcompensation.* Most people are familiar with the person who puts off others by trying too hard, talking too much, laughing too hard, or coming on too strong. One reason this type of behavior occurs is that high motivation can impede control of verbal and nonverbal behaviors that people use to present desired images to others (DePaulo, 1992). Our view is that is what is most commonly meant by overcompensation is the unskilled or inappropriate use of primary compensatory strategies. The unskilled use of strategies is most likely to occur when people use latent or new skills to compensate for prejudice. It requires time and practice to hone these skills. A great deal of trial and error may be involved in finding out which strategies are most effective in which situations.

Another more positive connotation of overcompensation is the pursuit of precisely the goal that seems most out of reach. The classic example is Demosthenes in ancient Greece who became a great orator despite a speech impediment that he overcame through extraordinary effort. More recent examples include a swimmer in the 1996 summer Olympics who earned a gold medal despite having asthma so severe that he often was in danger of passing out in the water as he pushed himself for greater speed. The implication of these examples is that people may strive in a particular domain *because* of rather than despite obstacles that exist in that domain.

There is some evidence that stigmatized people may exhibit this type of overcompensation. Zebrowitz, Collins, and Dutta (1996) used longitudinal archival data to examine the confirmation of appearance stereotypes in the personality traits of physically attractive and baby-faced people. A finding of interest for the present discussion is that boys' baby-faceness during childhood was *negatively* correlated at adolescence with personality traits associated with the baby-face stereotype (e.g., irresponsible, immature, and naive). Similarly, in a study of baby-face and personality traits among military personnel, Collins and Zebrowitz (1995) found that baby-faceness was positively correlated with military rank and with winning a military award (for example, for bravery in combat). As Zebrowitz and colleagues (1996) pointed out, this is not simply a compensation effect. If boys and men are simply compensating for stereotypes about baby-faceness there should be no relationship between baby-faceness and displaying traits and behaviors consistent with the baby-face stereotype. Instead, the baby-face stereotype may have become a self-defeating prophecy (Jussim, 1991). The expectation of babyish characteristics may have resulted in the opposite, which is what often is meant by overcompensation.

PREJUDICE: WHOSE PROBLEM IS IT?

One common secondary compensatory strategy of stigmatized people is to reframe the situation as being the prejudiced person's problem. This strategy is appealing because it defines the stigmatizing encounter as a problem created by people who are prejudiced who are then assumed to have responsibility for correcting it. Growing support for the "fat acceptance" movement throughout the United States exemplifies the view that it is prejudiced people who must change their ways. Groups like the National Association to Advance Fat Acceptance (NAAFA) and publications like *Radiance* magazine exhort heavyweight individuals to give up dieting and reclaim pride in themselves, while simultaneously coming together to fight fat prejudice in society at large.

If one accepts the view that prejudice is the problem of the stigmatizer and not the stigmatized, any discussion of compensation strategies that stigmatized individuals use runs the risk of being perceived as victim-blaming. For example, encouraging heavyweight individuals to be more assertive and socially outgoing can be criticized for focusing upon the wrong issues, because fat stigma will not be eliminated by helping people to cope with it.

It is true that using primary compensatory strategies such as trying harder, being more persistent, or using new or latent skills does place a burden on stigmatized people that they should not have to bear. However, this same objection applies to any form of compensation and to any individual or collective efforts to reduce prejudice and discrimination. None of these strategies is problem free, and some may be costly or even dangerous. They require committing psychological, cognitive, or behavioral resources that could otherwise be used to negotiate the challenges that everyone faces.

The facts are that stigma exists now (despite many efforts to eradicate it) and stigmatized people already may have developed compensatory strategies for dealing with it. We believe that some people become quite adept at compensating for the unique problems that stigmatized people face because of prejudice, and that therefore much can be learned by understanding what they do.

SUMMARY

We began with an analogy between the barriers that stigmatized people face to those that people with impairments face in meeting life's challenges. The main advantage of this comparison is that it directs attention to actions that stigmatized people may take to achieve the outcomes they desire despite the existence of prejudice in a particular situation. Most studies of how people cope with prejudice are premised on the assumption that they are not able to cope very well, falling victim to forces such as expectancy confirmation (Harris & Rosenthal, 1985; Jussim, 1986; Miller & Turnbull, 1986; Snyder, 1984) and stereotype threat effects (Steele & Aronson, 1995). This attention to poor outcomes resulting from prejudice may explain why secondary compensation strategies such as self-protective attributions, social comparisons, and devaluation of goals (Crocker and Major, 1989; Crocker et al., 1993; Crocker et al., 1991) also are well documented. If there is little that stigmatized people can do to avert negative outcomes, their fallback position has to be softening the blow that these outcomes have on their psychological well-being. Similarly, collective and individual actions aimed at redressing discrimination or eliminating prejudice could, if successful, eliminate the threat of negative interaction outcomes due to prejudice (Lalonde & Cameron, 1994). Prospects for success may be discouraging, however, especially over the relatively short span of a person's life.

Primary compensation is important because it may help stigmatized people obtain desired interaction outcomes in situations in which prejudice has not yet been successfully eliminated. Theory and research about how people compensate for physical or cognitive impairments suggests that avenues for obtaining desired outcomes despite the existence of prejudice may include the development of new or latent skills and increases in effort or persistence that might render existing skills more effective in a particular situation. Our own research on how people compensate for the stigma of being heavyweight indicates that when they know that prejudice could affect their interactions, they are able to behave in ways that prevent some of the negative effects of prejudice.

One problem with primary compensation is that prejudice makes it difficult for stigmatized people to gauge precisely what level of skills are required to function well in a particular situation. This difficulty can result in an underutilization of skills (as is the case in slacking off) or an overutilization (as is the case in over-compensation). However, there are drawbacks associated with any effort to cope with prejudice. Our hope is that by expanding the range of alternatives we study, we may better understand how stigmatized people can control the outcomes they receive despite the effects of prejudice on those with whom they interact.

REFERENCES

Bäckman, L., & Dixon, R. A. (1992). Psychological compensation: A theoretical framework. *Psychological Bulletin, 112,* 259–283.

Baumeister, R. F. (1982). Self-esteem, self-presentation, and future interaction: A dilemma of reputation. *Journal of Personality, 50,* 29–45.

Bennet. W., & Gurin, J. (1982). *The dieter's dilemma.* New York: Basic Books.

Boyd, M. A. (1989). Living with overweight. *Perspectives in Psychiatric Care, XXV,* 48–52.

Bylsma, W. H., & Major, B. (1994). Social comparisons and contentment: Exploring the psychological costs of the gender wage gap. *Psychology of Women Quarterly, 18,* 241–249.

Canning, H., & Mayer, J. (1966). Obesity: Its possible effects on college admissions. *New England Journal of Medicine, 275,* 1172–1174.

Collins, M. A., & Zebrowitz, L. A. (1995). The contributions of appearance to occupational outcomes in civilian and military settings. *Journal of Applied Social Psychology, 25,* 129–163.

Crandall, C. S. (1994). Prejudice against fat people: Ideology and self-interest. *Journal of Personality and Social Psychology, 66,* 882–894.

Crandall, C. S. (1995). Do parents discriminate against their heavyweight daughters? *Personality and Social Psychology Bulletin, 21,* 724–735.

Critelli, J. W., & Waid, L. R. (1980). Physical attractiveness, romantic love, and equity restoration in dating relationships. *Journal of Personality Assessment, 44,* 624–629.

Crocker, J., Cornwell, B., & Major, B. (1993). The stigma of overweight: Affective consequences of attributional ambiguity. *Journal of Personality and Social Psychology, 64,* 60–70.

Crocker, J., & Major, B. (1989). Social stigma and self-esteem: The self-protective properties of stigma. *Psychological Review, 96,* 608–630.

Crocker, J., Voelkl, K., Testa, M., & Major, B. (1991). Social stigma: The affective consequences of attributional ambiguity. *Journal of Personality and Social Psychology, 60,* 218–228.

DeJong, W., & Kleck, R. E. (1981). The social psychological effects of overweight. In C. P. Herman, M. P. Zanna, & E. T. Higgins (Eds.), *Physical appearance, stigma, and social behavior* (pp. 65–87). Hillsdale, NJ: Lawrence Erlbaum.

DelPaulo, B. M. (1992). Nonverbal behavior and self-presentation. *Psychological Bulletin, 111,* 203–243.

Dion, K. K., & Stein, S. (1978). Physical attractiveness and interpersonal influence. *Journal of Experimental Social Psychology, 14,* 97–108.

Downey, K., & Miller, C. T. (1996). *A meta-analysis of being heavyweight and self-esteem.* Manuscript under review, Burlington, VT: University of Vermont.

English, H. B., & English, A. C. (1958) *A comprehensive dictionary of psychological and psychoanalytical terms.* New York: Longmans, Green.

Farina, A., Allen, J. G., & Saul, B. (1968). The role of the stigmatized person in affecting social relationships. *Journal of Personality, 36,* 169–182.

Feingold, A. (1981). Testing equity as an explanation for romantic couples "mismatched" on physical attractiveness. *Psychological Reports, 49,* 247–250.

Fiske, S. T., Morling, B., & Stevens, L. E. (1996). Controlling self and others: A theory of anxiety, mental control, and social control. *Personality and Social Psychology Bulletin, 22,* 115–123.

Frable, D. E. E., Blackstone, T., & Scherbaum, C. (1990). Marginal and mindful: Deviants in social interaction. *Journal of Personality and Social Psychology, 59,* 140–149.

Friedman, M. A., & Brownell, K. D. (1995). Psychological correlates of obesity: Moving to the next research generation. *Psychological Bulletin, 117,* 3–20.

Goldman, W., & Lewis, P. (1977). Beautiful is good: Evidence that the physically attractive are more socially skillful. *Journal of Experimental Social Psychology, 13,* 125–130.

Graham, S. (1992). "Most of the subjects were White and middle-class": Trends in published research on African-Americans in selected APA journals, 1970–1989. *American Psychologist, 47,* 629–639.

Hall, J. A. (1978). Gender effects in decoding nonverbal cues. *Psychological Bulletin, 85,* 845–857.

Harris, M. J., Milich, R., Corbitt, E. M., Hoover, D. W., & Brady, M. (1992). Self-fulfilling effects of stigmatizing information on children's social interactions. *Journal of Personality and Social Psychology, 63,* 41–50.

Harris, M. J., & Rosenthal, R. (1985). Mediation of expectancy effects: 31 meta-analyses. *Psychological Bulletin, 97,* 363–386.

Heatherton, T. F., Kiwan, D., & Hebl, M. R. (1995, August). *The stigma of obesity in women: The difference is Black and White.* Paper presented at the Annual Meeting of the American Psychological Association, New York.

Heckhausen, J., & Schulz, R. (1995). A life-span theory of control. *Psychological Review, 102,* 284–304.

Hilton, J. L., & Darley, J. M. (1985). Constructing other persons: A limit to the effect. *Journal of Experimental Psychology, 21,* 1–18.

Jussim, L. (1986). Self-fulfilling prophecies: A theoretical and integrative review. *Psychological Review, 93,* 429–445.

Jussim, L. (1991). Social perception and social reality: A reflection-construction model. *Psychological Review, 98,* 54–73.

Kral, J. G., Sjostrom, L. V., & Sullivan, M. B. E. (1992). Assessment of quality of life before and after surgery for severe being heavyweight. *American Journal of Clinical Nutrition, 55, (supplement),* 611S–614S.

Krantz, D. S. (1978). The social context of obesity research: Another perspective on its place in the field of social psychology. *Personality and Social Psychology Bulletin, 4,* 177–184.

Lalonde, R. N., & Cameron, J. E. (1994). Behavioral responses to discrimination: A focus on action. In M. P. Zanna & J. M. Olson (Eds.), *The psychology of prejudice: The Ontario Symposium,* (Vol. 7, pp. 257–288). Hillsdale, NJ: Lawrence Erlbaum.

Langer, E. (1989) *Mindfulness.* Reading. MA: Addison Wesley.

Linville, P. W. (1987). Self-complexity as a cognitive buffer against stress-related illness and depression. *Journal of Personality and Social Psychology, 52,* 663–676.

Lord, C. G., & Saenz, D. S. (1985). Memory deficits and memory surfeits: Differential cognitive consequences of tokenism for tokens and observers. *Journal of Personality and Social Psychology,49,* 918–926.

Major, B., & Crocker, J. (1993). Social stigma: The consequences of attributional ambiguity. In D. M. Mackie & D. L. Hamilton (Eds.), *Affect, cognition, and stereotyping: Interactive processes in group perception,* pp. 345–370. San Diego, CA: Academic Press.

Markus, H. (1977). Self-schemata and processing information about the self. *Journal of Personality and Social Psychology, 35,* 63–78.

Miller, C. T., Rothblum, E. D., Barbour, L., Brand, P. A., & Felicio, D. (1990). Social interactions of obese and nonobese women. *Journal of Personality, 58,* 365–380.

Miller, C. T., Rothblum, E. D., Brand, P. A., & Felicio, D. M. (1995). Do obese women have poorer social relationships than nonobese women? Reports by self, friends, and coworkers. *Journal of Personality, 63,* 65–85.

Miller, C. T., Rothblum, E. D., Felicio, D., & Brand, P. (1995). Compensating for stigma: Obese and nonobese women's reactions to being visible. *Personality and Social Psychology Bulletin, 21,* 1093–1106.

Miller, D. T., & Turnbull, W. (1986). Expectancies and interpersonal processes. *Annual Review of Psychology, 37,* 233–256.

Millman, M. (1980) *Such a pretty face.* New York: W. W. Norton.

Myers, A. M., & Rosen, J. (1996). *Fat, stigma, and coping: Relation to mental health symptoms, body-image, and self-esteem.* Unpublished manuscript. University of Vermont, Burlington, VT.

Nisbett, R. (1968). Taste, deprivation, and weight determinants of eating behavior. *Journal of Personality and Social Psychology, 10,* 107–117.

Pliner, P. (1973). Effect of external cues on the thinking behavior of obese and normal subjects. *Journal of Abnormal Psychology, 82,* 233–238.

Pliner, P. (1976). External responsiveness in the obese. *Addictive Behaviors, 1,* 169–175.

Rand, C. W., & MacGregor, A. M. C. (1990). Morbidly obese patients' perceptions of social discrimination before and after surgery for obesity. *Southern Medical Journal, 83,* 1391–1395.

Reis, H. T., Wheeler, L., Spiegel, N., Kernis, M. H., Wezlek, J., & Perri, M. (1982). Physical attractiveness in social interaction: II. Why does appearance affect social experience? *Journal of Personality and Social Psychology, 43,* 979–996.

Rodin, J., Silberstein, L. R., &. Striegel-Moore, R. H. (1985). Women and weight: A normative discontent. In T. B. Sonderegger (Ed.), *Nebraska symposium on motivation* (Vol. 32, pp. 267–307). Lincoln: University of Nebraska Press.

Rodin, J., & Singer, J. L. (1976). Eye-shift, thought, and obesity. *Journal of Personality, 44,* 594–610.

Rodin, J., & Slochower, J. (1974). Fat chance for a favor: Obese-normal differences in compliance and incidental learning. *Journal of Personality and Social Psychology, 29,* 557–565.

Rodin, J., & Slochower, J. (1976). Externality in the nonobese: Effects of environmental responsiveness on weight. *Journal of Personality and Social Psychology, 33,* 338–344.

Rothblum, E. D., Brand, P. A., Miller, C. T., & Oetjen, H. A. (1990). The relationship between obesity, employment discrimination, and employment-related victimization. *Journal of Vocational Behavior, 37,* 251–266.

Rothblum, E. D., Miller, C. T., & Garbutt, B. (1988). Stereotypes of obese female job applicants. *International Journal of Eating Disorders, 7,* 277–283.

Schachter, S., & Rodin, J. (1974). *Obese humans and rats.* Washington, DC: Lawrence Erlbaum.

Schulz, R., & Heckhausen, J. (1996). A life span model of successful aging. *American Psychologist, 51,* 702–714.

Showers, C. J., & Ryff, C. D. (1996). Self-differentiation and well-being in a life transition. *Personality and Social Psychology Bulletin, 22,* 448–460.

Snyder, M. (1974). Self-monitoring of expressive behavior. *Journal of Personality and Social Psychology, 30,* 526–537.

Snyder, M. (1979). Self-monitoring processes. In L. Berkowitz (Ed.), *Advances in experimental social psychology* (Vol. 12, pp. 85–128). New York: Academic Press.

Snyder, M. (1984). When belief creates reality. In L. Berkowitz (Ed.), *Advances in experimental social psychology* (Vol. 18, pp. 247–305). San Diego, CA: Academic press.

Snyder, M., & Haugen, J. A. (1995). Why does behavioral confirmation occur? A functional perspective on the role of the target. *Personality and Social Psychology Bulletin, 21,* 963–974.

Snyder, M., & Haugen, J. A. (1994). Why does behavioral confirmation occur? A functional perspective on the role of the perceiver. *Journal of Experimental Social Psychology, 30,* 218–246.

Snyder, M., Tanke, E. D., & Berscheid, E. (1977). Social perception and social behavior: On the self-fulfilling nature of social stereotypes. *Journal of Personality and Social Psychology, 35,* 656–666.

Sobal, J., & Stunkard, A. J. (1989). Socioeconomic status and obesity: A review of the literature. *Psychological Bulletin, 105,* 260–275.

Steckler, N. A., & Rosenthal, R. (1985). Sex differences in nonverbal and verbal communication with bosses, peers, and subordinates. *Journal of Applied Psychology, 70,* 157–163.

Steele, C. M. (1975). Name calling and compliance. *Journal of Personality and Social Psychology, 31,* 361–369.

Steele, C. M. (1988). The psychology of self-affirmation: Sustaining the integrity of the self. In L. Berkowitz (Ed.), *Advances in experimental social psychology* (Vol. 21, pp. 261–302). New York: Academic Press.

Steele, C. M., & Aronson, J. (1995). Stereotype threat and the intellectual test performance of African Americans. *Journal of Personality and Social Psychology, 69,* 797–811.

Stier, D. S., & Hall, J. A. (1984). Gender differences in touch: An empirical and theoretical review. *Journal of Personality and Social Psychology, 47,* 440–459.

Swann, W. B., Jr. (1984). Quest for accuracy in person perception: A matter of pragmatics. *Psychological Review, 91,* 457–477.

Walster, E., Walster, G. W., & Berscheid, E. (1978). *Equity: Theory and research.* Boston, MA: Allyn & Bacon.

Word, C. O., Zanna, M. P., & Cooper, J. (1974). The nonverbal mediation of self-fulfilling prophecies in interracial interaction. *Journal of Experimental Social Psychology, 10,* 109–120.

Younger, J. C., & Pliner, P. (1976). Obese-normal differences in the self-monitoring of expressive behavior. *Journal of Research in Personality, 10,* 112–115.

Zebrowitz, L. A., Collins, M. A., & Dutta, R. (1996). *The relationship between appearance and personality across the life span.* Manuscript under review, Waltham, MA: Brandeis University.

10

COPING WITH STIGMA THROUGH PSYCHOLOGICAL DISENGAGEMENT

BRENDA MAJOR AND TONI SCHMADER

University of California, Santa Barbara

Social stigma is a pervasive aspect of our culture. According to Goffman (1963), people who are stigmatized have a spoiled identity in the eyes of others; they bear a mark that renders them susceptible to social devaluation. Extensive research has shown that negative stereotypes about members of stigmatized groups are often widely known in a culture, even to individuals who do not endorse them (e.g., Devine, 1989) and even to those who are targets of these stereotypes (Steele, 1992; 1997). Recently, scholars have begun to examine how people who are targets of negative stereotypes, prejudice, and discrimination understand and interpret their experience as members of socially devalued and disadvantaged groups (e.g., Frable 1989; Major, 1994), how they attempt to cope with this experience, and the consequences of these coping strategies (e.g., Crocker & Major, 1989; Major & Crocker, 1993; Steele, 1992; 1997). The current chapter extends this focus by examining how negative stereotypes, prejudice, and discrimination can lead members of stigmatized groups to psychologically disengage from a self-evaluative domain as a way of maintaining their personal and collective self-esteem. In this chapter we first describe the theoretical antecedents and consequences of psychological disengagement among the stigmatized. We then describe a program of research examining these processes among African American and European American students in the domain of academic performance.

PSYCHOLOGICAL DISENGAGEMENT AND DISIDENTIFICATION AMONG THE STIGMATIZED

Most theories of self-esteem formation, such as the theory of reflected appraisals (Cooley, 1956; Mead, 1934), self-fulfilling prophecy (Darley & Fazio, 1980), and efficacy-based self-esteem (Gecas & Schwalbe, 1983) imply that members of stigmatized groups on average will have lower self-esteem than members of nonstigmatized groups because of the social devaluation, prejudice, and discrimination that they often experience. On the basis of a review of more than 20 years of empirical research on this issue, Crocker and Major (1989) concluded that these theoretical assumptions are often incorrect. For example African Americans and Hispanic Americans typically have levels of self-esteem equal to or higher than that of European Americans; likewise, research has failed to find consistently lower self-esteem among those with facial disfigurements, physical disabilities, or mental disabilities, to name a few groups (see Crocker & Major, 1989, for a review). This does not mean that all members of stigmatized groups have levels of self-esteem equal to or higher than the nonstigmatized, however. Some stigmatized groups have levels of self-esteem that are on average lower than those of the nonstigmatized; furthermore, there is substantial within-group variability in levels of self-esteem (Crocker & Major, 1994; see Quinn & Crocker, this volume).

Although a number of psychological processes can maintain self-regard in the face of threats to esteem (e.g., Baumeister, 1995; Steele, 1988; Tesser, 1988), our focus here is on self-esteem maintenance processes that may be particularly likely to occur among members of socially devalued groups. Crocker and Major (1989) attempted to explain the sometimes paradoxical relationship between stigma and self-esteem by examining three strategies that may afford members of stigmatized groups the opportunity to protect their self-esteem: (1) attributing negative outcomes to prejudice based on the stigma; (2) devaluing outcomes on which their group fares poorly relative to other groups; and (3) making ingroup social comparisons with similarly stigmatized others rather than with members of nonstigmatized and advantaged groups. The current chapter refines and extends this analysis of the coping strategies used by the stigmatized to protect their self-esteem.

We propose that an important determinant of whether individuals who are targets of negative stereotypes, prejudice, and disadvantage in particular domains maintain their self-image is whether or not they *psychologically disengage* their self-esteem from feedback received in those domains. We define disengagement as a detachment of self-esteem from external feedback or outcomes in a particular domain, such that feelings of self-worth are not dependent on successes or failures in that domain (Major, Spencer, Schmader, Wolfe, & Crocker, 1998). Individuals who are highly engaged in a domain link their self-evaluations and self-esteem to feedback received in that domain. Individuals who are disengaged from a domain, in contrast, are relatively impervious to feedback or outcomes received in that domain. We assume that disengagement is motivated by the desire to maintain either personal or collective self-esteem and is typically triggered by anticipated or experienced threats to personal or social identity in a given domain. Although we propose that disengagement is typically a temporary and situationally specific response to threats, we recognize that chronic exposure to threats in a given domain may lead to chronic disidentification from that domain (Crocker, Major, & Steele, 1998).

Our framework assumes that individuals who are psychologically engaged in a domain draw upon domain-relevant social feedback and outcomes to make inferences about their own abilities and competencies in that domain. That is, they use social information received in the domain as a basis for making domain-specific self-evaluations. These domain-specific self-evaluations then direct their overall sense of self-worth and value (e.g., Pelham & Swann, 1989; Rosenberg, 1979). Within this framework, psychological disengagement from a domain can occur at one of two points. First, the person may discount the diagnosticity, or validity, of social feedback received in the domain and thus reject this feedback as a true indicator of his or her competencies in the domain. Hence, the person may not use the feedback as a basis for making domain-specific self-evaluations. Alternatively, a person may regard the feedback as diagnostic and base his or her self-evaluations in the domain on this feedback, but reduce the centrality, or importance, of the domain in the self-concept and thereby break the connection between domain-specific self-evaluations and global feelings of self-worth. Either of these processes results in disengagement of self-esteem from domain-specific social feedback. These two processes are discussed more fully below.

DEVALUING

The proposition that the impact of evaluative feedback in a domain on self-esteem is moderated by the psychological centrality, or importance of the domain to the self-concept dates back at least to William James (1890/1950), who observed:

> I am often confronted by the necessity of standing by one of my empirical selves and relinquishing the rest . . . So the seeker of his truest, strongest, deepest self must review this list carefully, and pick out the one on which to stake his salvation. . . . I, who for the time have staked my all on being a psychologist, am mortified if others know much more psychology than I. But I am contented to wallow in the grossest ignorance of Greek. My deficiencies there give me no humiliation at all. Had I "pretensions" to be a linguist, it would have been just the reverse.

This proposition is also central to more recent models of self-esteem such as those by Rosenberg (1979; Rosenberg & Simmons, 1972), Harter (1986), Tesser (1988), and Pelham and Swann (1989). Each of these perspectives makes three assumptions: that individuals differ in the value they attach to various aspects of self, that individuals choose which self-aspects to value, and that the value accorded to any given self-aspect will determine the impact that success and failure in that domain has on self-esteem. Some correlational evidence is consistent with this perspective (e.g., Harter, 1986; Pelham & Swann, 1989; Rosenberg, 1979). For example, Rosenberg (1979) showed that individuals who possessed negative self-conceptions were more likely to be low in global self-esteem if they considered the negative characteristics to be personally important. Other research, however, suggests that the value or importance attached to various domains does not moderate the impact of standing in that domain on self-esteem (e.g., Marsh, 1986).

External evaluations or performance feedback can also *shape* the value an individual attaches to a given domain. For example, individuals often regard as most important those domains in which they are most proficient (Rosenberg, 1979; Taylor & Brown, 1988). Likewise, Tesser and Campbell (1980) demonstrated experimentally that individuals will devalue, or regard as less personally relevant, attributes on which they compare unfavorably relative to a close (similar) other compared to those attributes on which they compare favorably. Furthermore, people experience more negative affect when outperformed by a close other on valued dimensions than when they are outperformed on dimensions that are not personally valued (Tesser, Millar, & Moore, 1988).

Several authors, including Crocker and Major (1989), Tajfel and Turner (1986), and Steele (1992; 1997), have applied the devaluing hypothesis to explain the often paradoxical relationship between membership in a socially devalued group and self-esteem. Crocker and Major (1989) hypothesized that the stigmatized can protect their self-esteem by "selectively devaluing, or regarding as less important for their self-definition, those performance dimensions on which they or their group fare(s) poorly, and selectively valuing those dimensions on which they or their group excel(s) (p. 612)." Furthermore, they proposed that the psychological centrality of a given domain within the self-concept is socially produced, that is, results from performance feedback, comparisons with others, and treatment by others. In a similar vein, C. Steele (1992; 1997) hypothesized that individuals who are vulnerable to social devaluation and negative stereotypes in a specific domain (such as women in math courses and African Americans in school), and hence do not perceive "good prospects" in that domain, may alter their self-concepts such that the domain is no longer a basis of self-evaluation. Steele (1997) called this process disidentification, and observes that, "Disidentification offers the retreat of not caring about the domain in relation to the self."

Crocker and Major's (1989) and Steele's (1997) frameworks implicitly assume that the importance or centrality of a domain in the self-concept is affected to some extent by domain-relevant information about one's group, such as domain-specific stereotypes or the standing of one's own group in the domain relative to other groups. For example, Steele (1997) asserts that disidentification results from negative social stereotypes and social structures that limit group outcomes. There is surprisingly little evidence, however, that information about the performance of one's group, in the absence of personal performance information, affects personal values.

Schmader and Major (1997) conducted a series of studies to examine this hypothesis. In one study, we assigned individuals randomly to one of two minimal groups and gave them a test of a fictional personality trait. We then informed them that members of their own group tended, on average, to score either better than, worse than, or equal to the members of the other group on this personality trait. Importantly, their own personal score was ostensibly subtracted from the group averages, so that no personal performance feedback was provided. As predicted, individuals who learned that their group scored higher than the other group on the test valued the trait more and assumed that they personally had scored higher than did individuals who learned that their group scored lower than the other group. This study indicates that group-level performance information can shape personal values in the absence of direct evidence of personal standing in the domain.

The value that people attach to performance domains, however, occurs within a larger cultural context and cultural standards of what is important. Thus, it may be difficult for members of socially devalued groups to devalue domains in which they personally, or their group, are disadvantaged if those domains in are highly valued in the larger culture. Evidence consistent with this hypothesis was obtained in a second study (Peterson, Major, Cozzarelli, & Crocker, 1988). Men and women were given a test of a fictional personality trait, and then were given bogus feedback that their own sex did better, the other sex did better, or both sexes scored equally on the trait. Again, their own score was removed from the group averages. Consistent with the above study, both men and women valued the trait most and were most likely to believe they were personally high in the trait when they were told that their own sex group had outperformed the cross-sex group. However, when told that their own sex scored more poorly than the other sex on the trait, only men devalued the trait. Women (a lower status group) did not devalue the trait when they believed that men scored higher than women on it, even though they assumed that their personal score on the trait test was low. We observed a similar status asymmetry in devaluing in a third study where we manipulated the perceived status of experimentally created minimal groups (Schmader & Major, 1997). Together, these three studies indicate that devaluing occurs in response to feedback about the relative performance of one's group, but that it is more likely to be used by members of high status groups than by members of low status groups.

DISCOUNTING

A second route to psychological disengagement from a domain is to discount the extent to which social feedback or outcomes in that domain are valid and diagnostic indicators of one's true personal abilities or merits (e.g., Crocker & Major, 1994; Major & Crocker, 1993). Discounting the validity of feedback produces psychological disengagement by breaking the connection between the external evaluation and one's internal assessment of personal ability or competence. Because the evaluation is not internalized, it does not affect the individual's global feelings of self-worth.

Theories of self-concept formation typically assume that individuals use evaluations or feedback from others, social comparison information, or observations of their own performance to define their self-conceptions. For example, the theory of reflected appraisals (Cooley, 1956; Mead, 1934) proposes that individuals' evaluations of themselves are a reflection of how others evaluate them. Social comparison theory (Festinger, 1954) assumes that people infer their own abilities by comparing them with those of others, and self-perception theory (Bem, 1970) assumes that people infer their own attributes through observation of their own actions.

The relationship between the external world and internal self-conceptions, however, is often more complex. For example, the relationship between others' appraisals of an individual and the individual's self-appraisals, often has been found to be weak or nonexistent (see Shrauger & Schoneman, 1979, for a review). Likewise, the effects of social comparisons on self-evaluations depend on how those comparisons are construed (Major, Testa, & Bylsma, 1991; Tesser, 1988). For example, upward comparisons on dimensions perceived as controllable are less painful than upward comparisons on dimensions perceived as uncontrollable (Major *et al.*, 1991). Furthermore, appraisals of the situational constraints on one's behavior alter the extent to which inferences about the self are made from that behavior (Bem, 1970). An obvious question is, when is external feedback discounted as nondiagnostic, and when is it internalized as diagnostic of the self?

We believe that a critical determinant of whether socially distributed outcomes or evaluations are believed to be diagnostic of the self and/or one's group, and hence internalized, is whether or not those outcomes or evaluations are believed to be *deserved* (see also Crocker & Major, 1994; Major, 1994). The sense of deserving is a cognitive judgment with affective and motivational implications, and refers to the relationship between a person and his or her outcomes (Lerner, 1987). The cognitive component of the sense of deserving is "the judgment, often tacit, that someone, or some category of people, is entitled to a particular set of outcomes by virtue of who they are or what they have done" (Lerner, 1987, p. 108). According to equity theory (e.g., Adams, 1965) outcomes are judged as deserved when they are believed to accurately reflect the relevant contributions or qualities of the individuals or groups receiving those outcomes.

Although there is a pervasive tendency for people to believe that outcomes are deserved, even when this belief is disadvantageous to the self (e.g, Homans, 1974; Lerner and Miller, 1978), several factors can break or diminish the perceived connection between outcomes and inferences about the self. For example, information that explicitly or implicitly suggests that outcomes or evaluations were obtained as a result of an unfair procedure (e.g., a prejudicial evaluator or discriminatory test), should lead individuals to question whether their own, or their in-group's, outcomes are diagnostic of their own, or their in-group's, abilities or qualities. Beliefs that one does not have control over one's outcomes, or the conditions that produced them, also moderate whether one feels one's outcomes are deserved (Crocker & Major, 1994; Lind & Tyler, 1988; Major, 1994). In addition, not all people endorse ideological frameworks that hold people responsible for their outcomes, and those that do not are less likely to believe that their own, or their group's, outcomes or evaluations are genuinely diagnostic of their internal qualities and/or attributes (e.g., Crandall, 1994). The less individuals internalize external evaluations as truly characteristic of self, in turn, the less likely they will be to base their self-esteem on those outcomes or evaluations.

The discounting route to disengagement is exemplified by Crocker and Major's analysis of the consequences of attributional ambiguity faced by the stigmatized. Crocker and Major (1989; Major & Crocker, 1993) hypothesized that people who are members of socially devalued and stigmatized groups experience more attributional ambiguity about the causes of their outcomes than do those who are not stigmatized, because for the former, prejudice based on their stigma is a plausible alternative explanation for their treatment by others. Furthermore, being able to attribute negative feedback to prejudice could potentially protect the self-esteem of members of stigmatized groups from negative feedback via the attributional process of discounting (Kelley, 1972). Positive feedback might also be discounted by the stigmatized if it is believed to be motivated by factors other than genuine deservingness, such as pity or the desire not to appear prejudiced.

A number of studies have provided support for the basic tenets of this attributional analysis (e.g., Crocker, Voelkl, Testa, & Major, 1991; Major & Quinton, 1997; Ruggiero & Taylor, 1997). Collectively, these studies suggest that the perception that feedback or outcomes result from unfair procedures, such as a biased or prejudicial evaluator, or are based on outcomes not under one's control (Major, Feinstein & Crocker, 1994) weakens the belief that outcomes are deserved, and hence leads people to disengage their self-esteem from that feedback, regardless of its valence. This perception can be temporarily induced in a specific situation, as in the above studies, or can reflect a more chronic ideological belief that the system is unfair (Major, 1994).

Because of their more frequent exposure to objective instances of prejudice, bias, and discrimination, as well as their knowledge of negative stereotypes about their group, it is likely that both chronic beliefs in system unfairness, as well as more temporary, situation-specific suspicions of unfairness, will be more prevalent among members of socially devalued groups. Consistent with this hypothesis, Major, Levin, Schmader, and Sidanius (1997), found that African American and Latino/a college students were less likely than Asian American and European American students to believe that the American system is just (i.e., that individuals have status mobility, that hard work pays off, and that group differences in status are fair). Furthermore, the less that ethnic minority students believed that the system is just, the more likely they were to perceive both themselves personally, and members of their ethnic group, as experiencing discrimination.

SUMMARY

In sum, we propose that either devaluing the importance of a domain *or* discounting the diagnosticity of outcomes in a domain can lead to psychological disengagement from that domain. It is not necessary for both of these processes to occur simultaneously for a person to disengage his or her self-esteem from a domain. It is possible, for example, for people to disengage their self-esteem from a domain but still value that domain and see it as important. This should be especially likely to occur when feedback is perceived as biased, unfair, uninformed, or nondiagnostic of ability or merit. Likewise, it is possible for people to disengage their self-esteem from feedback that is perceived as highly diagnostic, if the domain is not valued or central to the self-concept. Although we maintain that either devaluing or discounting can result in disengagement of self-esteem from a domain, it is possible that other processes also produce disengagement.

Recall that at the outset of this chapter we noted that although members of many stigmatized groups have levels of self-esteem equal to or higher than the nonstigmatized, this is not true of all groups. Furthermore, there is substantial within-group variability in levels of self-esteem (Crocker & Major, 1994; see Quinn & Crocker, this volume). The analysis that we have presented here suggests the conditions under which individuals who are members of stigmatized groups will have lower self-esteem, and the conditions under which they will not. Stigmatized individuals who receive negative feedback and who believe that feedback is diagnostic of their attributes or abilities (i.e., who do not discount the feedback) are likely to incorporate that feedback into their own self-evaluations. This alone will not be sufficient to result in lowered self-esteem, however, unless these individuals also consider the domain to be highly important (i.e., do not devalue the domain). Individuals are psychologically engaged in a domain when they neither discount nor devalue negative feedback in that domain. These are the individuals who are most likely to be vulnerable to negative feedback, outcomes, and social devaluation within that domain. For example, the overweight woman who believes that her stigma (her weight) is under her own control, that her scale is accurate, and that social prescriptions to be thin are valid, may find it difficult to discount negative feedback and stereotypes associated with her stigma. Hence, rather than blame social rejection on prejudice and discrimination, she is likely to internalize it and blame it on herself (e.g., Amato, Crocker, & Major, 1995; Crandall, 1994; Crocker, Cornwell, & Major, 1993; see Quinn & Crocker, this volume). If in addition, the larger cultural context within which she lives places a high value on physical appearance and thinness, she may find it difficult to devalue the importance of this domain. Consequently, she is vulnerable to low self-esteem.

COPING WITH NEGATIVE STEREOTYPES THROUGH DISENGAGEMENT: THE CASE OF AFRICAN AMERICANS AND INTELLECTUAL ABILITY

In this section we describe a set of studies we have conducted to test several hypotheses derivable from the theoretical framework presented above. These studies examine whether African American students are more likely to disengage their self-esteem from self-evaluative feedback received in the context of performance on intellectual tests. African Americans in the United States experience racial bias, prejudice, discrimination, and relative disadvantage across a number of domains (e.g., Gaertner & Dovidio, 1986). The domain in which the racial devaluation of African Americans is perhaps most apparent, however, is that of intellectual ability. According to Steele (1992; 1997; Steele & Aronson, 1995) negative stereotypes about the intellectual abilities of African Americans are so conditioned in our culture, and so collectively known, that even those who are not strongly prejudiced, and even African Americans themselves, are aware of them. Thus, this context is a particularly appropriate one within which to examine disengagement processes.

There is substantial evidence that African American students, on average, are more likely to experience poor school-related outcomes (e.g., Steele, 1992; Graham, 1994), and to score more poorly on standardized tests of intellectual ability (Simmons, Brown, Bush, & Blyth, 1978), than do European American students. Academic success is a domain that is highly valued in the larger culture, and is, on average, highly predictive of important life outcomes such as standard of living and professional success. Thus, one might expect the self-esteem and academic self-concepts of African American students to be lower than that of European American students. Available research, however, suggests that the self-esteem and academic self-concepts of African Americans students typically is equal to or higher than that of European American students (e.g., Crocker & Major, 1989; Graham, 1994; McCarthy & Yancey, 1971; Porter & Washington, 1979; Rosenberg & Simmons, 1972). Furthermore, several authors have reported that the correlation between global self-esteem and measures of academic achievement, such as GPA and SAT scores, is lower among African American students than it is for European American students, especially if the students are doing poorly in school (e.g., Demo & Parker, 1987; Lay & Wakstein, 1985; Osborne, 1995; Rosenberg & Simmons, 1972).

Our theoretical framework posits that this pattern of results can be explained by examining the extent to which African American students, as compared to European American students, hinge their self-esteem on their performance in academic and intellectual domains. Specifically, we suggest that African American students are more likely to psychologically disengage their self-esteem from evaluative feedback on intellectual tests than are European American students.

Recall that disengagement is proposed to be a coping strategy adopted in response to threats to the self, such as the presence of negative stereotypes about one's ability, poor personal performance, observed poor performance of a group with which one is highly identified, or perceptions of unfairness directed toward oneself or one's group. Consequently, African American students, especially if they are doing poorly in school, must contend with a double threat to their self-esteem. For these students, a poor academic performance not only creates the threat to personal esteem that all students doing poorly might experience, but also creates what Steele (1997) calls "stereotype threat," that is, anxiety that their poor performance will confirm the negative stereotype of the intellectual ability of their group. We suggest that in response to the greater threats they face in the academic domain, African American students may be more likely than European American students to enact defensive strategies that help to disengage their self-esteem from this domain. This observation is similar to one made more than 20 years ago by Rosenberg and Simmons (1972) in trying to explain their finding of higher self-esteem among African American children despite poorer school performance. They hypothesized that the social environments that African American children find themselves in more easily permit them to mobilize psychological defenses that protect them against the negative esteem implications of performing poorly in school.

We suggest that disengagement of self-esteem from academic domains may occur via one or both of the two processes we have discussed above: (1) African American students may be more likely to devalue, or reduce the importance of, doing well on intellectual tasks than European American students, and/or (2) African American students may be more likely to discount feedback on intellectual tests, that is, perceive it as biased and not diagnostic of genuine intellectual ability.

Although a number of authors have speculated that African American students may be less achievement motivated, or place less value on education than European American students, results of empirical research on this issue are equivocal (see Graham, 1994, for a review). Steinberg, Dornbusch, & Brown (1992), for example, demonstrated that parents of African American school children place just as much value on education as do parents of European American school children. Furthermore, African American and European American high school students are similar in their endorsement of the belief that getting a good education will pay off. Steinberg and colleagues (1992) also found, however, that African American students are less likely than European American students to believe that bad consequences will follow from not getting a good education.

An alternative pathway by which African American students may disengage their self-esteem from evaluative feedback in academic contexts is by discounting the diagnosticity of that feedback. That is, they may regard their performances on tests, evaluations by teachers, or performances relative to other students as not especially diagnostic indicators of their actual ability level, especially if it is negative. Several experimental studies have observed that African Americans are more likely to overestimate their future performance, increase their expectancies of success following a failure experience, and report higher expectancies for future success following a success or failure than are European American students, leading some authors to conclude that African American students' expectancies for success and self-conceptions of ability are "overly optimistic" in light of their objective performance (see Graham, 1994, for a review). This disconnection of self-appraisals from external evaluations may occur in part because African American students are aware of negative stereotypes about their intellectual abilities, and have experienced the prejudice and discrimination that accompany those stereotypes. As consequence, they may expect intellectual tests and performance evaluations to be biased and unfair, and not a true indicator of ability, at least when race is salient.

In the following sections, we describe three studies that we have conducted to examine whether African American students are more likely than European American students to disengage their self-esteem from evaluative feedback received in the academic domain, and if so, the mechanisms through which this occurs.

STUDY 1

Our first study had three goals. First, we attempted to develop a measure of disengagement from intellectual tests and academic domains that assessed both devaluing and discounting processes. Second, we examined whether there are differences between African American and European American college students on this measure. Third, we examined the associations among academic performance, disengagement with intellectual tasks, and global self-esteem among African American and European American students. Based on the theoretical framework presented above, we hypothesized that African American students would score higher on a measure of disengagement of self-esteem from feedback on intellectual tests than European American students. We also examined whether this hypothesized greater disengagement among African American students results from a tendency for African American students to devalue the importance of academic excellence, or from a tendency for African American students to discount the diagnosticity of intellectual test scores as indicators of actual ability. Finally, we examined whether disengagement from evaluative feedback on intellectual tests predicted global self-esteem.

Method

One hundred and eighty-nine college students participated in this study, 129 of whom were European American, and 60 of whom were African American.[1] Students completed the Rosenberg Self-Esteem Scale (Rosenberg, 1965) to assess global, personal self-esteem, and completed a measure of intellectual engagement (described below). Students were also asked to provide us with their current college grade point average (GPA) and to give us permission to access their academic records, as a measure of performance in the intellectual domain. GPA was obtained for 125 European American students and 47 African American students.[2]

[1]Our measures were also administered to a sample of Asian American students. Asian Americans are in the interesting position of being a relatively high-status minority group. Their status as a socially devalued group, therefore, is ambiguous. For this reason, we do not discuss their data here.

[2]To maximize the number of participants retained in our sample we used students' actual grade point average obtained from their records, when possible. If we could not retrieve students' actual GPA, we used their reported grade point average, if given. Reported GPA was highly correlated with actual GPA (r = .87).

TABLE 10.1   Factor Analysis of the Intellectual Engagement Inventory

	Factor 1	Factor 2	Factor 3
Discounting *(a = .81)*			
I feel that standardized achievement tests are fair tests of my abilities. ®	.88	.09	−.13
In general, I feel that standardized achievement tests are a good measure of my intelligence. ®	.78	.13	−.20
Most intelligence tests do not really measure what they are supposed to.	.71	.00	−.27
I feel that standardized achievement tests are definitely biased against me.	.52	−.11	.03
Devaluing *(a = .66)*			
I always feel good about myself when I do well on an academic test. ®	.00	.58	.01
Being good at academics is an important part of who I am. ®	−.06	.56	−.12
Doing well on intellectual tasks is very important to me. ®	.09	.54	.01
I care a great deal about performing well on tests of my intellectual ability. ®	.26	.54	−.30
It usually doesn't matter to me one way or the other how I do in school.	−.26	.50	−.26
Disengagement *(a = .62)*			
I really don't care what tests say about my intelligence.	−.17	−.21	.74
No intelligence test will ever change my opinion of how intelligent I am.	−.20	.08	.51
How I do intellectually has little relation to who I really am.	−.07	−.18	.50

® Refers to reverse-scored.

Measuring Domain-Specific Disengagement

To assess engagement in the intellectual or academic domain, students were asked to indicate the extent to which they agreed or disagreed with twelve statements about intellectual test performance (see Table 10.1). Each statement was rated on a scale from 1 (disagree strongly) to 7 (agree strongly). The 12 statements were designed to assess the extent to which students said it was important to them to do well on intellectual tests, believed that standardized intellectual tests were diagnostic of genuine intellectual ability, and more generally based their self-regard on how well they did on intellectual tests.

Maximum likelihood factor analysis of this scale yielded three factors with eigenvalues greater than one. The 12 items of the scale, along with their factor loadings, are presented in Table 10.1. Items were included in a factor if they loaded above .50 on that factor and did not load that highly on any other factor.

The first factor consisted of 5 items, and appeared to measure the extent to which students said that it was important or unimportant to them to do well in academics. We labeled this factor *Devaluing*. The second factor consisted of the four items assessing the extent to which students discounted the diagnosticity of standardized tests of intellectual ability. We labeled this factor *Discounting*. The third factor consisted of three items that appeared to closely reflect the extent to which students say that their feelings about themselves are independent of their performance on intelligence tests. We labeled this factor *Disengagement*.

Comparisons by Ethnicity and GPA

The second goal of this study was to compare the responses of high and low performing African American and European American students on our intellectual engagement measures. Recall that we predicted that African Americans would be more disengaged from the intellectual domain than European American students, and that this might be especially true if they were doing poorly in school. To test this hypothesis, we divided the sample into those with relatively high (>2.5) and those with relatively low (<2.5) grade point averages. This resulted in an N of 47 European Americans and 27 African Americans in the low GPA cells, and an N of 78 European Americans and 20 African Americans in the high GPA cells.[3] We then performed a series of 2 (Ethnic Group: European American/ African American) × 2 (GPA: High/Low) ANOVAS on each of the three disengagement subscales, as well as on self-esteem.[4]

Disengagement Measures

Analyses of the three disengagement subscales revealed significant main effects for ethnicity and GPA on all subscales, and no significant interactions on any subscale. As expected, African American students scored significantly higher on the disengagement subscale ($M = 5.06$; $SD = 1.22$) than did European American students ($M = 4.48$; $SD = 1.38$); $F(1,168) = 4.52$, $p < .05$. African American students also discounted the validity of intelligence tests significantly more ($M = 4.91$; $SD = 1.44$) than did European American students ($M = 4.33$, $SD = 1.30$); $F(1, 168) = 9.20$, $p < .01$. However, African American students devalued doing well in school significantly *less* (i.e., valued the domain more) ($M = 1.99$; $SD = .75$) than did European Americans ($M = 2.23$; $SD = .89$), $F(1, 168) = 4.20$, $p < .05$.

As might be expected, students with low GPAs ($M = 4.92$; $SD = 1.37$) reported higher levels of disengagement than did students with high GPAs ($M = 4.43$;

[3]Results of a one-way ANOVA on GPA indicated that African American students had significantly lower GPAs ($M = 2.30$) than did European American students ($M = 2.67$), $F(1,171) = 11.82$, $p < .001$. This difference was significant regardless of whether ethnic groups were compared on reported, actual, or the combined GPA measure. The median combined GPA for African American students was 2.35, whereas the median for European American students was 2.67. A GPA of 2.5 was selected as a cutoff to create a more balanced distribution of low and high GPA African American and European American students.

[4]Regression analyses yield similar results to the ANOVA. The latter is reported for ease of interpretation.

$SD = 1.32$); $F(1,168) = 3.89$, $p = .05$, and said that doing well in the academic domain was significantly less important to them (devalued the domain more) ($M = 2.30$; $SD = .88$) than did students with high GPAs ($M = 2.06$; $SD = .83$); $F(1, 168) = 4.61$, $p < .05$. Students with high GPAs, however, also discounted the validity of intelligence tests more ($M = 4.67$; $SD = 1.22$) than did students with low GPAs ($M = 4.24$; $SD = 1.50$), $F(1, 168) = 7.12$, $p < .01$.

Self-Esteem

Analysis of global self-esteem revealed that African American students ($M = 6.01$; $SD = 1.06$) had higher global self-esteem than did European American students ($M = 5.64$; $SD = 1.07$), $F (1,168) = 3.75$, $p = .05$. This main effect was qualified, however, by a significant interaction with GPA, $F(1,168) = 5.32$, $p < .03$. Student-Newman-Keuls tests indicated that African American students doing poorly in school had significantly higher global self-esteem ($M = 6.29$, $SD = .83$) than did European American students doing poorly in school ($M = 5.53$, $SD = 1.10$), ($p < .05$). However, there were no significant differences in global self-esteem between African American students ($M = 5.63$, $SD = 1.23$) and European American students ($M = 5.71$, $SD = 1.05$) who were doing well in school.

Relations among Disengagement and Self-Esteem

The third goal of this study was to examine the relationships among the disengagement processes, academic performance, and self-esteem. We predicted that the more students discounted the validity of intellectual tests, and/or the more they devalued the importance of academics, the more likely they would be to say that their self-esteem was disengaged from (not dependent upon) evaluative feedback they received in the academic domain. Furthermore, we predicted that the more disengaged students were from evaluative feedback in this domain, the higher their self-esteem would be, especially if they were doing poorly in school.

Pearson correlation coefficients revealed that the relationships among the three disengagement subscales were quite similar for African American and European American students. As predicted, higher levels of discounting ($r = .33$, $p < .01$) and higher levels of devaluing ($r = .31$, $p < .01$) were positively and significantly correlated with higher levels of disengagement. Discounting and devaluing were positively but not significantly correlated ($r = .11$).

We next examined the association between global self-esteem and disengagement, devaluing, and discounting scores overall, and separately among African American and European American students doing well (GPA > 2.5) vs. poorly (GPA < 2.5) in school. Both Pearson correlation coefficients and moderator regression analyses indicated that the relationships between the three disengagement subscales and global self-esteem did not differ significantly by ethnic group or by GPA. Overall, higher disengagement was significantly associated with higher global self-esteem ($r = .32$, $p < .01$), whereas neither discounting ($r = .02$) nor devaluing ($r = -.06$) was related to global self-esteem. Contrary to our expectations, the correlation between disengagement and self-esteem was not significantly higher for students who were doing poorly in school ($r = .43$, $p < .001$) than it was for students who were doing well in school ($r = .23$, $p < .05$), $z = 1.44$, $p = .13$.

Summary

In sum, this study confirmed that discounting the validity of intellectual tests and devaluing the importance of doing well on intellectual tests are distinct psychological processes. Furthermore, as expected, both devaluing and discounting were significantly related to higher disengagement, and this was true for both ethnic groups. Only disengagement, however, was significantly related to global self-esteem. Thus, discounting and devaluing appeared to have indirect relationships with global self-esteem, whereas disengagement appeared to have a direct relationship with self-esteem.

We also observed the predicted differences between ethnic groups on our measures of discounting and disengagement. African American students were more likely to discount the validity of intellectual tests and say that their self-esteem did not depend on their performance on such tests than were European American students. Contrary to the devaluing hypothesis, however, African American students valued the academic domain more, not less, than European American students. Consistent with findings of other studies, African American students had higher global self-esteem than did European American students. However, the significant interaction observed between ethnicity and GPA revealed that this difference occurred only among students who were doing poorly in school. African American students doing poorly in school had higher self-esteem than did European American students doing poorly in school, whereas African American and European American students doing well in school did not differ in self-esteem.

Consistent with the idea that disengagement is a response to perceived threat in a given domain, students with low GPAs scored higher on the disengagement subscale than did students with high GPAs. Furthermore, the more students disengaged their self-appraisals from intellectual feedback, the higher their self-esteem. Although the difference between low and high GPA groups was not significant, this relationship between disengagement and self-esteem was somewhat stronger for students doing poorly in school than it was for students doing well in school. Perhaps students with "high" GPAs wish they had still higher GPAs, and so need to engage in the self-esteem protection that disengagement affords.

Because the correlational nature of this study precludes definitive statements about cause and effect, we conducted two experiments to test the hypothesis that disengagement of self-esteem from performance feedback is more likely to occur among African American students than among European American students. In addition, we examined whether disengagement is especially likely to occur when expectations of racial bias are triggered, or is a more chronic response of African American students in the context of intellectual tests. These two studies are described below.

STUDY 2

In our first experiment (Major *et al.,* 1998, Experiment 1), African American and European American college students were given predetermined success or failure feedback on a supposed standardized test of intellectual ability by a European American experimenter. Prior to taking the test, half of the students were told that the test was known to be biased against certain racial and ethnic groups, whereas the other half were told that the test was culturally unbiased. A pretest measure of global trait self-esteem (Rosenberg, 1965) and postfeedback measures of global trait self-esteem and performance state self-esteem (Heatherton & Polivy, 1991) were administered. In addition, students were asked to rate their performance on the test, and to rate the extent to which they felt that their performance on the test was affected by a biased test and disadvantages due to their race. In this study we operationalized disengagement as a relative nonresponsiveness of self-esteem to performance feedback. That is, we hypothesized that students who were disengaged from the intellectual domain would be less reactive to success and failure feedback on a supposed test of intellectual ability.

Based on the disengagement hypothesis, our first prediction was that the self-esteem of African American students would be less affected by negative and positive test score feedback than would that of European American students. That is, we predicted that European American students' performance self-esteem would be higher after success than after failure, whereas African American students' self-esteem would be less reactive to performance feedback. Our second prediction was that these differences in responsiveness of self-esteem to performance feedback would be especially apparent when the test was described as racially biased as opposed to culture fair. Our reasoning was that describing a test as racially biased against certain ethnic groups would be likely to prime negative stereotypes of racial abilities and anticipation of poor performance among African American students, but not among European American students. Furthermore, we reasoned that describing a test as racially biased would also be more likely to lead African American students, but not European American students, to discount the diagnosticity of performance feedback on that test. Either of these processes should result in African American students being more likely than African American students to disengage their self-esteem from performance feedback in the racially-biased condition than in the culture-fair condition.

Results were consistent with the disengagement hypothesis. Corrected for initial self-esteem, European American students' performance state self-esteem was more affected by feedback on the test (success or failure) than was that of African American students. Specifically, whereas European American students tended to have higher performance self-esteem following success than failure, African American students did not. European American students' perceptions of their performance also were more affected by the performance feedback they received than were those of African American students.

Contrary to our expectations, describing the test as racially biased or culture fair did not moderate the effect of performance feedback on European American and African American students' responses on the self-esteem measures. One interpretation of this surprising finding is that African American students already may have chronically disengaged their self-esteem from feedback on intelligence tests more than European American students. Consequently, regardless of whether we described the test as biased or not, their self-esteem would be less affected by performance feedback. This interpretation would be consistent with our finding, described in Study 1, that African American students score higher on a measure of chronic disengagement from feedback in the intellectual domain. A second interpretation of this finding is that our African American students may not have believed the culture-fair test description—they may have perceived the test, in both its biased and unbiased forms, as racially biased, and hence discounted its diagnosticity. This perception may have been buttressed by the presence of a European American evaluator. Consistent with this idea, African American students were more likely to attribute their performance (success or failure) to a biased test and to racial disadvantages than were European American students, regardless of how the test was described. A third explanation is that we caused African American students to temporarily disengage their self-esteem from their performance in both conditions simply by raising the issue of race and ethnic differences in performance in descriptions of both the biased and unbiased test conditions. Such an interpretation is consistent with Steele and Aronson's (1995) finding that simply priming race can raise stereotype threat among African American college students taking a difficult test of intellectual ability. Our third experiment was designed to investigate these alternative explanations.

STUDY 3

In this experiment (Major *et al.*, 1998, Experiment 2), African American and European American students again completed a supposed standardized test of intellectual ability and received bogus performance feedback on it. In this experiment, however, all participants received feedback that they had done poorly on the test. Prior to taking the test, half of the participants were told that the test might be biased against certain minority groups, whereas no mention was made of race or test bias to the other half of the participants. Participants also were pretested on the disengagement subscale of our Intellectual Engagement Inventory, described above, and scores on this measure were used to divide them into two groups of chronically intellectually engaged and chronically intellectually disengaged students. Pretest and postfeedback measures of self-esteem and postfeedback perceptions of the racial bias of the test were also assessed.

Our first hypothesis was that when the possibility of racial test bias was primed, African American students' self-esteem would be less negatively affected by a poor performance on the test than would that of European American students. When race was not primed, however, we expected African American and European American students' self-esteem to be similarly affected by negative performance feedback. Our second hypothesis was that the self-esteem of students who are chronically disengaged from their performance in intellectual domains, as assessed by our disengagement subscale, would be less negatively affected by failure feedback on the test than would that of chronically engaged students.

Results were consistent with our first prediction. After receiving failure feedback, African American students' self-esteem was higher if race had been primed than if it had not been primed, whereas European American students' self-esteem was unaffected by the prime. African American students had higher self-esteem than did European American students if race had been primed, but lower self-esteem than did European American students if race had not been primed. Our second prediction also was supported, but only among African American students. Adjusted for initial self-esteem, African American students who scored high on the chronic disengagement premeasure had higher self-esteem after failure than did African American students who scored low on this premeasure. In contrast, scores on this premeasure had no effect on the self-esteem of European American students. Regardless of whether racial bias was primed or not, and regardless of level of chronic disengagement, however, African American students were more likely to perceive the test as biased against minorities, to report having an unfair racial disadvantage on the test, and to believe that nonminorities do better than minorities on the test.

Summary

Taken together, the results of these studies provide support for the idea that under certain circumstances, African American students are more likely than European American students to disengage their self-esteem from performance feedback received in intellectual testing situations. This disengagement is especially likely to occur, we believe, in situations in which either negative stereotypes, expectations of racial bias, or expectations of poor performance are primed, but may take on more chronic features as African Americans continually confront prejudice and discrimination in their environment. European American students, in contrast, who are not affected by the same negative stereotypes and social devaluation, are relatively unaffected by primes of racial bias and are more likely to remain engaged by intellectual tasks. Although we were unable in these studies to specify the mediational pathway by which disengagement occurs, we suspect that African American students are likely to believe that intellectual tests are biased against them, especially when racial bias is primed, and thus do not consider their performance on these tests to be a legitimate basis on which to evaluate their self-worth.

FUTURE DIRECTIONS

Our goal in this chapter is to articulate the processes through which members of socially devalued groups disengage their global feelings of self-worth from external evaluations, feedback, and outcomes, and to present initial evidence in support of this general process of disengagement. Several interesting issues deserve further mention and research.

IS DISENGAGEMENT CHRONIC OR TEMPORARY?

Psychological disengagement from a domain may be conceptualized as a relatively fixed aspect of a person's self-definition, or as a context-specific response to particular situations (Crocker *et al.*, 1998). The former, "trait," conceptualization is consistent with the way that many self theorists, including James (1890/1950), Rosenberg (1986), Harter (1986), and Pelham and Swann (1989) conceptualized the process of defining, or redefining, the self, and is more consistent with Steele's (1992; 1997) concept of disidentification. The latter, "state," conceptualization of disengagement is consistent with more fluid views of the self (e.g., Markus & Wurf, 1987; Tesser, 1988) and research showing that individuals alter their self-definitions in response to the social environment (Markus & Kunda, 1986). It is likely that both forms of disengagement are demonstrated by members of stigmatized groups. The stigmatized may temporarily disengage their self-esteem from performance feedback in situations in which negative stereotypes are salient and poor outcomes are anticipated, and/or when feedback is suspected to be biased, unfair, or otherwise nondiagnostic of personal merit. Over time, repeated exposure to such situations may lead the stigmatized to chronically disengage, or disidentify, with those domains (see Crocker *et al.*, 1998). Whether temporarily induced or chronically experienced, disengagement from a domain should reduce emotional reactivity to evaluations in that domain.

DISENGAGEMENT AS A COLLECTIVE RESPONSE
TO DISADVANTAGE

Our discussion of disengagement and our own research has focused on individual-level reactions to negative stereotypes, feedback, and outcomes. We believe that disengagement can also evolve into a *collective* response to negative stereotypes, feedback, and outcomes. That is, socially devalued groups may develop a subcultural value structure that allows them to devalue and disengage from domains in which their group experiences prejudice and discrimination. Ogbu (1991) labels this phenomenon *cultural inversion* and describes it as occurring when a minority group develops norms against engaging in behaviors or holding beliefs that are characteristic of the dominant culture and instead places greater value on behaviors and beliefs that are uncharacteristic of the dominant culture. In ethnographic studies of African American teenagers, Fordham and Ogbu (1986) observed that African American students tend to define school success as "acting White" and not "African American" and thus are caught in a bind between performing well in school and being popular among their peers.

Interestingly, our data do not suggest that African Americans devalue success in the academic domain, a domain that is dominated and controlled largely by

European Americans, but may actually value academic success *more* than their European American counterparts. This finding must be interpreted with caution, however, because our sample consisted of African Americans college students, individuals who are likely to be invested in academic success. It is possible that this tendency for African Americans to value academic success more than European Americans would not generalize to the greater population.

Another way that members of socially devalued groups may collectively disengage from a given domain is by developing shared beliefs that discount the legitimacy of the status structure or the established system of reward allocations. Consistent with this idea, members of ethnic minority groups are less likely than are European American students to endorse ideologies that legitimize the system, such as the belief in individual mobility, the belief that hard work pays off, and the belief that group differences in outcomes are fair (Kleugel & Smith, 1986; Major *et al.,* 1997).

IS DISENGAGEMENT ADAPTIVE?

Although we conceptualize disengagement as a response to perceived threats to the personal or collective self, this should not be construed as implying that we believe that disengagement is a pathological or nonnormative response. Rather, as James' (1890) quote indicates, disengagement of self-esteem from domains in which one does not perceive good prospects is a normal process of healthy identity maintenance that all individuals, regardless of stigmatized status, may adopt (see also Crocker *et al.,* in press; Steele, 1992; 1997). Because the stigmatized face discrimination, prejudice, and objective disadvantage in domains that are negatively affected by their stigma, disengagement of self-esteem from feedback received in those domains is likely to be a highly appropriate and highly effective coping strategy. Both Crocker and Major (1989) and Steele (1992; 1997), however have noted that disidentification from a domain, may over time, reduce motivation to achieve in that domain. Thus, disengagement can have costs: the stigmatized may protect their self-esteem by disengaging from domains in which they are targets of negative stereotypes and social devaluation, but pay for this protection through its negative impact on their motivation to achieve in those very domains. If these domains are not ones that are highly valued by the wider social context, or are very limited in their scope (such as James' ignorance of Greek), disengagement is unlikely to have maladaptive consequences. If success in the domain is highly central to important life outcomes, however, the price tag of disengagement can be steep.

REFERENCES

Adams, J. S. (1965). Inequity in social exchange. In L. Berkowitz (Ed.), *Advances in experimental social psychology, 2,* New York: Academic Press.

Amato, M., Crocker, J., & Major, B. (1995). Paper presented at the annual meeting of the American Psychological Association, New York.

Baumeister, R. F. (1995). Self and identity: An introduction. In A. Tesser (Ed.), *Advanced social psychology*. New York: McGraw-Hill Book Company.

Bem, D. J. (1970). *Beliefs, attitudes, and human affairs*. Belmont, CA: Brooks/Cole.

Cooley, C. H. (1956). *Human nature and the social order*. New York: Free Press.

Crandall, C. S. (1994). Prejudice against fat people: Ideology and self-interest. *Journal of Personality & Social Psychology, 66,* 882–894.

Crocker, J., Cornwall, B., & Major, B. (1993). The stigma of overweight: Affective consequences of attributional ambiguity. *Journal of Personality and Social Psychology, 64,* 60–70.

Crocker, J., & Major, B. (1989). Social stigma and self-esteem: The self-protective properties of stigma. *Psychological Review, 96,* 608–630.

Crocker, J., & Major, B. (1994). Reactions to stigma: The moderating role of justifications. In M. P. Zanna and J. M. Olson (Eds.), *The psychology of prejudice: The Ontario symposium* (Vol. 7, pp. 289–314). Hillsdale, NJ: Erlbaum.

Crocker, J., Major, B., & Steele, C. (1998). Social stigma. In D. Gilbert, S. T. Fiske, & G. Lindzey (Eds.), *Handbook of social psychology* (4th ed.). Boston: McGraw Hill and Oxford University Press.

Crocker, J., Voelkl, K., Testa, M., & Major, B. (1991). Social stigma: The affective consequences of attributional ambiguity. *Journal of Personality and Social Psychology, 60,* 218–228.

Darley, J. M., & Fazio, R. H. (1980). Expectancy confimation processes arising in the social interaction sequence. *American Psychology, 35,* 867–881.

Demo, D. H., & Parker, K. D. (1987). Academic achievement and self-esteem among Black and White college students. *Journal of Social Psychology, 4,* 345–355.

Devine, P. G. (1989). Stereotypes and prejudice: Their automatic and controlled components. *Journal of Personality and Social Psychology, 56,* 5–18.

Festinger, L. (1954). A theory of social comparison processes. *Human Relations, 7,* 71–82.

Fordham, S., & Ogbu, J. U. (1986). Black students' school success: Coping with the "burden of acting White." *Urban Review, 18,* 176–206.

Frable, D. E. (1989). Sex typing and gender ideology: Two facets of the individual's gender psychology that go together. *Journal of Personality & Social Psychology, 56,* 1, 95–108.

Gaertner, S. L., & Dovidio, J. F. (1986). The aversive form of racism. In J. Dovidio & S. L. Gaertner (Eds.), *Prejudice, discrimination, and racism* (pp. 61–89). San Diego, CA: Academic Press.

Gecas, V., & Schwalbe, M. L. (1983). Beyond the looking-glass self: Social struction and efficacy-based self-esteem. *Social Psychology Quarterly, 46,* 77–88.

Goffman, E. (1963). *Stigma: Notes on the management of spoiled identity*. New York: Simon & Schuster, Inc.

Graham, S. (1994). Motivation in African Americans. *Review of Educational Research, 64,* 55–117.

Harter, S. (1986). Processes underlying the construction, maintenance, and enhancement of the self-concept in children. In J. Suls and A. G. Greenwald (Eds.), *Psychological perspectives on the self* (Vol. 3, pp. 136–182). Hillsdale, NJ: Erlbaum.

Heatherton, T. F., & Polivy, J. (1991). Development and validation of a scale for measuring state self-esteem. *Journal of Personality & Social Psychology, 60,* 895–910.

Homans, G. (1974). *Social behavior: Its elementary forms* (Rev. ed.). New York: Harcourt Brace Jovanovich.

James, W. (1890/1950). *The principles of psychology* (Vol. 1). New York: Dover.

Kelley, H. H. (1972). Causal schemata and the attribution process. In E. E. Jones, D. E. Kanouse, H. H. Kelley, R. E. Nisbett, S. Valins, & B. Weiner (Eds.), *Attribution: Perceiving the causes of behavior* (pp. 151–176). Morrison, NJ: General Learning Press.

Kleugel, J. R., & Smith, E. R. (1986). *Beliefs about inequality: Americans' view of what is and what ought to be*. Hawthorn, NJ: Aldine de Gruyer.

Lay, R., & Wakstein, J. (1985). Race, academic achievement, and self-concept of ability. *Research in Higher Education, 22,* 43–64.

Lerner, M. J. (1987). Integrating societal and psychological rules of entitlement: The basic task of each social actor and fundamental problem for the social sciences. *Social Justice Research, 1,* 107–125.

Lerner, M. J., & Miller, D. T. (1978). Just world research and the attribution process: Looking back and ahead. *Psychological Bulletin, 85,* 1030–1051.

Lind, E. A., & Tyler, T. R. (1988). *The social psychology of procedural justice.* New York: Plenum.

Major, B. (1994). From social inequality to personal entitlement: The role of social comparisons, legitimacy appraisals, and group membership. In L. Berkowitz (Ed.), *Advances in experimental social psychology* (Vol. 26, pp. 293–355). New York: Academic Press.

Major, B., & Crocker, J. (1993). Social stigma: The affective consequences of attributional ambiguity. In D. M. Mackie & D. L. Hamilton (Eds.), *Affect, cognition, and stereotyping: Interactive process in intergroup perception* (pp. 345–370). New York: Academic Press.

Major, B., Feinstein, J., & Crocker, J. (1994). Attributional ambiguity of affirmative action. *Basic and Applied Social Psychology, 15,* 113–141.

Major, B., Levin, S., Schmader, T., & Sidanius, J. (1997). *Effects of justice ideology, group identification, and ethnic group membership on perceptions of personal and group discrimination.* Manuscript submitted for publication.

Major, B., & Quinton, W. (1997). *Group identification, justice beliefs, and attributions to discrimination.* Manuscript in preparation.

Major, B., Spencer, S., Schmader, T., Wolfe, C., & Crocker, J. (1998). Coping with negative stereotypes about intellectual performance: The role of psychological disengagement. *Personality and Social Psychology Bulletin, 24,* 34–50.

Major, B., Testa,, M., & Bylsma, W. H. (1991). Responses to upward and downward social comparisons: The impact of esteem-relevance and perceived control. In J. Suls & T. Wills (Eds.), *Social comparisons: Contemporary theory and research* (pp. 237–260). Hillsdale, NJ: Erlbaum.

Markus, H., & Kunda, Z. (1986). Stability and malleability of the self-concept. *Journal of Personality and Social Psychology, 51,* 858–866.

Markus, H., & Wurf, L. (1987). The dynamic self-concept: A social psychological perspective. In M. R. Rosenweig & L. W. Porter (Eds.), *Annual Review of Psychology* (Vol. 38, pp. 299–337) Palo Alto, CA: Annual Reviews, Inc.

Marsh, H. W. (1986). Global self-esteem: Its relation to specific facets of self-concept and their importance. *Journal of Personality and Social Psychology, 51,* 1224–1236.

McCarthy, J. D., & Yancey, W. L. (1971). Uncle Tome and Mr. Charlie: Metaphysical pathos in the study of racism and personal disorganization. *American Journal of Sociology, 76,* 648–672.

Mead, G. H. (1934). *Mind, self, and society.* Chicago: University of Chicago Press.

Ogbu, J. U. (1991). Minority coping responses and school experience. *The Journal of Psychohistory, 18,* 433–456.

Osborne, J. W. (1995). Academics, self-esteem, and race: A look at the underlying assumptions of the disidentification hypothesis. *Personality and Social Psychology Bulletin, 21,* 449–455.

Pelham, B. W., & Swann, W. B., Jr. (1989). From self-conceptions to self-worth: On the sources and structure of global self-esteem. *Journal of Personality and Social Psychology, 57,* 672–680.

Peterson, B., Major, B., Cozzarelli, C., & Crocker, J. (1988, April). *The social construction of gender differences in values.* Paper presented at the annual meeting of the Eastern Psychological Association, Buffalo, NY.

Porter, J. R., & Washington, R. E. (1979). Black identity and self-esteem: a few of studies of black self-concept. 1968–1978. *Annual Review of Sociology, 5,* 53–74.

Quinn, D., & Crocker, J. (1998; this volume). Vulnerability to the affective consequences of the stigma of overweight. In J. Swim & C. Stangor (Eds.), *Prejudice: The target's perspective.* San Diego: Academic Press.

Rosenberg, M. (1965). *Society and the adolescent self-image.* Princeton, NJ: Princeton University Press.

Rosenberg, M. (1979). *Conceiving the self.* New York: Basic Books.

Rosenberg, M., & Simmons, R. G. (1972). *Black and White self-esteem: The urban school child.* Washington, DC: American Sociological Association.

Ruggiero, K., & Taylor, D. (1997). Why minority group members perceive or do not perceive the discrimination that confronts them: The role of self-esteem and perceived control. *Journal of Personality and Social Psychology, 72,* 373–389.

Schmader, T., & Major, B. (1997). *The social construction of personal values.* Manuscript in preparation.

Shrauger, J. S., & Schoneman, T. J. (1979). Symbolic interactionist view of the self-concept: Through the looking glass darkly. *Psychological Bulletin, 86,* 549–573.

Simmons, R. G., Brown, L., Bush, D. M., & Blyth, D. A. (1978). Self-esteem and achievement of Black and White adolescents. *Social Problems, 26,* 86–96.

Steele, C. M. (1988). The psychology of self-affirmation: Sustaining the integrity of the self. In L. Berkowitz (Ed.), *Advances in experimental social psychology* (Vol. 21), 261–302.

Steele, C. M. (1992, April). Race and the schooling of Black Americans. *The Atlantic Monthly,* 68–78.

Steele, C. M. (1997). A threat in the air: How stereotypes shape intellectual identity and performance. *American Psychologist, 52,* 613–629.

Steele, C. M., & Aronson, J. (1995). Stereotype threat and the intellectual test performance of African Americans. *Journal of Personality and Social Psychology, 69,* 797–811.

Steinberg, L., Dornbusch, S. M., & Brown, B. B. (1992). Ethnic differences in adolescent achievement: An ecological perspective. *American Psychologist, 47,* 723–729.

Tajfel, H., & Turner, J. C. (1986). The social identity theory of intergroup behavior. In S. Worchel & W. G. Austin (Eds.), *The psychology of intergroup relations* (pp. 7–24). Chicago: Nelson-Hall.

Taylor, S. E., & Brown, J. D. (1988). Illusion and well-being: A social psychological perspective on mental health. *Psychological Bulletin, 103,* 193–210.

Tesser, A. (1988). Toward a self-evaluation maintenance model of social behavior. In L. Berkowitz (Ed.), *Advances in Experimental Social Psychology* (Vol. 21, pp. 181–227). San Diego: Academic Press.

Tesser, A., & Campbell, J. (1980). Self-definition: The impact of the relative performance and similarity of others. *Social Psychology Quarterly, 43,* 341–347.

Tesser, A., Millar, M., & Moore, J. (1988). Some affective consequences of social comparison and reflection processes: The pain and pleasure of being close. *Journal of Personality and Social Psychology, 54,* 49–61.

11

COPING WITH

GROUP-BASED

DISCRIMINATION:

INDIVIDUALISTIC VERSUS
GROUP-LEVEL STRATEGIES[1]

NYLA R. BRANSCOMBE

University of Kansas

NAOMI ELLEMERS

Free University, Amsterdam

Social groups can differ widely in terms of the degree of power and status that they are accorded, and such intergroup relational factors have consequences for the outcomes that individual group members receive (Eagly, 1987; Oakes, Haslam, & Turner, 1994; Taylor & Moghaddam, 1994). Some groups are considerably more privileged or advantaged, while others are targets of discrimination. In this chapter, we employ social identity and self-categorization theories as vehicles for better understanding how disadvantaged group members achieve a positive identity (Tajfel, 1978; Turner, 1985; Turner, Hogg, Oakes, Reicher, & Wetherell, 1987). Depending on the individual's level of identification with a disadvantaged group, different types of strategies—either individualistic or group-based—can be employed as means of coping with perceived discrimination.

[1]This chapter is the result of a collaborative effort on the part of both authors which occurred while the first author was a sabbatical visitor at the Free University, Amsterdam. Completion of this chapter was facilitated by a NWO (Dutch Organization for Scientific Research) Award to Nyla R. Branscombe.

243

LEVELS OF GROUP IDENTIFICATION
AND COPING STRATEGY USE

A major goal of social identity theory (Tajfel, 1974, 1975, 1981; Tajfel &
Turner, 1979) has been to understand how people respond to their position in the
social structure. Which of the several *different* identity management strategies will
be employed by disadvantaged social group members, and under what circumstances each will be favored, has received considerable research attention. Three
general types of strategic options have been distinguished: (1) individual mobility;
(2) social creativity; and (3) social competition. In this chapter, we discuss each
of these options according to whether they imply the operation of different underlying goals—to maintain a positive social identity or a positive personal identity.
While any given attribute can be potentially conceptualized in either personal or
group terms, whether an individual in a given social context considers that attribute to be a defining feature of the self at the individual or group level has important
implications for what strategy will be pursued (see Simon, 1997; Turner, 1985).

Individual mobility can be conceptualized as a strategy that is aimed at maintaining a positive *personal* identity, and it is likely to be preferred by people who
self-categorize at the individual level in a given social context. Social competition,
in contrast, can be seen as a group-based means of maintaining a positive *social*
identity, and it is employed by persons who categorize and identify themselves in
terms of a specific group membership. However, social creativity is an umbrella
term that has been used to cover a broad range of indirect responses that could
potentially reflect either individualistic or group-based self-conceptions and goals.
Therefore, our first task in this chapter is to distinguish between the different
forms of social creativity responses that have been investigated in terms of the
different goals and self-categorizations that are likely to be operating. We will
then turn to what impact perceiving discrimination has on feelings of self-worth
among disadvantaged group members who have different primary goals—to protect the value of their group identity or their personal self.

While lower status groups acknowledge the superior performance of higher
status comparison groups on dimensions that define the status difference between
the groups, they also simultaneously favor the ingroup on alternative dimensions
(cf. Lemaine, 1974; Mummendey & Schreiber, 1983; 1984; Mummendey &
Simon, 1989; Spears & Manstead, 1989; Van Knippenberg, 1989). By focusing
on such alternative dimensions, lower status groups can maintain the belief that
their group is, in fact, different from the higher status group in some valuable
ways (even if the higher status group might deem those alternative dimensions to
be relatively unimportant). This tactic, which is one of a variety of types of social
creativity responses that have been examined, we argue, constitutes a *group-level*
strategy. By emphasizing dimensions on which the ingroup does well, and by
decreasing the importance of dimensions on which the outgroup clearly excels, a
more positive identity for the ingroup as a whole, rather than only for the personal
self, can be achieved. Thus, for example, homemakers may claim that as a group,

"we are valuable because we have the very important job of rearing the next generation and this task is ultimately more important than making money." Consistent with the hypothesis that use of this form of social creativity is actually a group-level strategy, recent research has found that individuals who are highly identified with their ingroup are more likely to claim ingroup superiority on such alternative comparative dimensions, and enhance the importance of them, compared to those who are low in group identification (Ellemers, Van Rijswijk, Roefs, & Simons, 1997).

Other forms of social creativity, such as choosing to restrict one's social comparisons to other ingroup members (e.g., "I make more money than other women"), can be seen as primarily *individualistic methods* of coping with disadvantaged social status. Such an emphasis on how well the self is doing compared to other ingroup members allows for the maintenance of a positive personal identity, but it will not facilitate a positive view of the ingroup as a whole. Furthermore, negative self-implications that might accrue from comparisons between the groups (see Major, 1994), as well as the action implications that might flow from acknowledging relative ingroup disadvantage, can be avoided with this form of social creativity. In fact, people who do pursue a positive personal identity by setting themselves apart from their fellow ingroup members (i.e., those who see the self as distinctly different from other members of the ingroup) may be motivated, at times, to derogate other ingroup members because they do not fare as well as the self (cf. Doosje, Ellemers, & Spears, 1995; Lewin, 1948; Wills, 1981).

Thus, all three of the options proposed by social identity theory as possible means of coping with devalued group status (e.g., individual mobility, social creativity, and social competition) may be described as deriving from two fundamentally different goals: individual versus collective identity improvement (cf. Hogg & Abrams, 1988). Empirical efforts that have assessed people's use of different behavioral strategies have confirmed that a basic distinction can be made between responses that are aimed at improving one's personal situation, and attempts to change the position of the group as a whole (Doosje & Ellemers, 1997; Ellemers, 1993). The highly identified employ group-level strategies, whereas those who are low in identification employ individualistic strategies. However, as with use of the term social creativity, the varied forms of individualistic and group-level responses that can be displayed have not always been explicitly or consistently distinguished in the literature, resulting in some conceptual confusion. For example, some individualistic responses will be direct (e.g., social mobility), and others will be indirect and subtle (e.g., presenting the ingroup as heterogeneous and differentiating the self from other ingroup members). Likewise, some group-level responses can be difficult to mistake (e.g., social competition), while others can be considerably less obvious (e.g., stereotyping the self in terms of the ingroup's prototype). Furthermore, under some conditions, similar social behaviors may be displayed for fundamentally different purposes by those high or low in group identification. For instance, low group identifiers may align themselves with their fellow ingroup members, and as a result *temporarily* behave in terms of that group membership, as long as this is the best way to serve their own personal self-esteem goals in that particular situation. Thus, Wann and Branscombe (1990) found that both low- and high-identified individuals bask in the glory of the group when the group performs successfully and can therefore reflect well on low identifiers' personal selves. However, when the group performs poorly and might reflect negatively on low identifiers' personal self-images, those low in group identification distance themselves from the ingroup, while high identifiers do not dissociate themselves from the group, even when it performs poorly. In this sense, low identifiers can be said to be relatively opportunistic— they will temporarily align themselves with the group when it serves their personal interests, but distance themselves when that serves their individualistic purposes, resulting in some potential ambiguity when only a single action is considered. In this chapter, therefore, we aim to develop a model that explicitly considers the overall pattern of cognitive, emotional, and behavioral responses that will be exhibited by individuals who are coping with perceived discrimination, depending on their ultimate goal—either to salvage personal or group-based self-esteem.

INDIVIDUALISTIC AND GROUP-LEVEL RESPONSES TO DISCRIMINATION[1]

DO ATTRIBUTIONS TO PREJUDICE PROTECT SELF-ESTEEM?

To the extent that devalued group members do not categorize themselves in terms of their group membership, but instead at the individual level of categorization, it is reasonable to suppose that they might try to evade associations with a negatively evaluated ingroup. Several investigations have provided support for the idea that when a group is not particularly important to their identity, people are motivated to pursue individualistic strategies (Ellemers, Van Knippenberg, De Vries, & Wilke, 1988). In such artificially created and short-term laboratory groups, when people are presented with the opportunity to gain membership in

---

[1]Social discrimination can be conceptualized in several ways. People can feel they are rejected or are disadvantaged because of features of themselves that they consider to be personal. Those features might even be ones that observers could easily use to categorize people into groups. However, the possibility of categorizing people in a particular way does not necessarily imply that the people involved categorize *themselves* as such, or identify themselves as members of a group that shares the particular feature in question (cf. Simon, 1997; Tajfel & Turner, 1986). For example, recent research (Major & Crocker, 1993) has investigated the pain that overweight women experience when they are rejected because of their size in a dating context. Although this is clearly a form of social disadvantage, and these women do perceive themselves as being overweight, they are keenly aware that it is a personal feature of themselves that has brought about the rejection. Therefore, they are unlikely to perceive this kind of rejection as stemming from a group membership per se, and are unlikely to categorize or identify themselves as members of the group "fat people." In our model of coping, we will be exclusively concerned with social disadvantage that is seen by the targets as stemming from a group membership per se, rather than rejection that is likely to be interpreted in these more personal terms.

another higher status group, they will attempt to separate themselves from their devalued group and pursue individual mobility (cf. Jackson, Sullivan, Harnish, & Hodge, 1996; Lalonde & Silverman, 1994; Taylor & McKirnan, 1984; Wright, Taylor, & Moghaddam, 1990).

The question of whether such individualistic strategies, where the self is distanced from a devalued ingroup, are likely to be employed *among historically disadvantaged group members,* and whether doing so effectively provides self-esteem protection, has been examined in only a few studies thus far. Crocker, Voelkl, Testa, and Major (1991) hypothesized that externalizing negative outcomes and not seeing them as self-relevant, via attributions to prejudice, would protect self-esteem among devalued group members. While this possibility may seem intuitively appealing, these investigators failed to obtain strong support for the idea that attributions to prejudice among devalued group members actually protect self-esteem. In their first study, although women did attribute the negative feedback they received to prejudice when they were told the man who evaluated them held sexist attitudes, no significant differences in self-esteem were observed as a function of whether an attribution to prejudice was made or not. In a second study, the responses of African Americans were investigated using a similar paradigm. Again, no significant self-esteem differences were obtained as a function of whether the *negative* outcome received could be plausibly attributed to prejudice or not. However, when a *positive* outcome could be attributed to a motive reflective of the evaluator's goals rather than the participant's performance (i.e., the evaluator might be trying to appear unprejudiced), then personal self-esteem was not increased as it was when the evaluator was believed to be unaware of the participant's group membership. In other words, although the effect of a positive outcome on personal well-being appears to be undermined by external attributions, no reliable evidence was obtained in this research for the prediction that attributing negative evaluations to prejudice, and the distancing from a devalued group identity that would entail, protects self-esteem in historically disadvantaged group members.

In fact, a variety of studies have suggested that the opposite effect—under-estimating the degree to which one is a victim of discrimination—may facilitate well-being in devalued group members (cf. Crosby, 1982, 1984). For example, recent research has revealed that the more women perceive themselves to be victims of gender discrimination (Landrine, Klonoff, Gibbs, Manning, & Lund, 1995) or African Americans see themselves as victims of racial discrimination (Landrine & Klonoff, 1996), the more they exhibit debilitating psychiatric and physical health symptoms. Likewise, Kobrynowicz and Branscombe (1997) found that greater perceived discrimination in women was predicted by high levels of depression, and not by positive personal self-esteem. Furthermore, in a recent experiment, Branscombe (in press) found that women who were randomly assigned to think about the ways that they have been discriminated against because of their gender, tended to show *reduced* self-esteem compared to when thoughts of gender-based advantages were considered. Although participant ratings assessing the perceived illegitimacy of the events described were not collected (see Crocker & Major, 1994), the tone of the womens' written descriptions made it clear that they did consider their outcomes to be due to unjust group-based discrimination. Finally, in terms of willingness to make attributions to prejudice for negative outcomes, Ruggiero and Taylor (1995, 1997) have found that disadvantaged group members are rather reluctant to do so. In their studies, unless participants were given essentially no other option (i.e., they were told that it is a virtual certainty that they have been a victim of gender discrimination), women preferred to attribute their poor outcomes to their own personal inadequacies rather than to group-based discrimination.

Some empirical evidence supporting the idea that making attributions to prejudice can be protective of personal self-esteem has been obtained, however, with members of *historically privileged* groups. Specifically, when men were asked to think about the ways they have been discriminated against because of their gender (Branscombe, in press), and European Americans were asked to consider the disadvantages they have experienced because of their race (Branscombe, Schiffhauer, & Valencia, 1997), higher self-esteem was reported than when group-based advantages were contemplated. In addition, evidence from several studies that have employed artificial groups has revealed that the strongest tendency to use individual-level strategies, involving a separation of the self from the ingroup, occurs in *high*-status groups rather than low-status groups (cf. Doise, 1988; Smith, Spears, & Oyen, 1994). Thus, based on the studies that have been conducted so far, it would appear that attributions to prejudice are generally avoided by members of historically disadvantaged social groups, partly because such attributions undermine feelings of control. Such attributions may be, however, favored by and be protective of personal self-esteem among dominant group members.

In order for us to explain why attributions to prejudice among disadvantaged group members might not be particularly protective of personal self-esteem, the theoretical argument that suggests they *should* do so needs to be examined more closely. According to Crocker and Major's (1989) analysis, the harm to one's well-being that would otherwise result from the experience of exclusion can be psychologically ameliorated as long as the correct attribution—an external one—is made. However, the categorizations involved, such as gender, race, or age, are very pervasive, and recipients are aware that they are likely to be employed by perceivers in a number of situations (cf. Deaux & Major, 1987; Kite, Deaux, & Miele, 1991; Van Twuyver & Van Knippenberg, 1995). Consequently, prejudice attributions may not only imply that one's personal attributes have not been taken into account, but also that such experiences may be stable across both time and situations (cf. Weiner, 1982). Thus, given the pervasive influence that these group identities are likely to have, attributions to prejudice are unlikely to only imply external causation; they are also likely to be interpreted as global, stable, and uncontrollable, especially if made with any frequency.

For this reason, attributions to prejudice may well be more successful as a means of protecting personal self-esteem among members of *dominant* social groups. Because of their socially advantaged position, situations where dominant group members can plausibly claim to be victims of discrimination are likely to be relatively rare. Hence, in the case of dominant group members, attributions to prejudice represent external attributions that are unlikely to be either global or stable, as they are in the case of disadvantaged group members. Thus, for dominant group members, such attributions can be "seized on and used to explain away" potential personal inadequacies as stemming from their group membership, precisely because they can be only employed in very limited circumstances (see Kobrynowicz & Branscombe, 1997). Furthermore, identification with dominant groups tends to be lower than it is for minority groups, which makes separation of the self from the ingroup easier and more likely among the former than the latter (see Brewer, 1991; Mullen, Brown, & Smith, 1992).

For the disadvantaged, perceived discrimination represents external conditions that cannot be controlled and that can be expected to be encountered again in the future. In other words, such attributions imply that one's outcomes are caused by external, stable, and uncontrollable factors. Attributions of this sort have the potential to result in feelings of helplessness (cf. Seligman, 1975), and may even ultimately encourage low self-esteem and outgroup favoritism (cf. Clark & Clark, 1947; Jost & Banaji, 1994). Therefore, based on our multidimensional analysis of what attributions to prejudice may entail for historically disadvantaged groups, it is not surprising to find that they are generally quite reluctant to make them (Crosby, 1982; Kappen & Branscombe, 1997; Ruggiero & Taylor, 1995; 1997).

DOES PERCEIVED DISCRIMINATION ENCOURAGE INGROUP IDENTIFICATION AND DOES THAT PROVIDE WELL-BEING PROTECTION?

Ellemers, Van Knippenberg, and Wilke (1990) investigated the possibility that under some conditions group-level strategies of coping would be the preferred means of dealing with disadvantaged group status. They found that ingroup identification was increased when low-status group members believed that the position of their group could be improved, compared to when the low status of the ingroup could be expected to remain unchanged. In addition, a greater willingness to engage in collective efforts to address the group's position was observed when participants believed that their group's low status might be improved.

In two further studies, Ellemers, Wilke, and Van Knipppenberg (1993) manipulated whether the individual's inclusion in a lower status group or the assignment of inferior status to the ingroup were perceived as illegitimate. The results support our contention that, under some circumstances, group-level responses will be preferred over individualistic ones as a means of coping with low group status. Perception that the group's low status itself was assigned illegitimately resulted in increased identification with the low-status ingroup. When there was also a possibility that the low status position of the ingroup might improve, these group members displayed social competition towards the outgroup. In contrast, when the inclusion of the individual in the low-status group was perceived as illegiti-mate, ingroup identification was reduced. Moreover, when individual mobility was perceived as possible to achieve, these group members competed with each other, rather than the outgroup, for favorable outcomes. Thus, when illegitimacy is perceived in group terms, and group-level strategic behavior seems to be a feasible means of improving the ingroup's position, disadvantaged group mem-bers show high group identification and they prefer to collectively pursue social change rather than individual mobility. In fact, members of devalued groups may, at times, completely refrain from displaying behavior serving their own personal self-interests, if their common identity as ingroup members is sufficiently impor-tant (see De Gilder & Wilke, 1994; Ellemers, Doosje, Van Knippenberg, & Wilke, 1992; Mlicki & Ellemers, 1996). Therefore, to assume a uniform preference for individualistic strategies by the devalued underestimates the power of the need to belong and the importance of people's attachments to their groups for psycholog-ical well-being (see also Baumeister & Leary, 1995; Brewer, 1997; Bourhis, Giles, Leyens, & Tajfel, 1979; Bowlby, 1969; Branscombe & Wann, 1991; Phinney, 1990; Stevens & Fiske, 1995).

The question of whether a strong sense of identification with one's disadvan-taged social group can provide psychological protection when discrimination is perceived was investigated in a sample of African Americans (Branscombe & Harvey, 1996a). Participants were presented with a set of 10 ambiguous situations for which they were asked to indicate the extent to which they would attribute the outcome to racial prejudice (0–100%), if it happened to them. All of the events could be plausibly attributed to either racial prejudice or to other factors (e.g., not getting a job that you thought you were qualified for, a professor seems to be more helpful to other students than yourself, your boss tells you that you are not per-forming your job well). By averaging across these items, we were able to create an index of general willingness to attribute negative outcomes to racial prejudice (M=62%). A measure of degree of identification with the group African Ameri-cans was collected, as was a measure of disidentification with Whites (e.g., I don't like to associate with White people, I feel kind of hostile toward Whites because they have it easy, I think that Whites deserve to be held in contempt by Blacks). Finally, measures of psychological and social adjustment were assessed, including personal self-esteem. With these data, several structural equation models could be tested.

The model of greatest interest here assessed whether perceiving one's self as repeatedly likely to be discriminated against and excluded based on one's race protects well-being. Such protection could be either a direct effect of willingness to perceive prejudice, or an indirect one mediated by degree of minority group identification and disidentification with European Americans. Therefore a model assessing the impact of attributions to prejudice on self-esteem was tested with two mediators included—identification with the minority group and disidentifi-cation from the dominant group. For the completely mediated model, without any direct effect of attributions to prejudice on self-esteem being included, the comparative index of fit was .96, and the standardized residuals were .03, indicating that this model almost perfectly reproduced the data obtained. Adding the direct path from attributions to prejudice to self-esteem did not increase the degree of fit obtained. Thus, the relationship between willingness to make attributions to prejudice across a variety of situations and self-esteem among African Americans appears to depend on group identification processes. Increasing minority group identification and decreasing identification with European Americans appear to be important factors in the prediction of self-esteem in African Americans when increasing amounts of prejudice is perceived by them.

An alternative model, where the ordering of the initial predictor and the mediational variables were reversed was also examined. The possibility that high minority-group identification and hostility toward European Americans protect self-esteem because they encourage attributions to prejudice was not supported by these data. The fit for this second model, where attributions to prejudice was employed as the mediator of the two kinds of group identification effects on self-esteem, was significantly lower (comparative index of fit =.74) than was the previously tested ordering. Thus, we argue that when disadvantaged group members perceive themselves as being rejected in a variety of situations because of discrimination on the part of the dominant group, they feel both more hostility toward that outgroup, and they increasingly identify with their minority group. Such identification changes, especially increasing identification with one's minority group, predicts self-esteem in response to perceived discrimination.

Thus, strong attachment to one's devalued group can be an important buffer of the negative psychological effects that might otherwise accrue from feeling excluded by the dominant group. Banishment or rejection from important social groups and their activities leaves people vulnerable to alienation and a host of psychological disturbances (see Branscombe & Wann, 1991; Durkheim, 1897; Frable, 1993; Leary, Tambor, Terdal, & Downs, 1995). Therefore, those minority group members who perceive themselves to be victims of discrimination on the part of the mainstream and who also feel a lack of acceptance by the ingroup are likely to show significant signs of psychological impairment. Among Native Americans, low Indian identification and detachment from European American culture predict hopelessness and alcoholism (Berlin, 1987). Among Hispanic Americans, feeling rejected by mainstream culture and possessing a negative minority group identity is associated with the poorest self-esteem (Phinney, 1990, 1991). Finally, among African American women, we have found that those who feel excluded by their minority group and also perceive high discrimination from the majority exhibit significantly lower self-esteem than those who feel accepted by one group or the other (Branscombe & Harvey, 1996b). In other words, feeling accepted by a social group—either the minority or dominant group—appears to be critically important for well-being.

In sum, we argue that people who are highly identified with their group are not likely to dissociate themselves from the rest of the group when they perceive discrimination on the part of dominant group members. Although they may hold the conviction that they are being treated unjustly to the same degree as, or even more than, the low-identified person pursuing an individualistic goal, the highly identified are likely to defend their ingroup and derogate the outgroup when threatened (Branscombe & Wann, 1994; Turner, Hogg, Turner, & Smith, 1984; Wann & Branscombe, 1990). What is seen as unjust about discrimination, however, is likely to differ for these two types of group members. Discrimination will be perceived as wrong by the low identified because they believe that people should not treat them on the basis of a group membership. For the highly identified, anger will result from the belief that it is wrong to think of their group negatively. Therefore, we argue that the importance of a particular group to one's identity is a crucial determinant of how a discriminatory event will be perceived and how it will be coped with.

A MODEL OF STRATEGIC RESPONSES

In the remaining sections of the chapter, we briefly outline a theoretical model that details the multiple consequences that can flow from use of individualistic or group-level strategies of coping with discrimination. From our perspective, many different effects can follow from selecting different types of strategies, both immediately and across time. Although the model, shown in Table 11.1, points out the multiple effects that can occur when people are coping with disadvantage, this should *not* be interpreted as a stage model with a linear series of consecutive steps where processes that are described earlier constitute necessary conditions for later responses to occur. All of the possible indicators of the underlying processes will not be necessarily observed or tapped at the same time. Nevertheless, when multiple measures that should reflect use of the same strategy are employed in a single investigation, they should be correlated in a meaningful way. Thus, our model summarizes a wide array of different types of indices that can reflect the employment of the two classes of coping strategies.

ANTECEDENTS OF STRATEGY SELECTION

We have argued that strength of group identification is a crucial determinant of people's preferences for employing either individualistic or group-level strategies when faced with discrimination. An important question to consider then is how do differential levels of group identification arise? Low ingroup identification, and a resulting preference for pursuing personal self-esteem, are most likely to occur in majority groups (Brewer, 1991; McGuire, McGuire, Child, & Fujioka, 1978), groups in which members do not depend on each other for positive outcomes (Gurin, 1985; Rabbie, Benoist, Oosterbaan, & Visser, 1974), and those that have not suffered an unjust treatment or common failure (Ellemers *et al.*, 1993; Turner *et al.*, 1984). Conversely, strong ingroup identification, and a readiness to engage in group-level strategies to address social disadvantage, including pursuit

TABLE 11.1   Employment of Individualistic or Group-Level Strategies in Response to Group-Based Discrimination

	Type of Strategy	
	Group-level strategies	Individualistic strategies
Antecedents of strategy selection:		
Level of group identification	High group identification	Low group identification
Protection/enhancement goal	Group-based self-esteem	Personal self-esteem
Perceptual consequences:		
Preferred group social norms	Ingroup norms	Outgroup norms
Social judgments	Ingroup extremity	Outgroup extremity
Self-perception	Prototypical of ingroup	Atypical of ingroup
Interpretation of discrimination	Unjust group status	Unjust inclusion of self in group
Coping responses:		
Cognitive	Intergroup distinctiveness	Intergroup overlap
Emotional	Fraternal deprivation	Personal gratification
	Outgroup hostility	Ingroup hostility
Behavioral	Collective action	Individual mobility
	Work for group welfare	Work for own welfare
Long-term effects:		
Individual risks	Separatism	Marginalization
Individual benefits	Belongingness	Personal prestige and wealth
Social risks	Destabilize system	Legitimize system
Social benefits	Social change	Meritocracy

of group-based self-esteem, is most likely to occur in numerically smaller groups, and groups in which members experience outcome or fate interdependence (see Mullen, Brown, & Smith, 1992).

Cyclical Nature of Identification Processes

So far we have considered different responses as a function of initial level of identification. However, the psychological processes engaged in by disadvantaged group members may subsequently enhance or diminish ingroup identification. In other words, both from a theoretical and an empirical point of view, level of identification may be conceptualized as either an independent variable (cause of differential coping responses) or as a dependent variable (effect of strategy use). Consistent use of individualistic self-protection strategies is likely to further erode ingroup identification (Tajfel & Turner, 1986), while perceiving group-based discrimination and engaging in collective action can enhance a group identity (Branscombe & Harvey, 1996a; Klandermans, 1997). Group members who are initially highly identified with their group, maintain or increase their sense of identification over time, regardless of whether they believe the group's status can be improved or not (Spears, Doosje, & Ellemers, 1997). However, those who are initially low in identification, will *only* increase their identification with the ingroup when its low status is perceived as likely to improve in the future.

Because of the reinforcing nature of the use of individual versus group-level strategies, a basic incompatibility exists in employment of one of these two kinds of coping responses. In this regard, our model differs from other theoretical perspectives that maintain that there is a fixed order in which disadvantaged group members seek to address their plight, and that they will only undertake attempts at social change when individual mobility has proven to be almost completely impossible (cf. Taylor & McKirnan, 1984; Wright *et al.*, 1990). We argue, however, that highly identified group members will consistently prefer to employ group-level strategies rather than individualistic ones. Moreover, given the differential perceptions and responses involved, once people have committed themselves to one type of strategy or another, they may be unable to easily switch. Both because they may face sanctions from either their fellow ingroup members or the outgroup (depending on which strategy they have previously employed), and because doing so would require a fundamentally different conception of the self and the social structure, people may be locked into employing one class of strategies or the other.

PERCEPTUAL CONSEQUENCES

Preferred Group Social Norms and Social Judgments

People are generally inclined to adapt their social perceptions to the norms held by a group that they value (Hogg, Turner, & Davidson, 1990; Turner *et al.*, 1987). One recent investigation (Jetten, Spears, & Manstead, 1996) has revealed that highly identified group members are sensitive to the norms of their ingroup, whereas those who are low in identification are not. In fact, we would argue that, in the case of disadvantaged group members, those who are low in identification with the ingroup and who engage in individual mobility are likely to attend to and be guided by the norms of the higher status outgroup. For example, marginal group members who are uncertain about whether the powerful members of a group that they aspire to will accept them or not, conform to what they, at least, believe to be the norms of that group (Noel, Wann, & Branscombe, 1995). If derogation of their "former group" membership will convey to the powerful that they should be now considered one of them, then these aspiring group members will do so as long as the powerful can be expected to be aware of their actions. Thus, while people generally conform to the norms of the group in which they wish to gain or maintain acceptance, which group this is will vary for high- and low-identified disadvantaged group members. Those who are not identified with their low-status group will focus on and attempt to conform to the norms of the higher status outgroup, whereas those who are identified with the devalued group will focus on its norms.

Because of their heightened concern for the image of the ingroup, the highly identified exhibit ingroup extremity when judging the behavior of ingroup and outgroup targets, and this is especially the case when the value of the group is threatened (Branscombe, Wann, Noel, & Coleman, 1993). That is, the highly identified rate an ingroup member more positively when that target behaves in a desirable fashion compared to a similar outgroup member. When, however, an ingroup target's behavior reflects poorly on the group, such an ingroup "black sheep" is evaluated more negatively than a comparable outgroup target (see Marques & Paez, 1994, for a review). In contrast, low-identified group members show outgroup extremity in their evaluations of individuals, potentially because of their increased attentional focus on the outgroup and its norms. Accordingly, to the extent that minority group members are low in identification with their ingroup and are focused on being accepted by the higher status outgroup, they should evaluate dominant group members more extremely as a function of the consistency of their behavior with dominant group values that they too are striving to achieve, relative to comparable ingroup members. Thus, the social perceptions of disadvantaged group members are likely to vary depending on their level of identification with the ingroup, which dictates the group norms that are used as a guide when judging individual group members.

Self-Perception

Turning to the way people perceive themselves, there is evidence that the ingroup may either function as an ideal to which the person aspires, or as an image from which to distinguish the self. Again, level of ingroup identification constitutes the main determinant of how people are likely to define themselves in relation to the group prototype. Spears and colleagues (1997) conducted a series of studies demonstrating that, when confronted with a threat to their group membership, high- and low-identifying group members exhibit diverging self-definitions. Specifically, high identifiers showed more evidence of self-stereotyping in response to group threat, while low-identifying group members perceived themselves as less prototypical of the ingroup. Similar findings have been reported with national groups. Highly identified members of linguistic minorities, when faced with a threat from the dominant language group, are more likely to stereotype themselves as members of those groups by spontaneously adopting its language than are the low identified (Bourhis et al., 1979). Thus, depending on whether one identifies strongly with a group or not, self-stereotyping in terms of that group membership is differentially likely to occur.

Interpreting Discrimination

Devalued group members can elect to emphasize the personal qualities that they possess, as a means of differentiating themselves from other members of their ingroup. Thus, by thinking of themselves as independent individuals with valuable personal qualities, rather than as members of a disadvantaged social group, a positive *personal* identity can be achieved. This individualistic approach does, however, necessarily involve some amount of disidentification with the devalued ingroup. When persons using this strategy perceive themselves as experiencing discrimination from the dominant group, they are likely to interpret it as an affront to their ability to be considered in individualistic terms. As a consequence, perceived discrimination will be seen as illegitimate primarily because it involves *categorizing them as a member of a group* when they are not categorizing themselves at the group level.

Alternatively, one's sense of self-worth can be based on one's positive *social* identity. Brewer (1991) has suggested that group identification involves a shift in how the self is categorized: "What is painful at the individual level becomes a source of pride at the group level—a badge of distinction rather than a mark of shame" (p. 481). As a result of such group-level self-categorization, discrimination on the part of the dominant group, when experienced by disadvantaged group members, is likely to be perceived as illegitimate in a rather different sense than it is by those who think of the self at the individual level. When the self is conceptualized in group terms, the poor or discriminatory treatment that the *disadvantaged group as a whole experiences* will be focused on and seen as unfair or unjust. As a result, a sense of indignation on behalf of the group is likely to occur. Accordingly, we argue that collective action aimed at bringing about a change in the relations between the groups, as well as increasing hostility towards the outgroup, will both be more prominent in persons with a strong sense of group identification than in those who are less identified with the ingroup.

Such perceived "moral illegitimacy," which discrimination aimed at one's group can evoke, has played a powerful role in the historical development of social movements aimed at overthrowing colonial regimes and achieving civil rights for those who have been disenfranchised (see Davidson, 1992; Klandermans, 1997; MacKinnon, 1987; Steele, 1990). While it may be frustrating to be treated as a group member when the recipient would prefer to be responded to as an individual, it is unlikely to arouse such strong affective reactions or elicit sufficient commitment to engage in collective action. As Martin Luther King put it in his letter from a Birmingham jail in 1963, "human progress never rolls in on wheels of inevitability. It comes through the tireless efforts and persistent work of men [and women] willing to be co-workers with God." Such willingness to persist while working on behalf of a devalued group, even in the face of threats to the personal self, is significantly higher among high- versus low-group identifiers (Ellemers, Spears, & Doosje, 1997). Thus, high group identification, along with a focus on the the poor outcomes received by one's ingroup compared to another group (i.e., fraternal deprivation), are important precursors to participation in social protest actions that are aimed at improving the status of the ingroup as a whole (Guimond & Dubé-Simard, 1983; Tougas & Veilleux, 1988; Walker & Pettigrew, 1984).

COPING STRATEGIES

Cognitive Responses

Differential cognitive responses have been observed among low-status group members, depending on their level of ingroup identification. For example, Doosje and colleagues (1993) found that low-identified group members emphasize the hetereogeneity of the ingroup, as well as the outgroup. They also perceive the overlap between the two groups as greater than do those who are high in identification. Highly identified group members, in contrast, respond to their group's low status by accentuating the homogeneity within each of the groups, and by focusing on the distinctiveness of each group. Hence, the highly identified literally think more in intergroup terms than do the low identified. Such increased perceived homogeneity among the highly identified may encourage conformity to the ingroup's norms, partly because what the ingroup expects may seem more clear-cut than it does to the low identified who see the two groups as more similar.

Emotional Responses

When we turn to the emotional responses disadvantaged group members may show, again, we can distinguish between high identifiers who are more likely to be frustrated with the relative positions of the groups, and low identifiers who may report gratification with their own personal outcomes (see Smith *et al.*, 1994), but feel frustration as a consequence of inclusion of the self in the devalued group. In addition, emotional responses to the outgroup will vary by level of group identification. Branscombe and Harvey (1996a) found that hostility toward European Americans was significantly and positively correlated with degree of African American racial identification ($r = +.35$). Thus, high hostility toward the outgroup is more likely among disadvantaged group members who identify strongly with their ingroup. Likewise, in another social context entirely, differential emotional responses for negative outcomes have been observed, depending on degree of group identification (cf. De Weerd, Ellemers, & Klandermans, 1996). Farmers in two different European countries (the Netherlands and Spain), expressed more hostility about their perceived disadvantage when they were high versus low in identification with their occcupational group.

Behavioral Responses

A fundamental difference exists in terms of the behavioral responses that are displayed by high- and low-identifying members of disadvantaged groups. Specifically, low identification results in pursuit of individual mobility, while strong identification can result in action aimed at bringing about social change. For instance, Ellemers and colleagues (1993) found that low-identifying group members, who contest their inclusion in a lower status group, are relatively willing to leave their fellow ingroup members behind when presented with an opportunity to do so. When ingroup identification is relatively strong, however, and group members consider the inferior status of their group to be unjust, opportunities for social change elicit behavior that is aimed at improving the welfare of the ingroup. As Lalonde and Cameron (1994) report, those people who define themselves in terms of a group membership are more likely to take action rather than passively accept discrimination, relative to persons who do not define themselves in group terms, or compared to those who define the situation in interpersonal rather than intergroup terms.

Nevertheless, even if a high degree of group identification is present, if the means of bringing about social change are unavailable, the costs of protest are too high, or like-minded others are absent, then collective action may not be undertaken (Klandermans, 1997; Martin, 1986). Group identification may be only one of several preconditions that are necessary for collective action to actually occur, although identification may strengthen the belief that others will also join in if social protest actions are undertaken. Thus, those farmers who felt solidarity with other farmers in Europe, displayed higher expectations that others would join them and that collective action would be successful at bringing about improvements in their group's position (De Weerd *et al.*, 1996). Such perceptions, where other ingroup members are seen as experiencing the same unjust treatment as oneself, are similar conceptually to the notion of common fate, which has been found to be an important precursor of collective action among Hispanic Americans (Gurin, Hurtado, & Peng, 1994).

LONG-TERM EFFECTS

Individual Risks and Benefits

The disadvantaged person who attempts to evade the taint of a lower status group by engaging in individual mobility could be vulnerable on several fronts. First, it is uncertain whether attempts to separate the self from the group will be successful or not. When discrimination is prevalent, devalued group members may be actually rejected by the higher status group with some frequency, or they might only achieve marginal acceptance, both of which pose a threat to well-being. Second, it is not clear that attributing negative outcomes to prejudice will consistently result in self-esteem protection among disadvantaged group members. In fact, the use of such attributions may provoke problems of a different sort; in particular, dominant group members may be especially likely to reject devalued group members who voice prejudical explanations for their outcomes. Experiencing a self-presentational dilemma of this sort—making attributions to prejudice as an attempt to protect the personal self, which might potentially evoke the ire of dominant group members—could be stressful in its own right.

In addition, further reductions in ingroup identification, which are likely to be the result of using an individualistic coping strategy, might even leave the individual vulnerable to rejection by the ingroup. To the extent that previous attempts to distance the self from a low-status ingroup become known to other ingroup members, particularly if the low identifier has publicly derogated the ingroup, then that individual may be no longer welcomed by his or her ingroup. Because the ingroup may not accept an individual it perceives as a "traitor," the low identifier may find it impossible to subsequently realign the self with the ingroup after attempting individual mobility. Highly identified ingroup members may be especially vigilant at detecting individualistic responses in other ingroup members and reject them for their disloyal behavior (see Branscombe *et al.*, 1993). Therefore, those who use an individualistic strategy may be not only rejected by and experience discrimination from the dominant group, they may be also cut off from their ingroup, which could otherwise serve as a source of support and well-being. As a result of perceiving themselves as being rejected by both the dominant group that they aspire to, and the minority group that they have distanced themselves from, feelings of alienation and depression are a real risk for those who do disidentify with their disadvantaged group. On the other hand, persons employing an individualistic strategy can potentially gain a number of benefits, particularly if discrimination against them is not especially severe. Specifically, individually mobile persons may well achieve considerable personal prestige and wealth as a result of their successful adaptation to the higher status group, and they might even be admired by, or serve as role models for, other upwardly mobile ingroup members.

There is also a set of risks and benefits for the individual who employs group-level strategies. High group identification encourages attendance to ingroup norms, accentuation of ingroup distinctiveness on alternative dimensions, and hostility toward the outgroup. A self-imposed separation from the outgroup may be comforting for those who systematically experience discrimination because both validation of group-worth and a sense of belongingness can be provided, although such separatism is not without risk. To the extent that the dominant group defines the rules and controls access to valued outcomes, a lack of attention to outgroup norms and negation of possible intergroup similarities, can be harmful to the individual, precluding him or her from capitalizing on the opportunities that may actually exist (Steele, 1990). As is the case with individualistic strategies, these risks may prevent the individual from changing tactics after having worked to attain social change. The person who employs group-level strategies may gain a reputation among dominant group members as an "extremist" or a "troublemaker" which would block any hope that they might harbor of being accepted into the higher status group.

Social Risks and Benefits

Considering first the risks and benefits associated with the use of individualistic strategies, it is important to note that while individual mobility might seem to be a feasible option in principle, the actual reality often is that only a few token members are selectively admitted by the higher status group. Thus, the continuation of subtle discrimination is a risk of this strategy. Furthermore, instead of eventually providing an avenue for social change, as is often assumed, such selective individual mobility may mainly serve to suggest that existing status differences are just, while the system is not in fact providing equal chances for all (cf. Hogg & Abrams, 1988; Jost & Banaji, 1994). In fact, dominant groups may point to successful tokens as a means of substantiating their claim that the system is fair and only rewards individual merit. In this situation, disadvantaged group members who have not been admitted to the higher status group may be blamed for their predicament. On the other hand, the possible benefits that can be obtained, if individual mobility is achievable by all who are both capable and willing, is that it constitutes a meritocracy in its ideal form; such a just and tolerant society might breed high levels of loyalty and pride.

Employment of group-level strategies entails the risk of major social conflict within the larger society. When multiple groups undertake collective action to improve their social standing, it challenges the existing order, which can ultimately destabilize the overall social system. Tension between factions or different status groups has destabilized the economies of various countries recently, in varying degrees, including Canada, Lebanon, Rwanda, South Africa, and Yugoslavia, to name just a few. Such fundamental disagreements about what is just or unjust may undermine the bonds that are necessary to hold a multicultural society together, which can potentially escalate into violent conflict or total social disintegration. The reason such risks are taken, though, is the potential magnitude of the social benefits that group-level action may bring about. Successful achievement of social change obviously holds immediate rewards for the formerly disadvantaged group. In addition, in the long run, a more equitable society may be seen as desirable and beneficial to even those who stand to lose their group-based privileges (e.g., the White minority in South Africa), even though short-term sacrifices of personal benefits may be required (see Feagin & Vera, 1995; Smith & Tyler, 1996).

CONCLUSIONS

Disadvantaged group members can respond to perceived rejection and discrimination on the part of the dominant group by employing individualistic strategies that salvage their personal identities but that are also likely to encourage distancing from their ingroup. Alternatively, the use of group-level strategies can further elevate identification with the devalued group. Different goals encourage selection of one type of strategy over the other. Individualistic strategies are aimed at improving one's own personal status and self-esteem, whereas the aim of group-level strategies is to improve the overall welfare of the group and its position in the social structure.

Discrimination can be interpreted by its targets in different ways, resulting in fundamentally different types of threats to identity—either personal or social. We suggested that only when disadvantaged group members perceive prejudice as a threat to their personal identity will they attempt to distance themselves from their devalued group and be motivated primarily by the goal of protecting their personal self-esteem. When discrimination is interpreted as an offense against one's social identity, ingroup ties are likely to be strengthened, and this can provide an alternative route to well-being. Therefore, we suggest that level of group identification is a key determinant of how people respond to group-based discrimination.

We also speculated about the long-term consequences of these different types of responses to perceived discrimination, concluding that disidentification with the disadvantaged group can decrease the likelihood that the actual relations between the groups ultimately will be altered. Nevertheless, for the individuals involved, improving their personal social status and material wealth are obvious major benefits. When, however, the disadvantaged ingroup identity is made salient and the possibility of group-level change is cognitively available, negative evaluations of the ingroup on the part of a higher status outgroup, can result in responses that are directed at improving the social status of the ingroup as a whole. In the long run, such collective action may also elevate ingroup cohesion, which is needed if changes in the social system are to be brought about. Thus, attachment to a disadvantaged ingroup is an alternative, and an equally or even more important, means by which devalued group members can achieve a positive identity and sense of self-worth. However, compared to the disidentification of the upwardly mobile, engaging in social competition potentially involves psychological and material costs for the specific individuals involved. Dominant groups may respond defensively and attempt to strike back at those highly identified group members who push for social change. Increasing derogation in response to perceived threats to the status quo is possible (cf. Branscombe & Wann, 1994), as is the risk of physical harm (see Feagin & Vera, 1995; Klandermans, 1997).

Beginning with the different goals that drive the strategy selection of the high and low identified, we illustrated the different perceptual consequences that can follow from employment of these two types of strategies. Those who employ group-level strategies are guided by the norms of the ingroup, they exhibit ingroup extremity when making intergroup judgments, and they interpret perceived discrimination differently than those who are employing more individualistic strategies. Depending on whether discrimination is seen as a threat to the individual's personal or social identity, different cognitive, emotional, and behavioral consequences can be expected. Our analysis calls for a wider array of measures to be assessed in future research than has been thus far. Because well-being may be protected by employing either individualistic or group-level strategies, tapping the varied and multiple consequences that can result is essential if we are to develop new insights into the psychological processes that are operating when the disadvantaged cope with discrimination.

REFERENCES

Baumeister, R. F., & Leary, M. R. (1995). The need to belong: Desire for interpersonal attachments as a fundamental human motivation. *Psychological Bulletin, 117,* 497–529.

Berlin, I. N. (1987). Effects of changing Native American cultures on child development. *Journal of Community Psychology, 15,* 299–306.

Bourhis, R. Y., Giles, H., Leyens, J. P., & Tajfel, H. (1979). Psycholinguistic distinctiveness: Language divergence in Belgium. In H. Giles & R. St. Clair (Ed.), *Language and social psychology* (pp. 158–185). Oxford: Blackwell.

Bowlby, J. (1969). *Attachment and loss, Vol. 1: Attachment.* New York: Basic Books.

Branscombe, N. R. (in press). Thinking about one's gender group privileges or disadvantages: Consequences for well-being in women and men. *British Journal of Social Psychology, 37.*

Branscombe, N. R., & Harvey, R. (1996a). *Coping with perceived prejudice among African-Americans: Implications for minority group identification and well-being.* Unpublished manuscript, University of Kansas.

Branscombe, N. R., & Harvey, R. (1996b). *Attributions to gender and racial discrimination among African-American women.* Unpublished data, University of Kansas.

Branscombe, N. R., Schiffhauer, K., & Valencia, L. (1997). *Thinking about White privilege or disadvantage, degree of White racial identification, and intergroup relations beliefs for feelings about the ingroup and outgroup.* Manuscript submitted for publication.

Branscombe, N. R., & Wann, D. L. (1991). The positive social and self concept consequences of sports team identification. *Journal of Sport and Social Issues, 15,* 115–127.

Branscombe, N. R., & Wann, D. L. (1994). Collective self-esteem consequences of outgroup derogation when a valued social identity is on trial. *European Journal of Social Psychology, 24,* 641–657.

Branscombe, N. R., Wann, D. L., Noel, J. G., & Coleman, J. (1993). In-group or out-group extremity: Importance of the threatened social identity. *Personality and Social Psychology Bulletin, 19,* 381–388.

Brewer, M. B. (1991). The social self: On being the same and different at the same time. *Personality and Social Psychology Bulletin, 17,* 475–482.

Brewer, M. B. (1997). On the social origins of human nature. In C. McGarty & S. A. Haslam (Eds.), *The message of social psychology* (pp. 54–62). Oxford: Blackwell.

Clark, K., & Clark, M. (1947). Racial identification and preference in Negro children. In T. Newcomb & E. Hartley (Eds.), *Readings in social psychology* (pp. 551–560). New York: Holt.

Crocker, J., & Major, B. (1989). Social stigma and self-esteem: The self-protective properties of stigma. *Psychological Review, 96,* 608–630.

Crocker, J., & Major, B. (1994). Reactions to stigma: The moderating role of justifications. In M. P. Zanna & J. M. Olson (Eds.), *The psychology of prejudice: The Ontario symposium,* Vol. 7 (pp. 289–314). Hillsdale, NJ: Erlbaum.

Crocker, J., Voelkl, K., Testa, M., & Major, B. (1991). Social stigma: The affective consequences of attributional ambiguity. *Journal of Personality and Social Psychology, 60,* 218–228.

Crosby, F. (1982). *Relative deprivation among working women.* New York: Oxford University Press.

Crosby, F. (1984). The denial of personal discrimination. *American Behavioral Scientist, 27,* 371–386.

Davidson, B. (1992). *The Black man's burden: Africa and the curse of the nation-state.* New York: Random House.

Deaux, K., & Major, B. (1987). Putting gender into context: An interactive model of gender-related behavior. *Psychological Review, 94,* 369–389.

De Gilder, D., & Wilke, H. A. (1994). Expectation states theory and the motivational determinants of social influence. In W. Stroebe & M. Hewstone (Eds.), *European Review of Social Psychology,* Vol. 5 (pp 243–269). New York: Wiley & Sons.

De Weerd, M., Ellemers, N., & Klandermans, B. (1996). Rationele en emotionele determinanten van de intentie tot participatie in collectieve actie onder Nederlandse en Spaanse boeren. *Sociale Psychologie en haar toepassingen, 10,* 138–149. (Rational and emotional determinants of the intention to participate in collective action among Dutch and Spanish farmers.)

Doise, W. (1988). Individual and social identities in intergroup relations. *European Journal of Social Psychology, 18,* 999–1111.

Doosje, B., & Ellemers, N. (1997). Stereotyping under threat: The role of group identification. In R. Spears, P. Oakes, N. Ellemers & S. A. Haslam (Eds.), *The social psychology of stereotyping and group life* (pp. 257–272). Oxford: Blackwell.

Doosje, B., Ellemers, N., & Spears, R. (1995). Perceived intragroup variability as a function of group status and identification. *Journal of Experimental Social Psychology, 31,* 410–436.

Durkheim, E. (1897). *Suicide: A study in sociology.* New York: Free Press.

Eagly, A. H. (1987). *Sex differences in social behavior: A social-role interpretation.* Hillsdale, NJ: Erlbaum.

Ellemers, N. (1993). The influence of socio-structural variables on identity management strategies. In W. Stroebe & M. Hewstone (Eds.), *European Review of Social Psychology*, Vol. 4 (pp. 27–58). New York: Wiley & Sons.

Ellemers, N., Doosje, B., Van Knippenberg, A., & Wilke, H. (1992). Status protection in high status minorities. *European Journal of Social Psychology, 22*, 123–140.

Ellemers, N., Spears, R., & Doosje, B. (1997). Sticking together or falling apart: Group identification as a psychological determinant of group commitment versus individual mobility. *Journal of Personality and Social Psychology, 72*, 617–626.

Ellemers, N., Van Knippenberg, A., De Vries, N., & Wilke, H. (1988). Social identification and permeability of group boundaries. *European Journal of Social Psychology, 18*, 497–513.

Ellemers, N., Van Knippenberg, A., & Wilke, H. (1990). The influence of permeability of group boundaries and stability of group status on strategies of individual mobility and social change. *British Journal of Social Psychology, 29*, 233–246.

Ellemers, N., & Van Rijswijk, W. (1997). Identity versus social opportunities: The use of group level and individual level identity management strategies. *Social Psychology Quarterly, 60*, 52–65.

Ellemers, N., Van Rijswijk, W., Roefs, M., & Simons, C. (1997). Bias in intergroup perceptions: Balancing group identity with social reality. *Personality and Social Psychology Bulletin, 23*, 186–198.

Ellemers, N., Wilke, H., & Van Knippenberg, A. (1993). Effects of the legitimacy of low group or individual status on individual and collective status-enhancement strategies. *Journal of Personality and Social Psychology, 64*, 766–778.

Feagin, J. R., & Vera, H. (1995). *White racism*. New York: Routledge.

Frable, D. E. S. (1993). Being and feeling unique: Statistical deviance and psychological marginality. *Journal of Personality, 61*, 85–110.

Guimond, S., & Dubé-Simard, L. (1983). Relative deprivation theory and the Quebec Nationalist Movement: The cognition-emotion distinction and the personal-group deprivation issue. *Journal of Personality and Social Psychology, 44*, 526–535.

Gurin, P. (1985). Women's gender consciousness. *Public Opinion Quarterly, 49*, 143–163.

Gurin, P., Hurtado, A., & Peng, T. (1994). Group contacts and ethnicity in the social identities of Mexicans and Chicanos. *Personality and Social Psychology Bulletin, 20*, 521–532.

Hogg, M., & Abrams, D. (1988). *Social identifications: A social psychology of intergroup relations and group processes*. New York: Routledge.

Hogg, M. A., Turner, J. C., & Davidson, B. (1990). Polarized norms and social frames of reference: A test of the self-categorization theory of group polarization. *Basic and Applied Social Psychology, 11*, 77–100.

Jackson, L. A., Sullivan, L. A., Harnish, R., & Hodge, C. N. (1996). Achieving positive social identity: Social mobility, social creativity, and permeability of group boundaries. *Journal of Personality and Social Psychology, 70*, 241–254.

Jetten, J., Spears, R., & Manstead, A. S. R. (1996). Intergroup norms and intergroup discrimination: Distinctive self-categorization and social identity effects. *Journal of Personality and Social Psychology, 71*, 1222–1233.

Jost, J. T., & Banaji, M. R. (1994). The role of stereotyping in system-justification and the production of false consciousness. *British Journal of Social Psychology, 33*, 1–17.

Kappen, D., & Branscombe, N. R. (1997). *Reasons for gender-based exclusion: Impact on attributions and emotions*. Manuscript submitted for publication.

Kite, M. E., Deaux, K., & Miele, M. (1991). Stereotypes of young and old: Does age outweigh gender? *Psychology and Aging, 6*, 19–27.

Klandermans, B. (1997). *The social psychology of protest*. Oxford: Blackwell.

Kobrynowicz, D., & Branscombe, N. R. (1997). Who considers themselves victims of discrimination? Individual difference predictors of perceived gender discrimination in women and men. *Psychology of Women Quarterly, 21*, 347–363.

Lalonde, R. N., & Cameron, J. E. (1994). Behavioral responses to discrimination: A focus on action. In M. P. Zanna & J. M. Olson (Eds.), *The psychology of prejudice: The Ontario symposium,* Vol. 7 (pp. 257–288). Hillsdale, NJ: Erlbaum.

Lalonde, R. N., & Silverman, R. A. (1994). Behavioral preferences in response to social injustice: The effects of group permeability and social identity salience. *Journal of Personality and Social Psychology, 66,* 78–85.

Landrine, H., & Klonoff, E. A. (1996). The schedule of racist events: A measure of racial discrimination and a study of its negative physical and mental health consequences. *Journal of Black Psychology, 22,* 144–168.

Landrine, H., Klonoff, E. A., Gibbs, J., Manning, V., & Lund, M. (1995). Physical and psychiatric correlates of gender discrimination: An application of the schedule of sexist events. *Psychology of Women Quarterly, 19,* 473–492.

Leary, M., Tambor, E. S., Terdal, S. K., & Downs, D. L. (1995). Self-esteem as an interpersonal monitor: The sociometer hypothesis. *Journal of Personality and Social Psychology, 68,* 518–530.

Lemaine, G. (1974). Social differentiation and social originality. *European Journal of Social Psychology, 4,* 17–52.

Lewin, K. (1948). *Resolving social conflicts.* New York: Harper.

MacKinnon, C. (1987). *Feminism unmodified: Discourses on life and law.* Cambridge, MA: Harvard University Press.

Major, B. (1994). From social inequality to personal entitlement: The role of social comparisons, legitimacy appraisals, and group memberships. In M.P. Zanna (Ed.), *Advances in experimental social psychology,* Vol. 26 (pp. 293–355). New York: Academic Press.

Major, B., & Crocker, J. (1993). Social stigma: The consequences of attributional ambiguity. In D. M. Mackie & D. L. Hamilton (Eds.), *Affect, cognition, and stereotyping: Interactive processes in group perception* (pp. 345–370). Orlando, FL: Academic Press.

Marques, J. M., & Paez, D. (1994). The "black sheep effect": Social categorization, rejection of ingroup deviates, and perception of group variability. In W. Stroebe & M. Hewstone (Eds.), *European Review of Social Psychology,* Vol. 5 (pp. 37–68). New York: Wiley & Sons.

Martin, J. (1986). The tolerance of injustice. In J. M. Olson, C. P. Herman & M. P. Zanna (Eds.), *Relative deprivation and social comparison: The Ontario symposium,* Vol. 4 (pp. 217–242). Hillsdale, NJ: Erlbaum.

McGuire, W. J., McGuire, C. V., Child, P., & Fujioka, T. (1978). Salience of ethnicity in the spontaneous self-concept as a function of one's ethnic distinctiveness in the social environment. *Journal of Personality and Social Psychology, 36,* 511–520.

Mlicki, P., & Ellemers, N. (1996). Being different or being better? National stereotypes and identifications of Polish and Dutch students. *European Journal of Social Psychology, 26,* 97–114.

Mullen, B., Brown, R., & Smith, C. (1992). Ingroup bias as a function of salience, relevance, and status: An integration. *European Journal of Social Psychology, 22,* 103–122.

Mummendey, A., & Schreiber, H. J. (1983). Better or just different? Positive social identity by discrimination against or differentiation from outgroups. *European Journal of Social Psychology, 13,* 389–397.

Mummendey, A., & Schreiber, H. J. (1984). "Different" just means "better": Some obvious and some hidden pathways to ingroup favouritism. *British Journal of Social Psychology, 23,* 363–368.

Mummendey, A., & Simon, B. (1989). Better or just different? III: The impact of comparison dimension and relative group size upon intergroup discrimination. *British Journal of Social Psychology, 28,* 1–16.

Noel, J. G., Wann, D. L., & Branscombe, N. R. (1995). Peripheral ingroup membership status and public negativity toward outgroups. *Journal of Personality and Social Psychology, 68,* 127–137.

Oakes, P., Haslam, S. A., & Turner, J. C. (1994). *Stereotyping and social reality.* Cambridge, MA: Blackwell.

Phinney, J. S. (1990). Ethnic identity in adolescents and adults: Review of research. *Psychological Bulletin, 108,* 499–514.

Phinney, J. S. (1991). Ethnic identity and self-esteem: A review and integration. *Hispanic Journal of Behavioral Sciences, 13,* 193–208.

Rabbie, J. M., Benoist, F., Oosterbaan, H., & Visser, L. (1974). Differential power and effects of expected competitive and cooperative intergroup interaction upon intragroup and outgroup attitudes. *Journal of Personality and Social Psychology, 30,* 46–56.

Ruggiero, K. M., & Taylor, D. M. (1995). Coping with discrimination: How disadvantaged group members perceive the discrimination that confronts them. *Journal of Personality and Social Psychology, 68,* 826–838.

Ruggiero, K. M., & Taylor, D. M. (1997). Why minority group members perceive or do not perceive the discrimination that confronts them: The role of self-esteem and perceived control. *Journal of Personality and Social Psychology, 72,* 373–389.

Seligman, M. E. P. (1975). *On depression, development, and death.* San Francisco, CA: Freeman.

Simon, B. (1997). Self and group in modern society: Ten theses on the individual and the collective self. In R. Spears, P. Oakes, N. Ellemers, & S. A. Haslam (Eds.), *The social psychology of stereotyping and group life* (pp. 318–335). Oxford: Blackwell.

Smith, H. J., Spears, R., & Oyen, M. (1994). "People like us:" The influence of personal deprivation and group membership salience on justice evaluations. *Journal of Experimental Social Psychology, 30,* 277–299.

Smith, H. J., & Tyler, T. R. (1996). Justice and power: When will justice concerns encourage the advantaged to support policies which redistribute economic resources and the disadvantaged to willingly obey the law? *European Journal of Social Psychology, 26,* 171–200.

Spears, R., Doosje, B., & Ellemers, N. (1997). Self-stereotyping in the face of threats to group status and distinctiveness: The role of group identification. *Personality and Social Psychology Bulletin, 23,* 538–553.

Spears, R., & Manstead, A. S. R. (1989). The social context of stereotyping and differentiation. *European Journal of Social Psychology, 19,* 101–121.

Steele, S. (1990). *The content of our character: A new vision of race in America.* New York: Harper Collins.

Stevens, L. E., & Fiske, S. T. (1995). Motivation and cognition in social life: A social survival perspective. *Social Cognition, 13,* 189–214.

Tajfel, H. (1974). Social identity and intergroup behavior. *Social Science Information, 13,* 65–93.

Tajfel, H. (1975). The exit of social mobility and the voice of social change. *Social Science Information, 14,* 101–118.

Tajfel, H. (1978). *The social psychology of the minority.* New York: Minority Rights Group.

Tajfel, H. (1981). *Human groups and social categories.* Cambridge: Cambridge University Press.

Tajfel, H., & Turner, J. C. (1979). An integrative theory of intergroup conflict. In W. G. Austin & S. Worchel (Eds.), *The social psychology of intergroup relations* (pp. 33–47). Monterey, CA: Brooks/Cole.

Tajfel, H., & Turner, J. C. (1986). The social identity theory of intergroup behavior. In S. Worchel & W. G. Austin (Eds.), *Psychology of intergroup relations* (pp. 7–24). Chicago, IL: Nelson-Hall.

Taylor, D. M., & McKirnan, D. J. (1984). A five-stage model of intergroup relations. *British Journal of Social Psychology, 23,* 291–300.

Taylor, D. M., & Moghaddam, F. M. (1994). *Theories of intergroup relations: International social psychological perspectives* (2nd ed.). Westport, CT: Praeger.

Tougas, F., & Veilleux, F. (1988). The influence of identification, collective relative deprivation, and procedure of implementation on women's response to affirmative action: A causal modelling approach. *Canadian Journal of Behavioral Science, 20,* 15–28.

Turner, J. C. (1985). Social categorization and the self-concept: A social cognitive theory of group behavior. In E. J. Lawler (Ed.), *Advances in group processes: Theory and research,* Vol. 2 (pp. 77–121). Greenwich, CT: JAI Press.

Turner, J. C., Hogg, M. A., Oakes, P. J., Reicher, S., & Wetherell, M. (1987). *Rediscovering the social group: A self-categorization theory.* Oxford: Blackwell.

Turner, J. C., Hogg, M. A., Turner, P. J., & Smith, P. M. (1984). Failure and defeat as determinants of group cohesiveness. *British Journal of Social Psychology, 23,* 97–111.

Van Knippenberg, A. (1989). Strategies of identity management. In J. P. Van Oudenhoven & T. M. Willemsen (Eds.), *Ethnic minorities: Social psychological perspectives* (pp. 59–76). Amsterdam: Swets & Zeitlinger.

Van Twuyver, M., & Van Knippenberg, A. (1995). Social categorization as a function of priming. *European Journal of Social Psychology, 25,* 695–702.

Wann, D. L., & Branscombe, N. R. (1990). Die-hard and fair-weather fans: Effects of identification on BIRGing and CORFing tendencies. *Journal of Sport and Social Issues, 14,* 103–117.

Walker, I., & Pettigrew, T. F. (1984). Relative deprivation theory: An overview and conceptual critique. *British Journal of Social Psychology, 23,* 301–311.

Weiner, B. (1982). The emotional consequences of causal attributions. In M. S. Clark & S. T. Fiske (Eds.), *Affect and cognition: The 17th annual Carnegie symposium on cognition* (pp. 185–209). Hillsdale, NJ: Erlbaum.

Wills, T. A. (1981). Downward comparison principles of social psychology. *Psychological Bulletin, 90,* 245–271.

Wright, S. C., Taylor, D. M., & Moghaddam, F. M. (1990). Responding to membership in a disadvantaged group: From acceptance to collective protest. *Journal of Personality and Social Psychology, 58,* 994–1003.

12

THE EVERYDAY FUNCTIONS
OF AFRICAN
AMERICAN IDENTITY

WILLIAM E. CROSS, JR.

University of Massachusetts at Amherst

LINDA STRAUSS

The Pennsylvania State University

After I had outlived the shocks of childhood, after the habit of reflection had been born in me, I used to mull over the strange absence of real kindness in Negroes, how unstable was our tenderness, how lacking in genuine passion we were, how void of great hope, how timid our joy, how bare our traditions, how hollow our memories, how lacking we were in those intangible sentiments that bind [person to person], and how shallow was even our despair.

—*Richard Wright,* Black Boy, *p. 43*

But I am NOT tragically colored. There is no great sorrow dammed up in my soul, nor lurking behind my eyes. I do not mind at all. I do not belong to the sobbing school of Negrohood who hold that nature somehow has given them a lowdown dirty deal and whose feelings are all hurt about it. Even in the helter-skelter skirmish that is my life, I have seen that the world is to the strong regardless of a little pigmentation more or less. No, I do not weep at the world—I am too busy sharpening my oyster knife.

—*Zora Neale Hurston,* I Love Myself When I Am Laughing, *p. 153*

INTRODUCTION

Beginning in the late 1930s (Horowitz, 1939) and carrying over into the 1940s (Clark & Clark, 1947) and 1950s (Kardiner & Ovesey, 1951), stigma and internalized racism marked the starting point for the social scientific discourse on Black identity development and psychological functioning (Gordon, 1976). Complimenting the worldview of the famous novelist, Richard Wright, psychologists of his day took for granted that slavery had smashed the Negro's African culture and psychological foundation, forcing African Americans to construct a social identity that was imitative, shallow, barren of cultural integrity, and readily penetrated by the negative psychological messages of the larger white society. In effect, *stigma management and damage* became synonymous with Black identity. By analogy, it was as if one could discuss the nature of Jewish identity by solely focusing on anti-Semitism, without ever making reference to Jewish culture, suggesting that anti-Semitism and Jewish identity are one and the same.

In the aftermath of the Civil Rights (1954–1965) and Black Power (1965–1973) phases of the Contemporary Black Social Movement (1954–1975), researchers (Cross, 1991; Helms, 1990) and lay observers (Murray, 1970) alike began to reject the "Bigger Thomas" or as Wright's nemesis, Zora Neale Hurston, would say, the sobbing school of Negrohood, and replaced it with a complex, multifaceted conceptual scheme of Black psychological functioning that made possible effective stigma management, supportive social networking, collective indignation and protest, and Black cultural celebration. Reflective of this perspective was the wonderful article by the late Edward J. Barnes (1972) entitled: "The Black Community as a Source of Positive Self-Concept for Black Children." Barnes was ahead of his time, but in short order, the research literature began to keep pace, especially in the publication of study after study that showed that African Americans were capable of achieving average and sometimes higher than average levels of self-esteem despite everyday racist encounters (Rosenberg & Simmons, 1971; Cross, 1991).

In moving toward a more balanced depiction of Black identity dynamics, the role of stigma in the everyday experiences of Black people has not been lost on theorists, rather issues of stigma, pride, cultural resources as well as vulnerability are depicted as different aspects of the same phenomena, that is, Black identity. More importantly, it is no longer assumed that stigma and internalized racism are one and the same. Stigma is associated with a situation or predicament that has the potential for delimiting the response options of the person toward whom the stigmatization is directed, but as Crocker, Major, and Steele (1996) point out,

No internalization of the stigmatizing stereotype is necessary for this predicament to influence the persons experience. And coping responses that stigmatized individuals use in these situations are coping strategies that non-stigmatized individuals use when faced with self-threats. Although these coping responses have costs for the stigmatized, both psychological and otherwise, these costs are more context-specific, less internalized and permanent, and less inevitable and universal than is often assumed. (Crocker, Major, & Steele, 1996, p. 2)

The purpose of this chapter is to introduce a stigma management perspective associated with the lives of African Americans that is an outgrowth of Nigrescence theory (Cross, 1991; Cross, 1995; Cross, Parham, & Helms, 1991; Helms, 1990). Nigrescence is a French term that means the psychological and existential process of becoming Black. It is a process that maps the psychological steps some African Americans traverse in movement from a reference group orientation or social identity for which being Black and Black culture play an insignificant role in their self-concept dynamics, to a group identity for which race and black culture are central. Not every Black American is in need of Nigrescence, especially if their youthful socialization experiences fostered a rich set of perceptions about a multitude of race-related issues and challenges. However, for reasons that have been addressed elsewhere (Cross & Fhagen-Smith, 1996; Helms, 1990), many Blacks discover, at adolescence or some later point of the life span, that the worldview they evolved to date does not, in fact, address a number of cognitive and affective challenges that are related to one's perceptions about race and Black culture. Nigrescence is an identity conversion experience designed to increase the salience of race and Black culture in the organization of the person's worldview. Nigrescence models commence with an analysis of the types of identities found in Blacks for which race and Black culture are not a driving force, followed by a discussion of the types of triggering events which may cause the person to become more race and Black-culture sensitive. This triggering or encounter experience leads to an immersion experience during which the person tries to completely and radically change one's worldview, while making every effort to isolate and destroy, psychologically speaking, those aspects of the old identity from which the person now is estranged. If the transition stage is successful and the person cuts a successful psychological path toward a new identity, a final stage, internalization/commitment, is achieved, marking the habituation and internalization of the new reference group orientation. Once this foundational identity is intact, continued identity development is not precluded. Parham (1989) has modified basic Nigrescence theory to show how different identity challenges across the life span may stimulate a form of "recycling" through several of the middle stages, resulting in further expansion of the person's reference group orientation.

As an aside, we note that Nigrescence theory has stimulated the construction of identity development models that are applicable to the Latino/Latina, Asian American, disabled, feminist, and gay and lesbian experiences. For example, stage dynamics similar to those found in the original Nigrescence models have been successfully grafted to the phases of the coming-out process for gays and lesbians (Button, 1996).

IDENTITY FUNCTIONS

Recently three major Nigrescence theorists reviewed the theoretical and empirical literature associated with Nigrescence (Cross, Parham, & Helms, 1995), and part of their analysis focused on a multidimensional and psychodynamic interpretation of the way Black identity functions in everyday life, following a successful Nigrescence episode. Each function reticulates certain cognitions, feelings, and action plans. The cognitive component of a function refers to the ideas a person holds about racism, Black people, Black culture, and the Black experience, the affective component points to the emotions linked to such ideas, and finally, from a behavioral point of view, "function" means the action choices that logically follow from the fusion of ideas and emotions, as stimulated by various context variables. That their interpretation stresses not one but a series of functions, makes it multidimensional, and that it links the psychological properties (cognitions, emotions, and behavior) of an individual, with the characteristics of the situation, makes it psychodynamic. Contexts involving stigma are said to trip one type of function, while situations that are race and Black culture sensitive, but absent of stigma implications, are associated with other functions.

Clark, Swim, and Cross (1996) listed three functions (buffering, bonding, and bridging), to which Cross, Clark, & Fhagen-Smith added several more (code switching and individualism). As previously outlined, each function is a node in a person's multistranded racial worldview that organizes information, memories, experiences, expectations, feelings, and action tendencies designed to manage stigma (buffering); nurture and sustain an attachment to Black people and the Black experience (bonding); facilitate intense and open sharing with people, places, and things that lie beyond the Black experience (bridging); make possible temporary "passing," accommodation, or even assimilation (code switching); and demarcate behavior, thought, and action that is unique to one's self-concept and personality (individualism). A more detailed explanation of each node/function is as follows.

BUFFERING

The buffering function of Black identity provides psychological protection against racist situations, and facilitates stigma management. It provides a psychological buffer zone that has the effect of reducing the impact of the racist assault, when avoidance is not possible. Given that many racist and stigmatizing assaults are embedded in a larger situation that has nonracist elements, buffering can also mean the ability to "filter" out the racist elements of a situation, while being able to process and take advantage of nonracist information or opportunities. Not everything about life in America is racist, and one's buffering capacities must aid in the differentiation between stigma-tainted versus race-neutral information. Buffering requires (a) an awareness of the racist potential of a situation; (b) an anticipatory set that helps the person to appreciate that he or she may be the object of stigma, independent of one's private sense of self-worth or the credentials that one brings to the situation; (c) a response repertoire that is grounded in experience and practice, from which the person can quickly scan, retrieve and tailor a response that meets the characteristics of the stigma situation (i.e., one cannot apply the same reaction mode to every instance of stigma); (d) a proclivity toward system-blame rather than self-blame as a way of initially framing what appears to be a stigma assault (i.e., "I" am not the problem, but I may be forced to deal with the consequences of John Doe's stigma beliefs); and (e) a sense of spirituality, which in moments of duress can help a Black person maintain a balanced and hopeful orientation toward Whites as a group, even when faced with the most demonic behavior of a particularly crude White racist.

BONDING

The chapters in this volume focus heavily on "stigma." However, one of the messages of the perspective advocated by Cross, Parham, and Helms (1991) as well as Cross, Clark, and Fhagen-Smith (1998) is that, while stigma management is an important component of Black identity, it does not define Blackness, any more than anti-Semitism defines Jewishness, or homophobia the essence of gay-ness. At the core of Black identity is one's attachment and bonding to Black people, Black culture, and the historical and contemporary Black experience. This attachment can result from a crude, romantic, ethnocentric "gut" level sense of connection to Blackness, or it can be a linkage born of sustained socializa-tion, education, participation, and struggle. From Africa, the Deep South, the Caribbean, and South America, have evolved musical frames, artistic orienta-tions, unique foodstuffs, language styles, nonverbal communication patterns, hair styles, courting styles, courting, mating, and sexual-affectional preferences, which can engage and sustain many of the life choices of a Black person. These "Black" options, choices, or preferences may exist and/or operate independently of that which results from interactions with Whites and non-Blacks. If, as in Zora Neale Hurston's novels, Black people sometimes seem oblivious to Whites, it is be-cause, beyond the place of stigma, there is enough depth to the Black experi-ence that one can be both totally engaged and effectively reinforced by it. The issue here is not an "either-or-perspective," in which appreciation of say jazz, is pitted against "White classical music." Rather it is an understanding that to know jazz, to read its history, to immerse oneself in its experience, either through reproductions (cassettes, LPs, or CDs) or live performance, can result in a full plate.

From this vantage point we can see that the bonding function addresses the degree to which the person derives meaning and support, in life, from an affiliation or "attachment" to Black people and the Black experience. This attachment is made evident in one's hair style, clothing preferences, food tastes, church affilia-tion, friendship patterns, leisure time activities, formal cultural group member-ships, magazine subscriptions, historical perspective, music, art, and popular culture preferences, and self-attitudes toward one's body features (hair texture, lip thickness, skin color, size of buttocks, etc.). This attachment may take on a cate-gorical nature in the identity of Black nationalists, but for other Blacks, an equally strong attachment to aspects of American culture (biculturality), or a cluster of ethnic orientations (multiculturalism), may operate alongside the person's sense of bonding to the Black experience.

In speaking of jazz, the Black church, popular Black food dishes, and other qualities of the Black experience that make it intrinsically attractive, compelling, and engaging, we have set the stage to make an important distinction between intrinsic bonding and reactive bonding. Reactive bonding, or the tendency of Blacks to self-segregate in the face of an indifferent or hostile White presence, is a variation of buffering. The self-segregation is stimulated in reaction to a stigma threat, and not the intrinsic qualities of Black culture. Thus, the origins of the NAACP, SCLS, or Black Student Union Chapters on college campuses are expressions of reactive bonding or organized, collective buffering, but Duke Ellington's or Count Basie's creation of their jazz orchestras can hardly be explained by stigma threats. Of course, reactive bonding or collective buffering may lead to intrinsic bonding in that (a) in the face of a racial or stigma treat, Blacks may form a collective shield and self-segregate; however, (b) in coming together, Blacks may shift the focus to the exploration or celebration of those aspects of the Black experience that are intrinsically compelling. On the other hand, should Blacks self-segregate and then continue to focus on racism or other aspects of a stigma threat, their bonding is not motivated by the intrinsic qualities of Black life, but in reaction to an external threat.

BRIDGING

If bonding or attachment is a view into the private space of Black people, and buffering reflects protective mechanisms often employed, when that space is assaulted by a stigmatizing agent, there remains the question as to what aspects of Black identity facilitate communications with people and institutions outside the Black community? Close and intimate communications are said to be accomplished by a bridging function, while more controlled but necessary social intercourse is conducted through the code-switching function; let's begin the analysis with bridging. The bridging function refers to those social skills, interpersonal competencies, attitudes and behaviors that make it possible for a Black person to become deeply immersed in the emotions, attitudes, social perspectives, and worldview of a person who is not Black (including Whites). Bridging can be described as a two-way or reciprocal process, in which the other person is experiencing immersion in the worldview of her or his Black cohort. As importantly, there is the absence of any counterdemands that the Black person play down, mute or "hide" one's Blackness. On the contrary, a primary focus of the bridging relationship is *difference*. A core part of the relationship is the time spent deconstructing and trying to understand the other's worldview. Both people work to create a safe, and sometimes deeply intimate, space where each may share and "hear" each other's cultural, ethnic, religious, sexual, or gender voice. This exchange makes possible cross-racial friendships, multicultural alliances, and intimate cross-racial and trans-ethnic relationships or marriages. By definition, bridging relationships are exceptional, and not typically the chosen strategy used by Blacks, in the majority of their exchanges with Whites and others outside the Black community.

CODE SWITCHING

Clark, Swim, and Cross (1996) expanded the range of functions to include code switching and individualism. The code switching function of Black identity involves the capacity to suspend, in a calculated but highly effective fashion, the "open" and "natural" expression of those behaviors, verbal styles, attitudes, and other forms of presentation, which in the popular mainstream culture are labeled as "Black behavior." Code switching can be defined as the turning off or switching on of one's proclivity to present oneself in a "Black" way. Instead, this "Black" manner is temporarily replaced with a persona that is more in accordance with the norms and expectations of a particular person or institution. Unlike buffering which is triggered by stigma threats to one's personal or cultural integrity, the contexts for code switching is not a threat, but the "demand" to display behavior, attitudes, and competencies that are central to the dynamics of the context. Being Jewish, or female, or Black is considered "irrelevant" to the task at hand, and one must "turn off" one's cultural specificity and turn on the display of certain competencies.

The motivation for code switching stems from the fact that the Black person is trying to extract a service or to fulfill some need. Code switching, which Blacks also call "fronting," becomes necessary when an organization or group, while not openly hostile to difference, shows signs of discomfort with explicit expressions of difference. Situations calling for code switching (school, workplace, neighborhood, shopping centers, etc.) require that Blacks dress, think, act, and express themselves in ways that will optimize the comfort of the person, group, or institution, such that, in turn, Blacks will receive fair treatment, quality services, needed protection, and employment. Code switching makes it possible for a Black person not to be "seen" as Black, but as just another customer, student, citizen, applicant, or employee. In situations such as the workplace, school, or college, fronting is an "act" or "performance" that may last for hours on end, and may become a natural part of the Black person's everyday life (Goffman, 1959). Code switching, therefore, is not necessarily an unpleasant experience, as is the case of buffering, nor is it as open and freewheeling as bridging. Of course, to be effective, code switching requires that Blacks be as competent in the culture and norms of the "other" as he or she is when with other Black people. Code switching is an important function for those Blacks who go back and forth from a more authentic sense of self in the morning, code switching during the day, and back to the real self, after leaving the context for code switching. However, for Blacks who are assimilated, no such distinction between one's cultural self and context-specific self may be necessary; consequently, assimilated Blacks may have less of a need to front or code switch (or to front).

INDIVIDUALISM

This is the identity function a Black person employs when feeling, thinking, and acting in ways that are not obviously connected to Black culture, reflecting instead the manifestations of the person's distinctive personality dynamics. Nigrescence theory frequently associates "individualism" with an identity frame in need of transformation, and advanced Nigrescence is evidenced in Black self-concepts for which race is keenly salient. Consequently, the second author of this chapter was caught off guard, when, while facilitating a focus group, Blacks with high Black identity development stated that individualism was also a part of their "Black identity." They suggested that the clarity of the one dimension (individualism) was made possible by comparison with those behaviors they linked to "Black" expressions or behavior, as in a field-ground orientation. From this vantage point, the person perceives herself or himself to be acting in a race-neutral fashion, more in tune with the dictates and whims of the idiosyncratic aspects of one's self-concept and not necessarily motivated by race. While individualism may be a part of any Black person's identity structure, African Americans whose lives are organized around something other than race and Black culture may stress individualism across a broad range of situations, and seldom, if ever, employ buffering, code switching, or bonding functions. In a manner of speaking, such Blacks do not have a Black identity, given that their assimilated world view and philosophy of individualism, precludes any need for a "racial" or social identity.

Cross, Clark, and Fhagen-Smith (1998) have suggested the differences in social identity dynamics that one discovers between one Black person and another may reflect divergent identity profiles. That is, one person's Black identity may rely more heavily on functions buffering, bonding and individualism, while another may more frequent employ functions buffering, bonding, and bridging. For those Black persons whose reference group orientations are tied to something other than race and Black culture, their identity structure may be devoid of most or all the functions. Such differential configurations underscore what Cross, Clark, and Fhagen-Smith mean by "Black identity profile."

COMPARISONS WITH MECHANISMS
DISCUSSED IN THE SOCIAL AND
EDUCATIONAL PSYCHOLOGY LITERATURE

Our perspective on the functions of Black identity in everyday life has links to the mainstream social psychological and educational psychology literature. Oyserman and Harrison (see their chapter in this volume) speak of the components of black identity, one of which is connectedness, a concept that parallels our use of the term bonding. The notion of different functions is akin to different "selves" in the same person. Turner, Oakes, Haslam, and McCarty (1994) propose that individuals can utilize either a collective or an individual identity framework. The decision to use one over the other hinges on several factors, with one of the most salient being the context. Situational cues may help a Black person process which function will provide the best outcome or greatest degree of protection.

Allport (1954) anticipated our discussion of "buffering" in his suggestion that ego defenses function to offset the effects of victimization. A more explicit and modern link can be found in the work by Feagin and Sikes (1994), who proposed that one strategy for dealing with discrimination involves putting on a "shield" in the morning to protect oneself from incidences of discrimination. In their discussion regarding self-presentation, Taylor and Brown (1988) point out the functions of using positive images of the self as a way of maintaining self-control in stigmatizing situations. Crocker and Major (1989) have proposed that self-esteem is protected (buffered) by attributing negative feedback to discrimination against one's group and not oneself. Perhaps one could say that at the very foundation of the stigma literature is the concept of buffering.

Bridging serves as a conduit through which individuals, representing different races or ethnicities, may relate to one another in an intimate, sharing, open fashion. Theories and research on multicultural education (Banks & Banks, 1995), as well as social justice education (Adam, Bell, & Griffin, 1997), provide the most complementary support for the existence of this identity function. In their handbook on research inspired by multicultural education, Banks and Banks (1995) associate multiculturalism, not so much with concepts of "transcendence" or "color-blindness," but with the ability to hear, dissect, and reconstruct the frame of reference of another person. Rather than alienate, "difference" is transformed into something that is accessible, friendly, and engaging. In a similar fashion, the ground-breaking text on social justice education by Adams, Bell, and Griffin (1997) stresses that social justice theory assumes the possibility of movement from difference as strangeness and intimidation, to difference as uniqueness, for which intimacy is possible.

To date, our notion of bonding has only partially been captured by the existing stigma literature. The stigma literature focuses on instances of bonding that are stimulated by actual or potential rejection of Black by Whites, when Blacks are in predominantly White contexts. Crocker and Major (1989) provide evidence that such "self-segregation" can assist the individual in his or her everyday encounters, although "segregation" is an odd term to apply to Black within-group bonding. Specifically, they hypothesize that individuals who segregate themselves do not have to engage in as many intergroup comparisons. Members of the outgroup are not as available for comparison, and thus the differences in opportunities and treatment are not apparent. Lalonde and Cameron (1994) support this concept of togetherness in discussing the need to examine how African Americans seek out social support when discrimination is perceived. Taylor, Wright, Moghaddam, and Lalonde (1990), when measuring the effects of group membership and the attributions of discrimination in response to a discriminatory

event, found that individuals may tend to turn to the group as a means to deal
with the hostile affronts society provides. Additionally, Simon and Brown (1987)
found that a sense of solidarity and social support is achieved through the group.
From our vantage point, these examples of group solidarity in the face of discrimination have less to do with bonding than with buffering. In coming together
to form the Black Panther Party or the NAACP, Blacks were acting in a collective buffering mode. But when Blacks come together to marry, or to play jazz,
or, as happens on the coast of South Carolina, to make straw baskets in the
tradition of their African ancestors, they are bonding in the absence of Whites
or other "outside" group members. As discussed in an earlier section, it may
be necessary to differentiate between "reactive bonding" versus intrinsic bonding, with the former taking place in White contexts, and the latter in predominantly Black situations. In any case, the stigma research, by definition, has focused more on the "self-segregating' or reactive bonding actions of Blacks, and
what has remained understudied is what we are calling (intrinsic) bonding, or
the sense of attachment Blacks achieve with each other, independent of stigma
dynamics.

Code switching is analogous to impression management. Leary and Kowalski
(1990) discuss the idea that individuals are aware of the "roles" they need to
play. They try to be consistent with the expectations of the roles, to maximize
rewards and to minimize punishment. Within a racial framework, the rewards and
punishments could be thought of as the opportunities made available to African
Americans who "play the game." Additionally, Goffman (1959) spoke of the
suspension of impression management when the other is not present. Goffman
stated that the individual ". . . can relax; he [or she] can drop his [or her] front;
forgo speaking his [or her] lines, and step out of character" (p. 112). Additional
support for code switching is found in Allport's work (1954). Allport (1954)
introduced the contact hypothesis, about which he stated that, when equal status
is perceived between groups, prejudice can be diminished. Through code switching, African Americans may be attempting to create a more equal level of communication (i.e., they are attempting to interact with European Americans on their
terms). This in turn, Allport suggests, would decrease the prejudice incurred in
the situation.

There is little doubt that all individuals do, indeed, act as individuals. We
propose that African Americans still spend a large percentage of their time *not*
thinking about race. As previously underscored, Turner, Oakes, Haslam, and
McCarty (1994) claim that individuals may utilize either a collective or an individual identity framework, depending on the situation. Niedenthal and Beike
(1997) made note of the distinction between isolated (stand-alone) and interrelated
(social) self-concept representations. An isolated self-concept is one that has intrinsic meaning and is not grounded on concepts linked to other individuals, and
thus is an expression of individuality. Although individuality is a key theme in
American psychology, the actual number of studies that have studied individualism in Blacks is few and far between.

PRELIMINARY RESEARCH

We have conducted an exploratory pilot study to test the existence of the functions in everyday life. The participants were 10 African American students at a predominately European American institution. The intent of the focus group was to determine if the definitions of the functions were acceptable, and to determine the relationship between the definitions and actual applications of the functions. The focus group discussed the definitions and made one significant modification. They suggested the addition of the word "fronting" when discussing code switching. Although there were other minor disagreements, which were taken into consideration, the agreement for the definitions was high.

Additionally, students completed three questionnaires. The first questionnaire was designed to obtain demographic information. The second measure asked them to describe a meaningful event that had occurred to them during the day and to answer several questions about the event, including whether they engaged in any of the functions described in the present chapter, the racial composition of the situation they described, their relationship with other people present, and the emotions they felt in the situation. Finally, participants completed a questionnaire that recalled the frequency and importance of their use of each function over the previous day.

The results for the focus group indicated support for the hypothesis that context will influence the likelihood that individuals will use different functions. Specifically, there was a significant correlation between the number of European Americans in the situation identified and identifying the situation as one where they engaged in buffering function ($.89$, $p<.01$). There was a significant correlation between the perception that the situation was a stressful one and buffering ($.69$, $p<.05$).

Participants' recall of their use of the different functions indicated that they were most likely to recall having used the bonding ($M = 31.30$), and the individualism ($M = 19.00$) functions and least likely to recall having used the bridging ($M = 9.70$), buffering ($M = .40$), and code switching functions ($M = 1.40$). Similarly, on a 7-point scale from not very important (0) to very important (6), they were most likely to perceive the bonding ($M = 4.10$) and individualism ($M = 3.30$) functions as more important to them then the bridging ($M = 1.60$), buffering ($M = .60$), and code switching functions ($M = 0$).

Overall, the results of this pilot study support the existence of functions in everyday life, that participants use of the different functions are situationally dependent, and the use of the different functions serve different psychological needs. We are currently collecting data to test these and other relationships among a larger sample of African American students.

CONCLUSIONS

The concept of stigma has the tendency to truncate, if not overshadow, the identity integrity for the group under consideration. When this happens, identity and stigma appear to be one and the same. The identity functions that have evolved from Nigrescence theory help to differentiate between the important dimensions of *stigma management* found to be operative in the everyday lives of Black people, from those identity functions that show a limited relationship to stigma. A great deal of everyday Black behavior is in reaction to stigma situations that result from having to live in a White-controlled world, but there are other moments in the day when Black people are about living, sleeping, arguing, laughing, and just "being" with each other. While validation of the different functions is needed, the aim is to demonstrate the side-by-side existence of the stigma management and nonstigma driven aspects of everyday Black life.

REFERENCES

Adams, M., Bell, L. A., & Griffin, P. (1997). *Teaching for diversity and social justice: A source book.* New York: Routledge Press.

Allport, G. W. (1954). *The nature of prejudice.* Cambridge, MA: Addison-Wesley.

Banks, J. A. & Banks, C. A. (1995). *Handbook of research on multicultural education.* New York: Macmillan Publishing USA.

Barnes, E. J. (1972). The Black community as a source of positive self-concept for black children: A theoretical perspective. In R. Jones (ed.), *Black Psychology,* (1st ed., pp. 166–192). New York: Harper & Row.

Button, S. B. (1997, April 11). *Considering sexual diversity: Steps in the right direction.* Paper presented at the 12th annual convention of the society for industrial and organizational psychology, St. Louis, MO.

Clark, K. & Clark, M. (1947). Racial identification and preference in negro children. In T. M. Newcomb & E. Hartley (eds.), *Readings in social psychology,* pp.169–178. New York: Holt & Company.

Clark, L., Swim, J. K., & Cross, W. E. Jr. (1996). *Functions of racial identity in everyday life: A daily diary study.* Unpublished manuscript.

Crocker, J., & Major, B. (1989). Social stigma and self-esteem: The self-protective properties of stigma. *Psychological Review,* 96, 608–630.

Crocker, J., Major, B. & Steele, C. (1996) Social Stigma. In D. Gilbert, S. T. Fiske & G. Lindzey (Eds.), *Handbook of social psychology* (4th ed.). Boston: McGraw Hill.

Cross, W. E. Jr. (1991). *Shades of Black: diversity in African American identity.* Philadelphia: Temple University Press.

Cross, W. E., Jr. (1995). The psychology of Nigrescence: revisiting the Cross model. In Ponterotto, J. G. Casa, J. M. Suzuki, L. A. and Alexander, C. M. (Eds.), *Handbook of multicultural counseling* (pp. 93–122). Thousand Oaks, CA: Sage.

Cross, W. E., Jr., Clark, L., & Fhagen-Smith, P. (1998). Black identity development across the life span: Educational implications. In E. Hollins & R. H. Sheets (Eds.), *Race, ethnic, cultural identity and human development: Implications for schooling.* Hillsdale, NJ: Lawrence Erlbaum.

Cross W. E., Jr., & Fhagen-Smith, P. (1996). Nigrescence and ego identity development. In P. B. Pederson, J. G. Draguns, W. J. Lonner, & J. E. Trimble (Eds.), *Counseling across cultures.* (pp. 108–123). Thousand Oaks, CA: Sage Publications.

Cross, W. E., Jr., Parham, T. A., & Helms, J. E. (1991). The stages of black identity development: Nigrescence models. In Jones, R. (Ed.), *Black psychology* (3rd ed., pp. 319–338). Berkeley, CA: Cobb & Henry Publishers.

Cross, W. E., Jr., Parham, T. A., & Helms, J. E. (1995). Nigrescence revisited: theory and research. In R. Jones (ed.), *Advances in Black psychology,* pp.1–69. Berkeley: Cobb & Henry.

Demo, D. J., & Hughes, M. (1990). Socialization and racial idenity among Black Americans. *Social Psychology Quarterly, 53*, 364–374.

Feagin, J. R., & Sikes, M. P. (1994). *Living with racism; the Black middle-class experience.* Beacon Press Boston.

Goffman, E. (1959). *The presentation of self in everyday life.* Garden City, NY: Doubleday Anchor.

Gordon, V. V. (1976). *The self-concept of Black Americans.* Lanham, MD: University Press of America, Inc.

Graves, T. D. (1967), Psychological acculturation in a tri-ethnic community. *Southwestern Journal of Anthropology, 23*, 337–350.

Helms, J. E. (1990). *Black and White racial idenity development.* Westport, CT: Greenwood Press.

Horowitz, R. (1930). Racial aspects of self-identification in nursery school children. *Journal of Psychology, 7*, 91–99.

Kardiner, A., & Ovessey, L. (1951). *The mark of oppression: A psychological study of the Negro American.* New York: W.W. Norton.

Lalonde, R. N., & Cameron, J. E. (1994). Behavioral responses to discrimination: A focus on action. In M. P. Zanna, and J. M. Olson, (Eds.), *The psychology of prejudice: The Ontario symposium, Volume 7.* Hillsdale, NJ: Lawrence Erlbaum Associates.

Leary, M. R., & Kowalski, R. M. (1990). Impression management: A literature review and two-component model. *Psychological Bulletin, 107*, 34–47.

Murray, A. (1970). *The omni-Americans: New perspectives on Black experience and American culture.* New York: Outerbridge & Dienstrey.

Niedenthal, P. M., & Beike, D. R. (1997). Interrelated and isolated self-concepts. *Personality and Social Psychology Bulletin, 1*(2), 106–128.

Oyserman, D., & Harrison, K. (This volume). African American identity as social identity. In J. Swim, & C. Stangor (Eds.), *Prejudice: The target's perspective.* San Diego: Academic Press.

Parham, T. A. (1989). Cycles of psychological nigrescence. *Counseling Psychologist, 17*(2), 187–226.

Pettigrew, T. F. (1964). *A profile of the American Negro.* Princeton, NJ: D. Van Nostrand.

Reis, H. T., & Wheeler, L. (1991). Study social interaction with the Rochester interaction record. *Advances in Experimental Social Psychology, 24*, 269–318.

Rosenberg, M., & Simmons, R. G. (1971). Black and White self-esteem: The urban school child. *Arnold and Caroline Rose Monograph Series.* Washington, DC: American Sociological Association.

Simon, B., & Brown, R. (1987). Perceiving intergroup homogenity in minority-majority context. *Journal of Personality and Social Psychology, 53*, 703–711.

Taylor, D. M., Wright, S. C., Moghaddam, F. M., & Lalonde, R. N. (1990). The personal/group discrimination discrepency: Perceiving my group but not myself to be a target of discrimination. *Personality and Social Psychology Bulletin, 16*, 254–262.

Taylor, S. E., & Brown, J. D. (1988). Illusion and well-being: A social psychological perspective on mental health. *Psychological Bulletin, 103*, 193–210.

Turner, J. C., Oakes, P. J., Haslam, S. A., & McCarty, C. (1994). Self and collective: Cognition and social context. *Personality and Social Psychology Bulletin 20*(5), 454–463.

Walker, A. (1979). *I love myself* New York: The Feminist Press of CUNY.

Wright, R. (1945). *Black boy: A record of childhood and youth.* New York: Harper Collins.

13

IMPLICATIONS OF
CULTURAL CONTEXT
AFRICAN AMERICAN IDENTITY
AND POSSIBLE SELVES

DAPHNA OYSERMAN[1, 2]

University of Michigan

KATHY HARRISON

Wayne State University

INTRODUCTION

One's everyday choices and behaviors appear idiosyncratic, the result of highly personalized goals, desires, and motivations. Yet research and theorizing in social (e.g., Haslam, Oakes, Turner, & McGarty, 1996; Turner, Oakes, Haslam, & McGarty, 1994) and cultural psychology (e.g., Kagitcibasi, 1996; Markus, Kitayama, & Heiman, 1996; Oyserman & Markus, 1993) suggests that these choices may in fact be colored by social representations of what it means to be a successful person, a good or moral person, a person of worth. The ways we organize experience, how we make sense of ourselves, our goals and motivations, all importantly depend on the ways these concepts are socially represented within a society and the sociocultural niches we occupy within that society (e.g., Kagitcibasi, 1996; Oyserman & Packer, 1996; Oyserman, Gant, & Ager, 1995; Shaver, Wu, & Schwartz, 1992).

The role of cultural context in the everyday understandings of individuals has been highlighted in cross-cultural work suggesting that cultures differ both in the

[1]While writing this chapter, the first author was a W. T. Grant Faculty Scholar. Partial funding also came from the Michigan Prevention Research Center grant to the first author.

[2]Corresponding author.

ways life tasks are structured and the normative role of individual difference and social embeddedness (e.g., Hofstede, 1991; Markus & Kitayama, 1991; Triandis, 1989). More and more the insights gained from this cross-cultural work on individualism and collectivism are being utilized to make sense of the personal and social identities individuals within heterogeneous societies such as that in the United States create to organize experience, regulate affect, and control motivation and behavior (e.g., Cameron & Lalonde, 1994; Gurin, Hurtado, & Peng, 1994; Kowalski & Wolfe, 1994; Oyserman, 1993; Oyserman, Sakamoto, & Lauffer, in press). Thus, who one is and might become is importantly a social product that, we will argue, has important motivational and self-regulatory consequences.

In this chapter we first describe the individualism and collectivism as cultural frames, emphasizing the collectivist roots of racial and ethnic identity. Then we discuss the social representation of race and ethnicity and how this representation influences racial and ethnic identity for African Americans. We then explain how racial and ethnic identity can function to moderate the risk of individualistic cultural frames for minority group members, buffer individuals from racism, and motivate minority group members to achieve their goals. We propose that this resiliency-promoting function is most likely to happen when ethnic or racial identity is chronically or situationally salient and when this identity includes three components: a sense of connectedness to other African Americans, an awareness of racism or structural barriers, and achievement as centrally connected to being an African American. While African American identity is our specific focus, we see the insights gained from this work as providing insight into other ethnic identities and the broader social identity of being American (e.g., Hudson, 1995).

A CULTURAL PERSPECTIVE

AMERICAN INDIVIDUALISM AND COLLECTIVISM

Cultural psychology has highlighted the diverse nature of cultural assumptions as to what is considered central, moral, and good, and what is the basic unit of analyses in understanding human behavior. One of the more fruitful lines of research in this area has been contrast between cultural individualism and collectivism in terms of their divergent social representations of personhood (e.g., Oyserman, 1993; Schwartz, 1990; Shweder & Bourne, 1984; Triandis, 1995). What is the social representation of personhood within American society? American society is generally considered to be an individualistic one (e.g., Triandis, 1995). Individualism as a cultural lens focuses attention on the individual rather than the context within which the individual is embedded. That is, Americans are said to focus primarily on individual traits and attributes, to view personal independence as an important value, to believe that individuals are defined primarily by their achievements, and to believe that the individual is the causal agent, not his or her circumstances (Hsu, 1983). Within this cultural frame, individuals rather than contexts, roles, and processes are viewed as the nexus of causality. Following from this social representation of personhood, individuals are more likely to utilize information about the person than the situation in making causal attributions, often underestimating the influence of context (Ross & Nisbett, 1991).

Collectivism conversely is often portrayed as prototypically emanating from non-Western European societies. It involves a focus on the interdependence between individuals, a sense of common fate, the centrality of family, and the importance of the social unity (Chan, 1991; Fugita & O'Brien, 1991; Lee, 1994; Markus & Kitayama, 1991; Rosenberger, 1992; Takaki, 1994). Context is very important in the cultural lens of collectivism, each individual is viewed as part of the context, with a task of striving to fulfill his or her social roles as well as he or she can. Given this emphasis on fulfilling social roles, collectivists have been found less likely to make self-serving attributions. They are less likely to externalize causality for failure and internalize causality for success (e.g., Markus and Kitayama, 1991).

IMPLICATIONS FOR MINORITIES

Although America has often been used as the prototype of individualism, increased attention to the American multiethnic, multicultural population has led to consensus that many Americans, particularly minorities, are likely to be socialized into both individualistic and collectivist world views (e.g., Fowers & Richardson, 1996; Phinney, 1996; Sampson, 1988). Also, while individualism has been described as encouraging a focus on the individual and not the group, American society clearly does take social groups into account—especially ethnic and racial groups. This means that the collectivistic social representation of personhood continues to be elicited in American society. The social roles and memberships associated with ethnic and racial groups involve common fate and interdependence, aspects of collectivism (e.g., Phinney & Cobb, 1996). Ethnic and racial minority identity must take into account (1) the family-oriented focus of interdependence (e.g., Chan, 1991) and the more general influence of a collectivist world view on sense of common fate (e.g., Myers, 1993; Oyserman, 1993; Triandis, 1995); (2) a minority group member's need to take into account the possibility of negative stereotyping or devaluation of one's group by others in America (e.g., Crocker & Major, 1989); and (3) a minority group's need to integrate achievement and group identity (e.g., Oyserman, Gant, & Ager, 1995). In fact, our research with African American and Asian American youth and young adults suggests that racial ethnic identity often does contain these three components (i.e., family relatedness and pride in heritage-connectedness to traditions, awareness of discrimination-barriers, and achievement as integral to group membership; Oyserman, Gant, & Ager, 1995; Oyserman & Sakamoto, in press; Oyserman, Sanchez-Burks, & Harrison, 1997).

Given its collectivist roots, it is perhaps not surprising that racial and ethnic minority identity in the United States is likely to correlate positively with collectivism (Oyserman & Sakamoto, 1997). Thus feelings of connectedness, awareness of obstacles, and embedded achievement, components of ethnic identity, correlate with the belief that individuals can be best understood as parts of social groups. Using Crocker's collective self-esteem scale (e.g., Crocker & Major, 1989), we also found that collectivism is correlated with positive feelings about one's ethnic group generally (Oyserman & Sakamoto, 1997).

Our research suggests that acculturation leads to high levels of individualism among racial and ethnic minorities in the United States (Oyserman *et al.,* 1995; Oyserman & Sakamoto, 1997; Oyserman, Sakamoto, & Lauffer, in press; Rueda-Riedle & Oyserman, 1997). However, this research also suggests that collectivism continues to play a role in the life perspectives and everyday behaviors of minorities. That is, individuals are socialized in both worldviews and those high in collectivism have a greater sense of social obligation (Oyserman *et al.,* in press) and have a more detailed representation of the specific roles and obligations they have toward family and other in-groups (e.g., Coon & Oyserman, 1997).

SOCIAL REPRESENTATIONS OF RACE
AND ETHNICITY

In contemporary America, social representations of race and ethnicity carry with them presumptive knowledge about what an individual member of the race can or cannot do, should or should not do. Thus, young African American men are assumed to be ill-educated, non-middle class, dangerous, and potentially violent. Whether they choose this representation or not, that is who they *are* to others (Beale-Spencer, Cunningham, & Swanson, 1995). This social representation is so embedded into our popular culture that is used as part of the visual hook in a soft drink commercial that juxtaposes our fear of African American street youth with the commercial success of African American hip hop attire. Further, while individual assertion and striving achievement, intelligence, and academic skill are valued in the United States, those who are non-middle class, nonmale, and non-White are stereotyped as having fewer of these capacities (e.g., Steele, 1997). Yet these social representations of minorities do not necessarily take into account how minorities define themselves and their own group.

Class and race are deeply connected with larger society's social representation of race. Thus, in the course of his trial, O.J. Simpson was initially described as an "honorary White" to underscore his privilege. Later, his lawyers were accused of "playing the race card" when they reminded the jurors of his Blackness. Commentary and letters to the editor questioned whether O.J. was "Black enough" to be allowed use of this "card." Being African American, they felt, entailed a way of life that O.J. was perceived as not embodying.

IMPLICATIONS FOR MINORITIES

Minorities must make sense of themselves in terms of what it means to be a member of a racial or ethnic group in contemporary American. They face the simultaneous task of creating a sense of self in terms of their own personal characteristics, traits and competencies and the content and nature of their social identities (Oyserman *et al.*, 1997). To be effective, one's personal identity must involve some sense of competence and efficacy now and in the future. But for minorities, one's self-concept is not solely personal; it is importantly social as well. A key social identity is one's gendered racial–ethnic identity. We propose that ethnic identity can reduce risk and promote positive outcomes for minorities to the extent that it buffers individuals from feelings of depression and anxiety, promotes feelings of competence and efficacy, and focuses attention on culturally central goals such as school achievement.

However, research to date has not focused sufficiently on ways ethnic identity may function to motivate action in important life domains. The research literature suffers from lack of uniform definitions as to what ethnic identity is and how it can be measured. Ethnic identity is commonly defined as positive in-group attitudes and in-group identification. Thus defined, it is correlated with higher self-esteem, less stress, and less delinquent involvement (McCreary, Slavin, & Berry, 1996; Beale-Spencer, Cunningham, & Swanson, 1995). Further, Bat-Chava and Steen's (1996) recent meta-analysis of doctoral and master theses studies suggests a moderate connection between various measures of ethnic identity and self-esteem. Individuals who feel that being a member of their group is important, feel connected to their group, and carry out behaviors to make this connection clear, tend to feel good about themselves. However, we propose that ethnic identity is an important part of self-concept and as such does more than promote as sense of well being.

SELF-CONCEPT STRUCTURE AND FUNCTION

Self-concept contains a store of autobiographical memories but it is not simply a store of autobiographical memory. The self functions to (1) lend meaning and organization to experiences—thoughts, feelings, and actions; and (2) to motivate action by providing incentives, standards, plans, strategies, and scripts for behavior (Oyserman & Markus, 1993). Thus the self-concept is both content—who I am now, who I was and who I might become, and a motivated process—seeking out, organizing, and storing information about the self (Oyserman & Markus, 1993). Possible selves, the future oriented component of self-concept, are particularly important to this motivational function of the self. Possible selves can be one's positive expectations as well as one's feared or to-be-avoided selves. Having detailed positive expected selves provides one with a goal to approach. Having strategies to work toward these selves and believing that one is currently working toward becoming like one's positive expected selves is implicated with better outcomes (Oyserman & Saltz, 1993). Similarly, having strategies to avoid becoming like one's feared selves reduces risk of negative outcomes (Oyserman, Sanchez-Burks, & Harrison, 1997). Because possible selves often involve goals that can be attained or avoided only as the result of sustained action over time, preservation of motivation and the ability to seek out alternative routes to moving toward one's positive and away from one's negative possible selves over time is critical. We have termed "balanced" the situation in which one has both a positive expected self and a feared or to-be-avoided self in the same domain. Having both positive, approach motivation, and negative, avoidance motivation in the same domain is related to better attainments in that domain (Oyserman & Markus, 1990a).

IMPLICATIONS FOR MINORITIES:
THE TRIPARTITE MODEL OF IDENTITY

We propose that for African American and other racial and ethnic minority individuals, racial–ethnic identity is integral to the process of developing possible selves and reducing negative consequences of stereotypes. The sense one makes of what is possible and plausible in the future for oneself is contingent on one's vision of what is possible and plausible for people like oneself—one's sociocultural group. Other researchers have noted that a positive sense of one's group membership and connectedness to one's ethnic or racial group is central to well-being (e.g., Crocker, Luhtanen, Blaine, & Broadnax, 1994; Cross, 1991). Further, an awareness of racism and the obstacles that it may create provides a means of shielding ones' sense of competence by providing a nonself-denigrating explanation for failures and setbacks (e.g., Cose, 1993; Essed, 1990; Parham & Helms, 1985). However, these two components of identity alone do not provide motivational direction or goals. Because achievement is both central to individualism and a key component of stereotypes, issues related to achievement need to be answered at this basic level. We propose that by viewing achievement as part of being African American, identification with this goal is facilitated. Such identification promotes school and academic achievement and persistence and reducing risk of disidentification with school and "cultural inversion" of these values by which school is viewed as not "African American" (e.g., Ford, 1992; Fordham, 1988; Steele, 1988).

The importance of defining school and academic achievement as central to one's social identity as an African American, can be seen in case studies of successful male African American students as described by Bowser and Perkins (1991). These students describe the ways in which significant others in their lives centralized school success, making it an important part of what it meant to be a good son, brother, student, and so on. Within this relational context, youth came to view themselves as someone who could and must do well in school. Further, these African American males stated that it was in the context of these relationships that they came to believe that school success was possible for them in the future—that they could develop strategies to do well and avoid failure. In this way, working hard and getting good grades became integral to their social identity and resulted in academically focused possible selves that kept the youths focused and persistent in their efforts to attain school success. Similarly, in exploring underachievement at the university level, Steele and his colleagues (Aronson *et al.*, this volume; Steele *et al.*, 1995; Steele, 1997) have suggested that being African American is an example of a socially marked identity. Making marked identities such as femaleness or Blackness salient elicits vulnerability to academic underachievement. Those with marked identities who wish to succeed are not able to pursue success single-mindedly because their "marked" identity provides explanations for failures and setbacks, suggesting that failure is unavoidable.

Thus, for minorities, knowing how one is viewed by others allows one to take this into account in making sense of one's experiences, regulating affect and making choices about one's goals and behaviors. We propose that racial and ethnic identity require at least three components in order to fulfill these functions. These components have been alluded to above; they are: an awareness of obstacles, stereotypes, racism; a sense of connectedness; and embedded achievement. An awareness of racism must be incorporated into the self-concept because it is part of everyday life and therefore must be taken into account if one is to make sense of one's experiences. Such an *awareness of racism,* together with a sense of *connectedness*—a positive sense of one's group membership; serve the affect regulation function of the self—maintaining personal well-being. Further, knowing that one is likely to be viewed as a member of a stigmatized group rather than as an individual, knowing that feedback may be ambiguous or misleading due to one's category membership, and so on, provide a means to create a sense of self as competent and capable in spite of negative feedback one might receive due to group membership.

While an awareness of racism is important, this awareness alone does not foster self-regulatory focus on the achievement domains centralized by individualistic society. In order to do that, African American identity must contain a self-relevant goal of being smart and doing well in school and believing that school success is part of one's racial or ethnic identity ("It is important that we do well; We can succeed at school, we are smart"). Together with an awareness of obstacles brought on by the awareness of racism component, this *embedded achievement* component will organize experience and regulate affect in the service of this goal.

The content of African American identity can therefore motivate positive self-regulatory focus in the very domains that form the basis of stereotypes about African Americans. Because it is rooted in collectivist traditions, racial or ethnic identity is also likely to contain a sense of connectedness, obligation, and common fate with other group members. Although it is an identity and therefore can be studied within the same framework as other identities, we focus specifically on racial and ethnic identity due to the problematic and controversial nature of having a nonmajority race or ethnicity.

SOCIAL CONSTRUCTION OF SELF-CONCEPT

ETHNIC IDENTITY AS PUBLIC AND PRIVATE

In creating a sense of self, one must balance the selves one would like to become with those one believes one is likely to become (Oyserman & Markus, 1990b). But who does one want to be and how does one gauge the plausibility of attaining such a self? The process of identifying such self-guides is intimately socially embedded (e.g., Higgins, 1996; Oyserman & Packer, 1996). That is, the issues and vocabulary of one's time and place in the world are raw materials informing one of the selves that are worthy and important, the traits and attributes that go with these selves, and the nature of the relationship between individuals and situations (e.g., Hwang, 1987; Showers, 1995). In this way, like other identities, the content and structure of ethnic identity are a product of both micro contexts—here and now and face-to-face contexts; and macro contexts—historical and political, contexts within which individuals and groups create, maintain, and foster their identities (e.g., Oyserman & Packer, 1996). For this reason, both the specific content of one's racial and ethnic identity, one's valuation of the identity, and the chronic and situational salience of the identity are likely to vary across time and place. This socially constructed sense of self as having a racial or ethnic identity is especially important as individuals seek to make sense of what they are good at, and what they should be focused on. Thus, a student can know how many problems he or she solved on a math task or the number of homework assignments he or she handed in on time; but the meaning of these behaviors is a social construction that is linked to racial and ethnic identity.

As is illustrated in the following example, racial and ethnic identity are both uniquely personal and private and uniquely social and public in nature. Tiger Woods, the young golf star, described himself as Cablinasian rather than African American in order to demonstrate his multiracial background (see Pinderhughes, 1995). In doing so he unleashed highly vocal positive and negative responses in editorials, letters to the editor, and conversations among individuals. His claim to a multiethnic identity was welcomed by those who saw this statement by a public figure as legitimizing their own sense of self. Others decried his statement as a blow for Black racial solidarity, an effort on his part to ward off the subtle detrimental effect of being Black on assessments of excellence (see Biernat, Vescio, & Green, 1996) and therefore disloyalty to the group, an effort to reject group membership (see Ng, 1989). Being of African descent in America clearly is a marked category, it is a social category that is represented in the culture, it carries meanings and behavioral scripts. Numerous studies documenting popular knowledge of stereotypes about African Americans (e.g., Judd, Park, Ryan, Brauer, & Kraus, 1995) drive home the point that race and ethnicity are clearly social identities in that they carry shared meaning not only for members of the in-group but also to members of the larger society.

RACIAL AND ETHNIC IDENTITY AS SOCIAL IDENTITY

Like any other social identity, individuals both claim and are claimed by others to be bearers of racial and ethnic identities (e.g., Hinkle & Brown, 1990; Phinney, 1996). Social representations of race include who is and who is not a member and what that identity means in terms of the behaviors, characteristics, goals, and attributes of the individual (e.g., Brewer & Gardner, 1996; Banaji, Hardin, & Rothman, 1993; Phinney, 1996). Social psychological and sociological research and theorizing about the content and structure of racial and ethnic identity, often based in social identity theories (Taylor & Dube, 1986; Turner *et al.*, 1987), assumes that individuals have a basic need for a positive sense of self (e.g., Taylor & Brown, 1988; Tesser, 1986) and that social identities also serve this need. Individuals are assumed to strive to create a positive sense of themselves and their groups to the extent that the group is self-defining. This basic formulation of positive social identity is utilized explicitly in social psychological formulations of ethnic identity (e.g., Crocker & Major, 1989; Oyserman *et al.*, 1995). In addition, the situation of groups devalued by powerful others has been fruitfully examined within this model. Important insights from work in this tradition are that while individuals can discount both general and specific feedback from out group members (Landrine, 1992); they may face vulnerability to stereotypes and prejudicial attitudes when this is made salient (e.g., Steele, 1997).

Unfortunately, when the out-group is also larger society—the majority—it will naturally claim as self-describing those attributes most valued in the larger society (Oyserman, Gant, & Ager, 1995; see also Branscombe & Ellemers, this volume). Thus, for example, in the case of African Americans and European Americans, academic attainment and intellect, valued by both groups, were claimed by the European Americans. Some interesting work on African American youth asks whether being African American is a social identity that competes with a personal identity of being successful in school (e.g., Fordham, 1988; Fordham & Ogbu, 1986; Graham, 1994; Hudson, 1991; Ogbu, 1991; Tripp, 1991). As yet evidence for such competition is inconclusive (Ford, 1992; Wong & Eccles, 1996) in that it appears that African American youth value education and aspire to the kind of jobs that require higher education but they are also vulnerable to stereotypes about their ability as African Americans (Steele, 1988; Oyserman & Harrison, 1997).

Social identity theory in fact describes a number of identity management options that can be applied to the situation of minorities within a majority context (Haslam *et al.*, 1996; Ng, 1989; Tajfel, 1978; van Knippenberg, 1989): Individualization and individual mobility are individual strategies based on rejection of any group membership and personal movement to a more privileged social group respectively. Social change, social competition, and social creativity are collective strategies. Taken in order, they refer to methods of improving the in-group's valuation by changing the way one's group is viewed by society, directly challenging the position of the in-group on attributes valued by larger society, and improving the in-group's valuation by changing the attributes used to evaluate the in-group.

Following these collective strategies, African Americans could contest negative perceptions and stereotypes about individuals of presumed African heritage. They could contest academic achievement and intellect as defining individuals of presumed European heritage and claim these attributes as defining themselves. Or, alternatively, African Americans could contest the value of these attributes altogether, centralizing other traits and attributes. To the extent that these processes of social identity creation work, both groups could agree that African Americans were defined by a number of positive attributes. However, attributes centrally valued as part of the Protestant work ethic within American society— striving achievement, hard work, and pursuit of academic, intellectual, and work-related goals (e.g., Tropman, 1989), have also been preserved as European American social identities, particularly for middle class male European Americans. Because that which is quintessentially American had been co-opted as also White, male, and middle class, others have to create social identities that can integrate both American-ness and the other component of who they are, be that an ethnic, racial, or gender group. This in fact may be partially at least a reasonable model of some forms of identity construction among African Americans (see Oyserman, Sanchez-Burks, & Harrison, 1997, for a review).

Literature describing African American identity suggests that some positive yet less centrally valued attributes such as athletic and musical ability and personal style were centralized within African American identity. This process allowed African Americans to claim positive social identities as athletes, musicians, and arbitrators of personal style (Dyson, 1993). Yet it did not deal with the central issue of academic and intellectual achievement as main pathways to socio-economic and political power. In attempting to make sense of African American underachievement in academic domains, scholars in the area began asking if African American peer culture actively discouraged school success through a process of "cultural inversion." That is, being African American was understood to be that which was "not European American" such that when school success was claimed by European Americans, African American peer culture discouraged it. To the extent that academic achievement was not contained within the social identity of African American youth, then those youth who did attempt to do well in school might be labeled as "acting White," "oreos," and other terms meant to highlight the perception of others that they were attempting to be White or leave the group.

Individually, African Americans could attain academic achievement, thus improving their personal sense of self and perhaps gaining enough cultural and economic capital in the process to provide more flexibility in self-definitional choices (Lamont & Lareau, 1988; Ogbu, 1991) but such individual movement requires a particular stance with regard to the nature of the relationship between the in-group and larger society (see Cross, 1991). If doing well in school was defined as being White, an African American child could attempt to reconceptualize himself or herself as mostly defined by membership in a superordinate category such as "American" or member of humanity at large. But the chance to redefine oneself without regard to one's racial or ethnic group may be more genuinely afforded only to those who have sufficient cultural capital due to membership in middle and upper socioeconomic classes. Further, stereotypes about African Americans are class linked; when asked to describe middle class characteristics, respondents mention being White while when asked to describe lower class characteristics, being a minority member or an African American is a descriptor (Hoyt & Miller, 1996). Thus bringing to mind famous African Americans makes respondents view the category of Blacks more favorably (Bodenhausen, Schwarz, Bless, & Wanke, 1995). Success, middle class, and professional status are not part of majority social representations of African Americans. Thus, because their "fit" with the social representation of Blackness is problematic, middle- and upper-class African Americans may be less likely to be always perceived as and responded to in terms of their Blackness.

RACE AND ETHNICITY AS CHRONICALLY OR SITUATIONALLY SALIENT COMPONENTS OF IDENTITY

When race and ethnicity are perceived as likely to matter, to be used to make sense of who a person is, might do, think, or feel (e.g., Wittenbrink, Gist, & Hilton, 1997; Wittenbrink, Judd, & Park, 1997); then race or ethnicity is likely to be part of one's definition of oneself. In such circumstances, not defining oneself in terms of race or ethnicity would reduce one's ability to make sense of and to predict responses of others to the self, a key function of self-concept.

While racial and ethnic identity are ingroup products, they are constrained by social context (Hogg & Abrams, 1990). Under certain circumstances, race and ethnicity and therefore racial and ethnic identity may become a component of one's sense of self as a chronically salient self-schema (Markus, 1977). However, like any other component of self-concept, situational variation in accessibility of racial and ethnic identity as well as variability in the chronic salience and centrality of this component of identity are to be expected (e.g., Hogg & Abrams, 1990; Turner, Oakes, Haslam, & McGarty, 1994; Stryker & Serpe, 1994). In spite of this variability, we propose having some representation of oneself in terms of one's ethnic or racial group membership is likely because of the marked status of ethnic and racial group membership. Perhaps only those minority group members who are otherwise privileged may have a chance to consider having or not having racial identity as part of their self-concept. While race and ethnicity and the implications and meaning these constructs have for oneself may rarely be accessed as part of working self-concept (e.g., Markus & Kunda, 1986); racialized self-views can be accessed under certain conditions (e.g., Kunda, Sinclair, & Griffin, 1997).

Thus, like all components of self, racial and ethnic identity is situationally dependent and can be activated by constraints and demands in the context even when this identity is not chronically salient. While an individual may not always be defined by his or her racial and ethnic group membership, when membership is made salient, a racial or ethnic identity seems to be waiting in the wings and can easily be made situationally salient.

RESEARCH SUPPORT FOR THE
TRIPARTITE MODEL

Research and theorizing in sociological and social psychological traditions has made clear that identity is complex, and that components of identity can be chronically or situationally salient or central. From the early work of Rosenberg (1979) it was also clear that members of stigmatized groups can maintain a positive sense of personal esteem. Crocker and her colleagues showed that minorities can also maintain a positive sense of group or collective esteem in the face of prejudice (Crocker *et al.,* 1994). However, this research tradition has not provided specific insights into the content of ethnic or racial identity.

Some theorists of African American identity propose that it is the process of noticing that race matters and one's stance with regard to being African American, being a minority, and being a member of society at large that form the content of African American identity (e.g., Cross, 1991). More recent formulations of African American identity modify the specific ways in which African Americans can define what it means to be an African American; with responses ranging from assimilation into majority society to a humanistic approach (e.g., Sellers, 1993; Sellers *et al.,* in press). These formulations focus on the stance of the minority with regard to relations with the majority and with larger society. While useful, these formulations do not provide a basis for specific hypotheses about the ways ethnic and racial identity can serve the basic functions of self-concept—organize experience, regulate affect and motivation—promoting successful goal attainment within American individualistic society.

Therefore, we developed our tripartite model of African American identity, proposing that African American identity promotes a sense of well-being and effective self-regulation when it contains three elements: a belief that achievement is part of being African American, a sense of connectedness to the African American community and heritage, and an awareness of obstacles and the possibility of racism (Oyserman *et al.,* 1995). Specifically, we proposed that African Americans develop a gendered African American identity schema to (1) make sense of the self as a group member; (2) lend meaning and organization to current and historical racism, limited opportunities and successes of African Americans; and (3) organize self-relevant knowledge about personal effort and its meaning as an African American male or female (Oyserman *et al.,* 1995). We view these components of identity as serving the well-being and motivational functions of the self.

In a series of preliminary studies we found that African American identity is particularly important for youth low in academic efficacy. Using this tripartite model of racial–ethnic identity, we have shown that African American identity is related to having more achievement related possible selves, increased feelings of perceived competence and efficacy, reduced depressive symptomatology and increased school effort—more study time and more persistence on school tasks (Oyserman *et al.,* 1995; Oyserman *et al.,* 1997).

Specifically, we hypothesized that racial–ethnic identity can have a positive influence on both academic outcomes and psychosocial well-being if it contains three components—a sense of connection to and identification with African American community and heritage, identification with learning and school achievement as part of being African American, and an awareness of obstacles and barriers that one may encounter because of one's group membership (e.g., Oyserman *et al.,* 1995; Oyserman *et al.,* 1997).

We suggest that ethnic identity serves as a connecting link between the individualistic achievement frame of majority society and the more collectivist heritage of ethnic minority youth. In this way it makes achievement a part of social identity, enhancing its value and reducing possible conflict between personal and social goals. Ethnic identity is also posited to serve as a mechanism to highlight the possibility of racism, stereotyping, and prejudice, thereby framing causal reasoning along these lines and reducing vulnerability to stereotyping. Finally, ethnic identity is posited to enhance goal attainment by highlighting the importance of persistence.

In a series of studies (Oyserman *et al.,* 1995; Oyserman *et al.,* 1997; Oyserman & Harrison, 1997) using experimental and survey methodologies (both cross-sectional and prospective across one school year) and involving approximately 400 middle school youth in Detroit, we found evidence for the impact of African American identity on school performance, depressive symptoms, school attachment, and possible selves. First, when identity is made salient, youth whose sense of self as an African American contains all three identity components—connectedness, awareness of racism, and embedded achievement—persist significantly longer at school tasks than do youth whose sense of self as an African American does not contain all three components. The embedded achievement component was found to be of particular importance for persistence.

Second, repeated measures analyses of variance showed that being high in all three components of African American identity significantly predicted both more time spent in homework in the late fall and an increase in study time over the school year. In contrast, youth low in all three identity components both spent less time studying in the late fall and actually reported decreased time spent in homework over the school year. By the end of the school year, youth differing in African American identity reported widely divergent time in homework, with the low-identity group reporting an average of about 5 minutes a school night in homework and the high-identity group reporting an average of about 20 minutes a school night in homework.

Further, across the school year, African American identity was found to reduce vulnerability to depressive symptoms. Of particular importance were the connectedness and awareness of racism components. With regard to school bonding, the connectedness and awareness of racism components of identity were particularly important such that youth who felt connected and aware of racism also reported feeling closer to teachers and believed that school was relevant to their everyday lives. In addition, repeated measures analyses of variance showed that youth high in the three components of ethnic identity were significantly more likely to develop balanced possible selves across the school year. While feeling academically inadequate and having low academic efficacy was related to worse school outcomes, connectedness moderated this relationship, reducing risk of poor school performance among youth who felt academically inadequate. Finally, together with balance in academic possible selves, African American identity significantly predicted performance on standardized tests of academic ability as well as grade point average. These findings suggest that racial and ethnic identity can positively impact on academic outcomes as well as reduce the negative consequences of personal feelings of inadequacy.

In a separate study, we sought to explore the extent to which racial and ethnic identity may relate to feelings of academic efficacy. In this study, we manipulated identity salience and examined the impact of identity content and salience on feelings of academic efficacy. Using repeated measures analyses, we found that feelings of academic efficacy drop significantly over the course of 8th grade but that youth higher in African American identity have higher academic efficacy both in the fall and in the spring (Oyserman & Harrison, 1997). We further found that when racial and ethnic identity is made salient, youth low in African American identity feel less academically efficacious. This negative effect of identity salience is not found for youth high in African American identity. This effect was particularly strong in the end of the school year when youth may already have been more concerned about their academic competence as they faced the end of 8th grade and the transition to high school.

CLOSING REMARKS

In this chapter, we sought to highlight the social–cultural nature of the self-concept, with particular focus on the content and structure of racial and ethnic identity. Using the situation of African Americans as our prime example, we proposed that Americans who are also members of ethnic and racial minorities must forge a sense of self that takes into account a cultural heritage based in both collectivism and individualism. The collectivist social representation of personhood includes a focus on family relatedness, and interdependence among group members (e.g., Burlew et al., 1992; Min, 1995), while the individualist social representation includes a focus on striving independence, personal agency, and personal achievement (e.g., Oyserman et al., 1995; Oyserman & Sakamoto, 1997).

This integration of individualistic and collectivistic social representations occurs within a context that traditionally stereotypes minorities as lacking in the valued attributes of majority society. We proposed that the individualistic social representation of personhood, with its emphasis on the individual as the basic unit, is risky for minority group members' sense of well-being, efficacy, and goal attainment. A collectivist social representation of personhood may serve to buffer individuals because collectivism promotes processing of context as important in causal reasoning.

This focus on context is especially important for minorities because contexts may be structured in ways that reduce group members' ability to succeed. In addition, for minority group members, focusing on one's self as causal axis is risky because members of minority groups are stereotypically perceived as less able to attain culturally valued goals than are majority group members (e.g., Steele, 1997). Therefore one's failures will be viewed as consonant with social representations of members of one's group rather than as unusual or uncharacteristic events that must be explained. When failure is attributed to stable characteristics about the self, motivation drops and effort over time flags (Dweck, 1996). Individuals may then stop trying, stop learning and persisting even in tasks in which they might be able eventually to succeed and instead focus on alternatives where success seems more likely. Because of this, minority group members must develop a sense of self that can both provide a means to reduce vulnerability to stereotypes and make salient contextually embedded structural barriers and also maintain focus on attaining successful outcomes such as academic achievement rather than only avoiding problems and setbacks in these domains (e.g., Higgins, 1997).

Taking this interaction into account, we proposed a model of ethnic and racial identity that contains a sense of connectedness to one's group, an awareness of obstacles for members of one's group and a belief that one can attain culturally valued academic achievement as a member of one's group. We proposed that racial and ethnic identity is likely to be part of the self-concept of African Americans and that the content of racial and ethnic identity is likely to have consequences for the everyday functions of self-concept, especially when this component of identity is chronically or situationally salient.

In a series of preliminary studies, we showed that components of ethnic identity are related to both individualism and collectivism and thus, do serve to connect individuals to their cultural heritage and to American society at large. In addition, ethnic identity as conceptualized here, does relate to academic performance and well-being. Our research group is now exploring the extent to which these components of identity can also be found to function similarly for minorities in other individual achievement oriented countries. If the ethnic identity components can be found and if they function similarly in countries other than the United States, it will suggest that ethnic identity serves both as a bridge between collective traditions and individualistic current contexts and as a buffer between the self and a negatively appraising context.

REFERENCES

Banaji, M. R., Hardin, C., & Rothman, A. J. (1993). Implicit stereotyping in personal judgment. *Journal of Personality and Social Psychology, 65,* 272–281.

Bat-Chava, Y., & Steen, E. (1996). *Ethnic identity and self-esteem: A meta-analytic review.* Manuscript under editorial review. New York University.

Beale-Spencer, M., Cunningham, M., & Swanson, D. (1995). Identity as coping: Adolescent African-American males' adaptive responses to high-risk environments. In H. Harris, H. Blue, & E. Griffith (Eds.), *Racial and ethnic identity: Psychological development and creative expression,* (pp. 31–52). New York: Routledge.

Biernat, M., Vescio, T., & Green, M. (1996). Selective self-stereotyping. *Journal of Personality and Social Psychology, 71,* 1194–1209.

Bodenhausen, G., Schwarz, N., Bless, H., & Wanke, M. (1995). Effects of atypical exemplars on racial beliefs: Enlightened racism or generalized appraisals. *Journal of Experimental Social Psychology, 31,* 48–63.

Bowser, B., & Perkins, H. (1991). Success against the odds: Young Black men tell what it takes. In B. Bowser, (Ed.), *Black male adolescents: Parenting and education in community context,* (pp. 183–200). New York: University Press.

Branscombe, N., & Ellemers, N. (1998). Coping with group-based discrimination: Individualistic versus group-level strategies. In J. K. Swim & C. Stangor (Eds.), *Prejudice: The Target's Perspective.* San Diego: Academic Press.

Brewer, M., & Gardner, W. (1996). Who is this "We"? Levels of collective identity and self representations. *Journal of Personality and Social Psychology, 71,* 83–93.

Burlew, A., Banks, W., McAdoo, H., & Azibo, D. (Eds.). (1992). *African American psychology: Theory, research, and practice.* Newbury Park, CA: Sage.

Cameron, J. E., & Lalonde, R. N. (1994). Self, ethnicity, and social group memberships in two generations of Italian Canadians. *Personality and Social Psychology Bulletin, 20,* 514–520.

Chan, S. (1991). *Asian Americans: An interpretive history.* New York: Twayne.

Coon, H., & Oyserman, D. (1997). *Individualism revisited: American individualism and collectivism.* Unpublished manuscript. University of Michigan.

Cose, E. (1993). *The rage of a privileged class.* New York: Harper Collins Books.

Crocker, J., Luhtanen, R., Blaine, B., & Broadnax, S. (1994). Collective self-esteem and psychological well-being among White, Black and Asian college students. *Personality and Social Psychology, 20*(5), 503–513.

Crocker, J., & Major, B. (1989). Social stigma and self-esteem: The self-protective properties of stigma. *Psychology Review, 96,* 608–630.

Crocker, J., Voelkl, K., Testa, M., & Major, B. (1991). Social stigma: The affective consequences of attributional ambiguity. *Journal of Personality and Social Psychology, 60,* 218–228.

Cross, W. E. (1991). *Shades of Black: Diversity in African-American identity.* Philadelphia, PA: Temple University Press.

Dweck, C. (1996). Implicit theories as organizers of goals and behavior. In P. Gollwitzer & J. Bargh (Eds.), *The psychology of action: Linking cognition and motivation to behavior* (pp. 69–90). New York: Guilford Press.

Dyson, M. E. (1993). *Reflecting Black African-American cultural criticism.* Minneapolis, MN: University of Minnesota Press.

Essed, P. (1990). *Everyday racism.* Claremont, CA: Hunter House, Inc.

Ford, D. (1992). Self-perceptions of underachievement and support for the achievement ideology among early adolescent African-Americans. *Journal of Early Adolescence, 12*(3), 228–252.

Fordham, S. (1988). Racelessness as a strategy in Black students' school success: Pragmatic strategy or pyrrhic victory? *Harvard Educational Review, 58*(1), 54–84.

Fordham, S., & Ogbu, J. (1986). Black students school success: Coping with the "burden of acting white." *The Urban Review, 18,* 176–206.

Fowers, B. J., & Richardson, F. C. (1996). Why is multiculturalism good? *American Psychologist, 51*, 609–621.

Fugita, S. S., & O'Brien, D. J. (1991). *Japanese American ethnicity: The persistence of community*. Seattle: University of Washington Press.

Graham, S. (1994). Motivation in African Americans. *Review of Educational Research, 64*, 55–117.

Gurin, P., Hurtado, A., & Peng, T. (1994). Group contacts and ethnicity in the social identities of Mexicanos and Chicanos. *Personality and Social Psychology Bulletin, 20*, 521–532.

Haslam, S., Oakes, P., McGarty, C., & Turner, J. (1996). Stereotyping and social influence: The mediation of stereotype applicability and sharedness by the view of in-group and outgroup members. *British Journal of Social Psychology, 35*, 369–397.

Higgins, E. T. (1996). The self-digest: Self knowledge selving self-regulatory functions. *Journal of Personality and Social Psychology, 71*, 1062–1083.

Higgins, E. T. (1997). *Promotion and prevention: Regulatory focus as a motivational principle*. Donald T. Campbell Award Address, Society of Personality and Social Psychology Preconference, American Psychological Society 9th Annual Conference, Washington, DC.

Hinkle, S., & Brown, R. (1990). Intergroup comparisons and social identity: Some links and lacunae. In D. Abrams & M. A. Hogg (Eds.), *Social identity theory: Constructive and critical advances* (pp. 48–70). New York: Harvester/Wheatsheaf.

Hofstede, G. (1991). Empirical models of cultural differences. In N. Bleichrodt & P. Drenth (Eds.), *Contemporary issues in cross-cultural psychology* (pp. 4–33). Berwyn, PA: Swets & Zeitlinger, Inc.

Hogg, M., & Abrams, D. (1990). Social motivation, self-esteem, and social identity. In D. Abrams & M. Hogg (Eds.), *Social identity theory: Constructive and critical advances* (pp. 28–41). New York: Harvester/Wheatsheaf.

Hoyt, S., & Miller, A. (1996, May). *Social class stereotypes: Content, awareness, and beliefs*. Poster presentation at the annual meeting of the Midwestern Psychological Association, Chicago.

Hsu, F. (1983). *Rugged individualism reconsidered*. Knoxville: University of Tennessee Press.

Hudson, B. (1995). Images used by African-Americans to combat stereotypes. In H. Harris, H. Blue, & E. Griffith (Eds.), *Racial and ethnic identity: Psychological development and creative expression* (pp. 135–172). New York: Routledge.

Hudson, R. (1991). Black male adolescent development deviating from the past: Challenges for the future. In B. Bowser (Ed.), *Black male adolescents: Parenting and education in community context*. (pp. 271–281). New York: University Press.

Hwang, K. (1987). Face and favor: The Chinese power game. *American Journal of Sociology, 92*, 944–74.

Judd, C. M., Park, B., Ryan, C. S., Brauer, M., & Kraus, S. (1995). Stereotypes and ethnocentrism: Interethnic perceptions of African American and White American college samples. *Journal of Personality and Social Psychology, 69*, 460–481.

Kagitcibasi, K. (1996). *Family and human development across cultures*. Mahwah, NJ: Lawrence Erlbaum.

Kowalski, R. M., & Wolfe, R. (1994). Collective identity orientation, patriotism and reactions to national outcomes. *Personality and Social Psychology Bulletin, 20*, 533–540.

Kunda, Z., Sinclair, L., & Griffin, D. (1997). Equal rating but separate meanings: Stereotypes and the construal of traits. *Journal of Personality and Social Psychology, 72*, 720–734.

LaFromboise, T., Coleman, H.L.K., & Gerton, J. (1993). Psychological impact of biculturalism: Evidence and theory. *Psychological Bulletin, 114*, 395–412.

Lamont, M., & Lareau, A. (1988). Cultural capital. *Sociological Theory, 6*, 153–168.

Landrine, H. (1992). Clinical implications of cultural differences: The referential versus indexical self. *Clinical Psychological Review, 12*, 401–415.

Lee, S. J. (1994). Behind the model-minority stereotype: Voices of high- and low-achieving Asian American students. *Anthropology & Education Quarterly, 25*, 413–429.

Markus, H. (1977). Self-schemata and processing information about the self. *Journal of Personality and Social Psychology, 35*, 63–78.

Markus, H., & Kitayama, S. (1991). Culture and the self: Implications for the cognition, emotion and motivation. *Psychological Review, 98*, 224–253.

Markus, H., Kitayama, S., & Heiman, R. (1996). Culture and basic psychological principles. In E. T. Higgins & A. W. Kruglanski (Eds.), *Social psychology: handbook of basic principles* (pp. 857–914). New York, NY: Guilford Press.

Markus, H., & Kunda, Z. (1986). Stability and malleability of the self-concept. *Journal of Personality and Social Psychology, 51,* 858–866.

McCreary, M., Slavin, L., & Berry, E. (1996). Predicting problem behavior and self-esteem among African American adolescents. *Journal of Adolescent Research, 11,* 194–215.

Min, P. (1995). *Asian Americans: Contemporary trends and issues.* Thousand Oaks, CA: Sage.

Myers, L. (1993). *Understanding an Afrocentric world view: Introduction to an optimal psychology.* Dubuque, IA: Kendall/Hunt.

Ng, S. (1989). Intergroup behavior and the self. *New Zealand Journal of Psychology, 18,* 1–12.

Ogbu, J. U. (1991). Minority coping responses and school experience. *The Journal of Psychohistory, 18,* 433–456.

Oyserman, D. (1993). Who influences identity: Adolescent identity and delinquency in interpersonal context. *Child Psychiatry and Human Development, 23*(3), 203–214.

Oyserman, D., Gant, L., & Ager, J. (1995). A socially contextualized model of African American identity: School persistence and possible selves. *Journal of Personality and Social Psychology 69*(6), 1216–1232.

Oyserman, D., & Harrison, K. (1997). *The implications of social identity and perceived impact on external barriers on stereotype vulnerability.* Unpublished manuscript.

Oyserman, D., & Markus, H. (1990a). Possible selves and delinquency. *Journal of Personality and Social Psychology, 59*(1), 112–125.

Oyserman, D., & Markus, H. (1990b). Possible selves in balance: Implications for delinquency. *Journal of Social Issues, 46,* 141–157.

Oyserman, D., & Markus, H. (1993). The sociocultural self. In J. Suls & A. G. Greenwald (Eds.), *Psychological Perspectives on the Self* (Vol. 4, pp. 187–220). Hillsdale, NJ: Lawrence Erlbaum Associates.

Oyserman, D., & Packer, M. (1996). The socio-contextual construction of the self. In J. J. Nye & A. M. Brower (Eds.), *What's social about social cognition?* Thousand Oaks, CA: Sage Publications.

Oyserman, D., & Sakamoto, I. (1997). Being Asian American: Identity, cultural constructs and stereotype perception. *Journal of Applied Behavioral Science, 33(4),* 435–453.

Oyserman, D., Sakamoto, I., & Lauffer, A. (In press). Cultural hybridity and the framing of social obligation. *Journal of Personality and Social Psychology.*

Oyserman, D., & Saltz, E. (1993). Competence, delinquency, and attempts to attain possible selves. *Journal of Personality and Social Psychology, 65,* 360–374.

Oyserman, D., Sanchez-Burks, J., & Harrison, K. (1997). *Implications of ethnic identity: Possible selves, school performance and resilience.* Unpublished manuscript.

Parham, T. A., & Helms, J. E. (1985). Relation of racial identity attitudes to self-actualization and affective states of black students. *Journal of Counseling Psychology, 32*(3), 431–440.

Patel, N., Power, T., & Bhavnagri, N. (1996). Socialization values and practices of Indian immigrant parents: Correlates of modernity and acculturation. *Child Development, 67,* 302–313.

Phinney, J. (1990). Ethnic identity in adolescence and adulthood: A review of research. *Psychological Bulletin, 108,* 499–514.

Phinney, J. S. (1996). When we talk about American ethnic groups, what do we mean? *American Psychologist, 51,* 918–927.

Phinney, J., & Cobb, N. (1996). Reasoning about intergroup relationship among Hispanic and Euro-American Adolescents. *Journal of Adolescent Research, 11,* 306–324.

Pinderhughes, E. (1995). Bi-racial identity—Asset or handicap? In H. Harris, H. Blue, & E. Griffith (Eds.), *Racial and ethnic identity: Psychological development and creative expression* (pp. 73–94). New York: Routledge.

Rosenberg, M. (1979). *Conceiving the self.* New York, NY: Basic Books.

Rosenberger, N. (Ed.) (1992). *Japanese sense of self.* New York, NY: Cambridge University Press.

Ross, L., & Nisbett, R. (1991). *The person and the situation: Perspectives of social psychology.* Philadelphia: Temple University Press.

Rueda-Riedle, A., & Oyserman, D. (1997). *Implications of accultural for individualism and collectivism among Hispanic women.* Unpublished manuscript.

Sampson, E. (1988). The debate on individualism: Indigenous psychologies of the individual and their role in personal and societal functioning. *American Psychologist, 43,* 15–22.

Schwartz, S. (1990). Individualism-collectivism: Critique and proposed refinements. *Journal of Cross Cultural Psychology, 21,* 139–157.

Schweder, R., & Bourne, E. (1984). Does the concept of the person vary cross-culturally? In R. Schweder & R. LaVine (Eds.), *Culture theory: Essays on mind, self, and emotion* (pp. 158–199). New York: Cambridge University Press.

Sellers, R. (1993). A call to arms for research studying racial identity. *Journal of Black Psychology, 19,* 327–332.

Sellers, R., Rowley, S., Chavous, T., Shelton, J., & Smith, M. (In press). Multidimensional inventory of Black identity: Preliminary investigation of reliability and construct validity. *Journal of Personal and Social Psychology.*

Shaver, P., Wu, S., & Schwartz, J. (1992). Cross-cultural similarities and differences in emotion and its representation. In M. S. Clark (Ed.), *Review of personality and social psychology* (Vol. 13, pp. 175–212). Newbury Park, CA: Sage.

Showers, C. (1995). The evaluative organization of self-knowledge: origins, processes, and implications for self-esteem. In M. Kernis (Ed), *Efficacy, agency and self-esteem.* New York: Plenum Press.

Steele, C. (1988). The psychology of self-affirmation. *Advances in Experimental Social Psychology, 21,* 261–302.

Steele, C. (1997). A burden of suspicion: How stereotypes shape the intellectual identities and performance of women and African-Americans. *American Psychologist, 52,* 613–629.

Steele, C., & Aronson, J. (1995). Stereotype threat and the intellectual test performance of African Americans. *Journal of Personality and Social Psychology, 69,* 797–811.

Steele, C., Spencer, S., & Aronson, J. (1995). *Inhibiting the expression of intelligence: The role of stereotype vulnerability.* Paper presented at 103rd Annual Convention of the American Psychological Association, New York, NY.

Stryker, S., & Serpe, R. T. (1994). Identity salience and psychological centrality: Equivalent, overlapping, or complementary concepts? *Social Psychology Quarterly, 57,* 16–35.

Tajfel, H. (1978). *Differential between social groups: Studies in the social psychology of intergroup relations.* New York, NY: Academic Press.

Takaki, R. (Ed.). (1994). *From different shores: Perspectives on race and ethnicity in America. 2nd Ed.* New York: Oxford University Press.

Taylor, S., & Brown, J. (1988). Illusion and well-being: A social psychological perspective on mental health. *Psychological Bulletin, 103,* 193–210.

Taylor, S., Buunk, B., & Aspinwall, L. (1990). Social comparison, stress, and coping. *Personality and Social Psychology Bulletin, 17,* 74–89.

Taylor, D. M., & Dube, L. (1986). Two faces of identity: The "I" and the "we". *Journal of Social Issues, 42,* 81–98.

Tessor, A. (1986). Some effects of self-evaluation maintenance on cognition and action. In R. M. Sorrentino & E. T. Higgins (Eds.), *Handbook of motivation and cognition: Foundations of social behavior* (pp. 435–464). New York: Guilford Press.

Triandis, H. C. (1995). *Individualism and collectivism.* Boulder, CO: Westview Press.

Triandis, H. (1989). The self and social behavior in differing cultural contexts. *Psychological Review, 96,* 506–520.

Triandis, H., Kashima, E., Shimada, E., & Villareal, M. (1986). Acculturation indices as a means of confirming culturation differences. *International Journal of Psychology, 21,* 43–70.

Tripp, L. (1991). Race consciousness among African-American students, 1980's. *The Western Journal of Black Studies, 15,* 159–168.

Tropman, J. E. (1989). *American values and social welfare: Cultural contradictions in the Welfare State.* Englewood Cliffs, NJ: Prentice Hall.

Turner, J. C., Hogg, M., Oakes, P. J., Reichher, S., & Wetherell, S. (1987). *Rediscovering the social group: A self-categorization theory.* Oxford, England: Basil Blackwell.

Turner, J. C., & Oakes, P. J. (1986). The significance of the social identity concept for social psychology with reference to individualism, interactionism and social influence. Special Issue: The individual-society interface. *British Journal of Social Psychology, 25,* 237–252.

Turner, J. C., Oakes, P. J., Haslam, S. A., & McGarty, C. (1994). Self and collective: Cognition and social context. Special Issue: The self and the collective. *Personality & Social Psychology Bulletin, 20*(5), 454–463.

van Knippenberg, A. (1989). Strategies of identity management. In J. P. van Oudenhoven & T. M. Willemsen (Eds.), *Ethnic minorities: Social psychological perspectives* (pp. 59–76). Amsterdam: Swets & Zeitlinger.

Wittenbrink, B., Gist, P., & Hilton, J. (1997). Structural properties of stereotypic knowledge and their influence on the construal of social situations. *Journal of Personality and Social Psychology, 72,* 526–543.

Wittenbrink, B., Judd, C., & Park, B. (1997). Evidence for racial prejudice at the implicit level and its relationship with questionnaire measures. *Journal of Personality and Social Psychology, 72,* 262–274.

Wong, C., & Eccles, J. (1996). *The effects of racial discrimination on African American students' motivation and school achievement.* Paper presented at the Annual Meeting of the American Educational Researchers Association Meeting.

14

NEGOTIATING
SOCIAL IDENTITY

KAY DEAUX

City University of New York

KATHLEEN A. ETHIER

Yale University

Social identities—those constructions of self that relate the person to some collective group or category—exist in a continuous process of negotiation and renegotiation. Whether the result of changed goals or changed circumstances, people actively adjust their self-definitions, alter their reference groups, and modify their behaviors to deal with these changes. In this chapter, we consider this process of identity negotiation: a process that characterizes most social identity dynamics much of the time, and that is, more specific to the themes of this volume, a critical element in analyzing how targets respond to prejudice.

We define identity negotiation as agentic identity work carried out in response to contextual demands. Identity negotiation is an ongoing process, best conceived as continual efforts directed at maintaining existing identities as well as adapting to changing circumstances. Extreme changes or dramatic life events illuminate, in more sharply etched fashion, the nature of the negotiation process. Moving to a new location, for example, can challenge previously untested assumptions about one's identity (Hormuth, 1990), as tourists frequently observe when they enter a new culture. Taking on new roles, such as becoming a parent for the first time, illustrates another situation in which active identity work occurs (Ethier, 1995). Although the boundaries of identity negotiation are wide, we focus in this chapter on a particular set of conditions that prompt identity negotiation, specifically those situations in which a person is potentially the target of prejudice and discrimination because of a particular identification (either categorically imposed by others or claimed by the self).

Our coverage will emphasize several themes. First, we adopt the framework of social identification (Deaux, 1996). From this perspective, targets are considered not simply as individuals but rather as members of social categories. Accordingly, they are viewed by others as representative of a group of like people, and they see themselves as sharing specifiable attributes and concerns with those who share their social identity. Second, we focus on the dynamics of identity negotiation, regarding it as an agentic process in which people actively define the self and communicate their claimed identities to others. As noted above, we regard identity negotiation as "normal," ongoing social behavior. Third, we believe it is important to recognize that people function in varying contexts. In some of these contexts, a particular identity may be the target of considerable prejudice and discrimination; in other contexts, the same identity may be supported and strengthened or perhaps simply ignored. Shifts between these environments, both by chance and by choice, are important to examine.

We begin our analysis of identity negotiation by developing, in more detail and with more support, the general themes already stated. Next we review the major strategies that people use to negotiate their identities and consider some of the circumstances that prompt those negotiations. We then turn to a specific set of instigating conditions that are particularly relevant to the theme of this book, namely the concepts of threat and stigmatization. As we will argue, these conditions are not necessary to induce identity negotiation, but they do press for particular strategies of identity negotiation. Following these more general discussions, we introduce a specific case study to illustrate some of the issues raised. We use material gathered in a study of Hispanic students entering elite universities, a context that provides vivid examples of prejudice, perceived threats, and identity negotiation. Following this case study material, we will propose a model of identity negotiation in response to stigmatization and point to some research questions that remain to be explored.

IDENTITY NEGOTIATION: SETTING THE PARAMETERS

WHAT'S SOCIAL ABOUT IDENTIFICATION?

To understand the process of identity negotiation, particularly as it relates to the exercise of prejudice and discrimination, it is important to understand how the individual and the group or culture interact in the construction and maintenance of a social identity. From our perspective, a social identity is both a categorical definition or membership and a set of meanings associated with that category (Reid & Deaux, 1996). Thus, one places oneself in a particular category or takes on a particular label, such as feminist, African American, or pediatrician, and also associates that category with a set of attributes, behaviors, and meanings. These attributes, behaviors, and meanings are in large part socially defined, both by the society at large and by the experiences and agenda of the ingroup with which one is identified. In addition, individual experience with a particular identity can add or shape the meaning associated with a category, leading people to perhaps add to or substitute some of the cultural message with meaning of their own.

At the broadest level, the meanings associated with a particular identity category derive from the social representations of the culture (Breakwell, 1993; Moscovici, 1988). Thus, what it means to be a feminist, an African American, or a pediatrician is informed by the stereotypes, media representations, and communications that a society offers. Stereotypes are themselves a social product. As Spears, Oakes, Ellemers, and Haslam (1997) remind us, "sharedness is more than an important dimension to stereotypes, it is what makes them social—idiosyncratic 'stereotypes' are likely to be of little social consequence and to play only a marginal, if any, role in group life" (p. 8).

The shared aspects of meaning, derived from general social representations, provide the basis for assumed similarity among members of a category, both by outside observers and by members themselves. On the one hand, this shared meaning provides a "ready-made" definition of the identity to be used, facilitating communication within and between categories of membership. On the other hand, the consensual aspect of this definition can serve as a constraint to individual definition. It may be difficult to identify with a category while rejecting a substantial portion of the meanings associated with that category. The contemporary Catholic in the United States, for example, may struggle with which aspects of official church doctrine can be rejected while still maintaining a religious identity. In our own research, we have seen the role that language can play in identity definition. Can one claim to be Latino, for example, if knowledge of Spanish is minimal?

While individuals debate which aspects of the social definition to accept for themselves, outsiders viewing the person may too readily apply, in blanket fashion, the set of traits they associate with a membership category. The voluminous literature on stereotyping attests to the readiness of observers to assume characteristics and to act on the basis of those assumptions (Fiske, in press). The impact of these assumptions on the individual will vary as a function of their nature and their translation into action. In the case of stigmatization and prejudice, the assumptions held by outsiders are largely negative and their resultant actions can be exclusionary and/or detrimental. As a consequence, people who can be readily identified as being a member of one of these stigmatized categories must deal with a social world that, at least in part, can be seen as a hostile environment. At the same time, we know that while members of a stigmatized group may be aware of and acknowledge the negative images of others, they do not necessarily accept them as part of their group definition (Crocker & Major, 1989; Crocker, Luhtanen, Blaine, & Broadnax, 1994).

As suggested earlier, ingroups create their own set of meanings associated with group membership—a subcultural level of social representation that is shared and communicated among members of the identity category. Often, members of the outgroup will remain totally ignorant of the attributes and meanings that are shared by members of the ingroup. The rituals of fraternities and sororities, for example, are largely unknown to the non-Greek observer. The symbolic meanings of Kwanza remain unknown to the majority of North Americans. Such activities by the ingroup not only contribute to a sense of collective purpose, but they also can offer positively valued meanings to a category that is denigrated or stigmatized by outsiders.

Thus, it is within a decidedly social context that people negotiate their identities (a position advocated years ago by George Herbert Mead, among others). A given identity is shared with some (ingroup members) and reacted to by others (outgroup members). In neither case can the individual be realistically viewed as acting alone or in a vacuum, independent of norms and cultural beliefs. Identity negotiation is, by definition, a social activity.

DYNAMICS OF SOCIAL IDENTIFICATION

Social identification is a dynamic rather than static process. Within some limits, the meanings associated with an identity are subject to change as new experiences shape and modify the initial definitions. Much like the characterization of culture offered by Markus, Kitayama, and Heiman as "personalized, dynamic, and open-ended" (1996, p. 868), identity definition is an ongoing process that shifts over place and time. What causes these shifts in identity and what range of options is available to the person negotiating an identity are key issues that we explore in this chapter.

Agency is evident not only in the meanings that are associated with a particular category, but with the choice of which identities to claim and when to assert them. It is sometimes thought that one is "stuck" with certain identities, particularly those ascribed by demographic categories such as gender, age, or ethnicity. Yet in fact people vary significantly in their propensity to claim even these visible category memberships. In the case of ethnicity, for example, Waters (1990) reports considerable variation in the degree to which people claim their ethnic group membership. Ethier and Deaux (1990) reported that 13% of students in their sample who were identified as Hispanic by their universities did not personally claim that ethnic label. Biracial identity offers a particularly interesting example of identity choice (Kerwin & Ponterotto, 1995). People of multiracial background have a choice to claim the ethnic category of either parent, or to define themselves as neither, perhaps choosing an integrated ethnic category. Further, these choices can be altered over time, as personal goals and situational contexts vary.[1]

---

[1]One student interviewed in our project provided a striking example of identity change. When interviewed initially, he claimed both an African American and a Latino identity, reflecting his mixed parentage, and he rated the African American identity as the more personally important of the two. Approximately 6 months later, he claimed only a Latino identity, which he rated as more important than it had been earlier.

Over time, social identification often changes. The meanings associated with a particular category may change, the importance attached to an identity may change, or the existence of the category itself may be established or removed (Deaux, 1991). Stage theories of identification, especially as developed in reference to ethnic identity, specify particular sequences of change in the identity process. As one example, Phinney (1990) proposes three stages of development: first, a state in which ethnic identity is not explored or considered in any depth; second, a period of exploration and search; and third, a state of achievement in which one is confident about one's ethnicity. Other authors have proposed similar sequences of development for ethnicity (Cross, 1978, 1991), for gay and lesbian identity (Troiden, 1989), and for identity as a feminist (Downing & Roush, 1985). On the other side of the coin, authors such as Ebaugh (1988) have discussed the sequence of events leading to the weakening and eventual elimination of an identity. In both acquisition and relinquishment processes, the person engages in an ongoing negotiation of identity with self, others, and environment.

THE SIGNIFICANCE OF CONTEXT

Not only do identities shift over time, in a long-term sense, but people often make choices among various identities as they move from one circumstance to another. In some cases, a setting may shape a particular reaction or choice, as the classroom makes identities as student or teacher more salient. Self-categorization theory (Turner *et al.*, 1987) emphasizes contextual shifts in identity salience, positing that the accessibility of a category and its fit to the distribution of people in the immediate environment will determine which identity becomes operative. Brewer (1991, 1993), in her model of optimal distinctiveness, offers a more motivational basis for social identity choice, based on a person's competing needs for inclusion and differentiation.

In more agentic ways, people actively seek out contexts in which a particular identity can best be displayed. The work of Swann and his colleagues (Swann & Ely, 1984; McNulty & Swann, 1994) depicts the person as an active architect, presenting an identity to others and seeking to have that identity confirmed. Taking this process one step further, we can imagine that people not only describe themselves in ways that emphasize a particular identity, but they also place themselves in situations where those descriptions are most likely to be elicited. Thus, the would-be intellectual might frequent the library or selected coffee houses to convey the desired image.

Because identity negotiation is a social process, it is also important to consider how the views of others influence one's own identity claims. Others may, for example, assign a category that the person himself or herself does not claim, or which is of only secondary importance. Such possibly misdirected assignments may be particularly likely for categories that are visible to the other, such as gender, ethnicity, or age. Alternatively, others in the environment may not recognize an identity that is of central importance to the person. Occupational identities

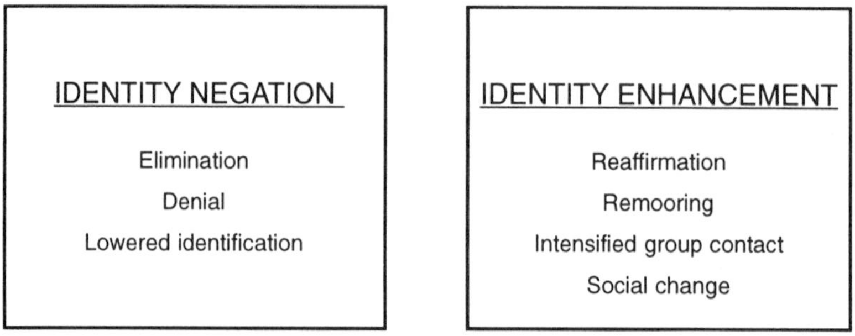

IDENTITY NEGATION	IDENTITY ENHANCEMENT
Elimination	Reaffirmation
Denial	Remooring
Lowered identification	Intensified group contact
	Social change

FIGURE 14.1   Identity negotiation strategies.

may be ignored or misattributed, for example, if ethnic or gender stereotypes predominate.

These examples suggest that questions of contextual change are particularly important to address when thinking about identity negotiation by those who are targets of prejudice, discrimination, and stigmatization. For people in these groups, mislabeling may be a common occurrence. At the same time, people subjected to these negative experiences frequently have options to find other environments in which the same identity is not stigmatized but rather is valued and supported. For many, these alternative environments are ones that are shared with others who have the same identification. Ethnic students may seek out cultural clubs on campus; deaf students may go to Gallaudet; and gays and lesbians may develop a network of clubs and vacation spots. In each case, an identity subject to stigmatization in one environment finds support and shared values in another environment.

STRATEGIES OF IDENTITY NEGOTIATION

With the ground rules in place—identity as a social phenomenon, actively constructed within specifiable contexts—we turn to a consideration of the mechanics of identity negotiation. What form does identity negotiation take, and how and why do people engage in the process? Identity negotiation occurs, we suggest, when there is a perceived need to adjust or in some way redefine a particular identity, as a consequence of some social, psychological or contextual demands. In the simplest taxonomy, negotiation strategies take one of two forms: (1) identity negation; and (2) identity enhancement. Within each category several more specific tactics can be described, which are listed in Fig. 14.1 and will be discussed in greater detail.

In several respects, these two general strategies resemble the options that social identity theory posits as ways of attaining positive self-esteem (Hogg & Abrams, 1990). From this particular theoretical perspective, a subjective belief in mobility of the social structure leads the dissatisfied individual to abandon the subordinate group and pass into the dominant group, that is, to negate the identity. Alternatively, if a person believes that the structural boundaries are fixed and relatively impermeable, social identity theory suggests that people will either choose social creativity, encompassing a variety of strategies that increase the value of the social identity, or social action, directed at altering the existent social structure (also see Branscombe & Ellemers, Chapter 11 this volume). Without necessarily adopting the language of dominant and subordinate group, the two forms of identity negotiation presented here are similar in their distinction between denial and affirmation.

IDENTITY NEGATION

For those tactics classified as forms of identity negation, the goal is to dissociate oneself from a social identity that is, for some reason, aversive or nonsatisfying. Attempts to dissociate show some variation in intensity and finality, ranging from total elimination of an identity to less dramatic shifts in the importance attached to a particular identity.

Eliminating an Identity

Perhaps the most extreme choice for identity negation is to simply abandon or eliminate a social identification. At least two conditions appear necessary for this strategy to be adopted: first, a negative evaluation of the identity, and second, a belief that one can escape the category. With regard to the first of these conditions, we stress that the negative evaluation of the identity must be subjective. Public derogation of a category, in the form of negative stereotypes and discrimination, is not sufficient to cause a person to devalue their category (Crocker & Major, 1989). Indeed, these two dimensions of evaluation are often independent of one another (Ethier & Deaux, 1990; Luhtanen & Crocker, 1992).[2]

A second condition for identity negation is a belief that one can get out of the category, similar to the belief in structural mobility posited by social identity theory. To accomplish this change, the individual must believe that the boundaries of an identity are permeable and that, with relative ease, he or she can pass from one category to another. At first glance, it might seem that identity elimination would be impossible for identities that are defined by demographic features, such as gender, ethnicity, or age. However, if one accepts the premise that social identification is a subjective rather than objective status (Deaux, 1993), then identity elimination is an option hypothetically available in all instances. Numerous examples, both anecdotal and empirical, attest to the possibilities of denying ethnic-

---

[2]Crocker and her colleagues (Crocker, Luhtanen, Blaine, & Broadnax, 1994) report that the relationship between public and private acceptance of ethnic identity, assessed by the Luhtanen and Crocker (1992) Collective Self-Esteem scale, varies between ethnic groups. Among Asian Americans, for example, these two measures were highly correlated, while there was no relationship between the two subscales for African Americans, suggesting that Asian Americans are more strongly influenced by the opinions of others than are African Americans.

ity and age in self-definition. At the same time, the propensity of others to use visible markers to define someone's categorical membership makes complete elimination less likely in these cases.

Ebaugh (1988) uses the term "role exit" in referring to the process of identity elimination. As she describes "becoming an ex-," people first begin to doubt their role commitment, often as a result of some event in their environment (e.g., reorganization or downsizing at the workplace, a change in the status of a relationship). They then begin to seek alternatives, and at some point realize that the old role is no longer desirable and that other attractive options exist. In the course of this process, people will make changes in reference groups and in contexts, as well as in self-definition. Ebaugh (1988) suggests that as part of this process individuals frequently maintain an identity as an "ex-member" of the group or category that they have abandoned.

This idea can be taken one step further when examining cases in which individuals change a stigmatized, negatively evaluated identity into a positive, socially accepted identity. Brown (1991), for instance, discusses the transition that some people make from being a drug addict to being a drug counselor as a process of becoming a "professional ex-." Similarly, advocates for the homeless, social workers, and counselors often have a personal history as members of the category of people they are trying to help.

It can be argued that this transformation of role, like becoming an "ex," is less the abandonment of an identity than its reinterpretation. Indeed, the creative possibilities for relabeling identities and reconstituting their meaning argue for considering some overlap among the suggested categories of identity negotiation. At the same time, the strategies of identity negation described here all imply a willingness to make significant changes in self-definition in order to decrease or eliminate the negative implications of an existent identification.

Denial of Identity

A slightly different strategy of identity negation is denial. Although the term could be considered a more psychological variation of identity elimination, we use denial here to refer to those cases in which some external source is applying a label with which the target does not identity. Stephen Carter, discussing affirmative action, illustrates this sense of discrepancy and denial with the following comments: "To be black and an intellectual in America is to live in a box. So I live in a box, not of my own making, and on the box is a label, not of my own choosing" (1991, p. 1).

Frequently, the identity imposed by others will be one cued by visible markers, such as gender, ethnicity, or age. Yet because of the subjective nature of social identification, the label, even if objectively valid, may not be acceptable to the person involved. Older people in the United States often experience this kind of discrepancy, as when a stranger on a subway offers to give up a seat to a white-haired but otherwise agile person, or when jokes are made about retirement status to someone who is strongly identified with his or her occupation.

For the target of mislabeling, denial is unlikely to fully resolve the dilemma. Particularly if cues are visible, the mislabeling is likely to be repeated in new situations. As a consequence, denial may be most successful if accompanied by enhancement strategies, directed at putting alternative identities in the foreground.

Decreasing Importance of an Identity

Less dramatic than elimination or denial, decreasing the importance of an identity is a way of reordering one's priorities. As in the case of identity elimination, some negative evaluations probably provide the impetus for change. However, either because of the perceived impossibility of abandoning the identification or a wish to maintain some connection with those for whom the identity is important (e.g., a parent who values a particular religious affiliation), the person can choose to retain an identity but to deemphasize its importance. Longitudinal studies of identity (Deaux, 1991; Ethier, 1995; Ethier & Deaux, 1994) have shown that although the basic set of identities claimed by a person is generally fairly stable over time, there are also fluctuations in importance. Often these changes are due to altered circumstances. After the birth of a first child, for example, many women rate their identity as spouse less important while their mother identity takes on more prominence (Ethier, 1995).

Decreasing (or increasing) the importance associated with a particular identity is a particularly flexible strategy of identity negation, allowing a person to respond to immediate situational pressures without relinquishing a well-established identification. The situational advantages of this strategy seem clear, though the longer term consequences for identity maintenance are less certain.

IDENTITY ENHANCEMENT

Under the general umbrella of identity enhancement, we consider a number of negotiation strategies that share the common goal of asserting or extending an existent identity. In contrast to a negation strategy, this family of strategies is adopted to strengthen an existent identity, to perhaps link it to a new context, or to extend the perimeter of the social network to include additional people into the category. Four specific strategies are discussed: reaffirmation, remooring, intensified group contact, and social change.

Reaffirmation

Reaffirmation refers to identity work in which the person proclaims or reasserts an identity that is already part of her or his self-definition. If the existent identification is relatively weak, reaffirmation efforts may reflect primarily a change in the importance or intensity of the identity relative to other bases of self-identification. Reaffirmation can also occur when some shift occurs in the meanings and connotations of an identity, which the person will then try to convey to others. Alternatively, reaffirmation can be a response to a social environment that is either unaware of or challenging to the identity in question.

"Black is beautiful" represents a clear case of reaffirmation within U.S. cultural history. In adopting this phrase, Blacks both affirmed a particular identity and attempted to alter the value associated with the category. Subsequently, the adoption of African American as a categorical label represented a new form of reaffirmation of this ethnic identity, bringing with it a new set of associated attributes (Philogene, 1996).

Early analyses of acculturation often assumed that people entering a new culture would readily adapt to that culture, giving up their original ethnic identity in preference to the new culture. Kosmitzki (1994) pitted this version of acculturation against predictions derived from social identity and self-categorization theory, which suggest that the contrast between self and others would accentuate self-stereotyping. Her sample consisted of Germans and Americans who were either monocultural (having lived continuously in their native countries) or bicultural (born in one country but currently living in the other). In terms of their endorsement of stereotypic traits to the self, biculturals saw themselves as more similar to the ingroup stereotype than did monoculturals, an outcome that Kosmitzki (1994) termed the reaffirmation effect. These results, consistent with self-categorization theory, suggest that one way of negotiating identity when the context changes is to accentuate the distinctiveness of the identity that one brings to the new environment and contrast it with the surroundings.

Remooring

Whereas reaffirmation primarily concerns cognitive adjustments and verbal statements of identity, remooring speaks to more active behavioral involvement. As defined by Ethier and Deaux (1994, p. 244), the process of remooring involves developing new bases for supporting an identity when the context has changed, and at the same time detaching the identity from its supports in the former environment. Techniques of remooring include seeking information about the group, associating with new group members, and participating in organized events associated with the social identity.

Context is critical to an analysis of remooring. Whether by choice or by circumstance, the environment in which an identity is exercised changes, and the person must decide how the identity can be maintained in the new context. A professor who moves to a new university, for example, may seek out the local chapter of the American Association of University Professors, set up a series of lunches with new colleagues, and develop courses that fit the curriculum of the new university. Each of these activities would be an attempt to place the identity of professor in a new context, rather than to rely on the inevitably weakening supports provided by the previous place of employment. Similar remooring strategies were used by the Hispanic students entering university in the Ethier and Deaux (1994) study, to be discussed in more detail later.

Remooring represents an attempt to reposition the self, often in response to some environmental change that demands this kind of reconsideration. The change itself can often be considered part of the remooring process, as the individual chooses to reposition a particular identity. Thus, the professor may move from a private to a public institution, or vice versa, as a means of adjusting the meaning of professor and/or researcher. Similarly, ethnic identity may motivate an African American in New York City to move to a new home in Harlem, where that identity can be connected to a set of cultural institutions, traditions, and neighbors that will nurture the identity.

Intensified Group Contact

Increased contact with other group members is closely related to remooring as a strategy of identity negotiation. The point of differentiation between the two is that whereas remooring typically involves some substantial shift in context, intensified group contact can be carried out in one's current environment. Often this strategy is a response to some particular threat or uncertainty in the ongoing context, which can be at least partially resolved by affiliation (Schachter, 1959) and the attendant social comparison processes. A new mother, for example, might make a point of going to a neighborhood park frequented by parents and children in strollers in order to affiliate and to compare experiences.

For people whose identities are stigmatized by some sectors of the population, contact with other group members can serve as a means of counteracting discrimination, enhancing self-esteem, and learning ways to adapt or cope with stigma. With the endorsement of others having the same identity, a person can affirm the value of group membership rather than incorporate the negative views of those who stigmatize.

Group contact can take place in organized as well as informal settings. The continuing growth of support groups is an example of how associating with others who share a stigmatized identity enables group members to cope with stigma and discrimination (Eastland, 1995; Harris, 1995). Organized groups serve as a basis of identity extension for those who are members of nonstigmatized groups as well. Parents or spouses of children with illness, for example, or the patients themselves often form groups both to acknowledge an identity group as well as to gain information and support for that identification.

A more contemporary example of group contact is provided in a recent study by McKenna and Bargh (1997) of internet news groups. For members of marginalized groups, these "virtual" communities were particularly important, providing a safe context for identity expression. As compared to members of nonstigmatized groups, those with stigmatized identities were more active in posting to their newsgroup and were more responsive to positive posts from other members. Further, to the extent that people with stigmatized identities participated in these groups, they were more accepting of their identity and more likely to "come out" to families and friends (with the link between activity and outcome mediated by the importance of the identity).

Social Change

A fourth type of enhancement strategy is one in which the focus is primarily on others rather than the self. The goal in this case is some form of social change: either to change the beliefs that others hold about one's social category, or to change the social system in some way that will facilitate the expression and recognition of the identity.

As suggested earlier, this strategy is most likely to be chosen when it is believed that identity boundaries are impermeable and unchangeable. Harris (1995), in his discussion of the impact of stereotypes on people with learning disabilities, suggests that individuals adopt collective strategies for social change as a means to maintain a positive self-concept. Social change is also more likely to be adopted as a negotiation strategy when the identity in question is associated with a high degree of collective involvement (Deaux & Reid, in preparation; Simon, Pantaleo, & Mummendey, 1995). Particularly when faced with threats to a group's fortunes, members of the group are likely to exert collective efforts to restructure the situation so that it becomes more favorable to their objectives.

Strategies for social change and social influence are varied, ranging from individual attempts to educate and change the attitudes of proximal outgroup members to the use of courts to change unfair institutional practices to large scale group demonstration (Watts, 1992). Members of stigmatized groups may choose any number of these strategies, depending on the degree to which they identify with the group, how much they experience stigma or discrimination, or the ways in which they define their group membership (Watts, 1992; Gutierrez & Ortega, 1991; Moore, 1991; Gurin & Townsend, 1986).

BALANCING ENHANCEMENT
AND NEGATION STRATEGIES

In sum, there are a variety of identity negotiation strategies that can serve the general goal of affirming or strengthening an existent identity. Some rely primarily on cognitive activities, while others involve behavioral choices and social interactions. Often, we suspect, they are used in combination to accomplish greater validation of identities that are important and potentially threatened by events and changes in environment.

In some cases, the enhancement of one identity may be accompanied by the negation of another. Thus, in identifying as a cult member, for example, many adherents will negate their previous roles as daughter or son, husband or wife. Steele (1988, 1992), in his work on self-affirmation theory, suggests that people will respond to threats to one identity by emphasizing another, a process which he uses to characterize the "dis-identification" of some minority youth with an academic identity.

The relation between enhancement and negation is not necessarily a one-to-one correspondence, however. Because most people hold a number of important identifications concurrently (Deaux, 1993), identities that can exist independently of one another, it is quite possible to affirm one identity without having an impact on other identities. It is equally possible for a person to affirm more than one identity during the same time period, or to negate more than one at a time.

Whether identity negotiation in one domain will influence identity work in another domain depends on a number of factors. The degree to which two identities are related or implicate each other is one such factor (Reid & Deaux, 1996), as implied by the traditional concept of role conflict. Also drawing from the literature of role theory, one can posit that if the time demands of two identities are both great, in the sense of role overload, then activities in one domain may impact the other. Ethier (1995), for example, found that new mothers were apt to decrease the importance of most nonfamily roles, as well as the role of spouse, in the months immediately following the birth of a first baby when the mother identity predominated. (Whether this pattern continues after the first 3 months of birth is unknown at this point.) The balance of identity negotiation strategies may also depend on the particular functions satisfied by any given identity (Deaux, Reid, Mizrahi, & Cotting, in press). Negation of an identity that serves important functions, such as for self-understanding or ingroup cooperation, might well motivate the person to enhance another identity that has the potential to satisfy these functions.

IDENTITY NEGOTIATION AS A CONSEQUENCE OF STIGMATIZATION AND THREAT

The negotiation strategies described here, either in the service of identity enhancement or identity negation, have a wide range of applicability. Presumably they are activated when there is some question about the status of a particular social identity. Those questions may be quite minor and nonthreatening, as when one converses at a dinner party and attempts to establish a desired identity to comparative strangers. Alternatively, the circumstances that lead to identity negotiation can present much more serious threats, requiring more intense and more sustained negotiation.

Given the focus of this volume, we will look more closely at the latter circumstances. In particular, we consider the situation in which an identity is stigmatized by others and the threats to identity that may (or may not) result. Further, we will propose that the perception of threat is a key mediator in the relationship between stigmatization and the choice of an identity negotiation strategy.

STIGMATIZATION

Although many circumstances can threaten an identity, stigmatization is one of the most pernicious and may indeed be one of the most common. As this volume documents, stigmatized identities include gender, ethnicity, sexual orientation, and obesity. Even more broadly, depending upon the particular context, it is possible to consider almost any social identification as a potential target of stigmatization. Thus, the intellectual academic may be a target of derision among more practically oriented workers; a member of a particular nationality group may be honored in some countries and negatively viewed in others.

The term stigma typically refers to some specific feature or characteristic of a target that is undesirable. As Goffman (1963) begins his classic work, "The Greeks, who were apparently strong on visual aids, originated the term *stigma* to refer to bodily signs designed to expose something unusual and bad about the moral status of the signifier. The signs were cut or burnt into the body and advertised that the bearer was a slave, a criminal, or a traitor—a blemished person, ritually polluted, to be avoided . . ." (p. 1). Subsequent layers of definition from medicine, zoology, and religion refer to marks, spots, and wounds. Each of these meanings conveys a sense of clarity and objectivity in defining stigma, providing a physical base from which more psychological understandings of stigmatization derive. Consequently, analyses of stigma often fall prey to the fundamental attribution error, pointing to the target or victim as the source of the stigmatized condition.

In fact, however, stigmatization must be defined both in terms of target and of perceiver. Crocker, Major, and Steele (in press) define stigma in the following way: "Stigmatized individuals possess (or are believed to possess) some attribute, or characteristic, that conveys a social identity that is devalued in some particular context" (pp. 2–3 of ms.). Crocker and colleagues go on to emphasize the social construction of stigma: both the decision as to what attribute is to be devalued and the judgment of who belongs to the stigmatized category are subjectively determined, not objective realities. Further, these authors, like others before them (e.g. Archer, 1985), recognize that a characteristic that might be stigmatized in one context can be ignored or even valued in another context.

Stigmatization represents a cognitive categorization process, in which a perceiver views a target person in a particular way. Such processes are of particular concern because they are often manifested in behavior toward the target, specifically discriminatory behavior. It is these actions, both subtle and blatant, that can lead to active strategies of identity negotiation. Whether stigmatization leads to identity negotiation and which strategies are chosen by the individual depend on his or her perceptions and interpretations of the stigmatization.

THREATS TO IDENTITY

Perceptions of discrimination are demonstrably subjective: what one person sees as blatant discrimination another person may ignore or be oblivious to. As Crocker and Major (Crocker, Voelkl, Testa, & Major, 1991) have shown, many situations involve a degree of attributional ambiguity in which judgments are difficult to assess. In addition, responses to discrimination or prejudice can be quite different. In terms of identity negotiation, although discrimination or prejudice may typically prompt identity negotiation by the target, the particular strategy chosen will depend on whether the target perceived that discrimination as threatening, as well as the magnitude of the threat. Thus, it is the subjective perception of threat that acts as a key mediator between stigmatization and the type of identity negotiation strategies used by the stigmatized target.

Felt threats to identity can take one of two forms, as Breakwell (1986) has described. The first is concerned with the evaluation of an identity category, as the value of the group or category to which one belongs is being negatively evaluated. A second form of identity threat takes the form of challenges to one's very claim to be a member of the group. A company plan to downsize, for example, can threaten the existence of an occupational identity. Changes in political boundaries, tragically illustrated by recent events in the former Yugoslavia, pose questions of both ethnic and national identity.

Stigmatization is best represented by the first of these forms of potential threat. In an experimental study of this effect, Phinney, Chavira, and Tate (1993) showed Hispanic students one of several videotaped interviews in which a Hispanic student talked about negative stereotypes of Hispanics, or positive features of Hispanic culture, or was neutral. Following these presentations, students who had viewed the negative presentation rated Hispanics less favorably than did other groups on a series of adjective traits, although they did not show significant decrements in ethnic self-concept, as assessed by the Private subscale of Collective Self-Esteem (Luhtanen & Crocker, 1992). Ethier and Deaux (1990, 1994) also assessed threats to Hispanic identity, in this case in a longitudinal interview study of students entering elite universities. Students experiencing threat (and only some of the students showed strong reactions) responded positively to statements such as "I feel that I have to change myself to fit in at school" and "I often feel like a chameleon, having to change my colors depending on the ethnicity of the person I am with."

Reactions to stigmatization depend in large part on the degree of one's identification with the stigmatized group. In an extensive program of research, Ellemers and her colleagues (Doosje & Ellemers, 1997; Ellemers, 1993) have shown that people who identify strongly with their group tend to engage in collective strategies. More generally, highly identified people are more likely to use enhancement strategies, maintaining their identity in the face of threat. People less strongly identified with a group are more inclined to dissociate from the group when confronted with threat, choosing to negate the identity and seek personal satisfaction elsewhere.

As the above studies suggest, not all people experience threat to identity in the face of discrimination. For some, the discrimination may simply not be noted. For others, the discrimination may be recognized but, through a variety of protective mechanisms and strategies, the target identity is resistant to threats. (See Crocker and Major, 1989 for a review of self-protective mechanisms used by members of stigmatized groups.) Perceptions of threat thus become central to a model of identity negotiation. As the following case study will illustrate in more detail, threats to identity are subjective experiences, often traceable to objective incidents of stigmatization and discrimination but not necessarily following from such events. As a result, responses to stigmatization will vary considerably, as will a person's choice of whether and how to negotiate a targeted identity.

HISPANICS IN IVY: A CASE STUDY
OF IDENTITY NEGOTIATION

To illustrate some of the themes discussed thus far, we turn to a study of identity negotiation during a particular contextual change—specifically, the case of Hispanic students who enter elite universities. We draw from this longitudinal study specific examples that provide a more general picture of the varying relationships between stigmatization, threat, and identity negotiation.

To explore the patterns and conditions of identity negotiation, we followed a cohort of Hispanic students throughout their first year of college at one of two Ivy League universities in which the majority of the students were Anglo.[3] These students were experiencing a dramatic change in context, often from an ethnic working-class neighborhood in the West or Southwestern United States to an elite university campus in the Northeast. Accompanying this change of ethnicity and class was the potential show of prejudice and discrimination from students and faculty at the new institution. In this context, we examined how our sample of Hispanic students defined their identities, changed both meanings and strength of ethnic identity across the first year of college, and selected strategies to negotiate their identities in response to perceived threat.

THE EXPERIENCE OF STIGMATIZATION AND THREAT

Pilot interviews helped us to identify ways in which stigmatization and threat were experienced by students in the study. Drawing from these interviews, we created a 6-item threat scale, which contained the following items: (1) I feel that I have to change myself to fit in at school; (2) I try not to show the parts of me that are "ethnically" based; (3) I often feel like a chameleon, having to change my colors depending on the ethnicity of the person I am with; (4) I feel that my ethnicity is incompatible with the new people I am meeting and the new things I am learning; (5) I cannot talk to my friends at school about my family or my culture; and (6) I cannot talk to my family about my friends at school or what I am learning in school.

Using a response scale that varied from 1 (not at all) to 7 (a great deal), we obtained scores at the initial interview ranging from 6, representing absolutely no perceived threat reported, to 30, which indicates a considerable degree of perceived threat. The mean for the sample at the initial interview was 12.1, a figure that increased measurably at the second and third occasions (midyear and at the end of the first academic year). These data suggest that for many students, the move to university was accompanied by an experience of identity threat.

Qualitative data obtained in interviews with students at the end of their first year provide a fuller picture of experienced stigmatization and perceived threat.

---

[3]The main findings of this study were previously reported in Ethier and Deaux (1990, 1994). Here we discuss some of the data reported in these articles as well as qualitative findings not previously published.

Most of the students did not feel that they were direct targets of prejudice or discrimination; at the same time, many were quick to recount instances that were more subtle evidence of the experience of stigmatization associated with their ethnicity.

Perceptions of discrimination took several forms. One student suggested that teachers do not expect as much from minority students, giving brief rather than informative comments on their papers or not calling on them in class. A woman said that "some guys won't ask you out"; a man said that his roommate often used derogatory slang words. Some students denied any experiences of discrimination, while others acknowledged the ambiguity of many situations. Not having any first-hand observation of the experiences of the students, we can not comment on the objective incidents that might have occurred. The variation in students' reactions, however, is consistent with the position that perceptions of threat are subjective and variable, with no clear one-to-one correspondence between perceptions and objective events.

We did not ask students directly about affirmative action policies at their university or their feelings about those policies. Nonetheless, the topic emerged frequently (among 47% of the students) and often served as a marker for perceptions of stigmatization. The following statement from one Puerto Rican man is illustrative:

> I came here thinking that . . . I got here because of affirmative action. Because I got told that, pretty much point blank, by people in my high school and by my guidance counselor in my high school. . . . And so when I got here that really had a big effect on me because . . . I just kind of felt like a second class student.

Another student reflected that "I wish I'd never put 'Hispanic' on the application form, because I sort of want to do it on my own. . . . I don't like to bring [affirmative action] up because I don't want them to take away from my own credentials."

Another source of conflict concerned stigmatization that some students experienced from other group members. Because we interviewed any student who was classified as Hispanic by the university, there was wide variation in the degree to which they came from culturally strong backgrounds—whether they and/or their parents were born in the mainland United States, whether Spanish was spoken in their home, and whether their friends and home community were predominantly Anglo or Hispanic. Students who came from less ethnically oriented environments often felt that they were not accepted by other Hispanic students. Language seemed to be a particularly influential factor. Students who were less fluent in Spanish felt that other Hispanics at the university did not accept them, and a number of students recounted specific incidents of discrimination regarding their lack of Spanish fluency as a marker of not belonging to the group.

Ironically, those students who experienced threat most strongly were those who were least involved with their Hispanic identity. On average, they were students who had weaker links to Hispanic neighborhoods, culture, friends, and language before they came to university, and they were less likely to connect to the Hispanic community at the university. In contrast, for those students who were more strongly linked to the Hispanic community, involvement in identity-related activities appeared to act as a buffer against threat and the negative effects of stigma. Specifically, we found that the strength of a student's cultural background was negatively related to their perceptions of identity threat.[4]

IDENTITY NEGOTIATION

Many of the identity negotiation strategies that we have discussed, both those of negation and those of enhancement, were observed in this study. In general, students made a choice between these two general categories, taking either a path that resulted in enhanced identity or one that moved away from the Hispanic label. For some, vacillation between these two general strategies was evident as the student struggled with his or her ethnic identity. Within a category, particularly in the case of identity enhancement, more than one tactic was typically adopted. In all, the findings suggest an intricate, dynamic process of identity negotiation that evolves and changes over time.

Identity Negation

Few students chose the route of complete elimination. Given their labeling by the universities, this choice would have been a difficult one although, from a subjective perspective, not impossible. However, there were one or two cases in which students denied the label assigned to them. One student, for example, had both Puerto Rican and Filipino parentage. He for the most part minimized his Hispanic identity and identified more as an Asian, choosing friends who were Chinese, Vietnamese, and Filipino.

More evident in terms of negation strategies was a decreased importance attached to the Hispanic identity. Although strength of ethnic identification for the sample as a whole remained constant over the year, a subset of the sample showed some detachment from the identity. Typically it was those students whose initial grounding in their ethnicity was weaker who deemphasized, even further, their identification as an Hispanic. As one woman described her reactions, "When I came here I probably didn't fit into the stereotype of being a Mexican American or Hispanic. And I don't speak Spanish. In a lot of ways, I'm very detached from that part of it."

Identity Enhancement

In contrast to this detachment or elimination pattern, many students, particularly those whose Hispanic cultural background was initially strong, chose ne-

---

[4]This buffer did not protect students from acknowledging that stigma is associated with their ethnicity; both groups (i.e., those who were strongly identified with their Hispanic identity and those who were not) recognized that others did not value their ethnic group. There were no differences between groups in the Public Acceptance subscale of the CSE scale that measures an individual's perception of others' feelings about their group.

gotiation strategies that extended their identification, through reaffirmation, remooring, intensified group contact, and, in a few cases, attempts at social change. For these students, it was important to establish their ethnicity in the new environment; over the course of the year, their identification became increasingly important.

Reaffirmation is clearly evidenced in the statement of this Mexican American woman: "It made me want to . . . get more Hispanic here. Doing the class stuff has gotten me to appreciate my heritage more." The process of remooring is vividly illustrated by a Puerto Rican woman:

> I became much more aware [of my ethnicity.] Something I always say is that you don't know what you have until you lose it. And when I came here I started missing all those things I have back home and the only chance I had to have that here was to emphasize my identity as a Puerto Rican, like to go out with my friends sometimes and to do the things we usually do.

As this statement suggests, ethnic identity was originally tied to the students' cultural background, as indexed by whether Spanish was spoken in their home, whether they had friends in high school who were also Hispanic, and whether they lived in a heavily Hispanic community. In leaving these communities, students who wished to continue to hold a strong ethnic identity were faced with the task of reconnecting the identity to their current environment. As evidenced in the interviews we conducted, students did this by making friends with other Hispanic students and by joining Hispanic clubs on campus, often ones specific to their particular ethnic group (e.g., Puerto Rican, Chicano).

The critical nature of this remooring process is shown by data indicating that the original links of identity to cultural background diminish over the course of the year, with the correlation dropping to less than .2 by the end of the year (Ethier & Deaux, 1994). Family was no less important to students, as assessed by other measures, but it could no longer sustain ethnic identity when context had changed so greatly. To replace those supports, students whose ethnic identity remained strong made links to the new context, indicated by a .6 correlation between identity and local involvement at the end of the year.

The more activist negotiation strategy of social change, although chosen less frequently, was also in evidence. Many of the students who wanted to maintain and strengthen their ethnic identification also saw a need to educate others around them, typically as part of a group-based strategy. One woman, for example, described how "you get together with all those people that are from Puerto Rico and you can work towards letting other people know how we are." "I had the opportunity to talk about Hispanics and in some way educate them to what being Hispanic is all about . . . and to change some stereotypes," said another Puerto Rican student.

Social change extended to political action groups, becoming involved in groups such as the Chicano Caucus and the Latino Task Force. As one Mexican American described her conversations with older Hispanic students, "they talked to us about how the ones who were here before us . . . fought and marched . . . or we wouldn't have been here." One might speculate that the strategy of social change would be more frequently adopted in subsequent years, as these now first-year students became settled in their new environment and aware of the options available to them.

Undoubtedly, the choice of a particular negotiation strategy is multidetermined, a product of past experience and current options. Yet, the options themselves, as well as the perceived threats to identity that might prompt one to look for options, are also influenced by past experience. Our results suggest that the selection of identity negotiation strategies depended on how strongly students were involved with the identity which, in turn, was related to the subjective experience of threat. Students who arrived at the university with a strong ethnic background were less likely to experience threats to their identity and made active efforts to maintain that identity and even to strengthen it through identity enhancement strategies. In contrast, students for whom ethnic identity was initially more tenuous were far more likely to experience threat and to choose strategies that weakened the identification further.

SUMMING UP

Identity negotiation is, as we have indicated, a dynamic and ongoing process, taking place and evolving in a complex social context. Although we have focused on one particular identity in the case of the Hispanic students entering university, it should be recognized that this identity undoubtedly coexists with numerous other identities (at least a half a dozen important ones, on the average, as reported by Ethier and Deaux, 1990). Thus, while students were working on their ethnic identity, they were in all probability negotiating other identities as well—redefining their role as a son or daughter, acquiring a new identity as university student, possibly discarding identities that were closely associated with their earlier years. How negotiations in one identity realm affect the status of other identities is a process that has only begun to be investigated (see Ethier, 1995, for one example).

The active nature of identity posited here does not ignore the constraints that society and social structures may impose. Because identities are inherently social constructions, they must be negotiated, not in an individual vacuum, but in ongoing contexts in which others affirm, deny, or ignore one's identity claims. The form that these external pressures take will shape the course of identity negotiation. Further, the rules and norms of a society to some extent constrain the choices any individual can make, or at the very least, set up barriers to some choices while making other choices quite easy. Because social identities are shared, the individual also inherits a set of meanings and assumptions that go with category labels. These social representations can be altered, fine-tuned and shaped for individual wear, but they are the raw material with which identities are built.

For targets of discrimination, the negative evaluations accompanying categorical judgments provide an additional burden. Yet these negative evaluations are also context-dependent and can be circumvented or reformed through active identity negotiation. A close look at the circumstances of negotiating the identity that may be stigmatized highlights the importance of social norms and specific contexts, issues that are central to all forms of identity work.

ACKNOWLEDGMENTS

We thank Pamela Lipp, San-Siang Sandy Lu, Gina Philogene, members of the Identity Research Group at the CUNY Graduate Center, and the editors of this volume for their helpful comments on an earlier version of this chapter.

The original research reported in this chapter was supported in part by a grant from the National Science Foundation (BNS-9110130) to Kay Deaux. We also thank Jose Lorenzo-Hernandez for his help in content analysis of the interview material.

REFERENCES

Archer, D. (1985). Social deviance. In G. Lindzey & E. Aronson (Eds.), *Handbook of social psychology* (Vol. 2, 3rd ed., pp. 743–804). New York: Random House.

Blanch, A., Penney, D., & Knight, E. (1995). "Identity politics" close to home. *American Psychologist, 5,* 49–50.

Branscombe, N. R., & Ellemers, N. (1998). Use of individualistic and group strategies in response to perceived discrimination among the disadvantaged. In J. K. Swim & C. Stangor (Eds.), *Prejudice: The target's perspective.* San Diego, CA: Academic Press.

Breakwell, G. (1986). *Coping with threatened identities.* London: Methuen.

Breakwell, G. M. (1993). Integrating paradigms, methodological implications. In G. M. Breakwell & D. V. Canter (Eds.), *Empirical approaches to social representations* (pp. 180–201). Oxford: Clarendon Press.

Brewer, M. B. (1991). The social self: On being the same and different at the same time. *Personality and Social Psychology Bulletin, 17,* 475–482.

Brewer, M. (1993). The role of distinctiveness in social identity and group behavior. In M. A. Hogg & D. Abrams (Eds.), *Group motivation: Social psychological perspectives* (pp. 1–16). New York: Harvester/Wheatsheaf.

Brown, J. D. (1991). The professional ex-: An alternative for exiting the deviant career. *The Sociological Quarterly, 32,* 219–230.

Carter, S. L. (1991). *Reflections of an affirmative action baby.* New York: Basic Books.

Crocker, J., Luhtanen, R., Blaine, B., & Broadnax, S. (1994). Collective self-esteem and psychological well-being among White, Black, and Asian college students. *Personality and Social Psychology Bulletin, 20,* 502–513.

Crocker, J., & Major, B. (1989). Social stigma and self-esteem: The self-protective properties of stigma. *Psychological Review, 96,* 608–630.

Crocker, J., Major, B., & Steele, C. (in press). Social stigma. In D. Gilbert, S. T. Fiske, & G. Lindzey (Eds.), *Handbook of social psychology* (4th ed.). Boston: McGraw Hill.

Crocker, J., Voelkl, K., Testa, M., & Major, B. (1991). Social stigma: The affective consequences of attributional ambiguity. *Journal of Personality and Social Psychology, 60,* 218–228.

Cross, W. E. (1978). The Thomas and Cross models of psychological nigrescence: A literature review. *Journal of Black Psychology, 4,* 13–31.

Cross, W. E. (1991). *Shades of Black: Diversity in African-American identity.* Philadelphia: Temple University Press.

Deaux, K. (1991). Social identities: Thoughts on structure and change. In R. C. Curtis (Ed.), *The relational self: Theoretical convergences in psychoanalysis and social psychology* (pp. 77–93). New York: Guilford.

Deaux, K. (1993). Reconstructing social identity. *Personality and Social Psychology Bulletin, 19,* 4–12.

Deaux, K. (1996). Social identification. In E. T. Higgins & A. W. Kruglanski (Eds.), *Social psychology: Handbook of basic principles* (pp. 777–798). New York: Guilford Publications.

Deaux, K., & Reid, A. (in preparation). Contemplating collectivism. In S. Stryker, T. J. Owens, & R. W. White (Eds.), *Self, identity, and social movements.*

Doosje, B., & Ellemers, N. (1997). Stereotyping under threat: The role of group identification. In R. Spears, P. J. Oakes, N. Ellemers, & S. A. Haslam (Eds.), *The social psychology of stereotyping and group life* (pp. 257–272). Oxford, England: Blackwell.

Downing, N. E., & Roush, K. L. (1985). From passive acceptance to active commitment: A model of feminist identity development for women. *The Counseling Psychologist, 13,* 695–709.

Eastland, I. D. (1995). Recovery as an interactive process: Explanation and empowerment in 12-step programs. *Qualitative Health Research, 5,* 292–314.

Ebaugh, H. R. F. (1988). *Becoming an ex: The process of role exit.* Chicago: University of Chicago Press.

Ellemers, N. (1993) The influence of socio-structural variables on identity enhancement strategies. *European Review of Social Psychology, 4,* 27–57.

Ethier, K. A. (1995). *Becoming a mother: Identity acquisition during the transition to parenthood.* Unpublished doctoral dissertation, City University of New York.

Ethier, K., & Deaux, K. (1990). Hispanics in ivy: Assessing identity and perceived threat. *Sex Roles, 22,* 427–440.

Ethier, K. A., & Deaux, K. (1994). Negotiating social identity when contexts change: Maintaining identification and responding to threat. *Journal of Personality and Social Psychology, 67,* 243–251.

Fiske, S. T. (in press). Stereotyping, prejudice, and discrimination. In D. T. Gilbert, S. T. Fiske, & G. Lindzey (Eds.), *The handbook of social psychology* (4th ed.). New York: McGraw-Hill.

Goffman, E. (1963). *Stigma: Notes on the management of spoiled identity.* New York: Simon & Schuster.

Gurin, P., & Townsend, A. (1986). Properties of gender identity and their implications for gender consciousness. *British Journal of Social Psychology, 25,* 139–148.

Gutierrez, J. M., & Ortega, R. (1991). Developing methods to empower Latinos: The importance of groups. *Social Work with Groups, 14,* 23–43.

Harris, P. (1995). Who am I? Concepts of disability and their implications for people with learning disabilities. *Disability and Society, 10,* 341–351.

Hogg, M. A., & Abrams, D. (1988). *Social identifications: A social psychology of intergroup relations and group processes.* London and New York: Routledge.

Hormuth, S. E. (1990). *The ecology of the self: Relocation and self-concept change.* Cambridge, England: Cambridge University Press.

Kerwin, C., & Ponterotto, J. G. (1995). Biracial identity development. In J. G. Ponterotto, J. M. Casas, L. A. Suzuki, & C. M. Alexander (Eds.), *Handbook of multicultural counseling.* Thousand Oaks, CA: Sage.

Kosmitzki, C. (1996). The reaffirmation of cultural identity in cross-cultural encounters. *Personality and Social Psychology Bulletin, 22,* 238–248.

Luhtanen, R., & Crocker, J. (1992). A collective self-esteem scale: Self-evaluation of one's social identity. *Personality and Social Psychology Bulletin, 18,* 302–318.

Markus, H. R., Kitayama, S., & Heiman, R. J. (1996). Culture and "basic" psychological principles. In E. T. Higgins & A. W. Kruglanski (Eds.), *Social psychology: Handbook of basic principles* (pp. 857–913). New York: Guilford.

McNulty, S. E., & Swann, W. B., Jr. (1994). Identity negotiation in roommate relationships: The self as architect and consequence of social reality. *Journal of Personality and Social Psychology, 67,* 1012–1023.

Moore, T. (1991). The African-American church: A source of empowerment, mutual help and social change. *Prevention in Human Services, 10,* 147–167.

Moscovici, S. (1988). Notes towards a description of social representations. *European Journal of Social Psychology, 18,* 211–250.

Philogene, G. (1996). *From Black to African American: The making of a new social representation.* Unpublished doctoral dissertation, Ecole des Hautes Etudes en Sciences Sociales.

Phinney, J. S. (1990). Ethnic identity in adolescents and adults: Review of research. *Psychological Bulletin, 108,* 499–514.

Phinney, J. S., Chavira, V., & Tate, J. D. (1993). The effect of ethnic threat on ethnic self-concept and own-group ratings. *The Journal of Social Psychology, 133,* 469–478.

Reid, A., & Deaux, K. (1996). Relationship between social and personal identities: Segregation or integration? *Journal of Personality and Social Psychology, 71,* 1084–1091.

Schachter, S. (1959). *The psychology of affiliation.* Stanford, CA: Stanford University Press.

Simon, B., Pantaleo, G., & Mummendey, A. (1995). Unique individual or interchangeable group member? The accentuation of intragroup differences versus similarities as an indicator of the individual self versus the collective self. *Journal of Personality and Social Psychology, 69,* 106–119.

Spears, R., Oakes, P. J., Ellemers, N., & Haslam, S. A. (Eds.) (1997). *The social psychology of stereotyping and group life.* Oxford, UK: Blackwell.

Swann, W. B., Jr., & Ely, R. J. (1984). A battle of wills: Self-verification versus behavioral confirmation. *Journal of Personality and Social Psychology, 46,* 1287–1302.

Troiden, R. R. (1989). The formation of homosexual identities. In G. Herdt (Ed.), *Gay and lesbian youth* (pp. 43–73). New York: Harrington Park Press.

Turner, J. C., Hogg, M. A., Oakes, P. J., Reicher, S. D., & Wetherell, M. S. (1987). *Rediscovering the social group: A self-categorization theory.* Oxford: Basil Blackwell.

Waters, M. (1990). *Ethnic options: Choosing identities in America.* Berkeley: University of California Press.

Watts, R. J. (1992). Racial identity and preferences for social change strategies among African Americans. *Journal of Black Psychology, 18,* 1–18.

INDEX